THE ULTIMATE BOOK OF JEWISH JOKES

I would like to dedicate this book to my special friend Andrea, who I love and who also happens to be my wife

THE ULTIMATE BOOK OF

JEWISH JOKES

DAVID MINKOFF

ROBSON

First published in Great Britain in 2005 by
Robson Books
151 Freston Road
London
W10 6TH

An imprint of Anova Books Company Ltd

ISBN 1 86105 821 7 (paperback)
1 86105 921 3 (hardback)

10 9 8 7 6 5 4 3 2

Printed and bound by Creative Print and Design (Ebbw Vale), Wales

This book can be ordered direct from the publisher
Contact the marketing department, but try your bookshop first

Contents

Introduction

I grew up in a Jewish household (my father was a kosher butcher and poulterer) so I was surrounded by Jewish culture. I started collecting jokes from the age of thirteen. Don't all boys get a book on Jewish customs and folklore as one of their Bar Mitzvah presents (as well as umbrellas, a *siddur* – or prayer book – and fountain pens)? I have continued to collect jokes and humour right up to the present day. My sources for jokes have been, and continue to be, numerous – schoolmates, family, friends, workmates, the changing rooms at the Maccabi football club, TV, radio, books, newspapers, magazines, emails, friends at my Israeli dance class – and even my rabbi.

A big change in my life came in the year 2000 when I set up a website (*www.awordinyoureye.com)* of Jewish jokes and humour to share what I feel are the best Jewish jokes around. The website has been enjoying the number-one position on Google for 'Jewish jokes' and has provided much of the material for this book. All of a sudden, not only did the website turn into a full-time job which required a lot of maintenance, but my new hobby took a large chunk out of whatever free time I had left in the evening. It involved, and still involves, a never-ending process of regularly adding jokes, new features, maintaining the website design, and conversing via emails with a great new bunch of contacts from all over the world. But I love doing it. Making people laugh, or even smile, is rewarding on a personal level.

I would like to single out a few of these new-found contacts, whose kind words have encouraged me to continually develop my collection: Stan Cohen (Stan the Man), Ed Kotler, Ian Sarsby, Uriah Yaniv, Hilary Ash, Marcos Sokiransky, Frank Reuben, Richard G Klein, Sylvia Suchall, Boris M Schein and Charles Kohnfelder – though there are many others too numerous to list here.

How do I choose and create my jokes? Most importantly, I have to like the joke. If I like a joke, I rewrite it in my own style. I try to keep the number of Hebrew and Yiddish words to a minimum so that as many of the jokes as possible can be enjoyed by Jews and non-Jews alike. I don't enjoy racist jokes or jokes about the Middle East, terrorists, etc. I don't find them funny and you won't see them in this book. In any case, there's enough humour around on this and every other subject to last a lifetime. I also try hard to filter out obscene jokes and jokes that might offend – though I have included a few that might be regarded as more risqué in a separate section called 'Naughtier Jokes' – and I try to balance out jokes made against men and husbands with those made against women and wives. I want to be fair to all.

So why did I compile this book? The success of the website was just one factor in my decision. I had been wondering for some time whether I should cater not only for people who prefer to see something in print rather than on screen, but also for people who do not have access to the Internet, or who are not computer literate. How could any of these groups enjoy the jokes if they were not available in printed form? And then I remembered the requests I had received from people all over the world to publish the jokes in book form. So here it is – what I hope is the indisputable heavyweight of Jewish joke books.

I have included over a thousand Jewish jokes. The classics are here as well as many I hope you will not already have heard. I've 'themed' the jokes under a number of categories. This has not been an easy task. For example, should a joke about a rabbi with a *davening* (praying) parrot come under rabbis, pets or prayers? It's very subjective. Nevertheless, if you are looking for a particular joke, hopefully you will only need to look under only few themes to find it. I've included jokes that can be told to or read by children; I've created a unique 'kosher-humour test' for dating couples; I've put together some humorous and barbed quips that can be included in various types of speeches for special occasions (weddings, birthdays, etc); and I've selected a number of punchlines from jokes included in the book that are funny to read just on their own.

I believe laughter to be the greatest of medicines, and I have been heartened in my labours by the responses I have been getting from around the world, particularly from those who have been using the jokes for 'medicinal' purposes! Here are a few examples:

> I have been sharing your jokes with a group of older single Jewish men (mostly retired doctors, lawyers, and one feisty, retired FBI man) who live in the high-rise tower where I work. We have all had a wonderful time for the past several weeks with me telling them a new joke now and then, and with them trying to top mine (yours). Your collection has brought much laughter and cheer to these guys, most of whom have lost their wives and have few friends due to their age and inability to get out much. Some of them have even grown closer to each other since we started exchanging jokes, and have begun having conversations with each other. I've even seen two former enemies start the process of forgiving past slights that have kept them apart for years!

> I needed some Jewish jokes to send to a friend who is recuperating from surgery. Thank you for this wonderful and expansive collection of jokes. I am hoping that a few jokes a day will expedite his recovery.

> I found your jokes at a low time. I am disabled and was having a bad pain day and now want to thank you. I am so much better. Everyday I read some of your jokes and have a real belly laugh. Thank you. For me, you are the Messiah. Laughter really is the best medicine, even if you are not sick.

I'll be honest and say that the above stories brought a few tears to my eyes. Now, when I visit my elderly mum, I regularly read her a selection of jokes – and it's music to my ears to hear her laughter. She even seems to understand every one of them (well, very nearly every one) – and that does me good, too!

The Jewish Jokes

EARLY YEARS

Babies

Sarah has recently given birth to her first child. Sarah is also a bit of a worrier, to say the least, and she hasn't been home long before she rings her doctor in a state of panic.

'So what's the problem, Sarah?' asks the doctor.

'My baby has a temperature of 102, doctor. Is he going to die?' shouts Sarah.

The doctor, needing to determine whether Sarah was taking the reading under the arm, in the mouth or elsewhere, says, 'I hope you don't mind me asking you this question, but – how are you taking it?'

Sarah replies, 'Oh, I'm holding up pretty well, doctor.'

***

Sadie is 65 years old and has always remained unmarried, yet she desperately wants a baby of her own. So with the help of modern science and with the help of a fertility specialist, Sadie has her miracle baby.

When she gets home, all her friends and relatives come to see her and meet the new member of her family. But when they ask to see the baby, Sadie says, 'not yet.'

A little later they again ask to see the baby and again Sadie says, 'not yet.'

Finally they ask, 'So when can we see the baby?'

Sadie replies, 'When the baby cries.'

'Why do we have to wait until the baby cries?' they say.
Sadie replies, 'Because I forgot where I put it.'

***

Rivkah went to her doctor for a check up. Afterwards, the doctor said to her, 'I must inform you that you have a fissure in your uterus, and if you ever have a baby it would be a miracle.'

As soon as she got home, Rivkah said to her husband, 'You vouldn't belief it. I vent to the doctah and he told me – "You haf a fish in your uterus and if you haf a baby it vill be a mackerel".'

***

Yitzhak and Melvyn live in a retirement home. One day, they are sitting on a bench under a tree, and Yitzhak turns to Melvyn and says, 'Melvyn, I'm 85 years old and I'm full of aches and pains. You're about my age. How do you feel?'

Melvyn replies, 'I feel just like a new-born baby.'

'Really? Like a baby?'

'Yes,' replies Melvyn, 'No hair, no teeth and I think I just wet myself.'

***

Sam had just picked up his wife Beckie and their new baby from hospital and brought them home. It was not long before Beckie suggested that Sam should try his hand at changing a nappy. 'I'm busy,' he said, 'I promise I'll do the next one.'

The next time soon came around so Beckie asked him again. Sam looked at Beckie and said, innocently, 'I didn't mean the next nappy, I meant the next baby.'

***

Ruth had just given birth to her tenth child in Edgware hospital. 'Congratulations,' said the nurse, 'but don't you think this is enough of the babies, already?'

Ruth replied, 'Are you joking? This is the only time I get to have a holiday each year.'

***

The time had arrived for Moshe to take his Leah to hospital to have their baby delivered. Upon their arrival, the doctor told them that he had invented a new machine that would transfer a portion of the mother's labour pain to the father. He asked if they were willing to try it out. They were both very much in favour.

The doctor set the pain transfer dial to ten per cent for starters, explaining that even ten per cent was probably more pain than Moshe had ever experienced before. But as the labour progressed, Moshe felt fine and asked the doctor to go ahead and bump it up a notch. The doctor then adjusted the machine to twenty-per-cent pain transfer. Moshe was still feeling fine. The doctor checked his blood pressure and was amazed at how well he was doing. At this point they decided to try for fifty per cent. Moshe continued to feel quite well. Since it was obviously helping out Leah considerably, Moshe encouraged the doctor to transfer ALL the pain to him. Leah delivered a healthy baby with virtually no pain. Leah and Moshe were ecstatic.

When they got home, they found their milkman dead at their front door.

***

Miriam gets on a bus with her baby. As she goes to pay her fare, the bus driver says to her, 'I've seen a lot of babies in my time but that's the ugliest one I've ever seen in my life.'

Miriam is shocked and very angry at this insensitive remark. She sits down and starts to cry. The man next to her asks her what's the matter.

Miriam replies, 'The bus driver just insulted me.'

The man replies, 'I wouldn't let him get away with it. You go and give him a piece of your mind. Go on – I'll hold your monkey for you.'

***

Little Benjy was in his Hebrew class and was learning all about how God created everything, including humans. He was especially interested when his teacher got to the bit about how Eve was created out of one of Adam's ribs. Later that day, Benjy's mother noticed him lying down as though he were ill, so she said to him, 'Benjy, darling, what's the matter with you?'

Benjy replied, 'I have a pain in my side, mummy. I think I'm going to have a wife.'

***

As his wife was expecting their first baby, Rabbi Bloom went to the synagogue committee and asked for a salary increase. After much deliberation, they passed a resolution that when the rabbi's family expanded again, so would his payslip.

Six children later, it began to get expensive for the *shul* and they decided to hold a meeting again to discuss the rabbi's salary situation. This time there was much arguing and shouting. Rabbi Bloom could take it no more, so he got up and said, 'Having children is an act of God.'

The chairman replied, 'Snow and storms are also "acts of God", but when it gets to be too much, we wear rubbers.'

Circumcision

'I'm getting operated on tomorrow.'

'Oh? What are they going to do?'

'Circumcise me!'

'I had that done when I was just a few days old.'

'Did it hurt?'

'I couldn't walk for a year.'

***

And Moses said unto the Lord, 'We are Your chosen people and You want us to cut the tips off of our WHAT?'

***

A rabbi and a minister decided to buy a new car together. The day after they bought it, the rabbi found the minister driving it. The minister explained that he had just gone to the carwash because, in his religion, it is customary to welcome a new member with the rite of baptism. The next day, the minister discovered the rabbi cutting the end off the exhaust pipe.

***

A tax official visited a rural synagogue for an inspection. Rabbi Gold accompanied him.

'So rabbi, tell me please, after you have distributed all your unleavened bread, what do you do with the crumbs?'

'Why, we gather them carefully and send them to the city and then they make bread of them again and send it to us.'

'Ah. So what about candles after they are burned? What do you do with the ends?'

'We send them to the city as well, and they make new candles from them and send them to us.'

'And what about circumcision? What do you do with those leftover pieces?'

The rabbi, wearily, replied, 'We send them to the city as well.'

'To the city? And when you do this, what do they send to you?'

'Today they have sent you to us.'

***

Q: If a doctor carries a black leather bag and a plumber carries a box of tools, what does a *mohel* carry?

A: A *bris* kit.

***

Q: What do you call an uncircumcised Jew who is more than eight days old?

A: A girl.

***

Morris was a very uneducated man, but by ruthless means became very rich. The older Morris got, the richer he got, the richer he got, the more women he had, the more women he had, the less use he was to them. One day, Morris went to the top surgeon in the business and said, 'I want to be castrated.'

'You want to be WHAT?'

'I said castrated, my sexual powers are failing. I insist you operate at once.'

The surgeon was a bit dubious, but in view of this last statement, and for a fee of £2,000, he carried out the operation.

Some weeks later, Morris was drinking in his local pub, listening to the conversation at the next table. 'I say, Barney,' said one of the group, 'Do you think there's any truth to the rumour that if a man gets himself circumcised, it improves his sexual performance?'

Morris quickly left the pub muttering to himself 'Circumcised, that was the word I've been trying to think of.'

***

Benjamin, a young Talmud student who had left Israel for London some years earlier, returns to visit his family.

'But Benjamin, where is your beard?' asks his mother upon seeing him.

'Mother,' he replies, 'In London, nobody wears a beard.'

'But at least you keep the Sabbath?' his mother asks.

'Mother, business is business. In London, everybody works on the Sabbath.'

'But kosher food you still eat?' asks his mother.

'Mother, in London, it is very difficult to keep kosher.'

Then silence, whilst his elderly mother gives thought to what she has just heard. Then she leans over and whispers in his ear, 'Benjamin, tell me, are you still circumcised?'

***

David's watch was not working. He remembered passing a little shop with clocks and watches in the window, so he took the watch in for repair.

'Can I help you?' asked the man behind the counter.

'I want this watch repaired,' said David.

'I'm sorry. I don't repair watches.'

'Well, how much for a new one then?' asked David.

'I don't sell watches.'

'You don't sell watches?'

'No, I don't sell watches.'

'Clocks, you sell clocks then? How much for a clock?'

'I don't sell clocks.'

David was getting exasperated. 'You don't sell watches, you don't sell clocks?'

'No, I'm a *mohel*,' replied the man.

'Then why do you have all those clocks and watches in the window?'

'If you were a *mohel*, tell me, what would you put in your window?'

***

'It won't be long now,' said the rabbi as he circumcised the little boy.

***

Harry and Victor are in the Gents toilet at King's Cross Station.

Harry says to Victor, 'Are you from Golders Green?'

Victor replies, 'Yes, how did you know that?'

Harry says, 'Do you belong to Holders Synagogue?'

Victor exclaims, 'Yes, how did you know that?'

Harry then says, 'Is Rabbi Levy, the *mohel*, still there?'

Victor replies, 'Yes, how did you know that?'

Harry answers, 'It's obvious. Rabbi Levy always cuts on a slant and you're peeing on my shoe.'

***

Tex Cohen lived in – you guessed it, Texas. One day, he bought a round of drinks for everyone in the pub because his wife Honeysuckle had just given birth to a typical Texas baby boy weighing twenty pounds. Everyone in the pub congratulated him and many told him that they found it hard to believe that his baby weighed in so heavy. But Tex assured them, 'It's true, it's really true.'

When Tex came back to the same pub three weeks later, the barman said to him, 'Say, you're the father of the typical Texas baby that weighed twenty pounds at birth aren't you? So tell us, how much does your baby weigh now?'

Tex proudly replied, 'Twelve pounds.'

The barman could not understand this, so he asked Tex, 'Why? Is he ill? What happened? He weighed twenty pounds at birth, why has he lost so much weight?'

Tex took a big swig from his beer, wiped his lips with the back of his hand, leaned into the barman and proudly replied, 'Had him circumcised.'

Children

Leah gives 50p to her daughter Sarah. The little girl goes outside and returns ten minutes later without the coin. Wondering what she has done with the money, Leah asks, 'Where is the 50p I gave you, darling?'

'I gave it to an old lady,' says Sarah.

'Oh, you sweet girl. I am so proud. Tomorrow you shall have one pound.'

The next day, true to her word, Leah gives Sarah a whole pound. Off Sarah goes outside and returns later without the coin.

'What did you do with the one pound?'

'Oh, today I saw the same old lady,' begins Sarah, as her mother beamed at her, 'and gave her the pound so she could buy me a bigger ice cream.'

***

Rabbi Bloom asked young Paul what his favourite Bible story was.

'I guess the one about Noah and the Ark, where they floated around on the water for forty days and forty nights' replied Paul.

'That was a good story,' said Rabbi Bloom, 'and, with all that water, I bet they had a good time fishing, don't you think?'

Paul thought for a moment, then replied, 'I don't think so – they only had two worms.'

***

Whenever four-year-old Miriam was asked her name, she replied, 'I'm Mr Levy's daughter.'

So her mother told her this was wrong and that she must answer, 'I'm Miriam Levy.'

Next Shabbes, after the service, the rabbi asked her, 'Aren't you Mr Levy's daughter, little girl?'

Miriam replied, 'I thought I was, but my mother says I'm not.'

***

Even though they were brought up strictly orthodox, Shlomo, eight, and Isaac, ten, were very naughty brothers. When anything went wrong in Golders Green, they were nearly always involved. One day, a friend visited their parents and mentioned a rabbi who was having great success with delinquent children. As they were finding it difficult to control their boys, they went to this rabbi and asked whether he could help.

He said he could and asked to see the younger boy first – but he must be alone. So Shlomo went to see the rabbi while Isaac was kept at home. The rabbi sat Shlomo down at a huge, solid mahogany desk and he sat down on the other side. For five minutes they just sat and stared at each other. Finally, the rabbi pointed his finger at Shlomo and asked, 'Where is God?'

Shlomo said nothing.

Again, in a louder tone, the rabbi pointed at Shlomo and asked, 'Where is God?' Again Shlomo said nothing.

Then the rabbi leaned across the desk, put his finger on Shlomo's nose and shouted, 'For the third time, Shlomo, where is God?'

Shlomo panicked at this, got up and ran all the way home. He went straight up to Isaac's room and said, 'We are in big trouble, Isaac.'

'What do you mean, big trouble, little brother?' said Isaac.

Shlomo replied, 'God is missing – and I'm sure they think we did it.'

***

As soon as the Shabbes service had ended, little Benjy walks up to Rabbi Bloom and says, 'When I grow up, Rabbi, I'm going to give you lots of money.'

Rabbi Bloom laughs and replies, 'That's really good to know, Benjy, but why do you want to do this?'

Benjy replies, 'Because my Dad says you're the poorest rabbi we have ever had!'

***

Sadie goes with her young son Moshe to visit her best friend Rifka and her young daughter Hannah, as they do every Sunday afternoon. When they arrive, the two mothers send their children upstairs so they can talk about their neighbours. The children are first given a stern warning not to fight. After about an hour, everything is too quiet upstairs so Sadie hollers out, 'Children, you're not fighting up there are you?'

Moshe's voice comes back, 'No mum, we're not fighting, we're *shtupping*.'

Sadie replies, 'That's good children, don't fight.'

***

Sadie was making some pancakes as a treat for her two young sons, Simon and Nicky. But the boys began to argue as to who should get the first pancake she made.

'Shame on you boys,' said Sadie. 'If the wise King Solomon were here today, he would say, "let my brother have the first pancake".'

Nicky looked at Simon and said, 'OK, Simon, you be King Solomon today.'

***

Rodney Dangerfield:

'I could tell that my parents hated me. My bath toys were a radio and a toaster!'

'I was such an ugly baby, my mother never breast fed me. She told me that she only liked me as a friend.'

'I remember the time I was kidnapped and they sent a piece of my finger to my father. He said he wanted more proof.'

***

Little Paul says to his father, 'Daddy, Daddy, I want to get married.'

His father says, 'For that son, you have to have a girlfriend.'

Paul says, 'But I've found a girl.'

'Who?' says his father.

'My grandma.'

'Let me get this straight.' the father says. 'You want to marry my mother? You can't do that.'

'Well, why not?' says Paul. 'You married mine.'

***

One morning, as little Hannah was sitting at the kitchen sink watching her mother wash and dry the breakfast plates, she noticed that her mother had several strands of white hair mixed in with her dark hair. Hannah looked at her mother and said, 'Why have you got some white hairs, mummy?'

Her mother replied, 'Well, darling, every time a daughter does something bad to make her mother cry or unhappy, one of her mother's hairs turns white.'

Hannah thought about this information for a few moments then said, 'Mummy, so how come all of grandma's hairs are white?'

***

Rebecca was a kindergarten teacher. One day, during her art lesson, as she was walking around the class observing the children while they were drawing, she stopped at little Leah's desk. Leah was working away very diligently.

Rebecca said, 'What are you drawing, Leah?'

Leah replied, 'I'm drawing God, teacher.'

Rebecca paused and then said, 'But no one knows what God looks like, Leah.'

Without looking up from her work, Leah replied, 'They will in a minute.'

Schools & teachers

A proud young mother sees off her son to school on the first day. 'Be a good boy, my *bubbeleh*! Be careful and think of mummy, sweetest! Come right home on the bus, honey! Mummy loves you very much, baby.'

At the end of the day, she's waiting for the bus and sweeps him into her arms. 'And what did my love learn on his first day at school?'

'I learned that my name is David.'

***

'Hyman, you had better come over here right away. There has been some trouble with your son.'

'Vy, vot's happened, teacher?'

'I can't discuss it over the phone, you had better come.'

So Hyman arrives at the school. 'I'm very sorry to tell you but we are expelling your son; we can't tolerate his sort of behaviour here.'

'But vy, vot's he done?'

'Well, to be quite frank, we found him playing with his genitals.'

'But dat's not such a terrible ting, some of my best friends are genitals.'

* * *

Yossi comes home from school and tells his mother he has been given a part in the school play.

'Wonderful,' says the mother, 'What part is it?'

Yossi says, 'I play the part of the Jewish husband.'

The mother scowls and says, 'Go back and tell your teacher you want a speaking part.'

* * *

On her first day in her new job, Christine, a new school teacher, thinks it would be a good idea to try to bond with the children by asking each of them their name and what their father did for a living.

The first little girl replies, 'My name is Celina, teacher, and my daddy is a dustman.'

The next little boy replies, 'I'm Peter and my dad is a gardener.'

But the next little boy says, 'My name is Moshe, teacher, and my father is a strip-o-gram during the day and works in a gay club at night.'

Christine quickly changes the subject.

Later on, in the school playground, Christine quietly goes over to Moshe and asks, 'Is it really true what you said about your father, Moshe?'

Moshe blushes and replies, 'I'm sorry teacher but he's a chartered accountant at Arthur Andersen. I was just too embarrassed to say so.'

* * *

The Sunday school lesson had just finished and the rabbi asked if the children had any questions. Little David quickly raised his hand. 'Yes, David? What question would you like to ask me?'

'I have four questions to ask you, Rabbi. Is it true that after the children of Israel crossed the Red Sea, they received the Ten Commandments?'

'Yes, David.'

'And the children of Israel also defeated the Philistines?'

'Yes, David, that's also true.'

'And the children of Israel also fought the Egyptians and fought the Romans and built the Temple?'

'Again you are correct, David.'

'So my last question is, Rabbi, what were the grown-ups doing all this time?'

***

Mr Henry, the maths teacher, enters the classroom. The students are playing around after the bell and are not in their seats, so Mr Henry decides to teach them a lesson.

He calls, 'Ivan, name a two-digit number.'

Ivan responds, '56.'

Mr Henry says, 'Why not 65? Sit down, you have a D minus.'

Peter, name a two-digit number.'

Peter responds, 'Eighteen.'

Mr Henry says, 'Why not 81? D minus for you, too.'

'Moshe, name a two-digit number.'

Moshe responds, '33.'

Mr Henry says, 'Why not – Moshe! Stop these Jewish tricks at once!'

***

A young, popular, but controversial teacher tells her third-year class that she is an atheist and asks if there are any other atheists in the class, that they put up their hands. Not really knowing what an atheist was, but wanting to follow their teacher, all but one of them immediately put up their hands. The exception is Natalie. The teacher asks Natalie why she wants to be different to all the others.

'Because I'm not an atheist,' she replies.

'So what are you then?' asks the teacher.

'I'm Jewish.'

The teacher asks Natalie why she is Jewish.

'I was brought up knowing and loving God. My Mother is Jewish and my father is Jewish, so I am Jewish.'

'That's not a good enough reason,' the teacher says loudly. 'What if your mum was a moron, and your dad was a moron. What would you be then?'

'Then I'd be an atheist,' says Natalie, smiling.

***

Little Sarah is attending her very first sex education class at her school. During the lesson, she asks her teacher, 'Miss, do you think my mother could get pregnant?'

The teacher asks, 'How old is your mother, Sarah?'

Sarah replies, 'She's 38 years old, Miss.'

The teacher then says, 'Yes, Sarah, your mother could get pregnant.'

Sarah then asks, 'Miss, can my big sister also get pregnant?'

The teacher asks, 'How old is your sister, Sarah?'

Sarah answers, 'She's eighteen, Miss.'

The teacher says, 'Oh yes, your sister certainly could get pregnant.'

So Sarah then asks, 'Can I get pregnant, Miss?'

The teacher asks, 'How old are you, Sarah?'

Sarah replies, 'I'm seven years old, Miss.'

The teacher says, 'No, Sarah, you can't get pregnant.'

Little Maurice, who is sitting behind Sarah, gives her a poke in the back and says, 'See, Sarah, I told you we had nothing to worry about.'

***

Little Moshe is doing his homework. As his mother walks past his room, she hears him saying, 'One and one, the son-of-a-bitch is two. Two and two, the son-of-a-bitch is four. Three and three.'

So she asks him, 'Darling, where did you learn that way of doing sums?'

Moshe replies, 'My teacher, Miss Anderson, taught us that way, mummy.'

Next day, Moshe's mother goes into his classroom, confronts Miss Anderson and tells her about Moshe's 'different' way of doing arithmetic. Miss Anderson is shocked. At first she can't understand why Moshe would say that she had taught it, but then suddenly it dawned on her.

'I know why,' she says, 'in our class, we say, one and one, the sum of which is two.'

***

The Student Letter and Its Reply

Dear Dad
Univer$ity life i$ really great and I'm beginning to enjoy it. Even though I'm making lot$ of new friend$, I $till find time to $tudy very hard. I already have $ome $tuff and I $imply can't think of anything el$e I need, $o if you like, you can ju$t $end me a $imple card a$ I would love to hear from you.
Love, your $on,
Mo$he

His father replies:

Dear Moshe
I kNOw that astroNOmy, ecoNOmics, and oceaNOgraphy are probably NOt eNOugh to keep even an hoNOurs student busy. But do NOt forget that the pursuit of kNOwledge is a NOble task and one can never study eNOugh.
Love, your father,
ArNOld

***

Two *yeshiva* students are discussing whether it is allowed to smoke while learning Torah. But they cannot reach any agreement. So Yankel says to Moshe, 'We will go and ask the Rebbe.'

When they find the rabbi, Yankel asks him, 'Rebbe, is it permitted to smoke while learning Torah?'

The rabbi replies in a severe tone of voice, 'Certainly not!'

Moshe then addresses the rabbi, 'Rebbe, let me ask you another question. May we learn Torah while we smoke?'

The rabbi immediately replies, with a warm smile, 'Yes, of course!'

***

Just before the class took their GCSE maths exams, their teacher asked them the following problem to test how well they would do in the real exam:

> A rich man dies and leaves £240 million in his will. One-third is to go to his wife; one-fifth is to go to his son; one-sixth to his chauffeur; one-eighth to his secretary; and the rest to charity. Now, what does each get?

After a long silence in the classroom, Saul raised his hand.

'Yes, Saul,' said the teacher.

'A good solicitor!' he replied.

***

Jacob from Russia had just completed a training course entitled 'Improve your English' and was taking an oral exam. The examiner asked him to spell 'cultivate'.

Jacob spelled it correctly.

Then the examiner asked Jacob to use the word 'cultivate' in a sentence.

Jacob thought about it for a while, then replied, 'Last vinter, on a very cold day, I vas vaiting for de bus but it vas too cultivate so I took an underground train home.'

***

Rifka told her daughter. 'You should read your Bible, Sarah, just like Grandma does.'

Sarah replied, 'I don't have to yet, mummy. Grandma's studying for her final exams.'

***

Q: What's a genius?

A: An average student with a Jewish mother.

***

One morning, the teacher asks her class, 'All those who want to go to heaven, please put up your hand.'

Everyone raises their hand except Benjamin, so the teacher asks, 'Why don't you want to go to heaven, Benjamin?'

'Because,' he replies, 'I heard my father tell my mother, "Business has gone to hell," and I want to go where the business went.'

***

It was lunchtime at the Jewish nursery school and all the children were lined up by the teachers. Then, as usual, they were led into the canteen. Little Moshe quickly noticed that at one end of the dining table was a large pile of apples with the message: 'Take ONLY ONE apple each, God is watching.'

At the other end he noticed was a large pile of kosher chocolate chip cookies. Moshe then whispered to his friend Sarah, 'We can take all the cookies we want. God is watching the apples.'

FAMILY EVENTS

Bar Mitzvahs

Young Bernie Gold was nearly twelve years old and although he had a lower than average IQ, he was a dutiful and caring son. One day, he was having a chat with his father. 'Dad, it's Father's Day on Sunday and I want to buy you something. Mum said I should ask you what you wanted.'

Mr Gold only needed to think for a moment. 'What do I want? I only want one thing – you are twelve months away from your Bar Mitzvah and I would be so very happy if you could learn at last to speak Hebrew.'

Bernie groaned aloud, 'You know how hard I'm finding it at school to learn new subjects, Dad. I'm such a slow learner. I just don't think I would be able to learn Hebrew.'

Mr Gold looked squarely at his son and said, 'Bernie, you're better than you think you are. I'll even help you, just as my father helped me. If you could do this for me, it would please me so very much!'

'OK, I'll try Dad, just for you, but please don't be angry with me if I fail.'

So next Sunday, they went to see the rabbi and soon after that Bernie was enrolled in the synagogue's Hebrew classes. Over the months that followed, Bernie kept his promise by attending regularly and trying as hard as he could. One day, Mr Gold decided to visit the synagogue and check on Bernie's progress. He entered the class in the middle of a lesson and when it came to Bernie's turn to read, Mr Gold was soon dismayed to discover how little Hebrew Bernie could manage after all the months that had gone by. Bernie was very slow and made many mistakes in his reading. But even worse, Mr Gold realised that what he was hearing from Bernie was the beginning of the Kaddish. He was shocked – the Kaddish is the prayer for the dead, the words that every son is expected to recite after his father's death.

'Rabbi, what on earth are you teaching my son?' argued Mr Gold after the lesson was over. 'I'm only in my forties – I'm a young man still in good health. I go jogging and Israeli dancing every week. Do I really look so ill that you are teaching Bernie to say the Kaddish now?'

The rabbi replied, 'Mr Gold, please God you should live so long that Bernie is able to say the whole of the Kaddish over you!'

***

Issy wanted something extra-special and memorable for his son Paul's Bar Mitzvah. He spent weeks checking out the swankiest venues and the best caterers in London and then settled on a very plush banqueting hall and an enormously expensive caterer who promised him a great surprise on the night.

'Issy,' said the caterer, 'don't worry. It will be such a special event that everyone who attends will talk about it for years to come.'

'OK, where do I sign?' said Issy.

The night of Paul's Bar Mitzvah party arrived. As soon as everyone was seated, the lights dimmed and to a fanfare from Sam Bloom's Symphony Orchestra, twelve powerful searchlights shone upwards whilst at the same time, an uncannily lifelike model of Paul slowly descended from the ceiling. But this was no ordinary sculpture. It was made entirely out of chopped liver. From all over the hall could be heard gasps of amazement. Then the toastmaster announced that the sculpture had been created by the great Henry Moore himself. Everyone cheered. At the end of the affair, Issy met with the caterer to settle the bill.

'This was indeed a very special night for me,' Issy said, 'but one thing upset me. Did you really have to get that Gentile Henry Moore to make the statue? Why didn't you get a Jew? Couldn't you have asked, say, Epstein?'

'Well, to tell you the truth,' said the caterer, 'I *did* ask Epstein, but he only works in egg and onion.'

* * *

Moshe was a bragger and loved to out-do his friends whenever he could and now it was coming up to the time of his son Isaac's Bar Mitzvah. He gave it a lot of thought and then, after studying many brochures and maps, he hit upon a perfect, unique way to celebrate – a safari. So Moshe went ahead with the detailed arrangements. He started off by hiring a special flight to Africa to accommodate all the invited family and friends. Then he chose a guide and his bearers. He phoned the guide in Africa and told him what he wanted.

'I want my entourage to be able to hear jungle chants; I want to be able to shoot some wild animals, on film of course; I need a clearing to be found where my rabbi can hold the service; and I want my son to be able to recite his prayers in Hebrew whilst standing on the body of an anaesthetised lion.'

'OK,' said the guide, 'no problem.'

The guests were ecstatic when they received details of the weekend and all accepted their invitation. Come the day of departure, they were all flown to Africa. On arrival, the guide and bearers were waiting for them, together with thirty elephants. Off they went with the guide leading the way and directing the elephants along the narrow trails through the rain forest. But then, just five hours into the journey, the column of elephants came to a sudden halt and the guide shouted, 'There will now be a delay of two hours.'

Moshe was angry at this. 'Why the delay?' he asked his guide.

'There's nothing I can do,' said the guide, 'there's another two Bar Mitzvah safaris ahead of us.'

Weddings & engagements

Sam tells his mum that he has got engaged at last. His mother is happy but a little bit worried as well. She just has to ask him, 'Is she Jewish?'

'Of course she is, mum. I'll bring her to dinner this evening so you can meet her.'

That night Sam arrives with three beautiful women – a blonde, a brunette and a redhead. 'Mother I want you to guess who is my fiancé,' says Sam smiling.

But his mother is not pleased at all. All she wanted to do was to speak to her son's fiancé one-to-one first without playing silly games. She doesn't know where to start.

She waits patiently and gives it some thought. When the meal is over, she calls Sam into the kitchen. 'I know which one she is,' she says.

'Which one, then, mum?' asks Sam.

'The blonde.'

'Yes, you're right. How on earth did you guess?'

'I knew as soon as I saw her, I couldn't stand the sight of her.'

***

Sadie was stopped by an usher at the entrance to the synagogue.

The usher asked, 'Are you a friend of the bride?'

Sadie quickly replied, 'No, of course not. I am the groom's mother.'

***

Q: Why is it so important for the groom at a Jewish wedding to stamp on a glass?

A: Because it's probably the last time he'll have a chance to put his foot down.

***

Q: You're at a Jewish wedding. How can you tell if it's Orthodox, Reform, or Liberal?

A: In an Orthodox wedding, the bride's mother is pregnant. In a Reform wedding, the bride is pregnant. In a Liberal wedding the rabbi is pregnant.

* * *

Sarah comes home from her long stay in Uganda and surprises her mother Bette, who is in the process of lighting the Friday night candles and serving the matzo ball soup. Bette is so thrilled she can't stop hugging and kissing Sarah.

Finally she says, 'Sit down, darling. Tell me all about what you were doing.'

Sarah says, 'Mum, I got married.'

'*Oy, Mazeltov*,' says Bette, 'But how could you do that without telling me? What's he like? What does he do? Where is he?'

'He's waiting outside while I tell you.'

'What are you talking about? Bring him in. I want to meet my new son-in-law.'

Sarah brings him in and to her consternation, Bette sees a black man standing before her wearing an evil grin, a feathered cod piece, an ornate head dress, animal tooth beads and holding a tall spear.

Bette says to Sarah, 'You stupid idiot. I said marry a *rich* doctor!'

* * *

Freda and Moshe were getting married at Edgware synagogue and all was going fine until the rabbi discovered that Freda and Moshe and their parents had disappeared. A search was immediately made throughout the synagogue and finally, the *chazan* found them sitting in the synagogue basement. All six of them were just sitting on the floor and crying. The rabbi approached Freda and said, 'Why are you all crying on this most happy and important day of your lives?'

Freda looked up at the rabbi and replied, 'My parents are alive and Moshe's parents are alive? Who are we going to name the baby after?'

* * *

Two Jewish aerials meet on a roof, fall in love and get married. The wedding ceremony was rubbish but the reception was brilliant!

***

Jeffrey, a rather innocent young man, is getting married. On the eve of his wedding night, he goes to his mother and asks, 'Mum, why are wedding dresses white?'

The mother looks at her son and replies, 'This shows everyone that your bride is pure.'

Thoughtful, Jeffrey goes to his father and asks, 'Dad, why are wedding dresses white?'

His father looks at Jeffrey in surprise – 'All domestic appliances are white!'

***

When Louis was younger, he just hated going to Jewish weddings. All his uncles and aunts used to come up to him, poke him in the ribs, giggle, and say to him, 'You're next, Louis.'

But they stopped doing that after Louis started doing the same thing to them at funerals.

***

'Congratulations, Moshe,' said the bridegroom's uncle. 'I'm sure you'll look back on today and remember it as the happiest day of your life.'

'But I'm not getting married until tomorrow,' replied Moshe.

'I know, I know,' replied his uncle.

***

Moshe, an elderly man, was listening to a dietician addressing a large audience in London. 'Did you know,' said the dietician, 'that the stuff we regularly put into our stomachs is harmful enough to eventually kill most of us here today? Well it's true. Red meat is terrible for us, soft drinks erode our stomach lining, Chinese food is loaded with monosodium glutamate and even vegetables can be disastrous to some of us. And most of us don't realise the long-term harm being caused by additives to our drinking water. But bad as these are, one thing is worse than all of these put together and we have all eaten it or will eat it. Can anyone here tell me what food causes the most grief and suffering for years after eating it?'

Moshe stood up and said, 'Wedding cake.'

***

Maurice and Rachel are sweethearts. Maurice lives in a small village out in the country and Rachel lives in town. One day, they go to see the rabbi and set a date for their wedding. Before they leave, the rabbi asks them whether they want a contemporary or traditional service. After a short discussion, they opt for the contemporary service.

Their day arrives but the weather is rotten and a storm forces Maurice to take an alternate route to the synagogue. The village streets are flooded, so he rolls up his trouser legs to keep his trousers dry. When at last he reaches the synagogue, his best man immediately rushes him up the aisle and up to the *chuppah*. As the ceremony starts, the rabbi whispers to Maurice, 'Pull down your trousers.'

Rabbi, I've changed my mind,' says Maurice, 'I think I prefer the traditional service.'

***

My dear Moshe,
I am writing to tell you that I have been unable to sleep ever since I broke off our engagement. Won't you please, please forgive me? Not being able to hug you any more is breaking my heart. I admit that I was a fool. Nobody can take your place. I really love you.
All my undying love,
Beckie

xxxxxxxxxxxxx

PS *Mazeltov* on winning the top lottery prize this week.

Honeymoons

Mr and Mrs Goldberg had just got married. On their way to their honeymoon, Mr Goldberg said to his new wife, 'Would you have married me if my father hadn't left me a fortune?'

She replied, 'Darling, I would have married you no matter who had left you a fortune.'

***

Shlomo and Rifka had just got married and were on honeymoon.

On the first night, as he was making love to Rifka for the first time, Shlomo looked down at her and asked, 'Am I the first man to make love to you, Rifka?'

Rifka looked up at him and replied, 'No Shlomo. I'm sure I would have recognised you.'

***

Maurice and Hannah got married and were on their honeymoon. On their first night, they began getting undressed together for the first time. As soon as Maurice removed his shoes and socks, Hannah quickly noticed how twisted and red looking his toes were.

'Whatever happened to your feet?' Hannah asked.

'I had a childhood disease called tolio,' replied Maurice.

'Don't you mean polio?'

'No, tolio, it only affects the toes,' Maurice said.

Maurice then took off his trousers to reveal badly deformed, lumpy knees.

'What happened to your knees?' Hannah asked.

'Well, I also had kneasles,' replied Maurice.

'Don't you mean measles?'

'No, kneasles, it only affects the knees,' Maurice said.

Finally Maurice removed his pants and stood there in all his glory.

Hannah gasped and said, 'Don't tell me, you also had smallcox!'

***

Fay and Cyril get married and on their first night in bed, Cyril puts his arm around Fay and very sweetly whispers, 'Fay, darling, please pull up your nightgown.'

Very sweetly Fay answers, 'Nooo.'

Cyril asks again, a little sterner, 'Fay, pull up your nightgown.'

Fay again says, 'No.'

Cyril is now angry and says, 'Fay, pull up your nightgown or I'm going out the door and you'll never see me again.'

'No,' says Fay.

So Cyril gets up and goes out the front door, slamming it behind him. Fay immediately gets up and locks the door. Not too long after, Cyril is back. He tries the front door but finds it locked. So he taps on the door and says, 'Fay, my darling, open the door, it's me.'

Fay says, 'Nooo.'

Cyril knocks a little louder, 'Fay, sweetness, please open the door.'

'No,' says Fay.

Cyril starts kicking the door and shouts, 'Fay, open this door right now or I'll break it down.'

Fay says, 'Really? A door you can break down, but a nightgown you can't pull up?'

Anniversaries

Benny and Max meet one Shabbes whilst parking their cars down a little road out of sight of the synagogue. As they begin their five-minute walk to the synagogue, Benny says, 'I'm glad I've bumped into you Max. It's my parents' golden wedding anniversary next week and I would like you to come to the party.'

'It's nice of you to ask,' replies Max, 'Thank you, yes, I will come.'

'And if you have some friends you can bring with you, please do so,' says Benny, 'It will be nice to have a lot of people at the party.'

'Yes. I can bring Hymie Cohen and Melvyn Levy.'

'Great, but don't forget to remind them to bring something gold.'

'OK.'

So Max brought a goldfish, Hymie Cohen brought a jar of Gold Blend coffee and Melvyn Levy brought Howard Goldberg.

***

Sadie and Maurice were celebrating their 25th wedding anniversary with a group of friends at Bloom's Restaurant in Golders Green. But Maurice looked unhappy so his best friend Michael, a solicitor, went over to him.

'What's the matter, Maurice,' he asked. 'Why do you look so sad?'

'Do you remember on my fifth anniversary I asked you what would happen if I murdered Sadie?'

'Yes,' answered Michael, 'I said you would get twenty years in jail.'

'Well,' said Maurice, 'I would have been a free man tonight!'

***

Shlomo asks his wife, 'Where shall we go to celebrate our anniversary, darling?'

Sarah replies, 'Somewhere I have never been!'

So Shlomo says, 'How about the kitchen, then?'

***

Shlomo and Ruth were celebrating their golden wedding anniversary. Their long-lasting and happy marriage was the talk of the Edgware community. So it was no surprise when a *Jewish Chronicle* reporter came to see Shlomo to ask him the secret of their successful marriage.

'Well, it dates back to our honeymoon,' explained Shlomo. 'We visited the Grand Canyon and took a trip down to the bottom of the canyon on mules. We hadn't gone very far when Ruth's mule stumbled. She looked at the mule and quietly said, "That's once." We had only proceeded a little farther when the mule stumbled again. Once more Ruth looked him in the eyes and quietly said, "That's twice." We hadn't gone more than a half-mile more when the mule stumbled a third time. This time, Ruth promptly removed a revolver from her rucksack and shot the mule dead. I started to protest over her treatment of the mule when Ruth looked at me and quietly said, "That's once."'

***

One day, Moshe goes up to his boss and says, rather timidly, 'Mr Gold, is it OK if I take tomorrow off? It's my golden wedding anniversary.'

'What a *chutzpah* you have,' replies Mr Gold, 'Is this what I'm going to have to put up with from you every fifty years?'

***

It was Hetty and Benjy's silver wedding anniversary. Hetty says, 'Do you remember when you proposed to me, Benjy? I was so overwhelmed and taken aback that I couldn't talk for an hour.' Benjy replies, 'Yes, of course I do, Hetty. How could I ever forget? It was the happiest hour of my life.'

***

Moshe and Sadie lived in a retirement home in Hendon and were celebrating their fiftieth anniversary. Although David, Henry and Alan, their three sons, had successful careers, they had been visiting their parents less and less in recent times. Nevertheless, the sons agreed to visit their parents at their home for a special Sunday lunch. As usual, they all arrived late and almost immediately their excuses began.

'Happy Anniversary, mum and dad,' shouted David, 'I'm sorry I'm late but I had an emergency at the hospital. You know how it is. So I didn't even have time to stop to get you both a present.'

'Don't worry,' said Moshe, 'the main thing is, we're together, aren't we?'

Henry then came over. 'Hi dad, you're looking great. And wow, mum, don't you look good also? You're looking just like a model. I just got in from Zurich where I closed the big deal I'd been working on for the last six months. So I came here straight from Heathrow and I'm sorry but I had no time to buy you both a gift. Next time, eh?'

'It's nothing,' said Moshe, 'the main thing is we're all together.'

Then Alan came in and said, 'Hi mum and dad. My firm is sending me to Paris for an important conference, so I'll have to leave as soon as we've finished dinner. I've been so busy packing that I didn't have time to buy you anything.'

Moshe sighed and replied, 'I don't care as long as I have my three sons together.'

Halfway through the meal, Moshe, in a reflective mood, said, 'Now might be a good time to tell you all something that has been on your mother's and my mind for years. Your mother and I, well, we came to England during the war. We had no money and were desperate and in our struggle to survive, I'm sorry to tell you that we never got around to getting married. We knew we loved each other and after a few years, it didn't seem so important, so - '

The three sons gasped, 'Dad, do you mean ... do you mean – we're bastards?'

'Yes,' replied Moshe, 'that's exactly what I do mean and cheap ones, too.'

MISHPOCHEH (FAMILY RELATIONSHIPS)

Dating

Sam is a nice young man who has fallen in love with a girl he has just met. When Sam tells his father about her, the father just wants to know her family name.

When Sam tells him that the girl's name is Ford, his father says that Ford is not a good Jewish name and he must forget her and go and find a Jewish girl.

Time passes and Sam finds another girl. Her name is Smith, so his father tells him to find a nice Jewish girl with a nice Jewish name.

More time passes and Sam finds another girl, but this time he is sure that he has solved the problem because the girl's name is Goldberg.

'Goldberg,' exclaims his father, 'this makes me very happy because it's a real good Jewish name, and from a good established family.'

Then his father asks, 'Is her first name one of my favourite names, like Rachael, or Rebecca?'

'No Father,' replies Sam, 'It's Whoopi.'

* * *

Did you hear about the guy who called his girlfriend 'Mezuzah' because she liked to be kissed?

* * *

Shlomo and Hetty, an elderly widow and widower, had been dating for about three years when Shlomo finally decided to ask Hetty to marry him. She immediately said 'yes.'

The next morning when he awoke, Shlomo couldn't remember what her answer was. 'Was she happy? I think so. Wait, no, she looked at me funny ...' After about an hour of trying to remember, but to no avail, he got on the telephone and gave Hetty a call. Embarrassed, he admitted that he didn't remember her answer to his proposal.

'Oh,' Hetty said, 'I'm so glad you called. I remembered saying 'yes' to someone, but I couldn't remember who it was.'

***

Benny is almost 32 years old. All his friends are now married but Benny just dates and dates. Finally his friend asks him, 'What's the matter, Benny? Are you looking for the perfect woman? Are you really that fussy? Surely you can find someone who suits you?'

'No I just can't,' Benny replies. 'I meet many nice girls, but as soon as I bring them home to meet my parents, my mother doesn't like them. So I keep on looking.'

'Listen,' his friend suggests, 'why don't you find a girl who's just like your mother?'

Many weeks go by and again Benny and his friend get together.

'So, have you found the perfect girl yet? One that's just like your mother?'

Benny shrugs his shoulders, 'Yes, I found one just like mum. Mum loved her right from the start and they have become good friends.'

'So, do I owe you a *Mazeltov*? Are you and this girl engaged yet?'

'I'm afraid not. My father can't stand her!'

***

Q: Why is it so difficult to find Jewish men who are sensitive, caring and handsome?
A: They already have boyfriends.

***

Howard, a young gay man, telephones his mother and says, 'Mum, I've decided to go back into the closet. I've met a wonderful girl and we are going to be married. What do you think of this news? You'll be happier now – I know that my gay lifestyle has been very disturbing to you.'

She responds, 'I'm very glad, Howard. I suppose it would be too much to hope that she's a Jewish girl?'

Howard replies, 'Not only is she Jewish, mum, but she comes from a wealthy Beverly Hills family.'

'So what's her name?'

'Monica Lewinsky.'

There is a pause, then his mother asks, 'What happened to that nice black boy you were dating last year?'

***

Suzie and Carol, two widows in a Hendon adult community centre, were curious about the latest arrival – a quiet, nice-looking man who, most of the time, kept himself to himself. Carol said to Suzie, 'You know I'm shy. Why don't you go over to him and find out a little bit about him. He looks so lonely.' Suzie agreed.

So she walked up to him and said, 'Excuse me, I hope you don't mind me asking, but my friend and I were wondering why you looked so lonely.'

'I'm lonely,' he said, 'Because I've spent the past twenty years in prison.'

'You're kidding me! What ever for?'

'For killing my third wife. I strangled her.'

'What happened to your second wife?'

'I poisoned her.'

'And, if I may ask, what about your first wife?'

'We had a fight and she fell out the window.'

'Oh my goodness,' said Suzie.

Then turning to her friend on the other side of the room, she shouted, 'Carol. It's OK, he's single!'

***

Beckie and Sadie have both lost their husbands and are hoping to find new partners. One day, Sadie says to Beckie, 'That nice Bernie Schwartz asked me out for a date the other day. I know you went out with him recently so tell me about him before we meet.'

Beckie replies, 'Well OK, I'll tell you. He shows up at my apartment exactly on time, just like a quartz clock. And like a *mensh* he is dressed – fine jacket, beautiful shirt and a smart tie. He brings me my favourite chocolates, you know, the ones I would die for. And he comes in an expensive Lexus car, no less, with a uniformed chauffeur wearing a peaked cap. So then he takes me out to dinner in Baker Street, a kosher restaurant even, just as I would have wanted. Then we go and see a West End show. Oh Sadie, I enjoyed that evening so much. But when we come back to my apartment for a coffee, everything changes. He suddenly goes completely crazy. He grabs hold of me, tears off my expensive Cerruti dress like it was made of paper and, and – he had his way with me!'

Sadie says, '*Oy Vay!* So are you telling me I shouldn't go out with him?'

Beckie replies, 'No. All I'm saying is if you do go out with him, wear *shmattas* [rags].'

***

Hannah comes home from her afternoon out with her boyfriend Arnold looking very unhappy. 'What's the matter, Hannah?' asks her mother.

'Arnold has asked me to marry him,' she replies.

'*Mazeltov!* But why are you looking so sad?' her mother asks.

'Because he also told me that he was an atheist. Oh mum, he

doesn't even believe in Hell.'

Her mother then says, 'That's all right Hannah, it really isn't a problem. I suggest you marry him and between the two of us, we'll show him how wrong he is.'

***

Melvyn goes to his girlfriend's house for the first time. Sharon shows him into the living room and then excuses herself to go to the kitchen to make them a drink. As he's standing there alone, he notices a colourful little vase on the mantelpiece and picks it up. As he's looking at it, Sharon walks back in.

Melvyn says, 'What's this?'

Sharon says, 'Oh, my father's ashes are in there.'

Melvyn is suddenly lost for words. He says, 'Jeez – oooh – I - '

Sharon then says, 'Yes, he's too lazy to get up off the couch and go to the kitchen to get an ashtray.'

***

Responses to kosher pick-up lines:

Abe: 'Haven't we met before? In Israel, maybe?'

Hetty: 'Yes, I'm the receptionist at the Tel Aviv VD Clinic.'

Abe: 'Haven't I seen you someplace before? At the Israeli dance class maybe?'

Hetty: 'Yes, that's why I don't go there anymore.'

Abe: 'I just love Jewish affairs – is this seat empty?'

Hetty: 'Yes, and this one will be too if you sit down.'

Abe: 'I live in Golders Green – shall we go to your place or mine?'

Hetty: 'Both. You go to yours and I'll go to mine.'

Abe: 'I'm an accountant – so what do you do for a living?'

Hetty: 'I'm a female impersonator.'

Abe: 'How do you like your eggs in the morning?'

Hetty: 'Unfertilised!'

Abe: 'I'm very experienced and I know how to please a woman.'

Hetty: 'Then please leave me alone.'

Abe: 'You're such a beautiful Jewish girl that I want to give

myself to you.'
Hetty: 'Sorry, I don't accept cheap gifts.'
Abe: 'I'm a stockbroker in the City and I can tell that you want me.'
Hetty: 'Ohhhh. You're so right. I want you – to leave.'
Abe: 'I'm a connoisseur of beautiful Jewish women and if I could see you naked, I'd die happy.'
Hetty: 'Yes, but if I saw you naked, I'd probably die laughing.'
Abe: 'My father is big in property and I'd go through anything for you.'
Hetty: 'Good! Let's start with your bank account.'
Abe: 'I have lots of money which I'd use to go to the end of the world for you.'
Hetty: 'Yes, but would you stay there?'

Matchmakers

Benny, the *shadchen* (matchmaker), goes to see Abe, a confirmed bachelor for many years.

'Abe, you mustn't wait too long. I have exactly the one you need. You only have to say the word and you'll meet and be married in no time!' says Benny.

'Don't bother,' replies Abe, 'I've two sisters at home, who look after all my needs.'

'That's all well and good,' said Benny, 'but all the sisters in the world cannot fill the role of a wife.'

'I said "two sisters". I didn't say they were mine!'

***

A *shadchen*, having sung the praises of a female client, brought his excited male prospect to see her. Cyril took one look at the girl to whom the *shadchen* elaborately introduced him and recoiled.

'What's the matter?' asked the *shadchen*.

'You said she was young,' whispered Cyril, 'but she's forty if she's a day! You said she was beautiful, but she looks like a back of a bus! You said she was shapely, but she's fat enough for two! You said - '

'You don't have to whisper,' said the *shadchen*. 'She's also hard of hearing.'

***

A *shadchen* goes to see a poor man and says, 'I want to arrange a marriage for your son.'

The father replies, 'I never interfere in my son's life.'

The *shadchen* responds, 'But the girl is Lord Rothschild's daughter.'

'Well, in that case - '

Next, the *shadchen* approaches Lord Rothschild. 'I have a husband for your daughter.'

'But my daughter is too young to marry.'

'But this young man is already a vice-president of the World Bank.'

'Ah, in that case - '

Finally, the *shadchen* goes to see the president of the World Bank.

'I have a young man to recommend to you as a vice-president.'

'But I already have more vice-presidents than I need.'

'But this young man is Lord Rothschild's son-in-law.'

'Ah, in that case - '

***

Benny had married off four of his children but the fifth was becoming a challenge. Young Solomon had no visible virtues that would make him a desirable husband. He had no charm, intelligence, manners nor conversation to make up for his poor looks. Yet, to Benny, it was unthinkable that Solomon remained single. In desperation, Benny met with a *shadchen* who listened and said, 'I have just the girl for Solomon – Princess Anne's daughter, Zara.'

'Who?'

'Zara, granddaughter of the Queen of England, that's who.'

'A *shiksa*?'

The *shadchen* sighed. 'In these enlightened times, what's wrong with a nice Gentile girl? She comes from a good family, with very little anti-Semitism – they fought Hitler, remember. They have excellent social connections, they're wealthy and the girl is a real beauty. Look, I'll write the names down together.'

SOLOMON GOLDMAN – ZARA PHILLIPS.

Benny thought the names looked very good together, but said, 'I also have to consider Aunt Bette. She is very religious and if she found out Solomon was marrying a *shiksa*, she'd kill herself.'

So an appointment was made to see Bette.

For several hours, the *shadchen* pleaded, argued, persuaded and slowly Bette began to change her mind. With tears in her eyes, Bette said, 'Well, maybe you're right and I shouldn't be so old-fashioned. If the girl really is a fine girl, and if she will make Solomon happy, and if the children will be brought up Jewish, I won't object. I can always move away from Edgware after the wedding and change my name so no one will know my shame.'

Even though he was worn out, the *shadchen* left Bette's house in high spirits. As soon as he got into his car, he opened his little book to the page where both names had been written and put a tick after the name 'Solomon Goldman.'

He then said, with a huge sigh of relief, 'Half done!'

***

Moshe the tailor felt it was time to get a wife so one day he plucked up courage to visit a *shadchen*. The *shadchen* immediately offered him a beautiful young lady. 'This girl is quite gorgeous. She's a real prize, especially as she wants to settle down with a husband right away. Yours would be a wedding made in heaven,' said the *shadchen*.

But Moshe was a businessman and he never made decisions quickly. 'Look, I need more information,' Moshe told her. 'Whenever I buy any cloth, I always ask to see some swatches first. So before I decide on a wife, I want to see a sample also.'

The *shadchen* said she would pass on Moshe's request directly to the lady in question. She then went to visit the intended bride. 'My client says he is a good businessman and needs to find out exactly what he's buying. He insists on a sample.'

'OK,' replied the girl, 'I understand – I am also good at business. Tell him that I don't give samples but I am prepared to give him references.'

***

A *shadchen* corners a poor student and says, 'Do I have a girl for you!'

'I'm not interested,' replies the student.

'But she's a very beautiful girl,' says the *shadchen*.

'Really?' says the student, a bit more interested now.

'Yes. And she's also very rich.'

'Are you serious?'

'Of course I am. Would I lie to you? And she has a long line of ancestry. She comes from a very noble family.'

'It all sounds great to me,' says the student, 'but why would a girl like that want to marry me? She'd have to be crazy.'

Replies the *shadchen*, 'Well, you can't have everything in life!'

Marriage

Son: 'How much does it cost to get married, Dad?'
Father: 'I don't know son, I'm still paying for it.'

***

Jacob and Rifka had been married for 65 years. When they were asked whether, in all those years, they had ever thought of divorce, they replied, 'Heavens, no. Murder, yes, but divorce never.'

***

Little Sam was out shopping with his mother, something he didn't like very much. But when they passed a toy store, Sam came to life. He saw a new toy in the window that he didn't have but wanted. Sam begged, pleaded and nagged but to no avail. He got so rude that his mother firmly said, 'I'm very sorry Sam, but we didn't come out to buy you a toy.'

Sam angrily said, 'I've never met a woman as horrible as you.'

Holding his hand gently, she replied, 'Sam, darling, one day you'll get married and then you will – you really will, I promise you.'

***

Jewish marriage advice:
'Don't marry a beautiful person. They may leave you. Of course, an ugly person may leave you too, but who cares?'

***

Negative views on marriage:
Bernie says marriage is not a word, it's a sentence – a life sentence.

Sadie says marriage is a three-ring circus – engagement ring, wedding ring and suffering.

Bernie and Sadie say that married life is full of excitement and frustration. In the first year of marriage, the man speaks and the woman listens; in the second year, the woman speaks and the man listens; in the third year, they both speak and the neighbours listen.

Sadie says that getting married is very much like going to a restaurant with friends – you order what you want but when you see what the other person has, you wish you had ordered that instead.

Bernie says a happy marriage is a matter of giving and taking – the husband gives and the wife takes.

Sadie says love is one long sweet dream, and marriage is the alarm clock.

Bernie says that when a man holds a woman's hand before marriage, it's love, but after marriage, it's self-defence.

Bernie told Sadie during their courtship that he would go through hell for her. They got married and now he IS going through hell.

Confucius, he say, 'Man who sinks into woman's arms soon have arms in woman's sink.'

Bernie says, 'When a man steals your wife, there is no better revenge than to let him keep her.'

Bernie and Sadie say that after marriage, a husband and wife become two sides of a coin. They can't face each other, but still they stay together.

Bernie and Sadie say marriage is when man and woman become one. The trouble starts when they try to decide which one.

Bernie says before marriage a man yearns for the woman he loves. After the marriage the 'Y' becomes silent.

Bernie says it's not true married men live longer than single men – it only seems longer.

Bernie says man is incomplete until he gets married – then he is finished.

Sadie says it doesn't matter how often a married man changes his job, he still ends up with the same boss.

Sadie says when a man opens the door of his car for his wife, you can be sure of one thing – either the car is new or the wife is.

***

Love versus marriage:

Love is holding hands in the street – marriage is holding arguments in the street.

Love is dinner for two at the Savoy – marriage is Chinese take-away.

Love is cuddling on a sofa – marriage is deciding which sofa.

Love is talking about having kids – marriage is talking of getting a break from kids.

Love is losing your appetite – marriage is losing your figure.

Love is a flickering flame – marriage is a flickering TV.

***

Victor and Leah were an elderly couple who had been dating for some time. One day, they decided it was finally time to get married. But first, they needed to discuss how their marriage might work. They talked about finances, living arrangements, health and finally, their conjugal relationship.

'How do you feel about sex?' Victor asked Leah, with a smile on his face.

'Oh, I like to have it infrequently,' replied Leah.

Victor thought about this and then asked, 'Was that one word or two?'

***

Q: Why are many Jewish girls still single these days?
A: They have not yet met Dr Right.

Q: Why are Jewish men with pierced ears well prepared for marriage?
A: Because they've experienced pain and bought jewellery.

Q: What do you instantly know when you see a well-dressed Jewish husband?
A: His wife is good at choosing his clothes.

Q: How many Jewish husbands does it take to change a roll of toilet paper?
A: We don't know – it's never happened.

Q: What's the best way to always remember your wife's birthday?
A: Forget it just the once.

Q: What do you call a Jewish man who's lost eighty per cent of his brain?
A: A widower!

***

Rachel and Moshe were invited to a posh masked, fancy dress Chanukah party. Unfortunately, Rachel had a terrible headache and told Moshe to go to the party alone. Being a devoted husband, Moshe protested, but she argued and said she was going to take some aspirin and go to bed and there was no need for his good time to be spoiled by not going. So Moshe put on his costume and mask and away he went to the party.

After sleeping soundly for an hour or so, Rachel awoke without pain and, as it was still early, decided to go to the party. She knew that Moshe didn't know what costume she was going to wear (how many husbands do?) and she thought she would have some fun by watching him to see how he acted when she was not with him. So Rachel put on her costume and mask and drove off to the party. Rachel soon spotted Moshe. He was fooling around on the dance floor, dancing with every girl he could, copping a little feel here and having a little kiss there. So Rachel sidled up to him and being a rather seductive lady, Moshe immediately left his partner and devoted all his time to her – to this new beauty who had just arrived. Rachel let him go as far as he wished, naturally, since he was her husband. So when he whispered a little proposition in her ear, she agreed. Off they went to one of the parked cars and made mad, passionate love. Just before midnight, when everyone at the party had to take off their masks, Rachel slipped away, went home, put her costume away, got into bed, and wondered what kind of explanation Moshe would make for his behaviour.

Rachel was sitting up reading when Moshe came in and she asked what kind of time he had. He said, 'Oh, the same old thing. You know I never have a good time when you're not there.'

Then she asked, 'Did you dance much?'

He replied, 'I'll tell you, Rachel, I never even danced one dance. When I got to the party, I bumped into Yossi, Roberto, David and some other guys, so we went into a back room and played cards all night. But I can tell you, Rachel, the guy I loaned my costume to sure had a real good time!'

***

A couple, preparing for conversion to Judaism, meet with the orthodox rabbi for their final session. The rabbi asks if they have any final questions. The man asks, 'Is it true that men and women don't dance together?'

'Yes,' says the rabbi, 'For modesty reasons, men and women dance separately.'

'So I can't dance with my own wife?'

'No.'

'Well, OK,' says the man, 'but what about sex?'

'That's fine,' says the rabbi. 'It's a *mitzvah* within the marriage!'

'What about different positions?' the man asks.

'No problem,' says the rabbi.

'Woman on top?' the man asks.

'Why not?' replies the rabbi.

'Well, what about standing up?'

'No, certainly not!' says the rabbi. 'That could lead to dancing!'

Husbands & wives

Moshe is talking to one of his friends. 'My wife Bettie will never have to work. All she needs to do is cook, clean, scrub, wash, iron and sew.'

His friend says, 'That's nice to hear, I am sure she appreciates you.'

'Well, I am not so sure,' replies Moshe, 'Bettie thinks I'm too nosy. Well, that's what she wrote in her diary, anyway.'

***

Moshe goes up to a beautiful woman he sees in Waitrose supermarket and says to her, 'I've lost my wife in here and I would be very happy if you could find some time to talk to me for a few minutes.'

She asks, 'Why on earth do you want me to do that?'

Moshe replies, 'Because every time I talk to a gorgeous woman, my wife always appears out of nowhere.'

***

Ethel was married to Harry, a very successful businessman. One day, Ethel decided to have her portrait painted as a gift to Harry. When she arrived at the artist's studio for her first sitting, Ethel told him exactly what she wanted, 'You should paint me like I really am. Even the little wrinkles, you put them on your canvas. And the lines under my eyes, my flabby arms, my crooked nose, even the mole on my cheek, they must all be included. But on my hands you should put lots of rings with big diamonds and emeralds and around my neck you should put chains of gold and diamonds. OK?'

The artist looked at Ethel and asked her why she should want such detail of real life in her physical appearance, but adorn herself with imaginary jewellery.

Ethel replied, 'When I die, I know Harry will re-marry and when he does, his new wife will go crazy looking for the jewels.'

***

As the doors shut and the crowded lift made its way down to the ground floor, Sadie got very angry with her Morris. She noticed that he was wedged up against a nice young girl and had a smile on his face that said he was delighted to be in that position. As the lift reached the ground floor and the doors were about to open, the girl suddenly slapped Morris's face and said aloud, 'I'm not that kind of girl. That will teach you not to pinch my bottom!'

Sadie and Morris didn't say a word as they made their way to the car park. When they got in the car, Morris turned to Sadie and said, 'You know, darling, I really didn't pinch that girl.'

'Of course you didn't,' said Sadie smiling, 'I did.'

***

Two rabbis were discussing the decline in morals in the modern world.

'I didn't sleep with my wife before I was married,' said one of them self-righteously. 'Did you?'

'I don't know,' said the other. 'What was her maiden name?'

***

Sadie sits down next to an attractive man on the train and says, 'You look just like my fourth husband.'

The man replies, 'Your fourth husband? So how many times have you been married, lady?'

'Three,' replies Sadie.

***

Old Jewish proverb:

'A Jewish wife will forgive and forget, but she'll never forget what she forgave.'

***

Peter, John and Shlomo were in the clubhouse talking about the amount of control they each have over their wives. Peter and John are doing all the talking whilst Shlomo remains silent. After a while, Peter turns to Shlomo and says, 'Well what about you, Shlomo, are Jewish men any different? What sort of control do you have over your wife?'

'Well, just the other night, my wife Hetty came to me on her hands and knees.'

Peter and John are amazed! 'What happened then?'

'Well,' replies Shlomo, 'Hetty then said, "Get out from under the bed and fight like a man."'

***

Hyman was a household efficiency expert and at the end of one of his lectures, he concluded with a note of caution. 'Please don't try these techniques at home.'

'Why not?' asked Benny, who was in the audience.

'I watched my wife's routine at breakfast for years,' Hyman explained. 'She made lots of trips between the refrigerator, oven, table and cupboards, often carrying a single item at a time. One day I told her, "Darling, why don't you try carrying several things at once?"'

'Did it save time?' Benny asked.

'Actually, yes,' replied Hyman. 'It used to take her twenty minutes to make breakfast. Now I do it in seven.'

In-laws

'I'm so upset,' said Benny to his rabbi. 'I took my son-in-law into my clothing business and yesterday I caught him kissing one of the models!'

'Have a little patience!' advised the rabbi. 'After all, men will be men. So he kissed one of the models, so what, it's not that terrible.'

'But you don't understand,' said Benny. 'I make men's clothes.'

***

Issy goes to meet his new son-in-law to be, Benjy.

He says to Benjy, 'So, tell me, Benjy my boy, what do you do?'

'I study the Torah,' he replies.

'But Benjy, you are going to marry my daughter, how are you going to feed and house her?'

'No problem,' says Benjy, 'I study Torah and it says God will provide.'

'But you will have children, how will you educate them?' asks Issy.

'No problem,' says Benjy, 'I study Torah and it says God will provide.'

When Issy returns home, his wife anxiously asks him what

Benjy is like.

'Well,' says Issy, 'he's a lovely boy. I only just met him and he already thinks I'm God.'

***

Two friends meet in the street. One says, 'Is it true, Isaac, that your mother-in law is ill?'

'Yes.'

'In fact, Isaac, I heard that she was in hospital.'

'Yes.'

'How long has she been in hospital, Isaac?'

Isaac replies, 'In three weeks' time, please God, it will be a month.'

***

Many years ago, a Jewish town had a shortage of single men of marriageable age and they used to bring them in from nearby towns. One day, when a suitable man arrived by train, not one but two mothers-in-laws-to-be were waiting for him and each claimed him for themselves. So the rabbi was called to sort it out.

After he heard the facts, he said to the two women, 'If you still both want him, then we'll have to cut him in half and each one of you can then have half of him.'

One kept quiet while the other said, 'In that case, give him to the other woman.'

When the rabbi heard this, he immediately said, 'OK, I agree. The other woman can have him. Anyone willing to cut him in half is obviously the real mother-in-law!'

***

There was a time when Pharaoh was repeatedly breaking his promise to release the children of Israel from bondage in Egypt. So Aaron said to his wife, 'You know Sarah, this Pharaoh is really turning out to be a first-class *momzer*.'

'Aaron,' said Sarah, 'You mustn't say such things. We are all one family. Don't forget we are all children of God, even Pharaoh.'

'I cannot deny that this is true,' replied Aaron, 'but this Pharaoh, he must come from your side of the family!'

***

Sadie and Rose were sitting under hair dryers at the hairdresser having a chat. Sadie says, 'So, Rose, how's that daughter of yours?'

Rose replies, 'She's OK, thanks. She married a fantastic man. He's got such a good job in the City that she gave up her secretary's job. She stays at home but never needs to cook, because he always takes her out, or clean the house, because he got her a maid, or worry about my two lovely grandchildren, because he got her a live-in nanny.'

Sadie then asks, 'And how's your son?'

Rose replies, 'His life is awful. He married a bitch from hell. She never cooks anything and makes him take her out to dinner every night. God forbid she should vacuum a carpet, so she made him get her a maid. He has to work like a dog because she refuses to get a job and she never takes care of my grandson because she made him get her a nanny.'

Marital strife

Sadie tells Maurice, 'You're a *shmuck*! You always were a *shmuck* and you always will be a *shmuck*! You look, act and dress like a *shmuck*! You'll be a *shmuck* until the day you die! And if they ran a world-wide competition for *shmucks*, you would be the world's second-biggest *shmuck*!'

'Why only second place?' Maurice asks.

'Because you're a *shmuck*!' Sadie screams.

***

Beckie and Morris had just had yet another of their flaming rows. At the end of this one, she said to him, 'You'll be sorry, I'm going to leave you.'

To which Morris replied, 'Make up your mind, dear, which one is it going to be? It can't be both?!'

***

Moshe had a fight with Sadie, his wife, and went to the cinema to cool off. Later that evening, he decided to phone home to see what the situation was and maybe even apologise.

'Hello, darling,' he said, 'what are you making for dinner?'

'What am I making, you bastard? Poison, that's what I'm making, poison.'

Moshe replied, 'So make just one portion, I'm not coming home.'

***

Morris was certainly not the most aggressive or demanding of husbands. During one argument with his wife, he told her, 'We're not going out tonight and that's semi-final!'

***

Moshe and his wife Sadie are having dinner at an upmarket restaurant in Golders Green when an attractive young redhead walks by, smiles at Moshe and says, 'Hello Moshe.'

Sadie immediately asks, 'And who was that girl who just spoke to you?'

Moshe replies, 'Oh her, that's my mistress.'

'You have a mistress? I don't believe you. How long has this been going on?' says Sadie.

'About ten years, on and off,' answers Moshe.

'Ten years?' says Sadie. 'You bastard! I'll see a solicitor tomorrow and start divorce proceedings. I'll ruin you, you wait and see.'

'Now hold on Sadie,' responds Moshe, 'just think about it for a minute. If we get a divorce, you will only get only half of what we have together now. You won't have our big house in Hampstead, you'll no longer get a new Lexus as your birthday present from me each year, you won't be able to play golf all day with your friends, you won't - '

But before Moshe can continue, a blonde walks past and says to him, 'Hello, nice to see you again.'

Sadie asks, 'And who was that, another of your "girls"?'

Moshe replies, 'No, that's Hymie's mistress.'

'You mean that Hymie also has a mistress?' says Sadie, surprised.

Moshe answers, 'Of course, she's been with him for nearly twelve years.'

Sadie then says, proudly, 'I like ours a lot better.'

* * *

Sadie was talking to her best friend Rachel. 'Is that a new ring I see you're wearing, Rachel?'

'Yes it is, Sadie,' replied Rachel. 'My husband Max bought it for me. It's special. I call it my mood ring.'

'Why do you call it that?' asked Sadie.

'Well, when I'm in a good mood it turns green and when I'm in a bad mood, it leaves a red mark on his forehead.

* * *

Moshe was talking to his friend. 'I had it all, Hymie – money, a beautiful house and the love of a beautiful woman. Then pow! It was all gone.'

'What happened?' asked Hymie.

'My wife found out about the beautiful woman.'

* * *

Isn't marriage wonderful?

'I married Miss Right. I just didn't know her first name was Always.'

'I haven't spoken to my wife for eighteen months. I don't like to interrupt her.'

The last fight was my fault. My wife asked, 'What's on the TV?' I said, 'Dust!'

In the beginning, God created earth and rested. Then God created man and rested. Then God created woman. Since then, neither God nor man has rested.

Why do men die before their wives? Because they want to.

A beggar walked up to a well-dressed woman shopping in Brent Cross and said 'I haven't eaten anything in four days.' She looked at him and said, 'God, I wish I had your willpower.'

Do you know the punishment for bigamy? Two mothers-in-law!

Son: 'Is it true, Dad, I heard that in some parts of Africa a man doesn't know his wife until he marries her?' Dad: 'Not just in Africa, son. That happens in every country.'

First guy (proudly): 'My wife's an angel!' Second guy: 'You're lucky, mine's still alive.'

Q: How do most men define marriage? A: An expensive way to get laundry done for free.

Just think, if it weren't for marriage, men would go through life thinking they had no faults at all.

If you want your wife to listen and pay undivided attention to every word you say, talk in your sleep.

Then there was a man who said, 'I never knew what real happiness was until I got married; and then it was too late.'

The trouble with some Jewish women is that they get all excited about nothing and then they marry him.

***

Moshe came home from work one day to find his wife, Yvonne, sitting on the front door step with her bags packed. Moshe asked her where she was going, and Yvonne replied, 'I'm going to Las Vegas.'

Moshe questioned her as to why she was going and Yvonne told him, 'I just found out that I can make £1,000 a night doing what I give you for free.'

Moshe pondered that for a while, went into the house, packed his bags and returned to the front door and his wife.

Yvonne said, 'And just where do you think you are going?'

Moshe replied, 'I'm going, too.'

'Why?' she asked.

Moshe said, 'I want to see how you are going to live on £1,000 a year.'

* * *

Moshe and Sadie are getting all snuggled up in bed one night and passions were heating up nicely. Suddenly, Sadie stops and says, 'I don't feel like it, I just want you to hold me.'

Moshe says, 'What?'

Sadie says, 'You're obviously not in tune with my emotional needs as a woman.'

Moshe quickly realises that nothing is going to happen that night.

The next day, Moshe takes Sadie to John Lewis department store. He escorts her into Ladies Fashions and makes her try on three expensive outfits. He then tells her, 'Why don't we take all three of them?'

He then makes her choose matching shoes for each outfit at £200 a pair. Then they go into Jewellery and he helps her choose some diamond earrings. Sadie is so excited. She thinks Moshe has flipped out, but she doesn't care. So she also chooses a lovely alligator bag.

Moshe says, 'But you don't even like alligators! OK, if you like it, then let's get it.'

Sadie is jumping up and down with excitement. She can't believe what is going on.

She says, 'I'm ready, Moshe, lets go and pay for all this stuff.'

But Moshe says,' No, darling, we're not going to buy all this stuff.'

Sadie's face drops.

'No darling, I just want you to hold all of this for a while.' Sadie's face gets red and she is about to explode but then Moshe says, 'You're obviously not in tune with my financial needs as a man.'

* * *

Moshe and Becky are sitting in a romantic restaurant in Soho.

Moshe says, 'Becky, I'm going to make you the happiest woman in the world.'

Becky replies, 'I'll miss you.'

***

'Listen to me, Moshe,' said the doctor. 'If you ever expect to cure your insomnia, you will have to stop taking your troubles to bed with you.'

'I know, but I can't,' said Moshe. 'My wife refuses to sleep alone.'

***

Rachel goes into a chemist and asks to see the pharmacist. 'How can I help you, madam?' he says.

'I need some arsenic, please,' Rachel replies.

'And what, may I ask, are you needing arsenic for?' the pharmacist says.

'I want to kill my husband.'

'Surely you know,' says the pharmacist, 'that I can't sell you any for such a use.'

Rachel gives him a photo of a naked man and naked woman clearly having sex. Rachel says, 'The man is my husband and the woman is, as I'm sure you have recognised, your wife.'

The pharmacist looks at the photo intently and says, 'Oh, I didn't know you had a prescription. I'll go and get you some arsenic.'

***

Hetty arrives home. She runs into the house, slams the front door, and shouts at the top of her voice, 'Harry, quickly pack your bags, I've just won £10 million on the lottery.'

Harry says, 'Oh my goodness, what fantastic news. Should I pack for Florida or skiing?'

Hetty yells back, 'I don't care where you go, just get out of my life.'

***

Moshe was sitting at the breakfast table one Sunday morning reading the *News of the World*. He had just read an article about a beautiful film star who had announced that she was going to marry a football player who was famous not only for his aggression on and off the field, but also for his lack of IQ and common sense. In fact he was as "thick as two planks".'

Like many men, Moshe loved hearing his own voice and liked to report aloud stories he read from the paper. So he turned to his wife Sadie and said, 'I'll never understand why the biggest *shmucks* get the most attractive wives.'

Sadie replied, 'Why thank you, darling.'

***

It was a terrible evening in Golders Green. The wind was blowing hard, it was snowing and it was very, very cold. The streets were almost deserted and Bagels Bakery was just about to shut when Sidney entered. He looked absolutely frozen. He was wearing two jumpers, a thick scarf and an even thicker coat. His umbrella had blown inside out and he looked thoroughly miserable. As he unbuttoned his coat, he said to the baker, 'Two bagels, please.'

The baker looked surprised. 'Only two? Don't you want anything else?'

'No. I only want two,' Sidney replied. 'One for Esther and one for me.'

'Is Esther your wife?' asked the baker.

'Don't ask silly questions,' replied Sidney, 'Of course she is. Do you think my mother would send me out on a night like this?'

***

Moshe had been away on a lengthy business trip and on the plane back home, he began thinking of all the romantic things he would do on his return. So when he came home, he quietly suggested to Beckie that they go to bed early that night for a bit of l-o-v-e. But Beckie said, 'Oh Moshe, I'm so tired from looking after the house all the time you were away. Please, another time if you don't mind.'

The next night Moshe asked again. Beckie said, '*Oy Vay*, Moshe, such a terrible headache I have got. I won't be able to do anything and it wouldn't be any good. Please, wait a bit longer.'

On the third night, Moshe had become just a little impatient. 'How about it?' he said, a bit abruptly.

Beckie snapped back at him, 'Moshe. This is the third night in a row you've asked me. What are you? Some kind of sex maniac?'

***

Louis was talking to his friend Morris. 'There's nothing I wouldn't do for my Beckie,' he said, 'and there's nothing Beckie wouldn't do for me. And that's how we go through life – doing nothing for each other.'

***

Bernie says to his wife Sarah, 'Let's go out tonight, darling and have some fun.'

Sarah replies, 'OK, but if you get home before me, please leave the light on in the hall.'

***

Isaac gets home late after attending his friend's leaving party in the City. As soon as he walks in, there is his wife, Sarah, waiting for him.

Sarah looks at Isaac and says angrily, 'Can you explain to me, Isaac, how this large red lipstick mark got onto your shirt collar?'

'No, I can't,' Isaac replies. 'I don't know how it happened – I distinctly remember taking off my shirt.'

***

Sarah and Isaac are arguing. Just before leaving for work, on his way out of the door, Isaac shouts at Sarah, 'You're not even good in bed.'

When Isaac returns home after work that day, he looks for Sarah. He goes upstairs and notices that the bedroom door is closed. He goes in and there is Sarah in bed with his best friend.

'What the hell are you doing?' he shouts at her.

'Getting a second opinion,' replies Sarah.

***

Bernard goes to see his rabbi. 'Something terrible is happening to me, Rabbi. I must talk to you about it.'

The rabbi asks, 'So what's wrong, Bernard?'

Bernard replies, 'I'm sure that my wife Sarah is poisoning me.'

The rabbi is surprised by this and says to Bernard, 'I'm sure you can't be right.'

But Bernard pleads, 'I'm telling you, Rabbi, I'm certain Sarah's poisoning me and I don't know what to do.'

The rabbi shrugs his shoulders and says, 'OK, if I can talk to Sarah, I might be able to find out what's happening. I can then let you know what I've discovered.'

Bernard says, 'Thank you, Rabbi. What would I have done without you?'

A week later, the rabbi calls Bernard and says, 'Well, I contacted Sarah – in fact I spoke to her on the phone for over three hours. Do you want my advice now?'

Bernard replies, 'Yes, please, Rabbi.'

'I think you should take the poison!'

***

This is what Sadie says (but really means):

We need (I want)

It's your decision (The correct decision should be obvious by now)

Do what you want (You'll pay for this later)

We need to talk (I need to complain)

Sure – go ahead (I don't want you to)

You're certainly attentive tonight (Is sex all you ever think about?)

You're – so manly (You need a shave and you sweat a lot)

I'm not upset (Of course I'm upset, you moron!)

I'm not emotional or overreacting (I've got my period)

Be romantic, turn out the lights (I have flabby thighs)

This kitchen is so inconvenient (I want new curtains, carpets and furniture)

Hang the picture there (No, I mean hang it there)

I heard a noise (I noticed you were almost asleep)

Do you love me? (I'm going to ask for something expensive)

How much do you love me? (I did something today you're not going to like)

I'll be ready in a minute (Kick off your shoes and turn on the TV)

Does my bottom look big in this? (Tell me I'm beautiful)

You must learn to communicate (Just agree with me)

I'm sorry (You'll be sorry)

Do you like this recipe? (It's easy to make so you'd better get used to it)

Was that the baby? (Get out of bed and rock him to sleep)

I'm not yelling! (Yes I'm yelling because I think this is important)

***

Lionel and Judith had just returned home from a party.

Judith said, 'Do you realise what you did tonight, Lionel?'

'No I don't,' Lionel replied, 'but I'll admit I was wrong. What did I do?'

***

Sidney says to his friend, 'We were so poor when I was young that I had to sleep in the same bed as my three brothers. We slept four-to-a-bed for many years. I didn't know what it was like to sleep alone until I grew up and married Sadie.'

***

Benny was fed up with being bossed around by his wife Leah so he went to see a psychiatrist. The psychiatrist told him that he was too much of a mild-mannered man and needed to build up his self-esteem. So he lent Benny a book on assertiveness. Benny started to read the book on the train and by the time he got home, he had finished the book.

Benny strode manfully into the house, walked over to Leah, pointed his finger at her and said, 'From now onwards you must get it into your head that I and not you make all the decisions in this house. Tonight, I want you to prepare me my favourite meal and I expect a special mouth-watering desserts afterwards. Then, after dinner, you're going to run me a hot bath so I can relax. And when I step out of the bath, guess who's going to dress me and comb my hair?'

'Abrahamson, the funeral director, that's who,' replied Leah.

Divorce

Even though Morris and Sadie have been married for a very, very long time, they still decide to visit a divorce lawyer in Camden Town. At the first meeting, the solicitor asks them, 'Why in the world do you want to get divorced? You each look well into your 90s. Why now of all times?'

Morris replies, 'Actually, I'm 102 and my wife Sadie is 101.'

The solicitor is totally bemused and asks them again 'So why do you want a divorce now?'

Sadie replies this time, 'Well, we wanted to wait until all of the children were dead.'

***

Shlomo and Hetty had been living apart for a number of weeks and decided to visit their rabbi to see whether he could help solve their problems and save their marriage. Following some lengthy counselling with the rabbi, they made a brief attempt to reconcile their differences, but in the end they failed. They quickly decided to end their union.

In court to finalise their separation, the judge asked Shlomo, 'So tell me, what has brought you to the point where you are unable to keep your marriage going?'

Shlomo replied, 'In the seven weeks we've been back together, your honour, we just haven't been able to agree on one little thing.'

Hetty interrupts, 'He means eight weeks, your honour!'

***

Hymie is telling his friends about his recent divorce. 'Yes, it's true. Sylvie divorced me for religious reasons. She worshipped money and I didn't have any.'

***

Rebecca goes to see her rabbi. He can see right away that she is angry. She immediately tells him that she wants a divorce. 'Why, what's the matter?' he asks.

Rebecca replies, 'I have a strong suspicion that he's not the father of our youngest child!'

***

Q: Why do Jewish divorces cost so much.

A: Because they are worth it.

***

Q. What is the technical term for a divorced Jewish woman?

A. 'The claimant.'

***

Q: What's the difference between a circumcision and a divorce?

A: With a divorce you're rid of the whole *shmuck*.

***

Issy is playing a round of golf with Sidney when suddenly, Issy announces, 'I want a divorce.'

'Why on earth do you want to do that?' says Sidney. 'Why do you want to divorce your lovely Hetty? She's beautiful. And if I may say so, she seems so warm and gentle, with a great figure to go with it.'

'Look at it this way Sidney,' replies Issy, as he removes one of his shoes. 'Just look at this shoe. The leather seems soft and gentle, it looks great on my foot and its shape is very modern. Don't you agree?'

'Yes,' replies Sidney, 'but I don't understand what you're getting at.'

'Well,' says Issy, 'I'm the only one who knows the shoe is pinching my toes and it hurts terribly.'

***

Moshe muttered a few words in the synagogue and found himself married. A year later he muttered something in his sleep and found himself divorced.

***

One day, Ethel tells her husband, Benjy, 'I've found myself another lover and I want a divorce.'

'Never,' says Benjy, 'I don't believe in divorce. But I'll tell you what you can do. If your new man is presentable, why not bring him home to live with us?'

Ethel accepts this arrangement. Her new lover comes to live with them and soon Ethel is pregnant. A few years later, the four of them are out walking when Benjy meets an old friend of his. 'Benjy! You're looking very well,' says his friend, 'who is that lovely lady?'

'That,' replies Benjy with pride, 'is my wife.'

'And who is the young boy?'

'That's my son Isaac,' answers Benjy.

'And who is that nice-looking young man with your wife?' asks his friend.

'Ah,' replies Benjy, 'that's my *shmuck*.'

Fathers

Morris calls his son in New York and says, 'Benny, I have something to tell you. However, I don't want to discuss it. I'm merely telling you because you're my oldest child, and I thought you ought to know. I've made up my mind, I'm divorcing your mother.'

The son is shocked, and asks his father to tell him what happened.

'I don't want to get into it. My mind is made up.'

'But Dad, you can't decide to divorce Mum just like that after 54 years together. What happened?'

'It's too painful to talk about it. I only called because you're my son, and I thought you should know. I really don't want to get into it anymore than this. You can call your sister and tell her. It will spare me the pain.'

'But where's Mum? Can I talk to her?'

'No, I don't want you to say anything to her about it. I haven't told her yet. Believe me it hasn't been easy. I've agonised over it for several days, and I've finally come to a decision. I have an appointment with my Edgware lawyer the day after tomorrow.'

'Dad, don't do anything rash. I'm going to take the first flight to London. Promise me that you won't do anything until I get there.'

'Well, all right, I promise. Next week is Passover. I'll hold off seeing the lawyer until after the Seder. Call your sister in New Jersey and break the news to her. I just can't bear to talk about it any more.'

Half an hour later, Morris receives a call from his daughter who tells him that she and her brother were able to get tickets and that they and the children will be arriving at Heathrow the day after tomorrow. 'Benny told me that you don't want to talk about it on the telephone, but promise me that you won't do anything until we both get there.'

Morris promises.

After hanging up from his daughter, Morris turns to his wife and says, 'Well, it worked this time, they're coming for Seder night, but we are going to have to come up with a new idea to get them here for Rosh Hashanah.'

***

The following was overheard at a recent 'high society' party.

'My ancestry goes back all the way to Alexander the Great,' said Christine.

She then turned to Miriam and asked, 'How far back does your family go?'

'I don't know,' replied Miriam, 'All of our records were lost in the Flood.'

***

Morris says to his teenage daughter 'There are two words I'd like you to drop from your vocabulary. One is "awesome" and the other is "gross".'

'OK,' she replies, 'what are they?'

***

Little Moshe asks his father, 'Dad, where do clouds come from?'

His father replies, 'Good question, son. I wish I knew that myself.'

Moshe then asks, 'Dad, how does rain come out of the clouds?'

His father replies, 'Interesting question, son. I must look that up later on.'

Moshe then asks, 'When lightning happens, Dad, why does it always come before the thunder?'

His father replies, 'I used to know that, son, but I've forgotten the answer.'

Then little Moshe asks, 'Do you mind me asking you all these questions, Dad?'

His father replies, 'No, of course not son. If you don't ask, you don't learn!'

***

Little Benny and little Sarah are at Edgware infants' school. One day during lunch, Sarah says, 'Benny, do you want to play mummies and daddies with me?'

Benny replies, 'OK. What do you want me to do?'

'I want you to communicate your thoughts,' she says.

'Communicate my thoughts?' says Benny, 'I have no idea what that means.'

Sarah instantly smirks and with a knowing look says, 'That's fine, then. You can be the daddy.'

***

Harry and his neighbour Joe often borrowed things from each other. One day, Harry asked to borrow Joe's ladder. Joe said, 'Sorry Harry, I've lent it to my son.'

Remembering an old saying that his grandma often used to tell him, Harry said, 'Joe, you should never lend anything to your children because you'll never get it back.'

Joe replied, 'Don't worry, it's not my ladder. It's my dad's.'

***

Jacob was an uneducated but hard-working immigrant who wanted a better future for his only son, David. He scrimped and saved for David's university education. In return, David worked hard and got accepted at a small university far from home. Every month, David received a cheque from his father for his living expenses and every month the cheque was attached to a piece of paper with the letters 'FUF' written on it. It regularly puzzled David, but he cashed the cheques anyway and went about his studies. Finally Passover came and David was able to travel home.

As he sat with his father after the Seder, David said, 'Dad, I want you to know how much I love you and how much I appreciate everything you're doing for me. I really couldn't get by without the cheque you send me every month. But I must ask, what does it mean when you write "FUF"?'

His father replied, '*Oy*, some scholar you're not. "FUF" means "From U Fadder".'

***

Maurice and Sarah were Londoners and were blessed with seven healthy children. After many months of discussion, they finally decided to move to New York. It should have been a simple enough move, but when they arrived, they had great difficulty finding a suitable apartment to live in. Although many were big enough, the landlords always seemed to object to such a large family living there. If only Maurice wasn't so honest about the size of his family! After several days of unsuccessful searching, Maurice had an idea. He told Sarah to take the four younger children to visit the local cemetery while he went with the older three children to find an apartment. After looking for most of the morning, Maurice found a place that was ideal.

The landlord asked him, 'How many children do you have?'

Maurice answered with a deep sigh, 'Seven – but four are with their dear mother in the cemetery.'

He got the apartment!

***

Abe, an elderly gentleman, was sitting on a bench in Brent Cross shopping centre when a priest sat down next to him. Because he had never had a chance to talk to a priest before, Abe asked, 'Excuse me, but vhy do you hev your shoyt collar on beckvurds?'

The priest replied, 'I wear this collar because I am a Father.'

Abe said, 'I am also a fadder but I vare my collar frontvays. So, vhy do you vare your collar differently?'

The priest replied, 'Because I'm the Father for many.'

'I am also the fadder for many,' said Abe. 'I have five sons, three daughters and many grandchildren, but I still vare my collar like normal. So vhy do you vare it yore vay?'

The priest was getting a bit fed up with this questioning and replied, 'Because I am the Father for over two hundred people.'

Abe was taken aback and was silent for a while. Then, as he got up to leave, Abe said to the priest, 'Mister, maybe you should vare your pents beckvurds instead.'

***

Benny has been wondering for some time why Sam, one of his five sons, is so different to his other children. So he plucks up courage and asks his wife, 'Tell me the truth, Sarah. Who is Sam's real father?'

Sarah replies, 'You are.'

Mothers

My Yiddishe Mama

My mother taught me to appreciate a job well done:

'If you two are going to kill each other, do it outside, I just finished cleaning!'

My mother taught me religion:

'If you don't learn Hebrew, you won't be Bar Mitzvah'ed and, if you're not Bar Mitzvah'ed, I'll die of embarrassment!'

My mother taught me about time travel:

'If you don't behave, I'm going to knock you into the middle of next week!'

My mother taught me logic:
'Because I said so, that's why.'
My mother taught me foresight:
'Make sure you wear clean underwear, in case you're in an accident.'
My mother taught me irony:
'Keep crying and I'll give you something to cry about.'
My mother taught me about the science of osmosis:
'Shut your mouth and eat your supper!'
My mother taught me about contortion:
'Will you look at the dirt on the back of your neck!'
My mother taught me about stamina:
'You'll sit there until all your spinach is finished.'
My mother taught me about the weather:
'It looks as if a tornado swept through your room.'
My mother taught me about hypocrisy:
'If I've told you once, I've told you a million times – don't exaggerate!'
My mother taught me the circle of life:
'I brought you into this world, and I can take you out.'
My mother taught me about behaviour modification:
'Stop acting like your father!'
My mother taught me about envy:
'There are millions of less fortunate children in this world who don't have wonderful parents like you do!'
My mother taught me medicine:
'If you don't stop crossing your eyes, they're going to freeze that way.'
My mother taught me to think ahead:
'If you don't pass your spelling test, you'll never get a good job!'
My mother taught me ESP:
'Put your sweater on – don't you think I know when you're cold?'
My mother taught me to meet a challenge:
'What were you thinking? Answer me when I talk to you! Don't talk back to me!'
My mother taught me humour:
'When that lawn-mower cuts off your toes, don't come running to me.'

My mother taught me restraint:
'Don't eat so fast. If you don't chew, you don't digest and the doctor will have to remove your stomach.
My mother taught me about the unknown:
'I gave you £2 last week. Where did it go? '

***

Rivkah sprang to answer the telephone, and heard, 'Darling, how are you? This is Mummy.'

'Oh Mummy,' Rivkah said crying, 'I'm having a bad day. The baby won't eat and the washing machine won't work. I've sprained my ankle and I'm hobbling around. On top of all this, the house is a mess and I'm supposed to have the Minkys and the Rokens for dinner tonight. I haven't even had a chance to go shopping.'

The voice on the other end said in sympathy, 'Darling, let Mummy handle it. Sit down, relax and close your eyes. I'll be over in half an hour. I'll do your shopping, tidy up the house and cook your dinner. I'll feed the baby and I'll call an engineer I know who'll fix your washing machine. Now stop crying. I'll even call your husband David at the office and tell him he should come home to help out for once.'

'David?' said Rivkah. 'Who's David?'

'Why, David's your husband – is this 020 8023 3374?'

'No, this is 020 8123 3774.'

'Oh, I'm so sorry. I must have dialled the wrong number.'

There was a short pause, then Rivkah said, 'Does this mean you're not coming?'

***

Q. What is a Jewish woman's idea of natural childbirth?
A. No make-up whatsoever.

Q: What did the Jewish Mother cash dispenser say to her customer?
A: You never write, you never call and you only visit me when you need money.

Q: What did the Jewish mother say when her daughter told her she was having an affair?
A: Who's doing the catering?

Q: Why did the Jewish mother want to be buried near Brent Cross shopping centre?
A: To be sure her daughter would visit her twice a week.

***

Henry invited his mother, Freda, over for dinner. During the course of the meal, Freda couldn't help but keep noticing how beautiful Henry's flatmate, Debbie, was. Freda had long been suspicious of a relationship between Henry and Debbie and this had only made her more curious. Over the course of the evening, while watching the two react, Freda started to wonder if there was more between Henry and Debbie than met the eye.

Reading his mother's thoughts, Henry said, 'I know what you must be thinking, mum, but I assure you Debbie and I are just flatmates.'

About a week later, Debbie said to Henry, 'Ever since your mother came to dinner, I've been unable to find the beautiful silver gravy ladle. You don't suppose she took it, do you?'

Henry replied, 'Well, I doubt it, but I'll write her a letter just to be sure.'

So he sat down and wrote: 'Dear Mother, I'm not saying that you did take the gravy ladle from the house, I'm not saying that you did not take the gravy ladle. But the fact remains that one has been missing ever since you were here for dinner.'

Several days later, Henry received a letter from his mother, which read: 'Dear Son, I'm not saying that you do sleep with Debbie, and I'm not saying that you do not sleep with Debbie. But the fact remains that if she were sleeping in her own bed, she would have found the gravy ladle by now. Love Mother.'

Lesson of the day – don't lie to a Jewish mother.

***

The remarkable thing about my mother is that for twenty years she served us nothing but leftovers. The original meal has never been found.

***

Moshe calls his mother and asks, 'How are you?'

'Not too good,' Hetty says. 'I'm feeling very weak.'

'Why, mother? '

Hetty says, 'Because I haven't eaten in 23 days.'

Moshe replies, 'That's terrible, mother. Why haven't you eaten in 23 days?'

Hetty answers, 'because I didn't want my mouth should be filled with food if you should call!'

***

Abe Caponovitch, a Jewish gangster, was dining at a kosher restaurant on New York's Lower East Side, when members of the mob burst in and shot him full of lead. Abe managed to stagger out of the restaurant and stumbled up the street to the block where his mother lived. Clutching his bleeding stomach, he then crawled up the stairs and banged on the door of his mother's apartment, screaming, 'Mama, Mama! Help me, Mama!'

His mother opened the door, eyed him up and down and said, '*Bubbeleh*, come in. First you eat, then you talk!'

***

Q: How do Jewish wives get their children ready for supper?

A: They put them in the car.

Q: What did the waiter ask the group of Jewish mothers?

A: 'Is anything OK?'

***

Although Miriam Cohen had a good job designing clothes in a top shop in Golders Green, she wasn't satisfied with being single. In fact she and her mother, Freda, shared the same wish – Miriam should marry a wealthy man, please God.

One day, Miriam came home from work with eyes red and sore from crying and went straight to Freda. 'Mum, I'm pregnant. Please don't get upset – the father is my boss.'

Miriam then began to cry again and Freda had to stay with her most of the night. The next morning, an angry Freda went with Miriam to see her boss.

'*Nu*,' she said. 'So what's going to happen to Miriam now?'

Miriam's boss was a handsome, single, well-dressed man of 32. He replied, 'Please take a seat Mrs Cohen and don't worry. I'm taking care of all the arrangements. Before the baby is born, Miriam will have the best doctor money can buy. Later on, she'll be booked into the best private clinic in London and after the baby is born, I will set up a trust fund for Miriam. She will receive £1,000 each week until the baby reaches 21. I can't do better than that.'

Freda was initially taken aback by this news but then responded, 'Tell me, God forbid Miriam should have a miscarriage, but if she does, would you give her a second chance?'

***

A Mother's Lament:
'Is one Nobel Prize so much to ask for from a child, after all I've done?'

***

Some motherly quotes you might not be aware of:
I don't care what you've discovered, you could have still written!
(Columbus' Jewish mother)
Of course I'm proud you invented the electric light bulb. Now be a good boy and turn it off and go to bed.
(Thomas Edison's Jewish mother)
But it's your Bar Mitzvah photo! Couldn't you do something

about your hair?
(Albert Einstein's Jewish mother)
That's a nice story. So now tell me where you've *really* been for the last forty years.
(Jonah's Jewish mother)

***

Q: What kind of cigarettes do Jewish mothers smoke?
A: Gefiltered.

Q: What is the most common disease transmitted by Jewish mothers?
A: Guilt.

Q: Why do Jewish mothers make such good parole officers?
A: They never let anyone finish a sentence.

Q: What is a genius?
A: An average pupil with a Jewish mother.

***

Letter to my son:

My dear darling Moshe and that-person-you-married-against-my-wishes,

Happy New Year and well over the Fast to you. Please don't worry about me – I'm well, considering I am having trouble breathing and eating. All I want is for you to have a nice holiday thousands of miles away from your mother.

Please find attached to this letter my last £20. I am just hoping that you will spend it on my grandchildren, poor babies – God knows their mother never seems to buy them anything nice. Maybe you'll buy some food, as they look so thin in the photos you sent me.

Thank you Moshe for the flowers you sent me on my birthday. To save you money, I have put them in the freezer in the hope that they will last until my funeral. And please don't think of sending me any more money. I realise you will need it yourself for your next who-knows-where-in-the-world expensive holiday.

I lost my walking stick last week beating off muggers, but don't worry – when I finish writing this letter, I shall crawl back to bed. I am even beginning to get used to the cold since the landlord turned off the heating. The frost helps to numb the constant pain.

Please give my love to my darling grandchildren and give my regards to 'her'.

Love from your devoted mother.

***

There are two theories on how to successfully argue with a Jewish mother.

Unfortunately, neither of them works.

***

If Mona Lisa's mother were Jewish, she'd have said, 'Mona, *bubbeleh*, after all the money your father and I spent on your braces, that's the biggest smile you can give us?'

***

You know your mother is Jewish when:

She cries at your *bris* – because you're not engaged already.

She shouts '*Mazeltov!*' – every time she hears some crockery break.

She does all her shopping for next Passover as soon as Passover ends – because she can buy the essential items at sale prices.

She calls you many times a day before 10 a.m. – because she wants to ask you how your day is going.

She takes an extra suitcase with her on holiday – because where

else can she put the hotel's face flannels, soaps, shampoos, bath oils, shower hats and shoe shiners?
She cries at your Bar Mitzvah – because you're not engaged already.
She goes to her doctor for every minor ailment – so she can show your photo to the young single doctors.
She won't let you leave home without a coat and some advice on dating – because 'mother knows best'.
She takes restaurant leftovers home with her – 'I should throw away?'
She cries on your twenty-first birthday – because you're not engaged already.
She serves you chopped liver every week – because just once, when you were young, you told her you loved chopped liver.
She makes an extra Shabbes table setting – because you just might have met your *beshayrt* (intended) on the way over.
She gets mad with you if you buy jewellery at full price – because she knows someone who could have got it cheaper in Tel Aviv.
She encourages you to do whatever you want with your life – as long as it includes grandchildren.
She's regularly heard muttering, 'Is one grandchild too much to ask for?'

Bragging mothers

Beckie, Sadie and Hannah are bragging about their sons.

Beckie says, 'My son is very successful. He is the best lawyer in London.'

Sadie says, 'My son has done better than that. He is the best doctor in London.'

Hannah says, 'My son has not done that well. He does not have a very good job and he is gay. But he has these two great boyfriends – one is the best lawyer in London and the other is the best doctor in London.'

***

Harry Goldberg has been elected the next President of the United States – the first Jewish boy to reach the White House. He is very proud and phones his mother in New York to invite her to the inauguration. 'Momma, guess what! I've just been elected President, won't you come to my inauguration?'

'Harry! You know I hate trains. I can't face the journey all the way to Washington. Maybe next time.'

'Momma. You will take no train. Air Force One will collect you. The journey will be over in thirty minutes. Come to my inauguration, please - '

'Harry, I hate hotels. The non-kosher food. No, maybe next time.'

'Momma. You will stay in the White House, with a kosher chef all to yourself. Please come.'

'Harry! I have nothing to wear.'

'I have someone on his way over to you now to take you to Macy's and Bloomingdale's to make you look perfect. You must come.'

'OK, OK, I suppose I'll come.'

Inauguration Day comes. Mother is in the front row, next to the Secretary of State. Harry is called up to become the next to take the oath of office as President. Mother digs the Secretary of State in the ribs and says, 'Do you see that boy Harry? His brother is a very successful doctor.'

***

'My son,' says Yetta, 'is a physicist.'

'My son,' says Sadie, 'is president of an insurance company.'

'My son,' says Beckie, 'is the head of a law firm and president of the Law Society.'

'My son,' says Hannah, 'is a rabbi.'

'A rabbi? What kind of career is that for a Jewish boy?'

***

Three mothers are sitting around and bragging about their children.

Freda says, 'Benny graduated with a first-class honours

degree from Oxford and he's now a doctor making £250,000 a year in Harley Street.'

Kitty says, 'Sidney graduated with a first-class honours degree from Cambridge and he's now a lawyer making £500,000 a year and he lives in the City.'

Ethel says, 'Abe never did well in school, never went to university but he now makes £1,000,000 a year working as a sports repairman.'

The other two women ask, 'So what's a sports repairman?'

Ethel replies, 'He fixes football matches, rugby matches, cricket matches - '

***

Rifka and Beckie are talking about their children. Rifka asks Beckie how her daughter is. Beckie says, 'Not too good. My daughter just divorced her husband. He was a doctor.'

Rifka replies, 'Oh, I am so sorry to hear that.'

Beckie continues, 'Yes, it is sad. Her first husband, whom she divorced three years ago, was a dentist. But she is OK now, she is dating a handsome lawyer.'

Rifka replies, 'A dentist, a doctor and a lawyer. *Oy Vay!* All this *naches* from just one daughter!

***

Four old school friends were having coffee. The first, a Catholic woman, says, 'My son is now a priest. When he walks into a room, everyone calls him "Father".'

The second Catholic woman then says, 'My son is a bishop. Whenever he walks into a room, people call him "Your Grace".'

The third Catholic says, 'My son is a Cardinal. Whenever he walks into a room, he's called "Your Eminence".'

The fourth woman, a Jewish lady, just sat there and sipped her coffee in silence. So the first three women give her this subtle 'Well - ?'

So she replies, 'My son is 6ft 6in, has plenty of money, broad square shoulders, terribly handsome, dresses very well, has a tight muscular body, tight hard bum and a very nice bulge. Whenever he walks into a room, women gasp, "Oh, my God."'

***

Bette and Freda are talking about their sons, both of whom were serving prison sentences. Bette says: '*Oy*, my son Michael has it so hard. He is locked away in maximum security, he never even speaks to anyone or sees the light of day. He has no exercise and he lives a horrible life.'

Freda says: 'Well, my son David is in minimum security. He exercises every day, he spends time in the prison library, takes some classes, and writes home each week.

'*Oy*,' says Bette, 'You must get such *naches* from David.'

***

Hetty was talking to her friend Sadie. 'My son Moshe,' said Hetty proudly, 'has first-class degrees in psychology, psychiatry and economics.'

'You must be proud of him,' said Sadie.

'Yes I am,' replied Hetty. 'He can't get a job – but at least he knows why.'

***

Sadie is out shopping in Brent Cross shopping centre when she bumps into Beckie, an old friend of hers. Beckie is looking after her two grandchildren while their mother does some shopping on her own.

Sadie says, 'Oh Beckie, what beautiful children, how old are they?'

'Well,' Beckie says proudly, 'The lawyer is six months and the doctor is two years.'

***

Jewish mothers don't differ from any other mothers in the world when it comes to bragging about their sons. Rivkah, trying to out-do another when it came to opportunities available to their just-graduated sons said, 'My Irving has had so many fine interviews, his C.V. is now in its fifth printing.'

Grandparents

Five-year-old Emma was sitting on her grandfather David's lap as he read her a bedtime story. From time to time, Emma would take her eyes off the book and reach up to touch David's wrinkled cheek. She was alternately stroking her own cheek, then his again. Finally Emma spoke up, 'Grandpa, did God make you?'

'Yes, darling,' he answered, 'God made me a long time ago.'

'Oh,' she paused, 'Grandpa, did God make me too?'

'Yes, indeed, *bubbeleh*,' he said, 'God made you just a little while ago.'

Feeling their respective faces again, Emma observed, 'God's getting better at it, isn't he?'

***

Rachel and Esther meet for the first time in fifty years since high school.

Rachel begins to tell Esther about her children. 'My son is a doctor and he's got four kids. My daughter is married to a lawyer and they have three great kids. So tell me Esther, how about your kids?'

Esther replies, 'Unfortunately, Morty and I don't have any children and so we have no grandchildren either.'

Rachel says, 'No children? And no grandkids? So tell me, Esther, what do you do for aggravation?'

***

Fay is wheeling her granddaughter in a pram when Rivkah stops her and says, 'What a beautiful grandchild, Fay.'

'Ach, Rivkah, this is nothing,' says Fay, 'you should see the photos.'

***

Talmud according to your grandmother:

The optimist sees the bagel, the pessimist sees the hole.

If you can't say something nice, say it in Yiddish.

If it tastes good, it's probably not kosher.

No one looks good in a *yarmulka*.

Why spoil a good meal with a big tip?

Twenty per cent off is a bargain; fifty per cent off is a *mitzvah*.

Israel is the land of milk and honey; North London is the land of Milk of Magnesia.

Never pay retail.

It's always a bad hair day if you're bald.

No one leaves a Jewish celebration hungry; but then, no one leaves with a hangover.

Wine needs to breathe so don't rush through the Kiddush.

Next year in Jerusalem. The year after that, how about a nice cruise?

The High Holidays have absolutely nothing to do with marijuana.

And what's so wrong with dry turkey?

Always whisper the names of diseases.

One *mitzvah* can change the world; two will just make you tired.

If you don't eat, it will kill me.

Anything worth saying is worth repeating a thousand times.

Where there's smoke, there may be smoked salmon.

Never take a front-row seat at a *bris*.

Never leave a restaurant empty-handed.

A bad matzo ball makes a good paperweight.

A *shmatta* is a dress that your husband's ex is wearing.

Without Jewish mothers, who would need therapy?

Before you read the menu, read the prices.

There comes a time in every man's life when he must stand up and tell his mother he's an adult. This usually happens at around 45.

According to Jewish dietary law, pork and shellfish may be eaten only in Chinese restaurants.
Tsouris is a Yiddish word that means your child is marrying someone who isn't Jewish.
If you're going to whisper at the cinema, make sure it's loud enough for everyone to hear.
If you have to ask the price, you can't afford it. But if you can afford it, make sure you tell everybody what you paid.

***

It was Benny's third birthday party and he was having a lovely time. Soon it was time to open his presents. One was from his grandma Freda and in it he discovered a water pistol. He jumped up and down with delight and then ran to the nearest sink to fill it up.

But his mother was not so pleased. She turned to Freda and said, 'I'm surprised at you, Mum. Don't you remember how we used to drive you crazy with water pistols when we were young?'

Grandma Freda smiled and then replied, 'I remember. Of course I remember.'

***

My Grandpa was very religious. He prayed three times a day and put on his *tefillin* every morning. One night, he heard a noise downstairs and having no fear for his safety went downstairs to see what it was. It was a burglar and he was putting my Grandpa's silver cutlery, wine goblets and candlesticks into a bag. This made my Grandpa very angry and he shouted at him to stop. He then tried to take the bag away but when he reached for it, the burglar pulled a knife out of the bag and was just about to stab my Grandpa when all of a sudden, my Grandpa screamed out '*Nisht mit der milchidic messer*!' (Not with the dairy knife!)

***

Rebecca is fifteen years old and tonight she has a date. When she finishes dressing, she comes downstairs and shocks her *bubbeh* because Rebecca is wearing a see-through blouse and she's clearly not wearing anything underneath it. Her *bubbeh* shouts at her and tells her she mustn't go out un-dressed like that. She looks like a tart. But Rebecca walks out the door anyway, saying, '*Bubbeh*, this is the twenty-first century, everybody lets their rosebuds show.'

The next day, when Rebecca comes home from school, there is her *bubbeh* sitting in the lounge wearing no top. Rebecca is very embarrassed and says, '*Bubbeh*, I have friends coming over and it's not appropriate for you to - '

Her *bubbeh* interrupts and says, 'Loosen up, Rebecca, this is the twenty-first century. If you can display your rosebuds, then I can certainly display my hanging baskets.'

DAILY LIFE

Food & restaurants

Manny goes into a restaurant and orders fried haddock. The waiter serves him a nice size piece of fish. As he's walking away the waiter overhears Manny talking to the fish. Soon Manny is deep in conversation with his lunch.

'What on earth are you doing?' says the waiter. 'Do you want to eat it or marry it?'

Manny replies, 'We're just *schmoozing*. It seems that the fish is from Herne Bay in Kent. I used to live there and I was asking the fish how things are back in my old home town.'

'What did he say?' asks the waiter.

'He said, "How should I know? I haven't been there in years!"'

***

Freda had just finished her fish dinner. She was not at all happy with it, however, so she called over the waiter.

'I've tasted fresher fish,' said Freda.

'Not in here,' replied the waiter.

***

Two Jewish students were living together in Manchester and they always shared the cooking of the evening meal. One day, when Sam came home, he did not find a hot meal waiting for them, only sandwiches. So he asked Moshe, 'What's with the cheese sandwiches? You promised to cook us roast beef for tonight.'

Moshe replies, 'I did! But the roast beef caught fire and it spread to the vegetables so I had to put it out with the chicken soup.'

* * *

Abe goes to a restaurant every day for lunch. He always orders the *soupe du jour*. One day the manager asks him how he liked his meal. Abe replies (with Yiddish accent) 'Wass goot, but you could give a little more bread.'

The next day, the manager tells the waitress to give him four slices of bread. 'How was your meal, sir?' the manager asks. 'Wass goot, but you could give a little more bread.'

Next day, the manager tells the waitress to give him eight slices of bread. 'How was your meal today, sir?' the manager asks. 'Wass goot, but you could give a little more bread.'

The manager is now obsessed with hearing Abe say that he enjoyed his meal, so he goes to the bakery and orders a six-foot long French loaf. When Abe comes in as usual the next day, the waitress and the manager cut the loaf in half, butter the entire length of each half and lay it out along the counter, right next to his bowl of soup. Abbe sits down, and devours both his bowl of soup and both halves of the six-foot loaf of bread. The manager now thinks he will get the answer he is looking for. When Abe comes up to pay for his meal, the manager asks in the usual way: 'How was your meal today, sir?'

Abe replies 'It wass goot as usual but I see you are back to giving only two slices of bread!'

* * *

Abe was a poor tailor whose shop was next door to a two-star Michelin restaurant. Every day for lunch, Abe would eat his black bread and herring in the small garden at the back of his shop. He would always smell the wonderful odours emanating from the next door restaurant's kitchen. One day, the restaurant sent Abe an invoice. Abe went to see the manager to ask why.

The manager replied, 'You're enjoying my food, so you

should pay for it.'

Abe refused to pay and the restaurant sued him. At the hearing, the judge asked the restaurant to present their side of the story.

They said, 'Every day, this man comes and sits near our kitchen and visibly smells our food whilst eating his. We are obviously adding value to his cheap food and we deserve to be recompensed for it.'

The judge then asked Abe, 'And what do you have to say about that?'

Abe said nothing but stuck his hand in his pocket and rattled around the coins he had inside.

The judge asked him, 'What's the meaning of that?'

Abe replied, 'I am paying for the smell of his food with the sound of my money.'

***

One morning, Shlomo and Sadie decided to go out for breakfast. The waitress at The Almond Tree told them that the special that morning was two eggs, tomatoes, mushrooms, hash browns and toast for £3.99.

'That sounds good,' said Sadie, 'but I don't want the eggs.'

'OK,' said the waitress, but I will then have to charge you £4.50.'

'Why,' asked Shlomo, 'it doesn't make sense.

'Because you will then in effect be ordering *à la carte*,' the waitress replied.

'Do you mean I'll have to pay for not taking the eggs?' Sadie asked.

'Yes, ' replied the waitress.

'OK then, I'll take the special,' says Sadie.

'How do you want your eggs done?' asked the waitress.

'Raw and in the shell,' Sadie replied.

At the end of the meal, Sadie took the two eggs home.

***

Freda and Moshe won £8 million on the National Lottery. They immediately went out to begin a life of living in luxury. They bought a luxurious mansion in Northwood, surrounded themselves with all the material wealth imaginable and decided to hire a butler. After much searching, they found the perfect one.

One day, they instructed the butler to set up a dinner for four because they were inviting their friends, the Cohens, over for dinner and they themselves would be going out for the day. When they returned that evening, they found the table set for six. When they asked the butler why six places were set when they specifically instructed him to set the table for four, the butler replied: 'The Cohens called and said that they were bringing the Bagels.'

***

Q: What do you call the steaks ordered by ten Jewish men?
A: Fillet *minyan*.

Q: What kind of cheese melts on a piece of matzo to make a Passover pizza?
A: Matzarella

Q: Why do Jewish women enjoy Chinese food so much?
A: Won Ton spelled backwards is 'Not Now.'

Q: How can you tell the gefilte fish from all the other fish in the sea?
A: It's the one swimming around with the little slice of carrot on its back.

***

Rabbi Landau has always been secretly sad that he's never been able to eat pork. So one day, he flies to a remote tropical island and books into a hotel. 'No one will find me here,' he says to himself. On the first evening, he goes to the best restaurant and orders the 'roast pork special'. While he's waiting, he hears someone call his name.

Rabbi Landau looks up and sees one of his congregants walking towards his table.

What unbelievably bad luck – they both had to visit the same restaurant on the same island at the same time! Just at that moment, the waiter puts on his table a whole roasted pig with an apple in its mouth and says, 'Your special, sir.'

Rabbi Landau looks up sheepishly at his congregant and says, 'Would you believe it – you order an apple in this restaurant and look how they serve it!'

***

Moshe goes into a restaurant and orders potato *latkes*. When they arrive at his table, he does not like the look of them and changes his order to strawberry *blintzes*. Later, when he had finished, he gets up to leave. 'Wait a second,' said the manager, 'You haven't paid for your *blintzes*.'

'What are you talking about?' Moshe replies. 'Those *blintzes* were only an exchange. I gave you the *latkes* for them.'

'Yes, but you didn't pay for them either.'

'Why should I pay for the *latkes*? I didn't eat them.'

***

Two Chinamen are leaving Bloom's restaurant and one says to the other: 'The problem with Jewish food is that two days later, you're hungry again'

***

A little something I'd thought you'd like to know . . .

5765	Year according to Jewish calendar
4702	Year according to Chinese calendar
——	
1063	Total number of years that Jews went without Chinese food

***

Shlomo went on holiday to Spain. One day, he sat in a Spanish cafe on Fiesta Day and watched the waiter serve a fragrant and attractive dish to a party at the next table.

'What is that?' Shlomo asked.

'*Señor*, those are the bull's testicles from today's bullfights.'

'They look excellent! Bring me some.'

'*Señor*, there is a wait! People sign up one year in advance for such a delicacy.'

'Then sign me up! I'll be here this time next year.'

A year of anticipation later and Fiesta Day arrives again. Shlomo is in the cafe anxiously awaiting his meal. Finally, the waiter appears with two leathery little lumps covered by gravy.

'And what is this?' cried Shlomo. 'Look at them! Do you call this a meal for a Jew?

Last year they were fragrant and big and fluffy! What happened?'

'*Señor*, the bull does not always lose.'

***

Howard came home from work one evening and there was his wife Miriam in the kitchen crying out loud. 'What's the matter, darling?' he asked her.

'I just don't know what to do,' said Miriam. 'Because we were eating in for a change, I cooked us a special dinner – but the dog has just eaten it.'

'Don't worry,' said Howard, 'I'll get us another dog.'

***

Moshe was talking to his friend Abe. 'Do you know, Moshe, that my friend David is so *frum* that he has two dishwashers in his kitchen!'

'That's nothing,' replied Abe, 'my friend Benjamin keeps such a kosher home that he has two smoke detectors in his kitchen!'

***

Sadie was taking her seven-year-old daughter Sarah and her friend Rifka to Hebrew classes one Sunday morning and was embarrassed to hear this conversation between them.

Sarah said to Rifka, 'Our family is kosher.'

Rifka asked, 'What's kosher?'

Sarah replied, 'That's when you can't have cheese with your ham sandwich.'

***

Rachel had not seen her Israeli relatives for years, so she was very excited when her Aunt Leah and Uncle Yitzhak came to visit her in London. To celebrate their visit, Rachel took them to an old-fashioned kosher restaurant in Hendon.

'I'll have the pickled brisket,' Rachel told the waiter.

'The brisket is from last night,' explained the waiter. 'Better you should order something made fresh today. How about stuffed peppers?'

'OK, let it be stuffed peppers.'

The waiter turns to Aunt Leah. 'And you?'

'Bring please the pot roast.'

'Look, lady, the pot roast is strictly for *goyim*. If you want something special, try the beef.'

'All right then, so bring the beef.'

Uncle Yitzhak studied the menu carefully then said to the waiter, 'I can't make up my mind. What do you suggest?'

'Suggest!' cried the waiter. 'On a busy night like this who has time for suggestions?'

***

Isaac was sitting at a table in his favourite restaurant when he called over his waiter.

'Yes?' asked the busy waiter.

'Are you sure you're the waiter I ordered from?' asked Isaac.

'Why do you ask?' replied the waiter.

'Because I was expecting a much older man by now,' replied Isaac.

***

This is what happens when Yitzhak decides to do a barbecue: His wife Hannah goes to the store to buy the food.

Hannah makes the salad, vegetables and dessert.

Hannah prepares the meat for cooking, places it on a tray along with the necessary cooking utensils and takes it to Yitzhak who is lounging beside the grill.

Yitzhak places the meat on the grill.

Hannah goes inside and sets the table and checks the vegetables.

Hannah comes out to tell Yitzhak that the meat is burning.

Yitzhak takes the meat off the grill and hands it to Hannah.

Hannah prepares the plates and brings them to the table.

After eating, Hannah clears the table and does the dishes.

Yitzhak asks Hannah how she enjoyed her 'night off'. Upon seeing her annoyed reaction, concludes that there's just no pleasing some women.

***

Moshe was eating in a Chinese restaurant and was chatting to his Chinese waiter. Moshe commented upon on what a wise people the Chinese are.

'Yes,' replied the waiter, 'we're wise because our culture is 4,000 years old. But Jewish people are also very wise, are they not?'

Moshe replied, 'Yes, we are. Our culture is 5,000 years old.'

The waiter was surprised to hear this. 'That can't be true,' he replied, 'Where did your people eat for a thousand years?'

***

A German comes to London and stays with Maurice and his family. The first morning they all have breakfast together and eat bagels. The German exclaims 'Wow, we don't have bagels like this in Germany.'

To which Maurice stands up and yells 'And whose fault is that?'

***

The Italian says, 'I'm tired and thirsty. I must have wine.'
The Mexican says, 'I'm tired and thirsty. I must have tequila.'
The Scot says, 'I'm tired and thirsty. I must have Scotch.'
The Swede says, 'I'm tired and thirsty. I must have aquavit.'
The Japanese says, 'I'm tired and thirsty. I must have sake.'
The Russian says, 'I'm tired and thirsty. I must have vodka.'
The German says, 'I'm tired and thirsty. I must have beer.'
The Greek says, 'I'm tired and thirsty. I must have ouzo.'
The Jew says, 'I'm tired and thirsty. I must have diabetes.'

***

Sadie says to her husband, 'Moshe, I'm fed up with frozen chickens. Please buy me a live chicken for a change. Then, when you bring it home, I'll get the rabbi to kosher it. Then I can make for us a lovely meal.'

So Moshe goes to the market and buys the chicken. On his way back, he sees that *Funny Girl* is showing at the Phoenix cinema, Finchley. So he rings Sadie on his mobile. 'Sadie,' he says, 'They're showing *Funny Girl* at the Phoenix. I think I'll see it before I come home. I missed it first time round and this is a new digitally enhanced release.'

'OK,' replies Sadie, 'but what about the chicken?'

'I'll take it inside with me,' Moshe answers.

So he stuffs the chicken down his trousers and goes in to see the film. Unfortunately, during the film, the chicken pokes its head out of Moshe's trousers. Two women are sitting next to Moshe and one turns to the other and whispers, 'There's a man next to me with his *shmuck* sticking out of his trousers.'

Her friend says, 'Why be shocked? If you've seen one, you've seen them all.'

'But this one's different. It's eating my popcorn.'

***

It's a lovely hot, sunny morning in the forest where the bear family Levine live. There was mummy bear Rifka, daddy bear Shlomo and baby bear Benny. Benny bear goes downstairs for breakfast and as usual sits down in his small chair at the end of the table. He looks at his small plate and guess what? It's empty. 'Who's been eating my bagel?' he squeaks.

Shlomo bear then makes an appearance and sits in his big chair. He looks at his big plate and guess what? It too is empty. 'Who's been eating my bagels?' he roars.

On hearing all this complaining, Rifka bear puts her head through the serving hatch and shouts at Shlomo and Benny. 'How many times do we have to go through this? It was mummy bear who got up first. It was mummy bear who woke up everybody else in the house. It was mummy bear who unloaded the dishwasher from last night and put everything away. It was mummy bear who set the breakfast table, who filled the cat's milk and food dishes, and who cleaned the litter box and took the dog for a walk. And now that you two have finally decided to get out of bed and grace me with your presence, listen carefully because I'm only going to say this one more time – I haven't made the damn bagels yet!'

* * *

Hymie is walking along Hendon Avenue carrying a large, heavy watermelon when he sees his friend Abe coming towards him.

'Hi Abe,' says Hymie. '*Nu?* How are you?'

'*Oy Vay*,' says Abe, throwing his arms up in the air, 'Don't ask! But tell me, how are you?'

'Me?' says Hymie, 'You ask how I am? You want I drop my watermelon?'

* * *

Simon is a lovely five-year-old who gives his parents Maurice and Hannah much *naches*. Their only worry is the fact that he hasn't spoken a word since he was born. But he appears happy and bright and he always does what he is told, so they live in hope. One day, at breakfast, Hannah realises that they have run out of corn flakes, so she gives Simon a bowl of grapefruit segments instead. As soon as Simon puts the first spoonful into his mouth, he spits it out and shouts, 'Yuck, what rubbish. It's not nice to start the day with such bitter-tasting food.'

'Simon, *bubbeleh*, you spoke,' cries Hannah, 'you've just said your very first words.'

'*Mazeltov*, son,' says Maurice.'

Hannah and Maurice dance around the room in joy. When they calm down a bit, Maurice says to Simon, 'Why has it taken you so long to speak? You've got such a lovely clear voice and you're already quite articulate.'

'Well,' answers Simon, 'until this morning, when you gave me this grapefruit, the food has always been excellent.'

Advertisements & announcements

Jewish personal adverts – part 1:

Divorced Jewish man, seeks partner to attend *shul*, light Shabbes candles, celebrate holidays, build *succah* together, attend *brisses*, Bar Mitzvahs. Religion not important.

Your place or mine? Divorced man, 42, with *flayshig* dishes only. Seeking woman with nice *milchig* set. Object: macaroni.

Desperately seeking schmoozing! Retired senior citizen desires female companion 70+ for *kvetching* and *kvelling*. Under 30 is also OK.

Conservative rabbi, 45. I count women for the *minyan* and call them up to the Torah. Seeking female to make *aliyah*.

Sincere rabbinical student, 27. Enjoys Yom Kippur, Tisha B'av, Taanis Esther, Tzom Gedaliah, Asarah B'Teves, Shivah Asar B'Tammuz (these are all fast days). Seeks companion for living life in the 'fast' lane.

Shul gabbai, 36. I take out the Torah Saturday morning. Would like to take you out Saturday night. Please write.

Attractive Jewish woman, 35, college graduate, seeks successful Jewish Prince Charming to get me out of my parents' house.

Worried about in-law meddling? I'm an orphan! Write.

Jewish male, 34, very successful, smart, independent, self-made. Looking for girl whose father will hire me.

All my friends are doing it, and quite frankly, I feel left out. Jewish woman, 37, never married. Seeks divorce.

***

The following signs have been spotted:

Over a gynaecologist's office: 'Dr Levy, at your cervix.'

On Yitzhak the plumber's truck: 'I repair what your husband fixed.'

Also on Yitzhak the plumber's truck: 'Don't sleep with a drip. Call me.'

On Cohen's Pizza shop: 'Seven days without pizza makes one weak.'

Also on Cohen's Pizza shop: 'Buy my pizza. I knead the dough.'

In Moshe the plastic surgeon's office: 'Hello. Can I pick your nose?'

On Hyman the electrician's truck: 'Let me remove your shorts.'

On a maternity-room door at a Jewish hospital: 'Push. Push. Push.'

At Benny the optometrist's office: 'If you don't see what you're looking for, you've come to the right place.'

In Abe the podiatrist's office: 'Time wounds all heels.'

In Shlomo the veterinarian's waiting room: 'Be back in five minutes. Sit! Stay!'

In Issy's restaurant window: 'Don't stand there and be hungry. Come on in and get fed up.'

On Benjy's radiator shop: 'Best place in town to take a leak.'

In the front yard of Isaac's funeral home: 'Drive carefully. I'll wait.'

***

Avrahom and Becky were very worried. They had just received an invitation to a very high-class wedding but couldn't figure out the meaning of the abbreviation RSVP.

'If only our son, the graduate, was here, he'd know,' sighed Becky, as she kissed Avrahom good-bye as he left for work.

She pondered the problem all day and finally in a moment of triumph called Avrahom at the shop.

'Darling, I've figured it out,' she said, 'RSVP means Remember, Send Vedding Present.'

***

Bernie died and his wife, Sarah, phoned the *Jewish Chronicle* to place an obituary. Sarah said to them, 'This is what I want you to print: Bernie is dead.'

The *JC* man said, 'But for £25, you are allowed to print six words.'

Sarah answered, 'OK, then print: Bernie is dead. Lexus for sale.'

***

There was an advert in the *Jewish Examiner* that read: 'Wife wanted. Please reply to Box Number 123.' Five thousand replies were received, all saying: 'You can have mine.'

***

Other adverts that have been spotted include:

'For sale by owner: complete set of *Encyclopaedia Britannica*, 45 volumes, excellent condition, £500 or nearest offer. No longer needed – just got married. Wife knows everything.'

'Mr & Mrs Moshe Levy are pleased to announce the birth of their beloved son, Doctor David Levy.'

***

Here are some announcements that have appeared in synagogue newsletters:

Join us for our celebration after services. Prayer and medication to follow.

Weight Watchers will meet at 8 p.m. at the Beck Hall. Please use the large double doors at the side entrance.

Remember in prayer the many who are sick of our congregation.

For those of you who have children and don't know it, we have a nursery downstairs.

We are pleased to announce the birth of David Bloom, the sin of Rabbi and Mrs Shlomo Bloom.

The Men's Club is warmly invited to the celebrations hosted by Wizo, the Women's International Zionist Organisation. Refreshments will be served for a nominal feel.
Our rabbi unveiled the synagogue's new fundraising campaign slogan last week 'I Upped My Pledge – Up Yours.'
If you enjoy sinning, the choir is looking for you.
Rabbi is on holiday. Massages can be given to his secretary.
Mrs Himmelfarb will be entering the hospital this week for testes.
The Ladies Guild have cast-off clothing of every kind and they may be seen in the basement on Thursdays.
We are taking up a collection to defray the cost of the new carpet in the Beck Hall. All those wishing to do something on the carpet, please come forward and get a piece of paper.
Don't let worry kill you. Let your synagogue help.

***

A Jewish telegram:
'Begin worrying. Details to follow.'

***

Many years ago, when Moshe was a young boy, he found a *mezuzah* on the wall of a deserted house near his street. As there was still time before he had to get home for his tea, he pulled it off the wall and opened it. Inside, he found a piece of old paper on which was written the words that he would never forget: 'Please help me. I'm being held prisoner in a *mezuzah* factory.'

***

Jewish personal adverts – part 2:
I've had it all: herpes, syphilis, gonorrhea, chlamydia, and four of the ten plagues. Now I'm ready to settle down. So where are all the nice Jewish men hiding?
Yeshiva bucher, Torah scholar, long beard and sidelocks. Seeks same in woman.

Nice Jewish guy, 38. No skeletons. No baggage. No personality. Are you the girl I talked to at the Kiddush after *shul* last week? You excused yourself to get more horseradish for your gefilte fish, but you never returned. How can I contact you again? (I was the one with the cholent stain on my tie.)
Jewish businessman, 49, manufactures Sabbath candles, Chanukah candles, Havdalah candles, Yahrzeit candles. Seeks non-smoker.
Eighty-year-old *bubbeh*, no assets, seeks handsome, virile Jewish male, under 35. Object matrimony. I can dream, can't I?
I am a sensitive Jewish prince whom you can open your heart to. Share your innermost thoughts and deepest secrets. Confide in me. I'll understand your insecurities. No fatties, please.
Single Jewish woman, 29, into disco, mountain climbing, skiing, athletics. Has slight limp.
Orthodox woman with *get*, seeks man who got *get*, or can get *get*. Get it? I'll show you mine, if you show me yours.
Couch potato *latke*, in search of the right apple sauce. Let's try it for eight days. Who knows?
Female graduate student, studying Zohar, Kabbalah [Jewish mysticism], exorcism of *dybbuks* [demons], seeks *mensh*. No weirdos, please.
Israeli professor, 41, with eighteen years of teaching in my behind. Looking for American-born woman who speaks English very good.

***

Kitty has just bought her first telephone answering machine and guess what she decided to record on it?

> If you want me to make smoked salmon when you come round, press 1; if you want chopped liver press 2; if you want chicken soup, press 3; if you want chicken soup with matzo balls, press 4; if you want to know how am I feeling, you must have dialled the wrong number because nobody ever asks me how I am. Who knows, I could even be dead by now.

***

Jacob was listening to Kosher FM on his radio when he heard the announcer say, 'We now have a request for a favourite record from a Mr Weinberg – goodness! – who is 111 and off work this week.'

Then, almost immediately, Jacob heard the announcer make this correction, 'Sorry, listeners, I got it wrong. The next request is from Mr Weinberg who is ILL and off work this week.'

***

There are three signs on the wall in Moshe's Furniture Warehouse:

'There are two very good reasons why we won't cash your cheque. Either we don't know you, or we DO know you.'

'We have an agreement with all the local banks. They don't sell furniture and we don't cash cheques.'

'We don't blame our competitors for charging less for their furniture. After all, they should know what their stuff is worth.'

***

Lionel is walking home one Friday afternoon feeling quite downcast because he is starting a new job on Monday and desperately needs a new suit, but he can't afford to buy one. Just then he passes the Hendon Menswear Shop and sees a large sign in the window:

> What d'ya think, my name is Fink
> And I sell clothes for nothink!

Lionel goes into the shop and chooses a new suit. He is very pleased with it – it's just right for his new job. He is about to leave the shop, looking good and feeling lucky, when his joy is cut short. Fink stops him and demands payment for the suit.

Lionel says, 'But your sign in the window says, "What d'ya think, my name is Fink and I sell clothes for nothink." So how come you want payment?'

'You are reading my sign wrong,' replies Fink. 'It actually says,

'What d'ya think, my name is Fink?
And I sell clothes for nothink?'

Charity

Abe and Janine, an elderly Jewish couple, are sitting together on an aeroplane flying to the Far East. Suddenly, over the public address system, the Captain announces, 'Ladies and Gentlemen, I am afraid I have some very bad news. Our engines have ceased functioning, and this plane will be going down in a few minutes' time. The good news is that I can see an island below us that should be able to accommodate our landing. The bad news is that this island appears to be uncharted – I am unable to find it on our maps. So the odds are that we will never be rescued and will have to live on the island for a very long time, if not for the rest of our lives.'

Abe turns to Janine and asks, 'Janine, dear, did we turn off the oven?' and Janine replies, 'Of course.'

'Janine, are our life insurance policies paid up?'

'Of course.'

'Janine, did we pay our pledge for the Kol Nidre Appeal?'

'Oh my God, I forgot to send off the cheque.'

'Thank Heavens. They'll find us for sure.'

***

One day, Jacob, a Russian Jew slipped on the wet riverbank and fell into the water. Unfortunately, Jacob could not swim and was in serious danger of drowning. Two Tsarist policemen heard cries for help and rushed over. But when they saw that it was a Jew, they laughed and just stood there watching him drown.

'Help, I can't swim,' shouted Jacob.

'Then you will just have to drown,' they replied.

Suddenly Jacob shouted with his last breath: 'Down with the Tsar!'

The policemen immediately rushed into the river, pulled Jacob out, and arrested him for trouble-making.

***

Nathan and Leah Levy went on holiday to Switzerland. As soon as they arrived, Nathan told Leah that he would go skiing whilst she unpacked.

'Don't worry about me,' he said, 'I'll be back within two hours.'

Three hours later, he still hadn't returned and Leah was getting very worried. So she rang the Red Cross. After four hours, a search party, with guides, dogs and army mountaineers, went out looking for Nathan. As they climbed the slopes, they began calling out, 'Mr Levy, Mr Levy, it's the Red Cross. Where are you Mr Levy?'

When they got to the top of the glacier, they tried one more time, 'Mr Levy, where are you? It's the Red Cross.'

And then they heard a faint voice say, 'It's OK. I've given already.'

***

Issy rings the bell of a very wealthy person's house in Hampstead Garden Suburb and when the owner comes to the door, Issy greets him. '*Sholom aleichem*, Mr Goldstein. I'm collecting for the Loads of Money Yeshiva, and I'm wondering if a nice wealthy Jewish person like yourself wouldn't want to make a little contribution.'

'The name is Gold, not Goldstein, and I am not Jewish.'

'Are you sure?' asks Issy.

'I'm positive.'

'But,' says Issy, 'it says here that you're Jewish and my records are never wrong.'

'I can assure you that I am certainly not Jewish,' replies Mr Gold impatiently.

'Look sir, I know that my records are never wrong. You must be joking. Are you sure you aren't Jewish?' demands Issy.

'For the last time, I am not Jewish, my father is not Jewish, and my grandfather, *alav hasholom*, wasn't Jewish either!'

***

One Sunday morning, Rabbi Rabbinovitz goes to visit Samuel Lyons. 'Shalom, Sam. I'll come straight to the point. I've come here because our synagogue needs your help. You've been a member for over twenty years and I realise that you're always quick to pay your membership fees in full. But as you are aware, we are in a financial crisis. I've come here to ask you for a little extra for the new school building fund.'

'How much are you looking to get from me – how big is little?' asks Sam.

'I'll be honest. £10,000 would be a tremendous help to us,' replies the rabbi.'

Sam responds, 'Rabbi, my daughter Rebecca is soon getting married and she has asked me for £25,000 to help her buy that house she saw in Hampstead. And my son David is just starting at Manchester University and he wants £25,000 to see him through the difficult first year there. My wife Sadie wants a hysterectomy and she has asked for £30,000 for the doctors' fees and in-patient facilities. And that's not all. You know from your own experience that to keep my mother in a nursing home, they are asking £35,000. So, Rabbi, if I can say "no" to them, I can say "no" to you.'

***

Sharon lives in a block of flats. One afternoon, she starts to worry because she hasn't heard anything for days from the elderly widow who lives next door.

So Sharon says to her son Paul, '*Bubbeleh*, be a good boy. Go and find out how old Mrs Himmelfarb is.'

A few minutes later, Paul returns.

'*Nu*?' asks Sharon, 'Is she OK?'

'She's fine mum, but she's quite angry with you,' replies Paul.

'Angry with me?' says Sharon, 'What has she got to be angry about?'

'Well,' says Paul, 'she said, 'It's none of your business how old she is.'

***

Rabbi Rabinovitz answers his phone.

'Hello?'

'Hello, is this Rabbi Rabinovitz?'

'It is.'

'This is the Inland Revenue. Can you help us?'

'I'll try.'

'Do you know Sam Cohen?'

'I do.'

'Is he a member of your congregation?'

'He is.'

'Did he donate £10,000 to the synagogue rebuilding fund last year?'

'He will!'

***

Hetty had just got back home after a trip to Brent Cross shopping centre when she was shocked to find her husband Bernie lying in their bed with a beautiful young woman at his side. Hetty was speechless and ran from the room crying. Bernie went after her and caught her just as she was opening the front door to escape.

Bernie said, 'Before you leave me, Hetty, please let me explain. I was driving home this afternoon when I saw this woman sitting on a wall at the bottom of our road. Her clothes were in tatters and she looked so tired and sad that I just had to stop and ask whether she needed any help. She told me she was hungry so I brought her back home and gave her the piece of last night's roast chicken you said you didn't want. Her shoes were so worn out that I gave her a pair of your shoes that you don't wear any more. She was so cold that I gave her that sweater you said was no longer in fashion that you were going to give to the charity shop. Her skirt was also worn out so I gave her a new skirt from your wardrobe – one that you said didn't fit you anymore.'

'Then just as she was about to leave the house, she asked me, 'Is there anything else that your wife doesn't use anymore?' And so, here we are!'

***

A beggar knocked on the door of a house in Golders Green. 'What do you want?' said the owner.

'Can you spare some money to help a poor person?' said the beggar.

But as soon he was given a few coins and told to go on his way, the beggar complained, 'Your son gave me twice as much when I called here last week.'

'Well, my son can afford to,' said the owner, 'he has a very rich father.'

***

One afternoon, Maurice, a wealthy solicitor, was driving his Rolls Royce when he passed two poor looking men by the side of the road eating grass. Maurice quickly stopped his car, backed up to the men, wound down his window and asked, 'What on earth are you two doing?'

'I'm starving, I have nowhere to live and I don't have any money to buy food,' said one of them.

'You can come with me to my house, then,' said Maurice.

'But I've got a wife and three kids just up the road.'

'So we'll bring them along, too,' replied Maurice.

'And what about my friend?'

Maurice turned to the other man and said, 'You can come with us, too.'

'But, sir,' said the friend, 'I've got a wife and six children just up the road.'

'OK. So we'll bring them as well,' said Maurice. 'Now get in my car, both of you.'

Soon, everyone had been picked up. They had been travelling for only a few minutes when one of the men said to Maurice, 'You're very kind. Thank you for taking all of us with you.'

Maurice replied, 'I'm happy to be able to do it. And you'll love my place – the grass is almost a foot tall.'

***

It's 3 a.m. in the morning in Golders Green and Maurice and Golda are woken up by a loud banging on their front door. Maurice gets up and opens the door to a drunken stranger standing in the pouring rain. 'Can I have a push?' says the drunk.

'No you can't,' says Maurice, 'it's three o'clock in the morning. Please go away, you'll wake the children.'

Maurice shuts the door and goes back to bed.

'Who was that?' asks Golda.

'Just some drunk, dear, asking for a push,' Maurice replies.

'So did you help him?' Golda asks.

'No I didn't. It's 3 a.m. and it's pouring with rain,' replies Maurice.

Golda says, 'Shame on you, Maurice. Have you already forgotten when our car broke down about six months ago in Bournemouth and those two men helped us? I think you should help the man outside.'

So Maurice reluctantly does as he is told. He gets dressed, goes out into the pouring rain and calls out, 'Hello, are you still there?'

'Yes,' comes back the answer.

'Do you still need a push?' Maurice shouts.

'Yes, please!' comes the reply from the dark.

'So where are you?' asks Maurice.

'Over here on the swing,' replies the drunk.

***

Hetty, a little old lady, gets onto a crowded bus in Hendon in the middle of a heat-wave and stands in front of a seated young girl. Holding her hand to her chest, Hetty says to the girl, 'If you knew what I have, you would give me your seat.'

The girl gets up and gives up the seat to Hetty. The girl then takes out a fan and starts to fan herself. Hetty looks up and says,

'If you knew what I have, you would give me that fan.'

The girl gives Hetty her fan.

A short while later, Hetty gets up and says to the driver, 'Stop, I want to get off here.'

The driver tells her he has to drop her at the next bus stop, not in the middle of the road. Her hand across her chest, Hetty tells the driver, 'If you knew what I have, you would let me out here.'

The driver pulls over and lets Hetty out. As she's walking out of the bus, he asks, 'Madam, what is it that you have?'

'*Chutzpah*,' Hetty replies.

Men vs. women

Jewish women's rules:

The female always makes the rules.

The rules are subject to change at any time without prior notification.

No male can possibly know all the rules.

If the female suspects the male knows all the rules, she must immediately change some or all of the rules.

The female is never wrong.

If the female is wrong, it is due to a misunderstanding, which was a direct result of something the male did or said wrongly.

If the above applies, the male must apologise immediately for causing the misunderstanding.

An apology without flowers is not an apology.

The female may change her mind at any time.

The male must never change his mind at any time without the express consent of the female.

The male may not point out that the woman has changed her mind.

The female has every right to be angry or upset at any time.

The male must remain calm at all times, unless the female wants him to be angry or upset.

The female must, under no circumstances, let the male know whether or not she wants him to be angry or upset.

The female is ready when she is ready.

The male must be ready at all times.
If the female has PMS, all rules are null and void.
The male may not inquire if the woman is angry or upset.
The male may not inquire when the woman will be ready.
The male may not inquire about the woman's time of the month.
The male is expected to mind-read at all times.
The male must earn the respect of the woman by giving his life up in service to her needs and nurturing of her character.

* * *

Once upon a time, a perfect man and a perfect woman met. After a perfect courtship, they had a perfect wedding at the London Hilton. Their life together in Golders Green was, of course, perfect. One snowy, stormy Christmas Eve, this perfect couple was driving their perfect Lexus car along a winding road in Hendon, when they noticed someone at the side of the road in distress. Being the perfect couple, they stopped to help. To their surprise, there stood Santa Claus with a huge bundle of toys. Although Jewish, they did not want to disappoint any children on the eve of Christmas, no matter what their religion. So the perfect couple loaded Santa and his toys into their car and soon they were driving along delivering toys.

Unfortunately, the driving conditions deteriorated and the perfect couple and Santa Claus had a bad accident. Only one of them survived the accident.

The mind-numbing question is: who was the survivor?

The perfect woman survived. She's the only one who really existed in the first place. Everyone knows there is no Santa Claus and there is no such thing as a perfect man.

Women: stop reading here. This is the end of the joke.

So, if there is no perfect man and no Santa Claus, the perfect woman must have been driving. And that explains why there was a car accident.

By the way, if you're a woman and you're reading this, this illustrates another point: Women never do what they are told.

* * *

One day, three men were hiking and unexpectedly came upon a large raging, violent river. They needed to get to the other side, but had no idea of how to do so. The first man prayed to God, saying, 'Please God, give me the strength to cross this river.' Poof! God gave him big arms and strong legs, and he was able to swim across the river in about two hours, but only after almost drowning a couple of times.

Seeing this, the second man prayed to God, saying, 'Please God, give me the strength and the tools to cross this river.'

Poof! God gave him a rowing boat and he was able to row across the river in about an hour, but only after almost capsizing the boat a couple of times.

The third man had seen how this worked out for the other two, so he also prayed to God saying, 'Please God, give me the strength and the tools and the intelligence to cross this river.'

And poof! God turned him into a woman. She looked at the map, hiked upstream a couple of hundred yards, then walked across the bridge.

***

Ask any man and he will tell you that any woman's ultimate fantasy is to have two men at once. While this has been verified by a recent sociological study, it appears that most men do not realise that in the Jewish version of this fantasy, one man is cooking and the other is cleaning.

***

Avrahom was reading an article out loud to his wife. 'Did you know that women use about thirty thousand words a day, whereas men only use fifteen thousand words?'

Sadie replies, 'The reason has to be because a woman has to say everything twice.'

Avrahom turns to Sadie and asks, 'What?'

***

Jewish men's rules:

Birthdays and anniversaries should not be challenges to see if we can again find the perfect present for you.

Sometimes we are not thinking about you. Live with it.

Sunday is sports day. It's like gravity or a full moon. Let it be.

Just ask for what you want. Let's be clear on this. Subtle hints don't work. Nor do strong or even obvious hints. So just simply tell us what you want.

We don't remember dates. So write birthdays and anniversaries on the calendar and remind us frequently before the event.

Learn to work the toilet seat. You're a big girl now, so if it's up, don't moan, just put it down. We need it up and you never hear us complaining when you leave it down.

Shopping is not a sport and we are never, ever going to think of it as such.

Yes and No are perfectly acceptable answers to most questions.

Christopher Columbus didn't need directions and neither do we.

Only come to us with a problem if you really want help solving it. That's what we do. Sympathy is what your girlfriends do.

Anything we said over three months ago is inadmissible in an argument. In fact, all comments become null and void after seven days.

If you think you're fat, you probably are. Don't ask us. We won't answer.

Most men own at most three pairs of shoes. So what makes you think we're any good at helping you decide which pair of your shoes, out of forty, goes best with your dress?

If something we said can be interpreted two ways, and one of the ways makes you sad or angry, we meant the other one.

Men see in only sixteen colours, like Windows default settings. Peach, for example, is a fruit, not a colour and we have no idea what mauve is.

We are not mind-readers and never will be. Our lack of mind-reading ability is not proof of how little we care about you.

If you ask a question to which you don't want an answer to, expect an answer you don't want to hear.

When we have to go out somewhere, anything you wear is fine. Really.

If we ask what is wrong and you say 'nothing', we will act like nothing's wrong. We know you are lying, but it is just not worth the hassle.

Let us ogle. If we don't look at other women, how can we know how pretty you are?

Don't rub the lamp if you don't want the genie to come out.

You can either ask us to do something OR tell us how you want it done – not both.

Whenever possible, please say whatever you have to say during the commercials.

Women who wear Wonderbras and low-cut blouses lose their right to complain about having their boobs stared at.

When we're turning the wheel and the car is nosing on to the motorway exit, your saying 'This is our exit' is not necessary.

Don't fake it. We'd rather be ineffectual than deceived.

Thank you for reading this. Yes, I know I have to sleep on the couch tonight, but did you know we really don't mind that? It's like camping.

***

To be happy with a man, you must understand him a lot and love him a little. To be happy with a woman, you must love her a lot and not try to understand her at all.

Accidents & emergencies

Maurice and Sadie were in a terrible accident in which Sadie's face was severely burned. The doctor told Maurice that they couldn't graft any skin from her body because she was too thin. So Maurice offered to donate some of his own skin. However, the only skin on his body that the doctor felt was suitable would have to come from his *toches*. Maurice and Sadie agreed that they would tell no one about where the skin came from, and requested that the doctor also honour their secret.

After the surgery was completed, everyone was astounded at Sadie's new beauty. She looked more beautiful than she ever had before! All her friends and relatives just went on and on about her youthful beautiful skin!

One day, she was alone with Maurice and she was overcome with emotion at this sacrifice. She said, 'Dear, I just want to thank you for everything you did for me. There is no way I could ever repay you.'

'My darling, ' he replied, 'think nothing of it. I get all the *naches* I need every time I see your mother kiss you on the cheek.'

* * *

Moshe is a member of Hendon synagogue. One day he calls on Rabbi Goldman of Golders Green synagogue to ask him for help. 'Everything I had and owned, Rabbi, was lost when my house burned down recently in a raging fire. I've nothing left but the clothes I'm wearing.'

'Do you have a letter from your own rabbi attesting to this fire?' Rabbi Goldman asks.

'Yes, I did have such a letter, but unfortunately, that was also lost in the fire.'

* * *

One day, Moshe is crossing the street and gets knocked down by a car. Although only slightly hurt, an ambulance is called. When it arrives, the attendant puts a blanket over Moshe and a pillow under his head and asks, 'Sir, are you comfortable?'

Moshe looks up and says, 'Vell, I make a living!'

* * *

Bernie was unfortunate enough to be hit by a ten-ton lorry and landed up in hospital in intensive care. His best friend Morris came to visit him. Bernie struggled to tell Morris, 'My wife Sadie visits me three times a day. She's so good to me. Every day, she reads to me at the bedside.'

'What does she read?'

'My life insurance policy.'

* * *

Beckie and Lou decided to take their little son, Sam, on his first visit to the beach. Dressed in his little swimming trunks and hat and bucket and spade in hand, Sam happily played at the water's edge as his mother and father spread their picnic blanket. Then suddenly, to his parents' horror, a huge wave crashed down on Sam and then dragged him far out to sea. As neither Beckie nor Lou could swim, Beckie began to wail and cry, 'Dear God, be merciful. Return our son to us!'

Suddenly another huge wave cast Sam back up on the sand at his parents' feet. Beckie inspected her son, then quickly looked back towards the heavens and said, 'He had a hat!'

***

Eighty-four-year-old Morris is hit by a car and lies bleeding on the pavement. A policeman arrives on the scene and seeing the state Morris is in, immediately calls for a priest and an ambulance. The priest arrives first. He bends over Morris and asks, 'Do you believe in the Father, the Son and the Holy Ghost?'

Morris lifts his head, opens his eyes wide, turns to the crowd that had gathered around him, and says, 'Here I am, laying here dying and this *shmendrick* is asking me riddles!'

Law & order

Morris walked into a solicitor's office for some advice. Before he started, however, he quite rightly asked the solicitor about his rates.

'How much do you charge for advice?'

'A hundred and fifty pounds for three questions,' replied the solicitor.

'Isn't that very expensive?' asked Morris.

'Yes,' replied the solicitor, 'and what was your third question?'

***

Abe, an elderly man, was in the witness box. 'How old are you?' asked the prosecution lawyer.

'I am, *kinahora* [may I be protected from the evil eye], 82.'

'What did you say?'

'I said I am, *kinahora*, 82 years old.'

'Please just give a simple answer to my question,' said the lawyer. 'How old are you?'

'*Kinahora*, 82,' replied Abe.

The judge then intervened and said to Abe, 'If you don't want to be held in contempt of court, you will answer the question and only the question.'

The defence lawyer then got up and said to the judge, 'Your Honour, may I ask the witness?' and turned towards Abe. '*Kinahora*, how old are you?'

Abe replied, '82.'

***

Some thieves broke into the Joint Israel Appeal offices. They got away with over £1 million in pledges.

***

A member of the jury is about to be sworn in but he tells the Court that he is deaf in one ear. The judge tells him, 'You really can't serve on the jury.'

'Why not?'

'Because you can only hear one side.'

***

A policeman spots two youngsters riding a motorcycle in Stamford Hill. They are unmistakably Chassidic: skullcaps, long sidelocks, prayer shawls, the works. He is unmistakably a bigot, so he follows them intending to catch them doing some kind of wrong. After a long ride during which they go on to the North Circular Road and then on to many side roads, he can find nothing wrong with their driving. Frustrated, he stops them anyway.

'I have been following you two for a long time now, watching every move you have made and hoping to catch you breaking the law, but you two seem to be doing perfectly. How do you do it?'

'*HaShem* is with us,' they reply.

'That's it! Now I've got you!' exclaimed the policeman, 'Three people on a motorcycle.'

***

Harry and Freda get stopped by a police car. When the police officer gets to their car, Harry says, 'What's the problem, officer?'

Officer: You were going at least 65mph in a 50mph zone.

Harry: No sir, I was going fifty.

Freda: Oh, Harry, You were going seventy.

Harry gives his wife a dirty look.

Officer: I will also give you a ticket for your broken brake light.

Harry: Broken brake light? I didn't know about a broken brake light!

Freda: Oh, Harry, you've known about that brake light for months.

Harry gives Freda a really dirty look.

Officer: I am also going to book you for not wearing your seat belt.

Harry: Oh, I just took it off when you were walking up to the car.

Freda: Oh, Harry, you never wear your seat belt.

Harry turns to his wife and yells, 'Shut your damn mouth!'

The police officer turns to the woman and says, 'Madam, does your husband talk to you this way all the time?'

Freda replies, 'No, only when he's drunk.'

***

Michael and Hetty, an elderly couple, are on holiday in Devon when they decide to take a drive into the countryside. Hetty is driving when she gets stopped by a traffic policeman. The officer comes up to the car and says to her, 'Madam, did you know you were speeding?'

Hetty turns to Michael and asks him, 'What did he say?'

Michael yells back at her, 'He says you were speeding.'

The policeman then says to Hetty, 'May I see your driving licence?'

Hetty turns to Michael and asks him, 'What did he say?'

Michael yells back at her, 'He wants to see your driving licence.'

So Hetty gives the officer her licence.

The policeman looks at the licence and then says, 'Ah. I see you are both from Golders Green in London. I spent some time there many years ago and I'll always remember the time that I went on a blind date with the ugliest woman I have ever seen in my life.'

Hetty turns to Michael and asks him, 'What did he say?'

Michael yells back at her, 'He says he thinks he knows you.'

***

It is midnight and a cold night in Golders Green when all of a sudden a burglar alarm goes off. The police are immediately called and surprisingly arrive just in time to catch the thief as he is leaving the jewellers with a bag full of Rolex watches and other valuable items. When he is brought to the police station, the officer on duty immediately recognises him. He is known as Morris the Catman. One week later, Morris appears in Court.

'Did you have an accomplice?' the judge asks him.

'What's an accomplice?' asks Morris.

'A partner,' replies the judge. 'In other words, did you commit this crime by yourself?'

'Of course, what else?' says Morris, 'Who can get reliable help these days?'

***

Moshe and Bernie were in court and standing before the judge.

'Why can't this case be settled out of court?' the judge asked.

Moshe looked up at the judge and said, 'That's what we were trying to do, your honour, when the police interfered.'

***

Shlomo's business had done so well that he treated himself to a brand new 5-litre Mercedes convertible. When he picked up the car from the dealers, he decided to take it out on a spin on the motorway. Soon he was driving at 80mph with the wind blowing through his hair. 'This is brilliant,' he said to himself and increased his speed a bit more. But a quick look in his rear-view mirror showed him a police car with flashing lights coming up quickly behind him.

Shlomo thought, 'I can easily get away from him,' and he started to accelerate away. But then he had another thought, 'What the hell am I doing? This is madness,' so he quickly pulled over to the side of the road and waited.

The police car pulled up behind him and a policeman got out. He walked up to Shlomo and said, 'This just might be your lucky day, sir. Today is Friday the thirteenth and my shift ends in three minutes. If you can give me one good reason why you were speeding that I've never heard before, I'll let you off with just a warning.'

Shlomo looked at the policeman and said, 'Last week, my wife Sadie ran off with a policeman and I thought you were bringing her back. That's why I was trying to get away from you.'

The policeman said, 'Enjoy the rest of your day sir.'

***

Moshe goes into his local post office to buy some stamps. As he walks up to the counter, he sees a man methodically sticking stamps onto a pile of pink envelopes. He was also placing 'I Love You' heart-shaped stickers onto the envelopes. When he had finished, the man took out a bottle of French perfume and sprayed all the envelopes with it.

Moshe had to find out why, so he goes up to the man and asks. The man replies, 'I'm sending out a hundred scented

Valentine cards, each one signed, "From you know who".'
'Why so many?' Moshe asks.
'Because I'm a divorce lawyer and business is not so good.'

***

'Mr Issy Levy,' says the divorce court judge, 'I have reviewed this case very carefully indeed, and as a result of the facts, I've decided to award your wife Rifka £350 a week.'

'That's very fair of you, your honour,' says Issy, 'and every now and then, I'll try to send her some money too.'

***

A classic example of *chutzpah* is someone who kills his mother and father and then throws himself on the mercy of the court because he is an orphan.

***

It was Christmas and Judge Levy was in a merry mood as he asked the defendant, 'What are you charged with?'

'Doing my Christmas shopping early,' replied the defendant.

'But that's not an offence,' said Judge Levy.

'It is if you do it before the shop opens,' said the defendant.

***

Did you see the recent story in the *Jewish Chronicle* about the theft of egg-enriched dough from a north London warehouse? Unfortunately, the theft happened just before Shabbes and it forced many local bakeries to bake their *challahs* with plain, white flour. A leading rabbi was quoted as saying, 'I'm appalled by the rise in white-*challah* crimes.'

***

Solly is serving time in Holloway prison for a securities fraud. Even so, he is still loved by his father Maurice. One day, Maurice writes Solly a letter:

> My darling Solly,
> It looks like I won't be able to plant anything in the garden this year. I am growing too old to do any digging without your help. Looking forward to your early release.
> Love from your Dad

Solly replies:

> Dearest Dad
> Please don't dig up the garden – that's where I hid the money and the securities. Be patient. Wait until I get out.
> Love as always, Solly

At 4 a.m. in the morning, the police show up at Maurice's house and dig up the entire garden. Two days later, Maurice receives another letter from Solly:

> Dearest Dad,
> Now the garden has been dug over, you can start to plant your garden. It's the best I could do from here.
> Your devoted son Solly

***

Benjy had been arrested and was now up before the judge.

The judge asks, 'Do you admit you broke into the same clothes shop three times?'

'Yes,' replies Benjy.

'Could you please tell the court what you stole,' asks the judge.

'I stole a dress, your honour,' replies Benjy.

'Just one dress? But you admitted to breaking in three times!' says the judge.

'Yes I did, your honour,' says Benjy, 'but on two of those

occasions, I broke in to return the dress I took before.'

'Return the dress? Why? I don't understand,' says the judge.

'Because my wife Bette didn't like the design, your honour.'

* * *

When Rivkah was called up for jury service, she asked the judge whether she could be excused. 'I don't believe in capital punishment,' she said, 'and I wouldn't want my views to prevent the trial from running its proper course.'

The judge liked her thoughtfulness but had to tell her that she was perfectly suitable to serve on the jury. 'Madam,' he explained, 'This is not a murder trial, it's just a simple civil lawsuit. Mrs F is bringing this case against her husband because he gambled away the entire £15,000 he had promised her for her birthday so that she could carry out a make-over on her kitchen.'

'OK,' said Rivkah, 'I'll join your jury – I could be wrong about capital punishment after all.'

* * *

Two solicitors, Levy and Cohen, opened an office in Kilburn. As this was a Gentile part of London, they decided to call their firm Christian and Christian in order to attract non-Jewish clients. But on their opening day, they forgot to tell their switchboard operator what to say. When anyone phoned in and asked for Mr Christian, she answered, 'Which Christian do you want, Levy or Cohen?'

Money

Issy walks into a central London bank and says he's going to America for two weeks and needs to borrow £5,000. For collateral, he offers his new Rolls Royce. The bank is satisfied and parks it in their secured underground garage. Two weeks later to the day, Issy returns to the bank and repays the £5,000 plus interest of £9.41.

The loan officer says inquiringly, 'Sir, we were delighted to have your business but checking your credit, we learned you are a multimillionaire. Why ever did you need to borrow £5,000?'

'Where else in central London could I park my car for two weeks for £9.41?'

***

Did you hear about the Jewish Mother ATM? When you take out some money, it says to you '*Nu*, what did you do with the last £50 I gave you?'

***

Shlomo said to his friend Moshe, 'Moshe, did I tell you that Hetty had plastic surgery the other day?'

'No you didn't,' replied Moshe.

'Yes,' said Shlomo, 'I cut up her credit cards.'

***

Abe's son arrived home from school puffing and panting, sweat rolling down his face.

'Dad, you'll be so proud of me,' he said, 'I saved a pound by running behind the bus all the way home!'

'*Oy Vay!*' said Abe, 'You could have run behind a taxi and saved £10.'

***

A Hebrew teacher in Chelm declared one day: 'If I were Rothschild I would be richer than Rothschild.'

'Why?'

'Because I would give Hebrew lessons on the side.'

***

The Government is going to put a special tax on *tzitzit*. They are being classed as fringe benefits.

***

Young David asked his rich grandfather, Paul, how he had made his money. Paul said, 'Well, David, it was 1955, and I was down to my last 5p. I went to the local market and invested that 5p in a large apple. I spent the entire day polishing the apple and, at the end of the day, I sold the apple for 10p. The next morning, I invested the 10p in two large apples. I spent the entire day polishing them and I sold them at 5 p.m. for 20p. I continued this system for a month. Then Grandma's father died and left us £2 million.'

***

Morris Schwartz was the oldest of seven children. Unfortunately, he had to quit school and work to help support his younger brothers and sisters. He never learned to read. So, when he married and opened a bank account, he signed his cheques just 'XX'. Morris then started his own business, which soon prospered. He became a very rich man.

One day, he got a call from his bank. 'Mr Schwartz, I wanted to ask you about this cheque. We weren't sure you had really signed it. All these years, you've been signing your cheques, 'XX'; this one is signed with three X's - '

Morris replied, 'Since I've become rich, my wife thought I should have a middle name.'

***

Jacob is talking to his friend Morris. 'A terrible thing,' says Jacob. 'my daughter Rifka is getting married tomorrow and I promised a dowry of £25,000. Now, half the dowry is missing.'

'So what?' replies Morris. 'One usually pays only half of the promised dowry at the beginning of the wedding.'

'I know, but that's the half which is missing.'

***

Paul and Bernard are out enjoying themselves one afternoon on a lake when their boat starts sinking. Bernard says to Paul, 'So listen, Paul, I have a problem, you know I don't swim at all well.'

But luckily, Paul remembers how to carry another swimmer from his lifeguard class years ago when he was just a youngster and so he begins pulling Bernard towards safety. After fifteen minutes of this, however, Paul begins to grow quite tired – all his energy has left him. And finally, just 100 feet from land, Paul asks Bernard, 'So Bernard, do you suppose you could float alone?'

Bernard replies, ' Paul, this is a hell of a time to be asking about money!'

***

It's nearly four o'clock in the morning and Sadie wakes up to see her husband pacing up and down the bedroom floor.

'Moshe, come back to bed, it's not yet morning,' she tells him.

Moshe replies, 'I can't go to sleep. You know the £10,000 I borrowed from our next door neighbour Bernie? Well, it's due to be repaid tomorrow and I don't have the money. I just don't know what I'm going to do.'

So Sadie gets out of bed and opens the bedroom window. 'Bernie!' she shouts on top of her voice, 'Bernie, Bernie!'

Finally a very tired looking Bernie opens his window and shouts, 'You're crazy, Sadie. Don't you know it's nearly four o'clock in the morning? What the hell do you want?'

Sadie shouts back, 'Bernie, you know the £10,000 my husband owes you? Well, he doesn't have it.'

Then she slams the window shut, turns to Moshe and says, 'Now you can go to sleep and let Bernie pace the floor.'

***

Shlomo and Sidney are walking home late one night when they see a crowd of drunken yobs coming towards them.

'Sidney,' says Shlomo, 'do you know that £500 you lent me

recently?'

'Yes,' replied Sidney.

'Well,' said Shlomo, 'here, you can have it back now.'

* * *

Moshe and his Scotsman friend enter a bar with a group of their friends. Soon everyone is eating and drinking like it's going out of style. Eventually, it comes time to pay the bill.

'I'll pay!' shouts McTavish, and with a scowl, pays the bill.

The next day, the headline in *The Times* reads, 'Jewish ventriloquist found murdered in alley.'

* * *

Helen and Issy were having a hard time financially and needed to keep their spending to a minimum. To keep her household account as low as she could, Helen decided not to have her dress dry-cleaned. Instead, she washed it by hand. When Issy returned from work, Helen proudly told him of her idea to save money.

She said, 'Just think, Issy, we are £3 richer because I washed this dress by hand.'

'Great,' Issy quickly replied. 'Wash it again!'

* * *

Moshe was 88 years old and went to see his financial advisor. 'So what do you think is an appropriate investment for me?' asked Moshe.

'Well,' replied the advisor, 'I have found a terrific investment that will double your money in five years.'

'Are you crazy?' said Moshe, 'A five-year investment? Why, at my age, I don't even buy green bananas.'

* * *

Maurice and Sadie were having a heated discussion about family finances. Finally Maurice exploded, 'If it weren't for my money, this house wouldn't be here.'

Sadie replied, 'Darling, if it weren't for your money, I wouldn't be here.'

* * *

Moshe goes to Brent Cross shopping centre with his ten-year-old son, Paul. Paul is flicking a 20p coin up in the air with his thumb and each time catching it between his teeth. But then someone bumps into Paul and the 20p coin goes straight down his throat. Paul starts to choke and soon begins to turn blue. Moshe starts to panic and shouts and screams for someone to help him. An ordinary looking man in a blue suit is sitting on a bench drinking coffee and reading his newspaper. He puts down his cup and paper, gets up and walks towards Paul, who is now close to collapse. When he gets to him, the man takes hold of Paul's testicles and squeezes them gently but firmly. Straight away, Paul coughs up the 20p coin into the man's free hand. The man gives the coin to Moshe and walks back to his bench to finish off his coffee. Not a word is said during this event.

Moshe is overwhelmed with gratitude and quickly goes over to the man to thank him. The man looks embarrassed and tells Moshe he doesn't have to thank him. But Moshe says, 'You're a hero. I've never heard of anyone doing what you just did – it was pure magic. What are you, a doctor?'

'Oh, no,' the man replies, 'I work for the Inland Revenue.'

* * *

Shlomo was a miser and his friend Isaac knew this. One evening, Shlomo and Isaac went out for a meal with their girlfriends. At the end of the meal, Isaac overheard Shlomo say to his girl, 'Marry me, darling, and I'll buy you the sun, the moon and the stars.'

Shlomo immediately called over the waiter and said, 'Separate bills please.'

* * *

'Hello, that's you, Abe?'

'Yes, dis is Abe.'

'It doesn't sount like Abe.'

'Vell, dis is Abe all right.'

'You're positive it's Abe?'

'Absolutely.'

'Vell, listen Abie, dis is Moe. Can you lend me feefty punds?'

'Ven Abe comes in, I'll tell him you called - '

***

Gary was having a good time in Tel Aviv and was invited to a party. Unfortunately, during the evening, he lost his wallet. So Gary, not being the shy kind, stood on a chair and shouted, 'Excuse me ladies and gentlemen, I've just lost my wallet with over £500 in cash in it. To the person that finds my wallet, I will give £50.'

A voice from the back of the hall shouted, 'I will give £75.'

***

A man dies and his three best friends, Shlomo, Patrick and Peter are looking at his body in the coffin.

Patrick says, 'He was such a good friend to me that I don't want him to go to his maker empty handed.' He then throws £200 in £20 notes into the coffin.

Peter says, 'I agree, so I'll match that,' and he also throws £200 in notes into the coffin.

Shlomo then says, 'What cheap-skates you both are. I'm ashamed to know you. I'm going to give him £1,000.' Shlomo then writes out a cheque for £1,400, throws it in and takes the £400 in change out of the coffin.

***

Harry went for a job interview. It seemed to go well because before he left, he was told, 'We would like you to work for us.

We'll give you £10 an hour starting today and in three months' time we'll increase it to £15 an hour. So when would you like to start?'

Harry replied, 'In about three months from now.'

***

Moshe the farmer had made out a will that stipulated how his prize cows would be shared out to his three sons on his death. He decided that half the cows should go to his eldest son, one third to his second eldest son and one ninth to his youngest son. He thought this was fair.

Some years later he died and his sons knew that there were seventeen cows. But they just couldn't divide them according to their father's wishes. So they had to call in the learned rabbi. After much thought, the rabbi went away and returned with one of his own cows, making eighteen cows. Then the rabbi gave the oldest son nine cows, the second son got six cows and the youngest two cows. There was still one cow left over, so the rabbi took his cow back home with him.

***

Angela was nearing sixty and was in her final year of teaching. She was a devout Christian who missed teaching from the Bible. Because she was worried at how little her class knew about religion, Angela decided she was going to disregard the new regulations and teach some religion. She told her class that she would run a contest. She would give £50 to whoever could tell her who was the greatest man who ever lived.

Immediately Moshe began to wave his hand, but Angela ignored him in favour of those in her Sunday school class. As she went around the room, Angela was disappointed with the answers she got. Jane, her best scholar, picked Noah because he saved all the animals. Others said, 'I think the greatest man who ever lived was Alexander the Great because he conquered the whole world.' and 'I think it was Thomas Edison, because he invented the light bulb.'

Finally, she called on Moshe who still had his hand in the air.

'I think the greatest man who ever lived was Jesus Christ,' said Moshe.

Angela was shocked but still gave him the £50 reward. As she did so, she said, 'Well, Moshe, I'm very surprised that you should be the only one with the right answer. How come?'

'Well, to tell you the truth,' Moshe replied as he pocketed the money, 'I really think it was Moses, but business is business.'

Shopping

Harry was walking down Regent Street and stepped into a posh gourmet food shop. An impressive salesman in a smart morning coat with tails approached him and politely asked, 'Can I help you, sir?'

'Yes,' replied Harry, 'I would like to buy a pound of *lox*.'

'No, no,' responded the dignified salesman, 'you mean smoked salmon.'

'OK, a pound of smoked salmon then, and make it wild salmon.'

'Anything else?'

'Yes, a dozen *blintzes*.'

'No, no, you mean crêpes.'

'OK, a dozen crêpes.'

'Anything else?'

'Yes. A pound of chopped liver.'

'No, no, you mean pâté.'

'OK,' said Harry, 'A pound of pâté then and I'd like you to deliver all of this to my house on Saturday.'

'Look,' retorted the indignant salesman, 'we don't schlep on Shabbes!'

***

Max is having a cup of tea in his best friend Morris's house. Morris was commenting on the time and the fact that his wife had not yet returned home from her shopping.

'Beckie's two hours late, Max.'

'She's probably been kidnapped or she's been involved in a terrible car crash,' replies Max, 'or maybe she's still shopping.'

'*Oy Vay!*' says Morris, 'I hope she's not shopping!'

***

Moshe says to his friend, 'My Sadie and I, we are always holding hands.'

'Why do you do this?' asks his friend.

'Because if I let go, she shops.'

***

Beckie is out doing her shopping. She goes into a supermarket and gets totally confused by the large selection of toilet paper they have on their shelves. So she goes up to one of the assistants and asks, 'Excuse me. Can you explain the differences between all these toilet rolls, please?'

'Of course,' he replies. He points out one brand, 'This is our best because it's as soft as a baby's kiss. It's £1.50 per roll.' He picks up another roll and says to her, 'This one is also good. It's nice and soft, strong but gentle and it's £1 a roll.' Then, pointing to the bottom shelf he tells Beckie, 'We call that roll our No Name brand, and it's 50p per roll.'

'Give me the No Name,' says Beckie.

One week later, Beckie goes back to the shop and seeks out the assistant.

'I've got a name for your No Name toilet paper. I call it John Wayne.'

'Why?' he asks.

'Because it's rough, it's tough and it don't take crap off anybody!'

***

Harry had some shopping to do at John Lewis department store. He walked into ladieswear, went up to the lingerie counter and quietly said to the women behind the desk, 'I'd like to buy a bra as a present for my wife.'

'Of course, sir, what type of bra would you like to buy?' she asked.

'What type?' replied Harry, 'do you mean to say there is more than one type?'

'Of course. Let me explain,' she said and began to show Harry bras in a variety of shapes, sizes, colours and materials. Harry looked bewildered. 'There's no need to be confused,' she said, 'there are really only four types of bra.'

When Harry asked her what the four types were, she replied, 'The Catholic type, the Salvation Army type, the Presbyterian type and the Jewish type.'

Still confused, Harry asked, 'What are the differences between them?'

The saleslady answered, 'The Catholic type supports the masses, the Salvation Army type lifts up the fallen, the Presbyterian type keeps them staunch and upright, and the Jewish type makes mountains out of mole hills.'

***

Latest inventions from Chelm:
A waterproof towel
Glow-in-the-dark sunglasses
A solar-powered torch
A book called 'how to read'
Waterproof tea-bags
A pedal-powered wheel chair
A full index for a dictionary

***

Did you hear about Moshe, who was sexually inexperienced? One day, he went into a bookshop and bought *How to Hug*. Later on, when he started to read his latest purchase, Moshe realised it was Volume 7 of the *Encyclopaedia Britannica*.

***

It's true. You've heard the joke about the Jewish mothers who want to be buried at Brent Cross shopping centre – so they can be sure that their daughters will regularly visit them? Well, these mothers had better start thinking again about where they want to be buried because scientists claim to have discovered a drug to combat the Jewish vice of shopaholicism. Trialists who took the drug found that their shopping impulses were reduced by at least 50 per cent – whether they were shopping in malls or via the Internet or TV shopping channels. The drug is normally used to treat depression.

***

It's true. Research has shown that women have just 72 minutes of shopping with their man before he starts to lose interest in the exercise. Women will happily spend 100 minutes roaming from shop to shop until something catches their eye; men, however, treat shopping as a project. Instead of looking around to compare prices, they know what they want and where to get it. So, for you Moshes and Sadies out there, it's a good idea to get your joint shopping expedition finished within 72 minutes of arriving at the shopping centre. Then, to avoid any flaming rows, go your own separate ways. That way you'll stay married longer!

***

Sadie walked into a print lab to have a photo of her deceased husband Moshe copied and retouched. She said to the technician, 'I have always hated the hat that my husband Moshe is wearing in the photo. Could you please retouch the hat out?'

'Of course,' said the technician, 'what colour hair did your husband have?'

'When you take the hat off, you'll see,' she said.

***

Morris's local manufacturing business was broken into last night and a large quantity of wigs was stolen. Police are currently combing the area for clues.

***

A man walks into Moshe's shoe shop and tries on a pair of shoes. 'How do they feel?' asks Moshe.

'Well the left one feels a bit tight,' replies the man.

Moshe looks down at the shoe on the man's left foot and says, 'Try it again, this time with the tongue out.'

'Well, theyth thtill feelth a bith tighth.'

***

Rivkah goes to the new shopping centre in Hendon. It's unique because it's only for Jewish women looking for Jewish husbands. Potential husbands are the only goods on display. This is why Rivkah is there. When she enters the building, there is a large sign which says:

> THE RULES OF THE HENDON JEWISH WOMEN'S SHOPPING CENTRE
> This centre is laid out over five floors.
> The men here have increasingly better attributes the higher up you go.
> You are only allowed in once.
> Once you open the door to a floor, you must choose a man from that floor.
> If you go up a floor, you can't go back down except to leave the centre.
> BEST OF LUCK

Rivkah goes to the first floor. The sign on the door says: 'Floor 1: All the men here have jobs, love children and are certainly not lazy.'

Rivkah thinks, 'Well, that's better than not having a job or not loving children, but I wonder what's further up?' So up she goes to the next floor. The sign says: 'Floor 2: All the men on this floor have executive jobs, love children, are certainly not lazy and are extremely good-looking.'

'That's better,' thinks Rivkah, 'but I wonder what's further upstairs?' Up she goes. The sign says: 'Floor 3: All the men on this floor have executive jobs, love children, are certainly not lazy, are extremely good-looking, help with the housework and are not strictly orthodox.'

'Wow,' thinks Rivkah, 'Almost perfect and very tempting. But I've come this far and there's more further up!' And so again, up she goes. The sign says: 'Floor 4: All the men on this floor have executive jobs, love children, are certainly not lazy, are extremely good-looking, help with the housework, are not strictly orthodox, are very romantic and know how to satisfy their partner.'

'*Oy*, wonderful,' she says aloud, 'But just think what could be waiting for me upstairs!' So up to the fifth and top floor she goes. The sign here says: 'Floor 5: This floor is just to prove that Jewish women are impossible to please. Thank you for shopping. Have a nice day.'

***

Q: Why were Gentiles invented?
A: Somebody has to pay retail.

Q: Why are Jewish men circumcised?
A: Because Jewish women won't touch anything unless it is 20 per cent off.

***

Old Yitzhak is standing in a Moscow street looking through the window of a huge grocery shop. He mutters, 'So they have no more beef – and no more lamb – and they don't even have any pork – or chicken – or sausage. In fact they have no meat at all. Nor do they have any milk or cheese or eggs or flour or - '

Suddenly, a man standing next to Yitzhak hisses in his ear, 'Shut up, you stupid Yid. Stop spreading anti-Soviet propaganda or I'll hit your stupid head with the butt of my gun. Have you understood me?'

'Yes, I understood, I understood you, comrade,' replies Yitzhak and he walks away as fast as he can. When Yitzhak arrives back at his house, he says to his wife, 'Leah, I really understood. They don't have any bullets either!'

* * *

Moshe walks into a post office to send a package to his wife. The postmaster says, 'This package is too heavy, you'll need another stamp.'

Moshe replies, 'And that should make it lighter?'

Presents

Beckie's grandson and his wife are coming to visit her for the first time. So she is giving him the directions to her flat. 'You come to the front door of the Golders Green block of flats. I am in flat number 32 on the fourteenth floor. At the front door, you'll see a big panel of buttons. With your elbow push button 32. I will buzz you in. Come inside, the lift is on the right. Get in, and with your elbow hit fourteen. When you get out, I am on the left. With your elbow, hit my doorbell.'

'Grandma, that sounds easy, but why am I hitting all these buttons with my elbow'?

'You're coming empty-handed?'

* * *

Moshe's mother, Hetty, once gave him two sweaters for Chanukah. The next time Moshe visited his mother, he made sure he was wearing one of them. As he entered her house, instead of the expected smile, Hetty said, 'What's the matter, Moshe? You didn't like the other one?'

* * *

Jeremy asks his wife Naomi what she wants for their fortieth wedding anniversary. 'Would you like a new diamond bracelet?' he asks.

'Not really,' says Naomi.

'Well how about a Lexus sports car?' says Jeremy.

'No,' she replies.

'What about a holiday home in the south of France?' he suggests.

She again rejects his offer with a 'No thanks'.

'Well what would you like for your anniversary?' Jeremy asks.

'I'd like a divorce, Jeremy,' answers Naomi.

'*Oy*, I wasn't planning to spend that much!' says Jeremy.

***

Abe came from a very poor family. One Chanukah, his father gave him an empty box and told him it was an Action Man Deserter Kit.

***

One year, Louis didn't know what to buy his mother-in-law for her birthday, so he bought her a large plot in Bushey cemetery. The following year, Louis bought her nothing for her birthday and his wife was quick to comment loud and long on his thoughtlessness to her mother.

'So, why didn't you buy her something?' she snapped at him.

'Well, she hasn't used the gift I gave her last year,' he replied.

***

David Levy and a beautiful woman walk into a very posh Hendon furrier.

'Show the lady your finest mink!' David says.

So the furrier goes into the storeroom and comes out with an absolutely stunning full-length coat. As the lady tries it on, the furrier goes over to David and discreetly whispers in his ear, 'Ah, sir, that particular fur coat goes for £20,000.'

'No problem! I'll write you out a cheque.'

'Very good, sir,' says the furrier. 'Today is Friday, you may come by on Tuesday to pick it up after the cheque has cleared.'

So David and the woman leave.

On Tuesday, David returns to the shop, on his own. The furrier is outraged to see him.

'How dare you show your face in here? There wasn't a single penny in your bank account.'

'I just had to come by,' grins David, 'to thank you for the most wonderful weekend of my life.'

***

Maurice, age 92, has just asked Sarah, age 89, to marry him and she has accepted. *Mazeltov!* They are both very excited and decide to go for a walk so that they can discuss the wedding arrangements. On their walk they pass a large chemist and decide to go in. Maurice asks to see the owner.

When a young man comes up to them, Maurice asks, 'Are you the owner?'

'Yes I am,' says the man, 'how can I help?'

'We're about to get married,' says Maurice. 'Do you sell heart medication?'

'Of course we do,' replies the owner.

'How about medicine for improving circulation?' asks Maurice.

'We stock all kinds, sir.'

'What about remedies for rheumatic conditions?' asks Sarah.

'Yes, no problem, madam.'

Maurice then asks, sheepishly, 'Do you stock that Viagra, then?'

'Of course, sir.'

Sarah then asks, 'What about vitamins, sleeping pills, antidotes for Parkinson's, medicine for memory problems, arthritis and jaundice?'

'Yes, we stock a large variety of all of these. The works, madam.'

Maurice then asks, 'Do you sell wheelchairs and Zimmer frames?'

'Our speciality. We have many sizes and all speeds.'

Maurice finally says to the owner, 'OK. We'd like to set up our wedding gifts list here, please.'

***

Shlomo was driving home one evening when he suddenly remembered that it was his daughter's birthday and he hadn't bought her a present. So he drove to Brent Cross shopping centre and ran all the way to the toyshop. 'How much is the latest Barbie doll?' he asked the manager.

The manager replied, 'Which one? We have "Barbie goes to the Gym" for £17.99, "Barbie goes to the Dance" for £16.99, "Barbie goes to the Shops" for £15.99, "Barbie goes to the Seaside" for £18.99, and "Barbie goes to the Bar Mitzvah" for £19.99. We also have "Divorced Barbie" for £350.'

Shlomo was confused and asked the manager, 'Why does "Divorced Barbie" cost £350 when all the others are less than £20?'

'It's simple,' replied the manager, 'Divorced Barbie comes with Ken's car, Ken's House, Ken's boat, Ken's dog, Ken's cat and Ken's furniture.'

***

Abe was well known for his meanness and his 'eye for a bargain'. One day he was looking for a cheap wedding present for his niece, so he went into a gift shop in Golders Green. As he was walking around, he noticed what was previously an expensive glass crystal vase lying in the corner. It was in three pieces. After some haggling with the owner, Abe bought the broken vase for £1. He then filled in the congratulations card, wrote out his niece's name and address and gave the owner a further £10 so that the broken vase could be gift wrapped and posted. Abe then left the shop feeling quite pleased with himself. He expected his niece to think the vase had broken in the mail.

A few days later, he rang his niece to see if the present had arrived.

'Yes, Uncle Abe, but unfortunately, it was in three pieces when it was delivered.'

'What terrible luck.' said Abe, 'The Royal Mail is getting worse all the time.'

'It's a shame,' she replied. 'It was so beautifully wrapped. Each piece separately.'

***

Hyman is a very rich and successful businessman. As it is coming up to his wife Rivka's birthday, he decides to buy her a really special birthday present. So he tells his chauffeur to take him to the best art shops in New Bond Street in London. He soon finds what he's looking for – a beautiful Rembrandt painting and he buys it without a moment's hesitation. As soon as Hyman gets back home, he opens his front door and shouts, 'Rivka, Rivka, have I got a Rembrandt for you!'

To which Rivka replies, 'God willing it will make a skirt.'

***

On his wedding day, Shlomo's father-in-law Louis came up to him and said, 'I'm a wealthy man, as you know, and for your wedding present I've decided to make you a partner in my business. All I need to know from you now is what department you would like to start work in. What about Accounts?'

'Me, in Accounts?' said Shlomo, 'why I can't even add two figures together.'

'All right then, what about IT?'

'What do I know about IT?' said Shlomo, 'for years I thought PC stood for police constable.'

Louis was confused. 'OK, what about joining the sales team?'

'Look dad, I have a much better idea. How about you buying me out?'

***

Avrahom walks into John Lewis department store and goes straight to the Perfumery Department. He says to an assistant, 'Today is my wife Sharon's birthday and I would like to buy her a nice bottle of French perfume.

The assistant says, 'That will be a nice surprise for her.'

Avrahom replies, 'It sure will – she's expecting a diamond necklace.'

***

Moshe was passing by a florist when he saw a sign in the window saying, 'Say It With Flowers'. He went into the shop and said to the assistant, 'Wrap up one rose for me.'

'Only one?' the assistant asked.

'Just one,' replied Moshe. 'I'm a man of few words.'

***

Three sons left England and went to live in the USA, where they prospered. One day, they met and discussed the gifts they had been able to give their old mother.

David said, 'I built a big house for mum.'

Henry said, 'I sent her a Lexus – with a driver.'

Alan said, 'You remember how mum enjoys reading the Bible? Because she can no longer see very well, I sent her a remarkable parrot that recites the whole Bible. All mum has to do is name the chapter and verse.'

Soon afterwards, a letter of thanks came from their mother.

'David, the house you built is so huge. I live only in one room, but I have to clean the whole house. Henry, I am too old to travel. I stay at home most of the time, so I rarely use the Lexus, and that driver is a fidget – he's a pain in the *toches*. But Alan, the chicken was delicious.'

***

Sadie is visiting her best friend Rose one afternoon for tea and notices a lovely vase of fresh flowers in the kitchen. 'Oh Rose,' says Sadie, 'what amazing flowers.'

'Yes, they are nice, aren't they,' said Rose. 'I get sent flowers every week.'

'So where do you get them from? Tell me, are you having an affair?'

'Don't be silly Sadie, of course not. My husband sends them to me.'

'What on earth do you have to do for them?'

'Do for them?' replied Rose, 'I have to spend my life on my back with my legs in the air, that's what.'

'Why,' asks Sadie, 'don't you have a vase?'

Looking good

Moshe is shouting at his wife, Beckie. 'Oh no, not another new dress and accessories. Just where do you think I am going to get the money to pay for it all?'

Beckie replies, 'I may be a lot of different things to many people, but I'm certainly not inquisitive!'

* * *

'**M**oshe, will you still love me when my hair is grey?' asks Yente.

'Of course,' says Moshe. 'I've loved you through blonde, brunette, red and every other colour. Why not grey?'

* * *

Sarah and Suzy have been married to their husbands for many years and are the best of friends. Sarah doesn't think her husband finds her attractive anymore.

'As I get older he doesn't even bother to look at me!' says Sarah.

'It's the opposite for me,' replies Suzy. 'As I get older, my husband says I get even more beautiful every day.'

'But that's because your husband is an antique dealer!'

* * *

Q. What's the name of a face lotion developed for Jewish women?

A. Oil of *Oy Vay*.

***

Q. What does Sadie do to keep her hands soft and her nails so long and beautiful?

A. Nothing, nothing at all.

***

One day, Benjy comes home from school, goes straight to his father and asks, 'What is fornication, Dad?'

And he gets the answer all Jewish fathers give – 'Why don't you ask your mother, son?'

So Benjy goes into the kitchen and asks his mother, 'What is fornication, Mum? Dad said you would know.'

His mother replies, 'I'm busy right now, Benjy, why don't you go and ask your *bubbeh*, she will tell you.'

So Benjy goes upstairs to his *bubbeh*'s room, knocks on her door and shouts, 'Please, *Bubbeh*, what is fornication? No one here seems to know.'

Bubbeh says, 'Come inside, darling,'

She then takes him to her wardrobe, opens the door, takes out a beautiful full-length pink beaded evening dress and says, 'This, my darling, is foranoccasion.'

***

Moshe telephoned his wife Sadie. 'Sadie, darling, I've got some good news. You know that Lloyd Webber musical you've always wanted to see?'

'Yes.'

'Well, I've just bought us two tickets to see it.'

'Oh Moshe, that's marvellous. I'll start dressing immediately.'

'Sadie, that's just what I wanted to hear you say. The tickets are for tomorrow night's performance.'

***

Benjamin was talking to his friend Isaac. 'Do you know, Isaac, that I married my Hetty for her looks, but not the ones she's been giving me lately! Ever since we got married, she has tried to change me. She got me to exercise daily, improve my diet, and to stop smoking. She taught me how to dress well and enjoy the fine arts. She introduced me to gourmet cooking, classical music and she taught me how to invest in the stock market. But between you and me, Isaac, I am now thinking of divorcing her. I'm already such a better person that she just isn't good enough for me any more.'

***

A Catholic woman, a Protestant woman and Hetty die and go to heaven. St. Peter meets them at the gate to heaven.

The Catholic woman says, 'I've been a good wife and mother, I took good care of my family and I want to go to heaven.' St. Peter tells her to go to the left.

The Protestant woman says, 'I've been a good woman. I kept my house clean and cooked and took care of my family, and went to church every Sunday.' St. Peter tells her to step to the left.

Hetty tells St. Peter, 'I've been a good woman, I made Shabbes every Friday, I went to the synagogue on the holidays and took care of my family.' St. Peter tells Hetty to step to the right.

Hetty immediately asks him, ' Why did you tell me to go to the right and you told the other two women to go to the left?'

St. Peter replies, 'Don't you want to go to the beauty salon first?

***

Shlomo and Yetta are getting ready to go out to dinner.

Yetta comes out of the bedroom and says to Shlomo,

'Darling, do you want me to wear this Chanel suit or shall I put on the Gucci outfit?'

'What do I care?' Shlomo replies.

Yetta then asks, 'Darling, shall I wear my Rolex or my Cartier watch?'

'Who gives a damn?' says Shlomo.

Yetta then says to Shlomo, 'Darling, shall I wear my five-carat pear or my six-carat round diamond?'

To which Shlomo responds, 'Hey, if you don't get your act together, and soon, we are going to miss the Early Bird Special at Benjy's Fish restaurant.'

***

Bernie was a very wealthy man indeed. One day in June, he went on holiday with his latest, much younger girlfriend, Sarah. As the days in the sun wore on, Bernie and Sarah began to talk about the differences in their ages and interests between them. Bernie took this opportunity to ask Sarah what was, to him, an important question. He asked, 'If I lost everything, all my money, my mansion, my Rolls Royce, tomorrow, would you still love me, Sarah?'

'Yes, darling,' said Sarah, 'and I'd miss you too.'

***

Freda and Kitty had been chatting for some time. After a while, Kitty said, 'I've got to rush, Freda, I'm off to a stone-setting.'

Freda replied, 'Oh, I'm sorry to hear that. Where are you going, Bushey?'

'No,' said Kitty, 'Hatton Garden diamond market.'

***

Shirley sat next to Hetty, a middle aged lady, in *shul* one Shabbes. She couldn't help but notice Hetty's wonderful, huge diamond ring on her wedding finger. Shirley sat there staring at it but couldn't hold out any longer and said to Hetty, 'I hope you don't mind me saying this, but I just have to let you know that I think that your ring is the most beautiful ring I have ever seen.'

'*Oy Vay*,' said Hetty. 'Thank you for saying that. This definitely is a beautiful diamond ring, but unfortunately, it has a curse as well.'

'What do you mean?' said Shirley.

Hetty replied, 'Don't you know that this is the Katz diamond?'

Shirley replied, 'The Katz diamond?'

'Yes, the Katz diamond, and the Katz diamond has a curse.'

'But whatever is this curse?' asked Shirley.

'Mr Katz.'

***

Morris had become a multi-millionaire during his successful working life. When he retired, he bought himself the largest and most expensive mansion in London that money could buy. Then he invited some friends to a house-warming party.

The day came and he naturally took them on a tour around his enormous home.

When they reached the dining-room, there was a gasp of amazement – the room was so large that they could hardly see the other end clearly. Morris proudly pointed to the exquisitely carved and polished mahogany table that ran from one end of the room all the way to the other and said, 'In this room, I can entertain as many as a hundred and twenty-five people – God forbid.'

***

When Sadie's husband dies, she has only £25,000 to her name. After all the expenses are paid, she tells her closest friend Ruth that she has no money left.

Ruth says, 'How can that be, Sadie? You told me you had £25,000 just a few days before Maurice died. How can you now be broke?'

Sadie replies, 'Well to tell you the truth, Maurice and I were not paid up members of any synagogue. So the funeral cost me £5,000, the hospital bill came to £3,000 and of course, I had to make the obligatory donation to the synagogue, another £3,000. All the rest went on the memorial stone.'

Ruth does some silent calculating and then says, '£14,000 for the memorial stone? My God, Sadie, how big was it, what was it made of?'

Extending her left hand, Sadie replies, 'Three and a half carats.'

***

Beckie was very rich. One day she telephoned a famous young artist and said she wanted to commission him to paint her. He said his fee would be £5,000, which she immediately accepted. When she arrived at his studio for the first sitting, she gave him a cheque for £7,000. The artist was very surprised and asked what the extra money was for.

'I want you to paint me in the nude,' she said, 'Do you have any objections?'

'Not for £7,000 I don't. But I would have to keep my socks on. I must have somewhere to put my brushes.'

Pets

Morris gets a new dog and can't wait to show him off to Shlomo. So when Shlomo arrives, Morris calls the dog into the house, bragging about how smart he is. The dog quickly comes running and stands looking up at his master, tail wagging furiously, mouth open, tongue hanging out, eyes bright with anticipation.

Morris points to the newspaper on the couch and commands, 'FETCH!'

Immediately, the dog climbs on to the couch and sits down. His tail wagging stops and the doggie-smile disappears. Looking balefully up at his master, the dog says in a whiny voice, 'You think this is easy wagging my tail all the time? *Oy Vay*. It hurts from so much wagging. And do you think that expensive organic dog food you're feeding me is tasty? You try it. It's rubbish – much too salty. And you just don't seem to care about me anymore. You just push me out the door to take a leak three times a day. I can't remember the last time you took me out for a walk.'

Shlomo is amazed. 'What the hell is that? Your dog is sitting there talking.'

'Oh, I know,' explains Morris, 'He's young and I'm still training him. He thought I said *KVETCH*.'

***

Q: How do you know when a Jewish dog is fully mature?

A: He has a Bark Mitzvah!

***

Solly took his happy little King Charles Spaniel dog to the vet. 'Dr Cohen,' he said sadly, I'm afraid I'm going to have to ask you to cut off my dog's tail.'

Dr Cohen stepped back in shock, 'Solly, why should I do such a terrible thing?'

'My mother-in-law's arriving tomorrow, and I don't want anything to make her think she's welcome.'

***

Sidney loved dogs. He thought nothing of approaching any breed of dog, no matter how vicious a reputation it had. One day, however, he tried to stroke a Rottweiler and it attacked him. So serious was the attack that Sidney died of the injuries he sustained.

If you ever come across Sidney's grave, you will find these words inscribed on his headstone: 'HE HAD NO MAZEL.'

***

Benny's dog has died and he goes to see his rabbi. 'Rabbi, I wonder whether you could find the time to say a special blessing at my dog's grave?'

The rabbi replies, 'I'm afraid it isn't possible, Benny. In fact, the rules don't really make any allowance for animals.'

Benny says, 'But I'm really upset, rabbi.'

'So maybe you should go to see the Reform rabbi over the road,' says the rabbi.

As Benny walks away dejectedly, he turns to the rabbi and says, 'What a shame. I was willing to donate £1,000 for such a service.'

At which point the rabbi shouts, 'Come back, come back.'

Benny turns round and says, 'I thought you couldn't help me.'

'Ah,' says the rabbi, 'but you didn't tell me your dog was Orthodox.'

***

Arnold and Abe are walking their dogs past the synagogue one Saturday morning.

Arnold says, 'Lets go in. I hear they have really nice chopped liver at the Kiddush on Shabbes.'

Abe says, 'They will never let us in with the dogs.'

'Just follow my lead,' says Arnold and goes into the synagogue.

As he thought, the *shammes* tells him, 'No dogs are allowed.'

Arnold says, 'But it's my seeing-eye dog.'

The *shammes* says, 'Sorry, I didn't know. OK, you can go in.'

Abe follows.

Again the *shammes* says, 'No dogs are allowed.'

Abe says, 'But it's my seeing-eye dog.'

The *shammes* says, 'This is your seeing-eye dog? A chihuahua!'

Abe looks startled and says, 'Is that what they gave me?'

***

Hymie walks into his synagogue with a dog. The *shammes* immediately comes up to him and says, 'This is a House of Worship, Hymie, you know you can't bring a dog in here.'

'What do you mean I can't?' says Hymie, 'Look at him, he's

a Jewish dog.'

The *shammes* then notices that the dog has a *tallis* bag round its neck.

Hymie then says to the dog, 'Benjamin, *daven* for me.'

The dog stands on his back legs and says, 'Woof, woof, woof,' then opens the *tallis* bag, takes out a *kippa* and puts it on his head, exactly in between its ears.

'Woof, woof,' says the dog who then pulls out a *tallis* and puts it round his neck.

'Woof, woof, woof,' says the dog who then takes out a *siddur* and starts to pray, rocking from side to side.

'That's brilliant,' says the *shammes*, 'totally incredible. You must get him on TV and the movies and you could make millions.'

'You speak to him, then,' says Hymie. 'He wants to be a doctor.'

***

And Adam said, 'Oh Lord, you do not visit me anymore in the garden. I am lonely here and it's getting hard for me to remember how much you love me.'

And God said, 'OK, I will create for you a companion who will be a reflection of my love for you and you will then know that I love you at all times. Regardless of how childish, selfish and unlovable you are, your companion will always accept and love you.'

And God created a new animal for Adam and God was pleased. And the new animal was pleased to be with Adam and wagged his tail.

And Adam said, 'Oh Lord, I can't think of a name for this new animal. All the good names in the animal kingdom have already been assigned.'

And God said, 'OK, because I created this animal, his name will be a reflection of mine and you will call him Dog.'

And Dog lived with Adam and was a good companion and loved him. And Adam was comforted. And God was pleased. And Dog was content and wagged his tail.

Later, it came to pass that Adam's guardian angel came to

the Lord and said, 'Oh Lord, Adam now struts around like a peacock and believes he is worthy of adoration. Dog has indeed taught him that he is loved, but no one has taught Adam humility.'

And the Lord said, 'OK, I will create another companion for Adam who will see him as he is. And this companion will remind him of his limitations and he will soon know that he is not worthy of adoration.'

And God created Cat. And Cat would not obey Adam. When Adam gazed into Cat's eyes, he was reminded that he was not the supreme being. And Adam learned humility. And God was pleased. And Adam was greatly improved. And Cat did not care one way or the other.

***

Rivkah, a little old lady, gets on an El Al flight to Israel. She's carrying a bag, a purse and a little dog in a box. She sits down and puts the box on the seat next to her. A stewardess approaches Rivkah and says, 'I'm sorry Madam, but you can't keep the dog here. I'll have to take it and put it in baggage.'

Rivkah agrees. What else can she do?

During the flight, the stewardess looks in on the little dog, and *Oy Gevalt*, the dog is dead. She informs the pilot who notifies Tel Aviv airport who tells the director who decides that they will get another dog to replace this one. The little old lady will never know. When the plane lands and Rivkah goes to the baggage hall to claim her box, they bring her a box with a new dog, an exact replica of her old dog.

'This is not my dog,' Rivkah exclaims.

'Why yes it is,' the captain tells her. 'See, it has the same markings.'

'This is not my dog,' Rivkah insists.

'How do you know this isn't your dog?' asks the captain.

'My dog is dead! I was bringing it here to be buried!'

***

David received a parrot for his birthday. This parrot was fully grown, with a bad attitude and worse vocabulary. Every other word was a swear word. Those that weren't were, to say the least, rude. David tried hard to change the bird's attitude and was constantly saying polite words, playing soft Israeli dance music, anything that came to mind. Nothing worked. He yelled at the bird, but the bird got worse. He shook the bird and the bird got madder and ruder. Finally, in a moment of desperation, David put the parrot in the freezer. For a few moments he heard the bird squawking, kicking and screaming and then, suddenly, all was quiet. David was frightened that he might have actually hurt the bird and quickly opened the freezer door.

The parrot calmly stepped out onto David's extended arm and said, 'I'm sorry that I offended you with my language and actions. I ask for your forgiveness. I will go to synagogue with you every week to pray and I will try to modify my behaviour.'

David was astounded at the bird's change in attitude and was about to ask what changed him when the parrot continued, 'May I ask what the chicken did?'

***

Meyer, a lonely widower, was walking home along Golders Green Road one day, wishing something wonderful would happen to his life when he passed a pet store and heard a squawking voice shouting out in Yiddish, 'Quawwwwk – vus macht du – yeah, du – outside, standing like a putzel – eh?'

Meyer couldn't believe what he was hearing and went inside, and was soon standing in front of an African Grey. The parrot cocked his little head and said, 'Vus? Kenst reddin Yiddish?'

Meyer turned excitedly to the owner. 'He speaks Yiddish!' In a matter of moments, Meyer had written out a cheque for £500 and carried the parrot, still in his cage, out of the shop. All night he talked with the parrot in Yiddish – about his family and his career, and the parrot's life in the pet shop.

The next morning, Meyer began to put on his *tefillin* while saying his prayers. The parrot demanded to know what he was doing, and when Meyer explained, the parrot wanted to do likewise. So Meyer went out and bought a hand-made miniature set of *tefillin* for the parrot. The parrot wanted to learn to *daven* and so Meyer taught him every prayer. He wanted to learn to read Hebrew so Meyer spent weeks and months sitting and teaching him the Torah. In time, Meyer came to love and count on the parrot as a friend and a Jew. He had been saved.

One morning, on Rosh Hashanah, Meyer rose and got dressed and was about to leave when the parrot demanded to go with him. Meyer explained that *shul* was not a place for a bird, but the parrot made a terrific row and was carried to *shul* on Meyer's shoulder. Needless to say, they made quite a spectacle and Meyer was questioned by everyone, including the rabbi and cantor. At first they refused to allow a bird into the building on the High Holy Days, but Meyer convinced them to let him in this one time, swearing that the parrot could *daven*. Some bets were made with Meyer. Thousands of pounds were bet that the parrot could not *daven*, could not speak Yiddish or Hebrew, and so on. All eyes were on the African Grey during the service. The parrot perched on Meyer's shoulder as one prayer and song passed – but Meyer heard not a peep from the bird. He began to become annoyed, slapping at his shoulder and mumbling under his breath, '*Daven!*'

Nothing. '*Daven* – parrot, you can *daven*, so *daven* – come on, everybody's looking at you!'

Nothing. After the Rosh Hashanah service was over, Meyer worked out that he owed over £4,000. He marched home angrily, saying nothing. Finally, several streets away from the *shul*, the bird began to sing an old Yiddish song and was happy as could be. Meyer stopped and looked at him.

'You miserable bird, you cost me over £4,000. Why? After I bought you your own *tefillin* and taught you the morning prayers and to read Hebrew and the Torah. And after you begged me to bring you to *shul* on Rosh Hashanah, why? Why did you do this to me?'

'Don't be a *shmuck*,' the parrot replied. 'The odds will be much better on Yom Kippur.'

***

Meyer's parrot had died and he was lonely once again. He quickly decided that life would be more fun if he had another pet. So Meyer went back to the Golders Green pet shop and told the owner that he wanted to buy another pet, but this time a bit more unusual. After some discussion, he finally bought a talking centipede, which came in a little white box to use for his house. Meyer took the box home. He found a good place to put it and decided he would immediately take his new pet to the local pub to have a drink and show it off. He asked the centipede in the box, 'Would you like to go to The Leather Bottle with me and have a beer?'

But there was no answer from his new pet. This bothered Meyer a bit, but he waited a few minutes and then asked his pet again, 'How about going to The Leather Bottle and having a drink with me?'

But again, there was no answer from his new friend and pet. So Meyer waited a few minutes more, thinking about the situation. He decided to ask one more time, this time putting his face up against the centipede's house and shouting, 'Hey, you in there! Would you like to go to The Leather Bottle and have a drink with me?'

A little voice came out of the box: 'I heard you the first time! I'm putting on my shoes.'

***

One day, Hetty approaches her rabbi after the service and says to him, 'Rabbi, I have a problem. I have two female talking parrots, but they only know how to say one thing.'

'What do they say?' the rabbi asks.

'They only know how to say, "Hello, we're prostitutes, want to have some fun?"'

'Why, that's terrible!' the rabbi says, 'but I have a solution to your problem. Bring your two female parrots over to my house tomorrow and I will put them with my two male talking parrots whom I taught to pray and read Hebrew. My parrots will teach your parrots to stop saying that terrible phrase and your female parrots will learn to praise and worship.'

'Oh thank you, Rabbi,' Hetty replies.

The next day Hetty brings her female parrots to the rabbi's house. His two male parrots are wearing tiny *yarmulkas* and praying in their cage. Hetty puts her two female parrots in with the male parrots and the female parrots say, 'Hello, we're prostitutes, want to have some fun?'

One male parrot looks over at the other male parrot and exclaims, 'Put away the Siddurs! Our prayers have been answered!'

***

Moshe wants to buy a parrot and goes to his local pet shop to see what they have. The assistant shows him a parrot and explains that this one is really quite special – it can speak most languages. So Moshe decides to test this out.

'Do you speak English?' asks Moshe.

'Yes,' replied the parrot.

'*Habla español?*' asks Moshe.

'*Si*,' replied the parrot.

'*Parlez-vouz français?*' asks Moshe.

'*Oui*,' replied the parrot.

'*Sprechen Sie Deutsch?*' asks Moshe.

'*Ja*,' replied the parrot.

'*Falas português?*' asks Moshe.

'*Sim*,' replied the parrot.

Moshe pauses for a while, then asks the parrot, 'Do you speak Yiddish?'

The parrot shrugs its shoulders and says, 'Vis a nose like dis, vot you tink?'

***

Sidney passes by a pet shop in Oxford Street and notices a parrot in the window selling for £1,000. He goes inside and asks why it costs so much. The salesman tells him the parrot speaks five languages.

'Five languages!' exclaims Sidney. 'Does it speak Yiddish?'

'Sure it does,' says the salesman.

As his mother lives by herself in Golders Green, Sidney decides to send her the parrot as a present – it'll keep her company. So he pays the £1,000 and arranges for the shop to deliver the parrot to his mother. The next day he phones his

mother. 'Mum, Did you like the parrot I bought you?'
'Mmm, it was delicious!' she says.
'What do you mean delicious?'
'I made soup out of it, it came out great!'
'But mum, the parrot wasn't for eating. It spoke five languages including Yiddish.'
'So why didn't it say anything?'

***

Moshe was one of those men who had very few girlfriends. When, on rare occasions, he was invited to parties, not only did people forget his name but also they did not take what he said seriously. Even when he tried to be funny, nobody laughed at his jokes! So naturally he was very depressed. When his counsellor suggested he should do something positive to impress his friends and neighbours, Moshe decided to rent a camel. He put on his khaki shorts and pith helmet and got on the camel. He then rode up and down Edgware looking very proud. Everywhere he and the camel went, there was a buzz of surprise. Passers by stared, pointed, shouted and talked about him. Moshe repeated this activity every day for a week. But then someone stole his camel and Moshe had to go to the police to report the theft.

'I have come to report the theft of a camel,' said Moshe.

'A camel?' said the sergeant, 'OK, let me have some details. How tall was it?'

'Maybe six or seven feet tall,' replied Moshe.

'What colour was it?'

'Light brown/grey.'

'Was it male or female?' asked the sergeant.

'Male,' replied Moshe.

'Are you sure?' asked the sergeant.

'Definitely,' replied Moshe, 'every time I rode it, I could hear passers by yelling, "Look at that *shmuck* on the camel."'

WORKING LIFE

Business

Two beggars are sitting on the pavement in Ireland. One is holding a large cross and the other a large Star of David. Both are holding out hats to collect contributions. As people walk by, they lift their noses at the guy holding the Star of David but drop money in the other guy's hat. Soon one hat is nearly full whilst the other hat is empty.

A priest watches and then approaches the men. He turns to the guy with the Star of David and says, 'Don't you realise that this is a Christian country? You'll never get any contributions in this country holding a Star of David.'

The guy holding the Star of David then turns to the guy holding the Cross and says, 'Hymie, look who's trying to teach us marketing.'

***

Avrahom is a fifty-year-old single guy who owns a successful gift shop in Edgware. He is very rich. One day, he somehow gets confused about how to pay an invoice he's just received, so he asks Sylvia, his secretary, to come into his office.

Avrahom sits her down next to him and says, 'Sylvia, if I were to give you £22,000, minus 17.5 per cent, how much would you take off?'

Sylvia pauses, looks him up and down and replies, 'Everything but my jewellery.'

***

Sam meets his friend Moshe in Brent Cross shopping centre. 'Hi Moshe, I haven't seen you for some months. So, *nu*? How is the company doing that you set up with Maurice last year?'

'Well, as I told you then, I put up the money and Maurice put in his business experience. But things have changed a bit since then.'

'What do you mean?' Sam asks.

'Now Maurice has the money and I have the business experience.'

***

Maurice has an appointment with his accountant, and he arrives a little early. The receptionist points to a comfortable easy chair and asks him to be seated for a while. Maurice settles down, picks up a glossy magazine, opens it and tries to read. However, he finds that he cannot concentrate because he is distracted due to a rumpus coming from behind one of the doors leading off the reception area. Maurice goes over to the receptionist and asks, 'What's going on in there?'

She replies, 'It's a partners' meeting.'

'But why are they shouting at each other?' Maurice asks.

'It's a battle of wits,' she replies.

Maurice asks, 'Who is in there?' and she answers, 'Horowits, Lebowits, Rabbinowits and Abramowits.'

***

Roberto is an art connoisseur and one day notices a mangy little kitten lapping up milk from a saucer in front of a delicatessen in Tel Aviv. He quickly realises with a shock that the saucer was a very rare and precious piece of pottery. He strolled into the store and offered £2 for the cat.

'It's not for sale,' said Abe, the proprietor.

'Look,' said Roberto, 'that cat is dirty and undesirable, but I'm eccentric. I like cats that way. I'll raise my offer to £10.'

'It's a deal,' said Abe, and pocketed the money.

'For that sum I'm sure you won't mind throwing in the

saucer,' said Roberto. 'The kitten seems so happy drinking from it.'

'Nothing doing,' said Abe firmly. 'That's my lucky saucer. From that saucer, so far this week, I've sold 34 cats.'

***

Moshe owned one of the biggest and fastest-growing businesses in north-west London: a furniture store. His friend convinced him that he needed to take a trip to Italy to check out the merchandise himself and because he was still single, he could check out all the hot Italian women, and maybe get lucky.

As Moshe was checking into a hotel, he struck up an acquaintance with a beautiful young lady. She only spoke Italian and he only spoke English, so neither understood a word the other said. He took out a pencil and a notebook and drew a picture of a taxi. She smiled, nodded her head and they went for a ride to the park. Later, he drew a picture of a table in a restaurant with a question mark and she nodded, so they went to dinner. After dinner he sketched two dancers and she was delighted. They went to several nightclubs, drank champagne, danced and had a glorious evening. It had become quite late when she motioned for the pencil and drew a picture of a four-poster bed. Moshe was dumbfounded, and to this day remarks to me that he's never been able to understand how she knew he was in the furniture business.

***

Abe walks into the local tavern and sees his friend Moshe sitting at the bar. He puts his hand to his heart and yells, '*Oy Vay*, Moshe! I'm so sorry to hear about your shop burning down.'

Moshe spins around quickly and whispers, 'Shhhh – it's tomorrow!'

***

The time is the French Revolution. Yossi lives in a small village and one day, his friend Roberto comes to see him after returning from a trip to Paris. Yossi asks Roberto what is happening in Paris as he has heard they are regularly using the guillotine.

'Yes, you heard right,' says Roberto, 'conditions there are as bad as can be. They are chopping off people's heads in their thousands.'

'*Oy Vay*,' moans Yossi, 'whatever will happen to my hat business?'

* * *

Moshe owned a PC shop in Golders Green. Unfortunately, the shop was robbed one night and much of the stock was taken. Henry, his friend heard of the robbery and went to visit Moshe.

'I'm very sorry to hear of the robbery,' said Henry. 'Did you lose much?'

'I did lose some big items but it's all OK, I'm quite lucky really. I'm glad it didn't happen one night earlier.'

'Why?' said Henry.

'Well,' replied Moshe, 'just on the day of the theft, I marked everything down by twenty per cent in readiness for my annual sale!'

* * *

A congregant asked his rabbi, 'Rabbi, you're a man of God. So why is it that you are always talking business when I, a businessman, am always talking about spiritual matters when I'm not at work?'

'You have discovered one of the principles of human nature,' the rabbi replied.

'And what principle is that, Rabbi?'

'People like to discuss things they know nothing about.'

* * *

Maurice, a young Jew comes to North London and applies for a job as caretaker at the Edgware Synagogue. The synagogue committee are just about to offer him the job when they discover that he is illiterate. They decide for many reasons that it would be inappropriate to have an illiterate caretaker. So Maurice leaves and decides to forge a career in another business. He chooses to sell plastic goods door to door. He does well and soon is able to buy a car and later, to open a store, and then a second. Finally he is ready to open five more stores and so applies to the bank for a loan. But when the bank manager asks him to sign the contract, it is obvious that he cannot write. Shocked to discover that this successful young man has had little education, the bank manager says, 'Just think what you could have been if you had learned to read and write!'

'Yes,' says Maurice, 'I would be caretaker at Edgware synagogue.'

***

Morris and Bernard met in a restaurant for a business lunch. Morris said, 'I have a good deal for you, Bernard. When I was in London Zoo recently, I happened to pick up an elephant they didn't need any more. I could let you have it for £3,000.'

Bernard sipped his gin and tonic and said, 'Morris, what am I going to do with an elephant? I live in a third-floor flat. I barely have room for my furniture. I can't even squeeze in a card table. So you think I'm going to buy an elephant?'

Morris said, 'I could let you have three of them for two grand.'

'Aha,' said Bernard, 'now you're talking!'

***

Issy owned a small deli in Hendon. One day, a tax inspector knocked on his door and questioned him about his recent tax return. Issy had reported a net profit of £50,000 for the year and he wanted to know all about it.

'It's like this,' said Issy. 'I work like a maniac all year round and all of my family help me out whenever they can. My deli is closed only five times a year. That's how I made £50,000.'

'It's not your income that bothers us,' said the taxman. 'It's the business travel deductions of £80,000 that worry us. You entered on the tax return that you and your wife made fifteen business trips to Israel.'

'Oh,' said Issy, smiling. 'I forgot to tell you that we also deliver.'

***

Maurice is a successful owner of a kosher meat-processing factory. His dream is that Louis, his only son, who is a bit dim-witted, will eventually take over the business.

One day Maurice shows Louis around the slaughterhouse. 'Look, son,' says Maurice, proudly pointing to one of the many pieces of advanced machinery on show, 'You see that machine? You put one whole ox into the front end and out the back come some little weenies. Great piece of British ingenuity, isn't it?'

He then looks to Louis for some kind of positive reaction but Louis just stares and says, 'Uh, duh ... do you have a machine where you put in a weenie and out comes an ox?'

Surprised, Maurice replies, 'There is a machine like that – your mother.'

***

Q: What business is a *yenta* in?

A: Yours.

***

Max was in the coats trade but unfortunately business was very bad. One day, his partner Benjy said to him, 'What are we going to do with these fifty coats? They're last year's style and even though we've knocked them down to £10 each, we still can't sell any.'

Max replied, 'Use your head, Benjy. Price them at £20 and send all our best clients five coats each. But here's the plan. Put in an invoice for £80 for only four coats. If I know them, my clients will think we've made a mistake. They'll jump at a bargain and pay the £80.'

'What a terrific idea,' said Benjy. 'I'll send them out today.'

Two weeks later, Benjy says to Max, 'What a stupid idea it was. Every one of our clients returned the parcel and the invoice, but only sent back four coats.'

***

Benny was talking to his best friend Harry. 'You know Harry, I can't understand why you failed in business. You had such good ideas.'

'Too much advertising was the main reason for my failure,' replied Harry.

'But I can't remember you spending a penny on advertising all your life,' said Benny.

'You're correct there,' said Harry, 'but all my competitors did.'

***

Moshe is talking to his friend, who is a marketing manager. 'Benny,' says Moshe, 'What's the difference between marketing and advertising? I've always wanted to know.'

'Well,' replies Benny, 'suppose you're at a party and you see a gorgeous lady across the room. Well, there are a number of things that could happen.

'One, you could go over to her and say, "Hi, I'm great in bed, so what about it?" That's direct marketing.

'Two, you could give your best friend £10 so he goes over to her and says, "Hello, see my friend over there? He's great in bed, so what about it?" That's advertising.

'Three, she could come over to you and say, "Hello, I've heard you're great in bed, so what about it?" That's brand recognition.

'Four, you could go over to her and get her telephone number. Then, next day, you could call her and say, "Hello, I'm great in bed, so what about it?" That's telemarketing.

'Five, you could walk over to her, pour her a drink and say, "May I?" You could then reach up to straighten her hair, at the same time brushing your groin against her leg, and say, "Hello, I'm great in bed, so what about it?" That's public relations.

'Six, you could talk her into going home with your friend. That's a sales rep.

'Seven, your friend might not be able to satisfy her and so she could then text you. That's tech support.

'Eight, you could leave the party and on your way home realise that there are probably many beautiful women in the houses you're passing. So you could shout out at the top of your voice, "I'm great in bed". That's junk mail.'

'Thanks, now I understand,' says Moshe.

***

One day, little Benny asks his father Harry a question, 'Dad, what is the stock market?'

'Benny,' replies Harry, 'you're too young to understand. Later.'

'I am not that young,' says Benny, 'I want to know now.'

'Please, wait a few years, then you will understand better.'

'Dad, I don't want to start life poor, like you did, selling second-hand furniture. That's why I want to know now.'

'Alright, already,' said Harry, 'It's like this. You buy two chickens and the two chickens lay eggs. So, next year, you have thirty chickens. These thirty chickens then all lay eggs and these eggs turn into chickens. So you end up having thousands of chickens and you're well off. You see, this is the stock market. You understand, Benny?'

'Yes, Dad.'

'And then, one day, the sky opens up and it rains. It rains like in the days of Noah. The floods come and they wash away all the chickens until they drown and you then have only two or three chickens left. You see, this is the stock market – you should have bought ducks.'

***

Daniel and Naomi go to bed and one hour later, Naomi is still awake. She is having great difficulty in getting to sleep so she decides to do what has worked before. She nudges Daniel and says to him in a soft voice, 'Daniel, turn over.'

Daniel replies, '£56,710.65.'

***

Fay is sitting at a hotel bar waiting for her husband to arrive when a man approaches her. 'Hi, honey,' he says. 'Want a little company?'

'Why?' asks Fay, 'do you have one to sell?'

***

Issy was the proud co-owner of the local dry cleaners. One day, during dinner, whilst he was finishing his chicken soup, his nine-year-old son Sam asked, 'Dad, what's ethics?'

Issy thought for a while, put down his spoon, looked at Sam and replied, 'OK, let's suppose someone comes into my shop and gives me his business suit to dry clean. Then suppose I find a £20 note in his trouser pocket.'

Sam looked expectantly at his father.

'So,' Issy said, 'to answer your question, Sam, do I tell my partner I found the money? That's ethics.'

Employment

There once lived a king who had an advisor called Hymie. The king relied so much on the wisdom of Hymie that one day he decided to promote him to chief advisor. But the other advisors objected.

They said, 'It's OK sitting in counsel with a Jew, but to allow him to boss us about would be unacceptable.'

The King accepted their argument and ordered Hymie to convert. Hymie had to obey. But soon after, Hymie felt great remorse and over the months that followed he became despondent, his health suffered and he grew weak. Finally, Hymie could take it no longer and made a decision. He went to the king and said, 'I was born a Jew and a Jew I will always be. So do whatever you want with me.'

The King had no idea Hymie had been feeling so strongly about his 'conversion'.

'OK,' said the King, 'if that's how you feel, go and be a Jew again. The other advisors will just have to live with it. You're too important for me to lose.'

On his way back home to tell the news to his family, Hymie felt the strength surge back into his body. When he arrived, he called out to his wife, 'Sarah, we can be Jews again, we can be Jews again.'

Sarah glared at him and said, 'Couldn't you have waited until after Passover?'

***

There once was a powerful emperor who needed a new chief Samurai. So he put up posters throughout the land saying he was searching for a new chief Samurai. But after two months, only three Samurai had applied for the job, a Japanese, a Chinese and Morris. So he interviewed all three.

The emperor first asked the Japanese to demonstrate why he should be his chief Samurai. The Japanese opened a little silver box and out flew a little fly. Whoosh went his sword and the fly dropped dead in two pieces. The emperor was impressed.

The emperor then asked the Chinese to demonstrate why he should be his chief Samurai. The Chinese opened a small pearl box and out flew a smaller fly. Whoosh, whoosh went his sword and the fly dropped dead in four pieces. The emperor was very impressed.

Then the emperor asked Morris to demonstrate why he should be his chief Samurai. Morris opened a small gold box and out flew a wasp. Whooooooossshhh, whooooooossshhh, whoooooooossshhh, whooooooossshhh, whooooooossshhh went Morris's sword, but the wasp was still alive and buzzing around the emperor.

The emperor was very disappointed and asked Morris, 'After all your sword play, why is the wasp not dead?'

Morris replied, 'A circumcision is never intended to kill.'

***

A rabbi took a job at a Duracell factory. His job was to stand on the production line and as the batteries went by, say, 'I wish you long life.'

***

Show me a Jewish boy who didn't become a doctor and I'll show you a lawyer.

***

A junior manager, a senior manager and Moshe their boss, are on their way to a meeting. On their journey through a park, they come across an oil lamp sticking out of the ground under a bush. They pick it up, rub it, and out pops a genie.

The genie says, 'Thank you very much. I normally grant three wishes but as there are three of you, I can only allow one wish each.'

Without waiting for the others, the eager senior manager shouts, 'I want the first wish. I want to be in the Bahamas, on a fast boat with loads of money and have no worries for the rest of my life.'

POW! and he disappears.

The junior manager can't keep quiet and shouts, 'I want to be in Florida with beautiful girls all around me and plenty of good food and champagne.'

KERPOW! and he disappears too.

Moshe the boss then calmly says, 'Here's my wish. I want those two idiots back in my office immediately after lunch.'

Moral: Always allow your boss to speak first.

***

There were four people who were in the final stages of interviewing for a prestigious job. One was Christian, one was Catholic, one was a Buddhist and the fourth was Bernie. The company decided to fly them all in for dinner and a final interview. Over dinner at a fine restaurant, the president of the company told them that all were very worthy applicants, and that he wished he could hire them all, but that they only had enough money budgeted to hire one person. He told them that the following day, he would call each of them in one at a time for a final interview and that he would ask each one of them the same question. Whoever answered the question the best would be the one hired. All applicants agreed that this was fair.

The next day the first applicant, the Christian, was called in. The president posed the question, 'What is the fastest thing in the world?'

He thought for a moment and replied, 'That would have to be a thought.'

'Why do you say that?' asked the president.

'Well, a thought takes no time at all – it is in your mind in an instant, then gone again.'

'Ahh, very good. Thank you,' replied the president.

Next the same question was posed to the Catholic woman.

'What is the fastest thing in the world?'

She paused and replied, 'That would have to be a blink.'

'Why?' asked the president.

'Because you don't even think about a blink, it's just a reflex. You do it in an instant.'

The president thanked her, then called in the next person.

The Buddhist was asked what the fastest thing in the world was, and after hesitating for a brief moment, he replied, 'I would have to say electricity.'

'Why?'

'Because a man can flip a switch and immediately three miles away a light will go on.'

'I see, very good,' replied the president.

Then, Bernie was called in. He, too, was asked, 'What is the fastest thing in the world?'

'That's easy – ' he replied, 'that would have to be diarrhoea!'

Rather stunned, the president asked, 'Why do you say that?'

'Well, last night after dinner, I was lying in my bed and I got the worst stomach cramps – and before I could THINK, BLINK, or TURN ON THE LIGHTS - '

(Bernie got the job)

***

Daniel is a Jewish actor who's so down and out that he's ready to accept any acting part that comes along. One day he sees an advert in the *Jewish Chronicle*: ACTOR NEEDED TO PLAY A GORILLA.

'I could do that,' says Daniel and he arranges an interview.

The employer turns out to be a local zoo who have spent so much renovating the grounds and improving the habitat that they can't afford the gorilla they need. Until they can get more funding, they've decided to use an actor in a gorilla suit. Needing the money, Daniel takes the job. At first, he feels not only dishonest by fooling the customers but also undignified in the ape suit, stared at by crowds who watch his every move. But after a few days on the job, he begins to be amused by all the attention and starts to put on a show for the spectators – hanging upside-down from the branches, swinging on vines, climbing up cage walls and roaring whilst beating his chest. Soon, Daniel is drawing a sizeable crowd.

One day, when Daniel is swinging on a vine to show off to some children, his hand slips and he goes flying over the wall into the lion's den. Terrified, Daniel backs up as far as he can from the approaching lion, covers his eyes with his paws and starts to pray aloud, '*Shma Yisrael Ado-nai Elokeinu Ado-nai Echad.*' (Hear O Israel, the Lord our God, the Lord is one.)

The lion opens its powerful jaws and roars, '*Baruch Shem k'vod malchuto l'olam va'ed!*' (Blessed is the name of His glorious kingship forever and ever.)

'Shut up you two *shmucks*,' shouts a panda from a third cage. 'You'll get us all fired.'

***

Quasimodo Levy had finally decided to retire and the Abbot placed an advert in the Church gazette for a new bell-ringer. One day a man with no arms came to the church to apply for the bell-ringer's position. The Abbot, being an equal opportunity employer, said he would consider the armless man for the position if he could prove he could do the job. The armless man was led to the bell-tower and when Quasimodo Levy asked him to do his stuff, the man took a running start and charged face-first into the bell. A beautiful melodious tone sang through the valley. So beautiful that all the townspeople came out of their houses crying, 'Who rang that bell – such a sound – hire him, hire him!'

Quasimodo Levy promptly asked him to ring the bell again. The man again took a running start but unfortunately slipped and plunged over the parapet to his death. The townspeople were aghast and one called out, 'Who was that man?'

Quasimodo Levy replied, 'I don't know but his face rings a bell.'

* * *

Unfortunately, the church was still without a bell-ringer. So the Abbot re-advertised the job. Another armless man showed up to apply for the position, claiming he was the dead man's brother and, having learned all he knew about bell-ringing from his brother, declared that it was only right that he take over the bell ringer's position and succeed where his brother could not (due to his untimely death, naturally). The Abbot gave the brother the same chance to prove his ability. The brother charged at the bell smacking it with his face and eliciting a lovely mellow tone, which was heard all throughout the valley.

The townspeople came running into the square calling out, 'Who rang that bell? Such tone, such vibrato – hire him, hire him!!'

Noting that it was nearing 3 p.m. and time to ring the bell for real, Quasimodo Levy instructed the man to do the same. The man backed up to start his run and misjudged how close he was to the edge of the bell tower. He stepped backward and fell to his death. The Abbott turned to Quasimodo Levy and asked, 'Who was that man?'

Replied Quasimodo Levy, 'I don't know, but he's a dead ringer for his brother.'

* * *

David had done well for himself and became mayor of a small town in Israel. One day, David and his wife Andrea were walking past a construction site. Suddenly, one of the construction workers stopped and called out, 'What's new, Andrea?'

'Why, it's nice to see you again Avi,' Andrea replied.

She turned to introduce David to the construction worker, and they talked for several minutes. After David and Andrea continued on, David turned to her and asked how she knew Avi.

'Oh,' Andrea said. 'We went to the same school. I even thought about marrying him.'

David laughed. 'You don't realise how lucky you are. If I hadn't come along, today you would be the wife of a construction worker!'

Andrea replied without hesitation, 'Not really. If I had married him, he'd now be a mayor!'

***

Isaac Rokenson was a new recruit in the British Army. On his first day, an officer came up to him and said, 'What is your name?'

'Isaac Rokenson,' he replied.

The officer shouted at him, 'You must say "Sir" when you answer an officer in the British Army. What's your name?'

'Sir Isaac Rokenson,' came the reply.

***

Sadie had worked as an accounts clerk for the Prague Candlesticks Company for nearly thirty years when she died. Everyone remembered how she would arrive at her desk every morning at exactly 8.30 a.m. She would put on her glasses, unlock her desk, and peer closely into the centre drawer. Then she would re-lock her desk and get on with her work. She did this every working day and no one, not even the senior accountant, knew what was in her centre drawer. Now she was dead, her work colleagues could find out her secret.

So they unlocked her desk and opened the centre drawer. Inside they found a small piece of paper with these words written on it: 'The Side Towards the Door is the Debit Side.'

***

Max, a *Vaadnik* (union leader) is addressing a union meeting at a certain unnamed Israeli government-owned company.

'Comrades. We have agreed on a new deal with the management. We will no longer work five days a week.'

'Hooray!' shouts the crowd.

'We will finish work at 3 p.m., not 4 p.m.'

'Hooray!' shouts the crowd, again.

'We will start work at 9 a.m., not 7 a.m.'

'Hooray!'

'We shall have a 150 per cent pay rise.'

'Hooray!'

'We will only work on Wednesdays.'

Silence – then a voice from the back asks, 'Every Wednesday?'

***

Solly, an orthodox Jew, goes for a job interview with a gentile employer. In the course of the interview, which is going well, the employer asks Solly what kind of salary he is looking for. Thinking of his large family and the many bills that have to be paid, Solly quickly replies that he'd needs around £50,000 per annum.

The employer replies that in today's market and with Solly's limited skill set, he is only prepared to pay £40,000 per annum.

Upon hearing this, Solly tells him, 'Listen, even though I am an Orthodox Jew and keep kosher, I still have to bring home the bacon.'

***

Abe goes to see his boss and says, 'We're doing some heavy house-cleaning at home tomorrow for Passover and my wife needs me to help with the attic and the garage, moving and hauling stuff.'

'We're short-handed, Abe,' the boss replies. 'I just can't give you the day off.'

'Thanks, boss,' says Abe, 'I knew I could count on you!'

***

Alf met his friend Bernie in the street one day. As Alf was interested in how Bernie's new job was going, especially as he was working for a Jewish firm, he asked. 'How's the new job going? Is it what you hoped it would be?'

Bernie replied, 'Working for a Jewish firm is not all it's cracked up to be. I handed in my notice yesterday.'

Alf asked, 'Why?'

Bernie replied, 'The firm is so keen to improve its profitability, it wants every part of me to contribute 24 hours a day, seven days a week.'

Bernie then gave Alf a page taken from his Office Manual and said, 'Read this, this is why I resigned.'

> HOLIDAYS. Employees' holidays are considered by the directors to be completely unnecessary. All employees should realise that they are lucky to be employed. Should anyone demand a holiday entitlement, this will be considered by the directors as being disloyal, the firm will assume that the employee must be unhappy in his/her work and will cease to be considered an asset to the firm. Dismissal will therefore have to be seriously considered by the directors.
>
> SICKNESS. The directors will consider it a sign of weakness should an employee fall ill. It is the duty of every employee to look after his/her health and therefore be available for duty on every working day. A visit to the doctor by an employee is considered totally unnecessary. If employees are well enough to visit the doctor, they are well enough to come to work.
>
> DEATH – OTHER THAN OF THE EMPLOYEE. If a relative or friend has died, unfortunate as this may be, there is obviously nothing more that can be done for them. Therefore, the directors will not accept such a death as a legitimate excuse for not coming in to work. Funerals, if employees must attend them, will have to be arranged outside of working hours.

DEATH – OF THE EMPLOYEE. If an employee's death should occur prior to the mandatory retirement age, the employee should have arranged a replacement for himself or herself before inflicting this inconvenience on the firm.

***

Yossi is the manager of an up-market menswear store in New Bond Street and is interviewing Abe for the recently advertised salesman role. Yossi looks at Abe's CV and notices that Abe has never worked in retail before. So Yossi says, 'What a *chutzpah*, if you don't mind me saying. For someone with no retail experience, you are certainly asking for a high salary.'

'Well I suppose I am,' Abe replies, 'but you must realise that the work is so much harder when you don't know what you're doing.'

***

The Kosher Leather Company feels it is time for a shake-up and advertises for a new managing director. Morris gets the job. He is determined to rid the company of all slackers. On his first tour of the factory, he sees a young man leaning against a wall. The area is full of production workers and he thinks this is a good time to let them all know he means business.

Morris walks up to the man and asks, 'How much money do you make a week then?'

The young man looks at Morris and replies, 'I make £240 a week. Why do you want to know?'

Morris then hands the man £240 in £20 notes and shouts, 'Here's a week's pay. Get out of here and don't let me see you here again.'

Feeling pretty good about his first dismissal, Morris looks around and asks, 'Does anyone want to tell me what that idiot did here?'

With a smile on his face, one of the workers replied, 'He's a pizza delivery guy from down the road.'

Builders & repairmen

One day, some builders are renovating an old building in Jerusalem when Solly, one of the workers, falls through the rotten floor into a previously undiscovered cellar. As the dust settles, Solly sees to his horror a skeleton lying in the corner. The skeleton is wearing a blue and white sash with these words written on it:

'ALL ISRAEL HIDE-AND-SEEK CHAMPION 1948'

***

Lionel is out of work and goes to a nearby building site to see what jobs are going. He goes up to the foreman and says, 'Do you have any vacancies?'

The foreman replies, 'What do you do?'

'I'm a handyman,' says Lionel.

'Can you do bricklaying?'

'No.'

'Can you do plumbing?'

'No.'

'Can you do carpentry?'

'No.'

'So why are you calling yourself a handyman, then?' says the foreman.

'Because,' replies Lionel, 'I live round the corner.'

***

Hymie, a wealthy American, retires to England and buys a fabulous English country home with over fifty rooms. He brings in a local workman to decorate the place.

When the job is finished Hymie is delighted but soon after realises that he's forgotten something. There are no *mezuzahs* on the doors.

He immediately goes out and buys fifty kosher *mezuzahs* and asks the decorator to place them on the right-hand side of each door except on the bathrooms. He's worried that the decorator won't put them up correctly. However, the job is carried out entirely to his satisfaction and so he gives the workman an extra bonus.

As the decorator is walking out of the door he says, 'Glad you're happy with the job mate. By the way, I took out all the guarantees that were in those little boxes and left them on the table for you.'

***

One day, as soon as she woke up, Hannah decided that she was sick and tired of all her husband Arnold's blonde jokes and how he thought that all blondes were stupid. To show Arnold how wrong he was and to prove to him that blondes really were smart, Hannah decided to decorate two rooms while he was at work.

When Arnold returned home that evening, he immediately smelled the distinctive aroma of wet paint. He went into the dining room and there he found Hannah lying on the floor in a pool of sweat. He couldn't help but notice that she was wearing her fur coat on top of her ski jacket.

He went over to her and asked, 'Are you OK, darling?'

She replied, 'Yes, of course I am.'

'So what on earth are you doing dressed like that?' he said.

'Darling,' she said, 'I wanted to prove to you that not all blonde women are dumb and I wanted to do it by painting some rooms in our house.'

'But why are you wearing your fur coat over your ski jacket?' he asked.

'I was reading the directions on the paint can,' she replied, 'and it said – FOR BEST RESULTS, PUT ON TWO COATS.'

***

Sarah sees an advert in the *Jewish Chronicle*:

Rebecca & Co, High Quality Decorators and Gardeners

So she contacts Rebecca for a quote to repaint the interior of her house. Rebecca arrives and Sarah walks her through her home explaining what colours she wants for each room. In the first room, Sarah says, 'I would like this room painted in cream.'

Rebecca writes it down, walks to the window, opens it and yells out, 'Green side up.'

She closes the window and follows Sarah to the second room.

Sarah is confused, but continues, 'I would like an off-blue colour for this room.'

Again, Rebecca writes it down, opens the window and yells out, ' Green side up.'

This baffles Sarah, but she is hesitant to say anything.

In the third room, Sarah says, 'I would like this room painted a rose colour.'

And once more, Rebecca opens the window and yells, 'Green side up.'

Sarah musters up courage and asks, 'Why do you keep shouting "Green side up" out of my window every time I tell you the colour I would like the room?'

Rebecca replies, 'Because I have a team of Jewish men laying new turf across the road.'

***

Like most Jewish wives, Rachel could never get her husband to do anything around the house. Issy would come home from work, sit in front of the TV, eat dinner and sit some more – and he would never do those little household repairs that most husbands take care of. This frustrated Rachel quite a bit. One day the toilet overflowed. When Issy got home, she said sweetly, 'Honey, the toilet is bunged up. Would you look at it?' Issy snarled, 'What do I look like – Mr Plumber?' and promptly sat down on the sofa to watch TV.

The next day, the vacuum cleaner wouldn't work. When Issy got home, Rachel said, very nicely, 'Honey, the vacuum cleaner won't work. Would you try to fix it for me?'

Once again, Issy growled, 'What do I look like – Mr Hoover?'

The next day, the washing machine went wrong. When Issy

got home, Rachel steeled her courage and said, 'Honey, the washing machine isn't running. Would you check on it?' And again she was met with a snarl, 'What do I look like – Mr Electrolux?'

Finally, Rachel had had enough. The next morning, she called three repairmen, one to fix the toilet, one the vacuum cleaner and the third the washing machine. When her husband got home, Rachel said, 'Honey, I had the repairmen out today.'

Issy frowned, 'Well, how much is that going to cost?'

'Well, honey, they all said I could pay them by either baking them a cake or having sex with them.'

'Well, what kind of cakes did you bake them?' he asked.

Rachel smiled. 'What do I look like – Mrs Kipling?'

***

When Abe returned home from work, his wife Ruth said, 'So how was your day?'

He replied, 'I met an artist and I've never met someone so talented. He said he painted a picture of a cobweb on his wall and it looked so real, the maid tried for over an hour to get it off.'

Ruth said, 'I don't believe him.'

'Why not?' said Abe. 'Some artists are very good indeed.'

'Maybe,' said Ruth, 'But maids aren't.'

***

Lionel and Sarah, a young, religious couple, had only recently set up house when an unfortunate incident occurred. Early one morning, Sarah, drowsy from bed, went to the toilet for the morning's relief but neglected to notice that the seat was up. She was very skinny and when she sat down, she literally fell in. She was just the right size and shape so that she became jammed into the toilet past her waist with her legs sticking straight up in front of her. Sarah cried for her husband, who rushed in, and for the next hour tried desperately to extricate her. In the process, they removed her nightgown, but this only left her naked and still stuck, with a particular part of her anatomy prominently visible between her splayed legs. Finally, Lionel had to call a plumber, despite the embarrassing nature of his wife's problem.

When the plumber arrived, Lionel let him in, but as they were walking to the bathroom, Lionel realised that his wife was exposed in a very compromising and humiliating way. Thinking fast, he ran ahead of the plumber and placed the first thing he could think of, his *yarmulka*, over Sarah's exposed privates.

The plumber walked into the bathroom, took one long look, and commented, 'Well, I think I can save your wife, buddy, but the rabbi's a goner.'

Tradesmen

Moshe is walking along Bond Street and sees a little tailor's shop named Cohen & O'Reilly. Moshe goes in and talks to the typical little Jewish tailor behind the counter, telling him how impressed he is that for once the Irish and the Jews, often at one another's throats, have come together like this.

The little Jewish man seems unmoved. 'You sopprised by dis?' he asks.

'Well, yes,' says Moshe, still oozing enthusiasm, 'I mean – Cohen and O'Reilly working together in the same shop. I mean, it's different! It's heart-warming!'

'Vell,' says the little Jewish tailor, 'here's anuder soprise for you – I'm O'Reilly!'

***

Maurice Gold took his new pair of trousers to a tailor in Stamford Hill to have them altered. But the next day, Maurice was called to Manchester on a last-minute job assignment. It was over five years before he was able to return to his Stamford Hill home. One day, while he was dressing, Maurice reached into his jacket pocket and to his surprise found the tailor's receipt for his trousers. So Maurice went straight away to the tailor's shop, which fortunately was still there.

Maurice handed him the receipt, and asked, 'Are my trousers here?'

'Yes, of course,' said the tailor. 'Be ready next Tuesday.'

* * *

Yossi goes to a tailor to try on a new custom-made suit. The first thing he notices is that the sleeves are too long. 'No problem,' says the tailor. 'Just bend them at the elbow and hold them out in front of you. See, now it's fine.'

'But the collar is up around my ears!'

'It's nothing. Just hunch your back up a little . . . no, a little more . . . that's it.'

'But I'm stepping on my cuffs!' Yossi cries in desperation.

'*Nu*, bend your knees a little to take up the slack. There you go. Look in the mirror – the suit fits perfectly.'

So, twisted like a pretzel, Yossi lurches out onto the street. Janine and Suzy see him go by. 'Oh, look,' says Janine, 'that poor man!'

'Yes,' says Suzy, 'but what a beautiful suit!'

* * *

Q: What is the difference between a tailor and a psychiatrist?

A: A generation.

* * *

In the middle of Whitechapel, London, there was a little street with just five shops in it. Every shop was a tailor's shop, except for one, which was empty.

The first was called George's Tailor Shop. On its sign was written, 'Best tailors in the area.'

The second was called Mick's Tailor Shop. Its sign read, 'Best tailors in London.'

Then came The Tailor Shop. Its sign read, 'Best tailors in the UK.'

The fourth was Baring & Gilow's Tailors. On its big sign

were the words, 'Best tailors in the world.'

So Moshe Cohen took a lease on the fifth shop, the empty one, and Moshe decided to call it 'Cohen's – Best tailors in the street!'

***

Isaac is out shopping in Golders Green when he sees a sign in a window saying JACOB'S CUSTOM-MADE CLOTHING.

He's not sure whether to go in – it looks an expensive shop. But Jacob, the owner, sees him hesitating and quickly invites him in. 'What are you looking for?'

'A suit.'

'Good,' said Jacob, 'you've come to the right place. When we make a suit here, you'll be surprised at how we go about it. First, digital cameras take pictures of your every muscle and we download the pictures to a special computer to build up your image. Then we cultivate sheep in Australia to get the very best cloth. For the silk lining, we contact Japan for their silkworms, and we ask Japanese deep-sea divers to get the pearl buttons.

'B-b-but,' said Isaac, 'I need the suit for a Bar Mitzvah.'

'When?'

'Tomorrow.'

'You'll have it.'

***

Yitzhak needed his *tallis* cleaned. Rosh Hashanah was over but there was time until Yom Kippur. So he called his friend Lionel to ask which dry cleaner to use. Lionel said, 'I always take my *tallis* to Moshe's Dry Cleaners on Golders Green High Road. He only charges £4.'

But when Yitzhak went to Moshe's, he discovered that the shop had changed ownership and was now called Kelly's Dry Cleaners. He asked the new owner, Sean, if he was keeping to the previous price list. Sean assured him that he was. Three days later, Yitzhak picked up his *tallis* and was given a bill for £12.

He was naturally angry and said to Sean, 'I thought you said you met Moshe's prices?'

'I do,' said Sean, '£4 for the prayer shawl and £8 to get all the knots out of the fringes!'

***

A man stormed into Moshe's Bakery and confronted Moshe.

'Do you know what happened to me?' he demanded. 'I found a fly in the raisin bread I bought from you yesterday.'

Moshe gave a palms-up shrug and replied, '*Nu*, so you'll bring me the fly and I'll give you a raisin.'

***

Rachel and Sarah meet one day in Brent Cross shopping centre.

'Is it true, Rachel,' asks Sarah, 'that your son Benjy has moved out of law?'

'Yes, it's true,' replies Rachel, 'he's now a salesman in a tailor shop.'

'*Mazeltov*,' says Sarah, 'But a salesman? Is he any good at it?'

Rachel replies, 'Is he any good? Why he's brilliant! Only yesterday a woman comes into his shop to buy a suit to bury her poor late husband in. And guess what my Benjy did? He talked her into buying an extra pair of trousers.'

***

Moshe worked in an upmarket men's clothing shop in London. One day, his boss Avrahom returned from lunch and noticed Moshe's hand was bandaged. Before he could ask what had happened, Moshe told him that he had some good news to report, 'I finally sold that ridiculous suit we've had in stock for such a long time.'

'Do you mean that repulsive bright orange-and-blue double-breasted thing?' said Avrahom.

'That's the one!' said Moshe.

'*Mazeltov!*' Avrahom shouted, 'I really thought we'd never

get rid, it – it had to be the ugliest suit we've ever had. But tell me, Moshe, why is your hand bandaged?'

'Simple,' Moshe replied, 'as soon as I sold the suit to the gentleman, his guide dog bit me.'

***

Shlomo and Moshe went to Pincus the tailor for new suits.

'Listen, Pincus,' Shlomo said, 'the last suits you made for us were sort of grey. We want black suits, the darkest black cloth that we can get.'

'See this cloth?' Pincus said, fingering a roll of fabric. 'This is the stuff they make nuns' habits from. There ain't no blacker cloth.'

A few weeks later, Shlomo and Moshe were walking down the street in their new suits when they passed two nuns. Impulsively, Moshe went up to the nuns and matched his suit against their habits. Becoming angry, he muttered something to Shlomo and they both walked off.

'What did that man want?' one nun asked the other.

'I don't know,' she replied, 'He looked at my garment, said something in Latin and left.'

'What did he say?'

'He said, "Pincus Fuctus".'

RELIGION

Biblical jokes

After Adam was created, there he was, all alone, in the Garden of Eden. Of course it wasn't good for him to be all by himself, so the Lord came down to visit.

'Adam,' He said, 'I have a plan to make you much, much happier. I'm going to give you a companion, a help mate for you – someone who will fulfil your every need and desire. Someone who will be faithful, loving and obedient. Someone who will make you feel wonderful every day of your life.'

Adam was stunned. 'That's sounds incredible!'

'Well, it is,' replied the Lord. 'But it doesn't come for free. This is someone so special that it's going to cost you an arm and a leg.'

'That's a pretty high price to pay,' said Adam. 'What can I get for a rib?'

* * *

The Recording Angel needed two new Executive Assistants to help him in the admissions office in Heaven. God sent him three applicants and the Angel began interviewing them immediately.

'I was senior partner in a law firm on earth,' said the first applicant 'and I'm sure I could be very helpful to you.'

'I'm sure you could,' said the Angel. 'I've looked over your CV and you certainly have more than enough credentials for the job. But I do have a little test I ask all applicants to take. Would you spell God, please?'

'A piece of cake,' said the applicant. 'G – O – D.'

'Fine,' said the Angel, extending his hand, 'I'll be in touch.' The fellow left and the second applicant came in.

'I was Chief Executive of a very successful business on earth,' he said. 'There were 16,000 people on my payroll. I think I'd make an excellent assistant.'

'Your record is certainly impressive,' said the Angel. 'And I think I'm going to hire you, but first there's a little test. Spell God.'

'G – O – D,' said the second applicant.

'Great!' said the Angel, shaking his hand. 'You'll be hearing from me.'

The man left and the third applicant, a woman, approached the Angel's desk. 'Tell me about yourself,' said the Angel.

'On earth,' she said, 'I was secretary to one of the most powerful men in Europe. You know, because you know everything, that I did most of the work for which he got credit. I'm certain I could do whatever is required.'

'Of course,' said the Angel, 'but there's one little test - '

'Oh, please, not a test,' said the woman. 'I've had it rough all my life. Because I'm a woman I had to fight for every promotion I ever got. I had to take lower pay for doing the same job as the men in the office. I was constantly harassed by male chauvinist bosses. I thought it would be different up here. Now I get the feeling that because the job title is Executive Assistant and not Secretary, you don't want to give me a chance at it.'

'No, no. Not at all!' said the Angel. 'This is just a little test that I give all applicants, regardless of sex.'

'All right,' sighed the woman. 'Go ahead.'

'Spell desuetude, parietals and chiaroscuro,' said the Angel.

***

The Hebrew people were sitting around Mount Sinai. You could hear only a subdued murmur among them, but you could feel the tension in the air. For hours now, Moses had been on top of the mountain, hidden from their gaze by clouds wafting around its top. Sometimes the clouds became dark and you could hear thunder rolling down. In spite of the warm weather this always caused a shudder among the waiting masses. The end of day was approaching and dusk was beginning to set in when suddenly a figure came through the clouds and walked down the steep mountainside carrying a heavy load. It was Moses.

Moses set down his load and raised his hands. 'Friends,' he said, 'friends, it was hard work and I have done my best. I have negotiated with Him. I used every possible argument, every trick I could think of – and I think I was successful. The good news is: I brought Him down from fifteen to ten. The bad news is: adultery is still in.'

* * *

Did you know that Moses had to make a third trip up to the top of Mount Sinai?

Well, on this third trip, Moses arrived at the burning bush after much climbing, removed his sandals, kneeled and prayed to God.

'Oh mighty God, King of the Universe, your people have sent me back here to ask you a question about the Ten Commandments.'

'What question do they have for Me?' roared the voice of God.

'They want to know whether the commandments are listed according to priority.'

* * *

And the Lord said unto Noah, 'Where is the ark which I have commanded thee to build?'

And Noah said unto the Lord, 'Verily, I have had three carpenters off ill. The gopher wood supplier hath let me down – yea, even though the gopher wood hath been on order nigh upon twelve months. What can I do, O Lord?'

And the Lord said unto Noah, 'I want that ark finished even after seven days and seven nights.'

And Noah said, 'It will be so.'

And it was not so. And the Lord said unto Noah, 'What seemeth to be the trouble this time?'

And Noah said unto the Lord, 'Mine sub-contractor hath gone bankrupt. The pitch, which Thou commandest me to put on the outside and on the inside of the ark, hath not arrived. The plumber hath gone on strike. Shem, my son who helpeth me on the ark side of the business, hath formed a rock group with his brothers Ham and Japheth. Lord, I am undone.'

And the Lord grew angry and said, 'And what about the animals, the male and the female of every sort that I have ordered to come unto thee to keep their seed alive upon the face of the earth?'

And Noah said, 'They have been delivered unto the wrong address but should arrive on Friday.'

And the Lord said, 'How about the unicorns, and the fowls of the air by sevens?'

And Noah wrung his hands and wept, saying, 'Lord, unicorns are a discontinued line; thou canst not get them for love nor money. And fowls of the air are sold only in half-dozens. Lord, Lord, Thou knowest how it is.'

And the Lord in his wisdom said, 'Noah, my son, I know. Why else dost thou think I have caused a flood to descend upon the earth?'

***

'Noah,' says the Lord, 'for the next flood, I want no animals on board, just fish. And not any old fish, but only carp, in glass tanks.'

'And this time,' says the Lord, 'think big. Eight decks at least.'

'I got you,' says Noah, 'what you want is a multi-storey carp ark.'

***

When young David was asked by his father to say the evening prayer, he realised he didn't have his head covered – so he asked his little brother Henry to rest a hand on his head until prayers were over. Henry grew impatient after a few minutes and removed his hand.

The father said, 'This is important – put your hand back on his head!'

Henry exclaimed, 'What, am I my brother's *kippa*?'

***

Q: What did God say after He created man?

A: 'I can do better than this.'

Q: Why was Elijah's mother so happy?

A: Because she not only had fun in bed, but she made a prophet!

***

Bernie and Yossi were down on their luck and decided to do some part-time external decoration work to earn extra money. To start off their new venture, they asked their rabbi if he would be interested in their painting the outside of his house – for a very keen price, obviously. The rabbi said 'yes' and so Bernie and Yossi went out to buy the paint. They drove to the local hardware store and bought some emulsion. It was cheap enough as paint goes and they planned to mix half-paint and half-water to further increase their profits. Then they went back to the rabbi's house and started work.

When they had finished painting the rabbi's house, Yossi called the rabbi and his wife to come out and inspect their work. 'It looks wonderful,' the rabbi said. But as he started to hand them their cheque, it started to rain quite heavily. All at once there was thunder and lightning, the rabbi's house was drenched, and the paint started running down the walls.

Suddenly, as the three of them stood there in disbelief, a voice from Heaven roared, 'Repaint. Repaint and thin no more.'

***

During some recent excavation work, a team of Israeli archaeologists discovered a previously undetected cave. They were very excited because the following five symbols were carved on one wall of the cave: a woman – a donkey – a shovel – a fish – a Star of David.

The archaeologists declared this a unique find – the carvings were thought to be at least three thousand years old. They carefully cut out the piece of stone holding the symbols and sent it to the Tel Aviv Museum. Soon, archaeologists from all over the world were invited to meet to discuss the meaning of the markings.

The chairman opened the meeting by pointing to the first symbol and saying, 'We can judge from the first symbol that this race was family oriented and held women in high esteem. You can also tell that they were smart enough to train donkeys to help them till the soil. The shovel symbol means they had tools to work with. Their intelligence is highlighted by the fish, which means that if their crops failed, they would take to the sea for food. The last symbol means they were evidently Hebrew.'

The audience applauded enthusiastically. Suddenly a little old man stood up in the back of the room and said, 'Idiots! Hebrew is read from right to left. This is what it says, "Holy Mackerel, Dig the Ass on that Woman."'

***

George W Bush was in an airport lobby and noticed a man in a long flowing white robe with a long flowing white beard and flowing white hair. The man had a staff in one hand and some stone tablets under the other arm.

George Bush approached the man and inquired, 'Aren't you Moses?'

The man ignored George and stared at the ceiling.

George Bush positioned himself more directly in the man's view and asked again, 'Aren't you Moses?'

The man continued to peruse the ceiling.

George tugged at the man's sleeve and asked once again, 'Aren't you Moses?'

The man finally responded in an irritated voice, 'Yes, I am.'

George asked him why he was so uppity and the man replied, 'The last time I spoke to a Bush I had to spend forty years in the desert.'

***

What would have happened if three wise Jewish women had

gone to Bethlehem instead of three wise men? They would have asked directions, arrived on time, helped deliver the baby, hired someone to clean the stable, cooked brisket and brought practical gifts.

And what would they have said to each other after they left?

'Did you see the sandals Mary was wearing with that *shmatta*?'

'That baby doesn't look anything like Joseph.'

'Virgin? I knew her in school.'

'Can you believe they let all of those disgusting animals in there?'

'I heard that Joseph doesn't have a job.'

'And that donkey they are riding has seen better days.'

'We'll just see how long it will take to get your brisket pot back.'

***

Here is why God gave the Jews the Ten Commandments.

God first went to the Egyptians and asked them if they would like a commandment.

'What's a commandment?' they asked.

'Well, it's like, THOU SHALT NOT COMMIT ADULTERY,' replied God.

The Egyptians thought about it and then said, 'No way. That would ruin our weekends.'

So then God went to the Syrians and asked them if they would like a commandment.

They also asked, 'What's a commandment?'

'Well,' said God, 'it's like, THOU SHALT NOT STEAL.'

The Syrians immediately replied, 'No way. That would ruin our economy.'

So finally God went to the Jews and asked them if they wanted a commandment. They asked, 'How much?'

God said, 'They're free.'

The Jews said, 'OK. We'll take ten.'

***

It's question time: who are the five most constipated men in the Old Testament?
1) Cain, because he wasn't Abel.
2) Moses, because he went up onto the mountain and took two tablets.
3) King David, because he sat on the throne for forty years.
4) Solomon, because neither heaven nor Earth could move him.
5) Noah, because he was at sea for forty days and forty nights and all he passed was water.

***

Adam and Eve had an ideal marriage. He didn't have to hear about all the men Eve could have married, and she didn't have to hear about how well Adam's mother cooked.

Conversations with God

Sidney was thinking about how good his wife had been to him, and how fortunate he was to have her. He asked God, 'Why did You make her so kind-hearted?'

The Lord responded, 'So you could love her, My son.'

'Why did You make her so good-looking?'

'So you could love her, My son.'

'Why did You make her such a good cook?'

'So you could love her, My son.'

Sidney thought about this. Then he said, 'I don't mean to seem ungrateful or anything, but why did You make her so stupid?'

'So she could love you, My son.'

***

Hetty has a heart attack and is taken to hospital. While on the operating table she has a near-death experience, during which she sees God and asks if this is the end for her. God says no and explains that she has another thirty to forty years to live. As soon as she has recovered, Hetty figures that since she's got another thirty or forty years, she might as well stay in the hospital and have the face-lift, liposuction, breast augmentation and tummy tuck that she had always promised herself. So she did and she even changed the colour of her hair!

But tragedy – some weeks later, just as Hetty is leaving hospital, she is knocked over and killed by a car. When Hetty arrives in front of God, she asks, 'I thought you said I had another thirty to forty years?'

God replies, 'I didn't recognise you.'

***

God: And remember, Moses, in the laws of keeping kosher, never cook a calf in its mother's milk. It is cruel.

Moses: So You are saying we should never eat milk and meat together?

God: No, what I'm saying is, never cook a calf in its mother's milk.

Moses: Oh Lord, forgive my ignorance! What you are really saying is we should wait six hours after eating meat to eat milk so the two are not in our stomachs together.

God: No, Moses, listen to me. I am saying, don't cook a calf in its mother's milk!

Moses: Oh, Lord! Please don't strike me down for my stupidity! What You mean is we should have a separate set of dishes for milk and a separate set for meat and if we make a mistake we have to bury that dish outside?

God: Moses, do whatever you want ...

***

One day, a poor woodcutter was cutting a branch of a tree above a river when his axe fell into the river. When he began crying, God appeared and asked him, 'Why are you crying?'

The woodcutter told Him that he had dropped his axe into water.

God went down into the water and reappeared with a golden axe.

'Is this your axe?' God asked. The woodcutter said, 'No.'

God again went down and came up with a silver axe.

'Is this your axe?' God asked. The woodcutter said, 'No.'

God went down again and came up with an iron axe. 'Is this your axe?' God asked.

The woodcutter said, 'Yes.'

God was so pleased with the man's honesty that He gave him all the three axes. The woodcutter went home happy. Many months later, while the woodcutter was walking with his wife along the river, she fell into the river. When he began crying, God appeared and asked him, 'Why are you crying?'

'My wife has fallen into the water and I can't swim.'

God went down into the water and came up with Jennifer Lopez. 'Is this your wife?' God asked.

'Yes,' he said.

God was furious, 'Now I am going to punish you.'

The woodcutter quickly said, 'Please forgive me, My Lord. It is a misunderstanding. If I had said "No" to Jennifer Lopez, you would have come up with Joan Collins. If I also said "No" to her, you would have finally come up with my wife and I would say "Yes". Then you would give all the three women to me. I am a poor man. I would not be able to look after all three of them, so that's why I had to say "'Yes".'

***

When God made man, She was only joking.

***

Adam is bored in the Garden of Eden, so he says to God, 'O Lord, I have a problem.'

'So what is your problem Adam?' replies God.

'O Lord, I know that You did create me and gave me all this wonderful food and put me in this beautiful garden, but I'm just not happy.'

'Why is that, Adam?'

'O Lord, even though I know You created this place for me and You gave me all these beautiful animals to be with, I am nevertheless still lonely.'

'OK Adam, I have the perfect solution – I shall create a woman for you.'

'What is a "woman", O Lord?'

'A "woman" will be such an intelligent creature that she will know what you want before you even ask for it. She will be so sensitive and caring that she will know your every mood and how to make you happy. Her beauty will be the equal of anything on earth. She will unquestioningly care for your every need and desire. She will be the ideal companion,' answers the Voice from Heaven.

'This woman sounds great to me, O Lord.'

'She will be, take my word for it, but she comes at a price, Adam.'

'So how much will she cost me, O Lord?' Adam asks.

'She will cost you your left arm, your right foot, one eye, one ear and your right testicle.'

Adam thinks about this for a good hour, working out all the pros and cons of having such a woman for company, but especially the cost to him. Finally Adam says, 'O Lord, what kind of woman can I get for just one rib?'

The rest, as they say, is history.

***

Jacob is a very religious man. One day, a nearby river floods its banks and rushes into town, forcing Jacob to climb on to his garage roof. Soon, a man in a boat comes along and tells Jacob to get in. Jacob says, 'That's very kind of you, but no thanks. God will take care of me.'

So, the boat leaves. The water rises and Jacob has to climb on to the roof of his house. Another man in a boat comes along and tells Jacob to get in. Jacob replies, 'That's very kind of you but no thanks. God will take care of me.'

The boat leaves. The water rises further and soon Jacob is clinging to his chimney. Then a helicopter arrives and lowers a ladder. The helicopter pilot tells Jacob to climb up the ladder. Jacob replies, 'That's very kind of you but no thanks. God will take care of me.'

The pilot says, 'Are you really sure?'

Jacob says, 'Yes, I'm sure that God will take care of me.'

Finally, the water rises too high and Jacob drowns. He goes up to Heaven and is met by God. Jacob says to God, 'You told me you would take care of me. What happened?'

God replies, 'Well, I sent you two boats and a helicopter. What else did you want me to do?'

***

Billy Graham went to see the Pope in Rome. While he was waiting, Billy noticed a red phone. As he was ushered in to talk to the Pope, he asked, 'What's the red phone for?'

'That's to talk to God,' came the reply.

'Really,' Billy gasped, 'how much does such a call cost – it's an awful long way?'

'Ten thousand pounds a minute, but it's well worth it,' answered the Pope.

Some weeks later, Billy Graham went to see the Chief Rabbi in Jerusalem. He noticed that he, too, had a red phone. 'I don't suppose,' asked Billy, 'that this phone is to talk to God?'

'Yes it is,' came the reply.

'And how much does that cost?' Billy inquired.

'Twenty pence a minute,' shrugged the chief rabbi.

'How come it's so cheap?' Billy asked, 'the Pope has a phone like that and it costs £10,000 a minute!'

'Well,' grinned the Chief Rabbi, 'from here it's just a local call.'

***

A man walked to the top of a hill to talk to God. The man asked, 'God, what's a million years to You?'

And God said, 'A minute.'

Then the man asked: 'Well, what's a million pounds to You?'

And God said, 'A penny.'

Then the man asked, 'God – can I have a penny?'

And God said, 'Sure – in a minute.'

Christmas

Father Christmas is on duty, working in the Brent Cross shopping centre. When a little girl comes up to his table, Santa asks her, 'What's your name, dear, and what do you want for Christmas?'

The girl replies, 'My name is Mary and I would like a new Barbie doll for Christmas, please.'

Santa tells her, 'I will add your Barbie doll to my list, but for now, please take a present from my toy sack.'

Then a little boy comes up to his table. Santa asks him, 'What's your name, boy, and what do you want for Christmas?'

The boy replies, 'My name is Peter and I want a Harry Potter remote control car for Christmas.'

Santa tells him, 'I will add your Harry Potter car to my list, but for now, please take a present from my toy sack.'

Then another little boy comes up to his table. Santa asks him, 'What's your name, handsome, and what do want for Christmas?'

The boy replies, 'My name is Moshe and I'm Jewish. I'm not allowed to ask for anything from Santa.'

Santa points to his toy sack and whispers in the boy's ear, '*Nem tz Vay*' [Take two].

***

Father Christmas was working at Brent Cross shopping centre when he noticed a young lady of about twenty years old, wearing a large gold Star of David pendant around her neck, who was walking towards him. He was surprised, therefore, when she sat on his lap. Now Santa doesn't usually take requests from adults, but as she gave him such a nice smile, he couldn't refuse.

He said to her, 'What's your name?'

'Hannah,' came the reply.

'And what does a nice Jewish girl like you want for Christmas, Hannah?'

'Actually, I want something for my mother, please,' said Hannah.

'Something for your mother? Well, that's very thoughtful,' smiled Santa. 'What do you want me to bring her?'

Without blinking, Hannah replied, 'A son-in-law.'

***

As little Rivkah climbed on to Santa's lap, Santa asked the usual question, 'And what would you like for Christmas?'

Rivkah stared at him, open mouthed and horrified, then gasped, 'Didn't you get my e-mail?'

The Church

Moshe got a new job with a firm of accountants. One afternoon in the second week, he entered Martin Lewis's office and declared: 'Boss, I know everybody in the world.'

Obviously, Martin didn't believe him and replied, 'Everybody in the whole world?'

Moshe said, 'Yes sir, and you can choose anyone, and I will prove it.'

After a moment, Martin said, 'I bet you don't know Madonna.'

Moshe said, 'I talk to her very often by e-mail, and what's more we've had dinner together. Now we are friends.'

Martin decided to uncover the ruse, so he bought two tickets to Hollywood and they went to Madonna's house. Madonna personally opened the door. She opened her arms and said, 'Oh Moshe, what a surprise! Come in, you and your friend.' They spent a very nice afternoon there. But Martin wasn't convinced. He thought that it could just have been a coincidence, so he said, 'How about President Bush?'

'George!' said Moshe. 'Of course. We were friends together when I lived in the USA. We always talked by phone.'

Martin almost lost his cool and decided that this one he had to see immediately. They flew to Washington and as soon as they landed they took a cab to the White House. There they went to a press conference where Bush was making a speech. At the end, Bush happened to take a look in Moshe's direction. Moshe shouted, 'George! George!' and Bush, with a smile, shouted back: 'Moshe, buddy, come on in and let's talk.'

Martin was bewildered – he couldn't believe it. But his mind didn't stop working. The chances that Moshe knew everybody in the world were billions to one. He decided to use a final test: the Pope. Moshe couldn't possibly know the Pope.

But Moshe said he knew the Pope from when he lived in Poland. So they flew to the Vatican. There, in the middle of thousands of people, the Pope interrupted his prayer. They could see his lips saying 'Moshe' with a smile in his face. The Pope opened his arms and called Moshe to come close to him by the veranda. Moshe was there, looking for Martin and he saw the exact moment when Martin fainted. The Pope blessed Moshe, Moshe kissed the Pope's ring and ran to where Martin was lying.

When Martin woke up, Moshe asked what had happened. Martin, sweating and still confused, looked at Moshe and finally said: 'I have accepted Madonna, I have accepted Bush. Even the Pope I have accepted! But I couldn't stand it anymore when here, in the middle of the crowd, a random person asked me, "Who is that guy dressed all in white, standing on the veranda next to Moshe?"'

***

Abe and Shlomo are strolling down the street one day when they happen to walk by a Catholic Church. They see a big sign posted that says: 'CONVERT TO CATHOLICISM AND GET £20.'

Abe stops walking and stares at the sign.

Shlomo turns to him and says, 'Abe, what's going on?'

'Shlomo,' replies Abe, 'I'm thinking of doing it.'

Shlomo says, 'What, are you crazy?'

Abe thinks for a minute and says, 'Shlomo, I'm going to do it.'

With that, Abe strides purposely into the church and comes out twenty minutes later with his head bowed.

'So,' asks Shlomo, 'did you get your £20?'

Abe looks up at him and says, 'Is that all you people think of?'

***

Bernard is not the brightest of men and is finding it very difficult to find a job. But one day, he applies for and gets a job as caretaker of the local Catholic Church. They decide to give Bernard a trial run and see what it is like for a Jewish man to work in a church. Bernard works very hard indeed.

After a week, he is called into the office. 'Bernard, things are working out fine. I just have a few corrections. First, when you wash your hands, use the bathroom, don't use the holy water. Second, when you hang your coat up, use the cloakroom, do not hang it on the cross. Third, my name is Mother Superior, not Mother Shapiro!'

***

Four young novice nuns were about to take their vows. Dressed in their white gowns, they came into the chapel where the Mother Superior was waiting to perform the ceremony to marry them to Jesus. Just as the ceremony was about to begin, four Chassidic Jews with skullcaps, long sidelocks and long beards, carrying Jewish prayer books, came in and sat in the front row.

The Mother Superior said to them, 'I am honoured that you would want to share this experience with us, but do you mind if I ask you why you came?'

One of the four Jews replied, 'We're from the groom's side.'

***

Moshe and Abe were partners in a very successful clothing factory. It had been in operation for many years and there wasn't much they didn't know about the *shmatta* business. One day, Moshe decided to take a trip to Rome. As Abe had many Catholic friends, he surprised Moshe by getting him an audience with none other than the Pope.

On Moshe's first day back at work after his Rome trip, Abe asked him, 'So, Moshe, what kind of a man is the Pope?'

Moshe replied, 'I would say he's a 44 regular.'

***

Moshe was fed up with life in Mokum (Amsterdam's Jewish name) so he decided to resettle in a new place. He moved to northern Brabant, the heart of the Roman Catholic part of Holland, and opened a small bazaar selling all sorts of things and at extremely low prices. As he wanted to become one of the community, he went to the local church every Sunday just to hear the sermons but without getting converted.

The local shop owners soon got fed up with Moshe's cut-price competition and attempts to fit in, and decided to ask the priest for his assistance. The priest listened to their story and told them to return the next day.

When they returned, the priest told them of his solution, and asked them to contribute €500 to the church-roof building fund.

Next Sunday, Moshe as usual was sitting in the front of the church near the pulpit to listen to the sermon. Suddenly in the middle of the sermon the priest looked straight at Moshe and said, 'I want all Jews to leave this church.'

Moshe wasn't sure he heard it correctly so he stayed seated. The priest repeated, 'I want all Jews to leave this church.'

Moshe stood up, went over to the cross, took Jesus off and said, 'Let's go. We're not wanted here!'

***

Jacob was a shy gentleman. One day, he was preparing to board a plane when he heard that the Pope was on the same flight. 'This is exciting,' thought Jacob. 'I know I'm Jewish but I've always been a big fan of the Pope. Perhaps I'll be able to see him in person.'

Imagine his surprise when the Pope sat down in the seat next to him for the flight. Still, Jacob was too shy to speak to the Pontiff. Shortly after take-off, the Pope began a crossword puzzle. 'This is fantastic,' thought Jacob. 'I'm really good at crosswords. Perhaps, if the Pope gets stuck, he'll ask me for assistance.'

Almost immediately, the Pope turned to Jacob and said, 'Excuse me, but do you know a four-letter word referring to a woman that ends in "unt"?'

Only one word leapt to mind – a vulgar one. 'My goodness,' thought Jacob, 'I can't tell the Pope that. There must be another word.'

Jacob thought for a moment, then it hit him. Turning to the Pope, Jacob said, 'I think you're looking for the word "aunt".'

'Of course,' said the Pope, 'Excuse me, but do you happen to have an eraser?'

Israel

On the sixth day, God turned to the Angels and said: 'Today I am going to create a land called Israel. It will be a land of mountains full of snow, sparkly lakes, forests full of all kinds of trees, and high cliffs overlooking sandy beaches with an abundance of sea life.'

God continued, 'I shall make the land rich so as to make the inhabitants prosper, I shall call these inhabitants Israelis, and they shall be known to most people on earth.'

'But Lord,' asked the Angels, 'don't you think you are being too generous to these Israelis?'

'Not really,' God replied, 'just wait and see the neighbours I'm going to give them.'

***

Maurice was a good, well-respected elderly Edgware man. He felt that death was close and asked his sons to take him to the Holy Land, to die there and be buried in Jerusalem. The loving sons did as he asked, brought him to Jerusalem, put him in a hospital and waited for death to come. However, once in Jerusalem Maurice started to feel better and better and after a few weeks was again strong, healthy and full of life.

He called upon his sons and said, 'Quickly, take me back to Edgware.'

The sons were somehow disappointed and asked, 'Father,

how come? You said you want to die in the Holy Land and be buried in Jerusalem!'

'Yes,' answered Maurice, 'to die it's OK – but to live here?'

***

Tony Blair was on holiday. He was walking along a beach one morning when he stumbled upon an old lamp. He picked it up and rubbed it and a genie appeared.

Tony asked if he got three wishes. The genie said, 'Nope, not these days. I'm only giving out one wish. So – what'll it be?'

Tony didn't hesitate. He said, 'See this map? I want Israel and the Palestinians to stop fighting with each other and start loving each other instead.'

The genie looked at the map and exclaimed, 'Are you crazy? These people have been at war for years! I'm good, but I'm not that good. I don't think it can be done. So make another wish.'

Tony thought for a minute and said, 'You know, for some minor reason, a lot of people are beginning not to trust me. It would be terrific if you would make everyone trust me more. That's my wish.'

The genie thought for a minute and said, 'Hmm. Let me see that map again - '

***

Israel's economy is in a bad way, inflation is getting higher and immigrants are flooding in from all over the world. Problems, problems, problems, but what should they do? So the Knesset holds a special session to come up with a solution. After several hours of talk without progress one member, Yitzhak, stands up and says, 'Quiet everyone, I've got it, I've got the solution to all our problems. We'll declare war on the United States.'

Everyone starts shouting at once. 'You're nuts! That's crazy!'

'Hear me out!' says Yitzhak. 'We declare war. We lose. The United States does what she always does when she defeats a country. She rebuilds everything – our highways, airports, shipping ports, schools, hospitals, factories – and loans us money, and sends us food aid. Our problems will be over.'

'Sure,' says Benny, another minister, 'that's if we lose. But what if we win?'

***

Q: How does an Israeli man commit suicide?

A: He jumps from his ego to his IQ.

***

Issy was part of a group being shown around the latest theatre in Tel Aviv by the owner. The theatre was enormous – the size of at least two soccer pitches. But Issy couldn't help noticing that it had only four rows of seats right at the front. So Issy asked the owner, 'Why are there only four rows of seats? You could have got thousands of seats in this space.'

The owner replied, 'The Jews here only want to sit in the front four rows. If they can't, they don't book to see the shows.'

***

Did you hear about the new dairy factory being built in Israel?

It's called 'Cheeses of Nazareth.'

***

Benny from Haifa passed away and was sent 'below'. He was amazed, however, to discover lush vegetation, running streams, waterfalls and beautiful lakes everywhere. Everyone seemed happy.

'You look surprised,' said a resident.

'Yes, I am,' replied Benny, 'I expected hell to be very dry and exceedingly hot. Like a desert. But all I can see are trees full of all kinds of fruit, beautiful flowers, lots of vegetables, lush grass and water everywhere. This is not hell.'

'Well,' said the resident, 'it used to be like you thought, but then the Israelis started to arrive and they irrigated the hell out of the place!'

Miracles

One Sunday morning, Rabbi Bloom's kitten climbed up a tree in his front garden and wouldn't come down. He tried everything. He pleaded with it – 'Here kitty kitty,' he said, many times over. He placed a bowl of milk by the tree and then placed his pet's basket by the tree, but the kitten would not budge. So the rabbi thought about the problem for a while and came up with a solution. He tied one end of a rope to the tree, attached the other end to his car and drove away slowly. The tree began to bend but every time he got out the car to check, he found he still couldn't reach his kitten. He tried one more time and drove on a little bit farther. But the rope suddenly broke, the tree snapped upright and the kitten sailed through the air out of sight.

Rabbi Bloom immediately went looking for his kitten. He asked everyone he saw if they'd seen a little kitten, but none had. He was very sad it had gone, it had become good company. Some days later, he met Freda in the Deli and was surprised to see some cat food in her basket – he knew she hated cats.

'Freda, why are you buying cat food when you hate cats?' he asked.

'You won't believe me, Rabbi,' she replied. 'My daughter Sarah had been begging me for weeks to buy her a cat, but I kept on refusing. A few days ago, Sarah nagged me yet again, and I told her that if God gives her a cat, she could keep it. I watched Sarah go out into the garden, look up to the sky, and ask God for a cat. Really, Rabbi, I know you won't believe this, but I saw it with my own eyes. A cat suddenly came flying out of the empty sky, with its paws spread out, and landed right in front of Sarah. And that's why I'm buying cat food!'

***

A group of rabbis were having lunch in Isaac's White House kosher restaurant. Unfortunately, Isaac served them watermelon spiked with whisky that he had prepared for another table and he realised his mistake too late to do anything about it. All Isaac could do was wait in his kitchen and expect the worst.

As soon as the waiter came back into the kitchen with the empty plates, Isaac grabbed hold of him and asked, 'What did they say, please tell me, what did they say?'

'Nothing at all, Mr Isaac,' replied the waiter. 'They were all too busy searching for the watermelon seeds and putting them into their pockets.'

***

Sadie had passed away and her funeral service was being held at Bushey cemetery. Morris, her husband for over forty years, had tears in his eyes. At the end of the service, as the coffin was being wheeled out, the trolley accidentally bumped into the doorframe and jarred the coffin. To everyone's total shock, they heard a faint moaning coming from the coffin. They quickly opened it and found that Sadie was alive. Wonder of wonders – a miracle if ever there was one.

Sadie and Morris lived together for ten more years and then Sadie died. The ceremony was again held at Bushey. At the end of the service, as the coffin was being wheeled out on the trolley, Morris shouted out, 'Watch out, don't hit the doorframe again!'

***

Sadie takes her sixteen-year-old daughter to see Dr Myers. The doctor says, 'OK, what's the problem?'

Sadie says, 'It's my daughter, Sarah. She keeps getting these cravings, she's putting on weight, and is sick most mornings.'

The doctor gives Sarah a good examination, then turns to Sadie and says, 'Well, I don't know how to tell you this, but your Sarah is pregnant – about four months would be my guess.'

Sadie says, 'Pregnant? She can't be, she has never ever been left alone with a man! Have you, Sarah?'

'No mother. I've never even kissed a man.'

Dr Myers walked over to the window and just stared out of it. Five minutes pass and finally Sadie says, 'Is there something wrong out there doctor?'

Dr Myers replies, 'No, not really, it's just that the last time anything like this happened, a star appeared in the east and three wise men came over the hill. I certainly don't want to miss it.'

Prayers

Moshe goes for a walk in the woods. Suddenly, a six-foot-tall grizzly bear appears and approaches him at quite a fast pace. Moshe stands there petrified and begins praying for his safety. But then Moshe notices that the bear has stopped, has put on a skullcap and has also started praying. Saved!

But as Moshe approaches the bear with an outstretched hand to greet a fellow Jew, he hears the bear concluding the *motzi*, the traditional prayer before eating.

***

A rabbi said to a precocious six-year-old boy, 'So, you tell me that your mother says your prayers for you each night. That's very commendable. What does she actually say?'

The little boy replied, 'Thank God he's in bed!'

***

Sadie was a Reuters journalist. One year, she was assigned to their Jerusalem office and her apartment overlooked the Wailing Wall. On her first morning, as she was getting ready to go to the office, she looked out her window and saw an old man praying vigorously, his head bobbing up and down rapidly. So Sadie, seeing an interesting story in the making, went down to talk to him.

Sadie asked him, 'How often do you come here to pray?'

'Every day,' he replied. 'I have come here to pray on this spot every day for the last twenty years.'

'You come every day to the wall? What are you praying for?' Sadie asked.

The old man replies, 'I pray for peace in this angry world in the morning. I tell God about my troubles and then I go home, have my lunch and come back in the afternoon. Then I pray for a world free of illness and disease.'

Sadie is amazed. 'How do you feel coming here every day for twenty years and praying for these things?' she asks.

The old man looks at her sadly. 'Like I'm talking to a wall.'

***

One night, Nathan overhears his son Benny saying his prayers. 'God bless mummy and daddy and grandma. Goodbye, grandpa.'

Nathan thinks this a bit strange. The next day, the grandfather dies.

About a month or two later, Nathan hears Benny saying his prayers. Once again, 'God bless mummy. God bless daddy. Goodbye, grandma.'

The next day the grandmother dies. Nathan gets more than a little worried about the whole situation.

Two weeks later, Nathan once again overhears Benny's prayers. 'God bless mummy. Goodbye, daddy.'

This nearly gives Nathan a heart attack. He doesn't say anything, but gets up early next morning to go to work to avoid the traffic. He stays out all through lunch and dinner and finally, after midnight, leaves his office. He's still alive!

When he gets home, he apologises to his wife, Sarah. 'I'm sorry, darling. I had a very bad day at the office.'

'You think you had a bad day?' Sarah says, 'The postman dropped dead on our doorstep this morning.'

***

Little Yossi and his family were having dinner at his *bubbeh*'s house. When everyone was seated, the food was served. As soon as little Yossi got his plate, he started eating from it right away.

'Yossi, please wait until we say our prayer,' said his father.

'I don't have to,' Yossi replied.

'Of course you have to,' said his mother. 'Don't we always say a prayer before eating at our house?'

'Yes, but that's our house,' Yossi explained. 'This is *Bubbeh*'s house and she knows how to cook.'

***

A marriage is arranged for a young Chassidic couple, as has been the tradition for centuries. The wedding takes place and Yossel and Annie are soon in bed ready to consummate their marriage. But Yossel is a novice.

'I've never done this before,' he tells Annie.

Annie quickly reassures him. 'Don't worry, darling, I will guide you through the process. First of all, remove your garments.'

He complies.

'No,' she says, 'all of them, not just your prayer shawl.'

A little embarrassed, Yossel does what he is told.

She says 'OK, Yossel, now you need to lie right on top of me.'

'Naked?' he asks.

'Yes' she says. So Yossel climbs on top of her, but just lies there.

'Now' she says, 'put it inside me.'

'You mean my - ?'

'Yes!'

Yossel again does what he is told but is still embarrassed and just lies there, rigid, on top of her, doing nothing. After five minutes of just lying there, it suddenly becomes clear to Annie what must happen next.

'Now,' she says to Yossel, '*Daven!*'

Rabbis

Benjamin woke up one Saturday morning in a bad mood. When he came down to breakfast, he put on his *yarmulka* and sat across the table from his visiting sister, Sarah. 'I'm not going to *shul* today!' he said to Sarah emphatically.

'Yes you are,' Sarah replied calmly.

'No I'm not ... I don't think I really want to ever go again!'

Benjamin said with obvious irritation. 'The people down there don't like me, they ignore me sometimes ... they don't appreciate me at all ... and I won't go back.'

'Yes, you will go today, and you will continue,' said Sarah with confidence. And, I'll give you two reasons. Number one, you're 45 years old – and number two, you're the rabbi!'

***

A poor Jew finds a wallet with £700 in it. At his *shul*, he reads a notice stating that a wealthy Jew has lost his wallet and is offering a £50 reward to anyone who returns it. Quickly he locates the owner and gives him the wallet. The rich man counts the money and says, 'I see you have already taken your reward.'

The poor man responds, 'What are you talking about?'

The wealthy Jew continues, 'This wallet had £750 in it when I lost it.'

The two men begin arguing, and eventually they come before the rabbi. Both men present their case. The poor man first, then the wealthy man who concludes by saying, 'Rabbi, I trust you believe me.'

The rabbi says, 'Of course.'

The rich man smiles, and the poor man is devastated. Then the rabbi takes the wallet out of the wealthy man's hands and gives it to the poor man who found it.

'What are you doing?' the rich man yells angrily.

The rabbi responds, 'You are, of course, an honest man, and if you say that your missing wallet had £750 in it, I'm sure it did. But if the man who found this wallet is a liar and a thief, he wouldn't have returned it at all. Which means that this wallet must belong to somebody else. If that man steps forward, he'll get the money. Otherwise, it stays with the man who found it.'

'What about my money?' the rich man asks.

'Well, we'll just have to wait until somebody finds a wallet with £750 in it.'

***

Rabbi Bloom is walking down the street one day when he notices a very small boy trying to press a doorbell on a house across the street. However, the boy is very short and the doorbell is too high for him to reach. After watching the boy's efforts for some time, Rabbi Bloom moves closer to the boy's position and calls out to him, 'Would you like some assistance?'

The little boy responds, 'Yes please.'

Rabbi Bloom continues to watch as he crosses the street and walks up behind the little fellow. He places his hand kindly on the child's shoulder leans over and gives the doorbell a solid ring. Crouching down to the child's level, Rabbi Bloom smiles benevolently and asks, 'Is there anything else I can help you with, my little man?'

To which the boy replies, 'Yes, run like hell.'

***

Did you hear about the dyslexic rabbi?

He went around saying 'Yo Yav!'

***

Moshe and Sadie suspected their rabbi had committed adultery, and decided to trap him by exposing his hypocrisy while his wife was away in Israel visiting her family.

The rabbi was working at home, as he usually did on Wednesday mornings, preparing his Shabbes sermon, when the doorbell rang. When he opened the door, there was Sadie standing outside. She opened her coat, revealing that she was nude, except for a small frilly white apron. 'Do you want to play games?' Sadie asked, 'I'll be Caron, the French maid.'

'Wonderful, wonderful,' the rabbi said, 'come right in and take off your coat.'

He looked Sadie over and said, 'OK, let's play. You're the maid and I'm the housewife. I'm going out to have lunch with a couple of my friends, and while I'm gone, you're going to start in the kitchen. Be careful with the crockery and don't mix up the silverware. OK?'

***

Rabbi Bloom of the United Orthodox Synagogue is playing golf one Sunday when he meets three members of the Reform Synagogue on the course. They talk and he invites them to come to his *shul* next Shabbes. They accept.

Next Saturday, they turn up some time after service has begun and all the main seats are filled. Several other latecomers are already seated on folding chairs. Rabbi Bloom calls over the *shammes*, 'Moshe, please get three chairs for my reform friends at the back.'

Moshe is a bit deaf so he leans closer and says, 'I beg your pardon, Rabbi?'

Rabbi Bloom again says, 'Get three chairs for my reform friends at the back.'

Moshe was puzzled but as there was a lull in the service, he goes to the front of the *shul* and loudly announces, 'The rabbi says, "Give three cheers for my Reform friends at the back!"'

***

Rabbi Bloom was having trouble getting a *minyan* together. Several families with strong anti-war views had recently left his synagogue and taken up the Quaker faith.

'It can't be helped,' Rabbi Bloom lamented. 'It seems some of my best Jews are Friends.'

***

One early winter morning, Rabbi Bloom was walking beside the canal when he saw a dog in the water trying hard to stay afloat. It looked so sad and exhausted that Rabbi Bloom jumped in and after a struggle managed to bring it out alive. A passer-by saw this and said, 'That was very brave of you. Are you a vet?'

Rabbi Bloom replied, 'Of course I'm a vet! I'm a freezing cold as vell.'

***

Letter to a synagogue secretary

Dear Sir,
We have a proposition to make. A recent survey – 'What makes the perfect rabbi?' showed that:

- the perfect rabbi's sermons last exactly fifteen minutes
- the perfect rabbi condemns sin but, at the same time, never upsets anyone
- the perfect rabbi works from 8 a.m. until midnight and is also synagogue handyman
- the perfect rabbi makes £250 pw, wears good clothes, buys good books, drives a good car and gives about £50 pw to the poor and needy
- the perfect rabbi has a burning desire to work with teenagers and spends all of his time with senior citizens
- the perfect rabbi smiles all the time but with a straight face because he has a sense of humour that keeps him seriously dedicated to his work
- the perfect rabbi makes fifteen calls daily to congregation families and the hospitalised, and is always in his office when needed.

If your rabbi does not measure up to the above, simply send this letter to six other synagogues that are also tired of their rabbi. Then bundle up your rabbi and send him to the synagogue on the top of your list. In one week, you will receive 1,643 rabbis and one of them will be perfect. Have faith in this procedure. One congregation broke the chain and got its old rabbi back in less than three weeks.
Yours faithfully -

***

Rabbi Bloom ran a Talmud class at a *yeshiva*. He was always so involved in the text being studied that he never looked up from his books. Often, when he called up a student for translation and explanation, without realising it, he chose the same student day after day. But out of respect, the students wouldn't point this out to him.

Hymie had already been called up on three consecutive days

when the rabbi once again said, 'Hymie Himmelfarb, come up here and translate and explain.'

Hymie replied, 'Himmelfarb is absent today, Rabbi.'

'OK,' said the rabbi, 'why don't you come up here and translate and explain instead.'

***

The little village was very poor. The people could hardly pay their rabbi. It was lucky that the rabbi was such a pious man who fasted twice a week, because if he wasn't, he would have starved.

***

Sadie goes to see her rabbi and complains about her bad headaches. She whines, cries, and talks about her poor living conditions for hours.

All of a sudden, Sadie shouts, overjoyed, 'Rabbi, your holy presence has cured me! My headache is gone!'

To which the rabbi replies, 'No Sadie, it is not gone. I have it now.'

***

A Polish town had just one cow to its name and its milk ran dry. The townsfolk did some research and bought a replacement cow from Minsk for only a thousand roubles. It was a great cow and produced lots of milk and lots of cream. Everybody loved it. Then the people decided they would mate the cow and get more cows and would never again have to worry about their milk supply. They bought a bull and led the cow and the bull into the pasture. But things were not that easy – when the bull came in from the right to mount the cow, the cow moved to the left and when the bull moved in to mount the cow from the left, the cow moved to the right. This went on all day. In desperation, the people asked their rabbi what to do – he was very wise.

'Rabbi, we've tried all day to mate our cow, but when the bull moves in from the right the cow moves left, and vice versa.

What shall we do?'

The rabbi said to them, '*Nu*, why did you buy a Minsk cow?'

'Rabbi,' they said, 'you are so wise. We never told you that we bought the cow from Minsk. How did you know?'

The rabbi said, 'My wife is from Minsk.'

***

One Sabbath afternoon, Jacob was in the rabbi's office and was looking out of the window when he said, 'Rabbi, if one sees a cow drowning on the Sabbath, is it permitted to save it or should one let it drown?'

The rabbi looked up and said, 'No, my son, it is not permitted to break the Sabbath over a cow.'

'That's a shame,' said Jacob. 'A cow has fallen into the lake and it's drowning.'

The rabbi replied, 'Yes, it's too bad.'

Jacob continued, 'Its head is now going under and it's certainly going to die. I feel sorry for the animal.'

'Yes,' said the rabbi, 'it is not a nice thing to happen, but what can one do on the Sabbath?'

'And I feel so sorry for you,' Jacob said.

'Why me?' said the rabbi looking up.

'It is your cow.'

Rabbis & priests

A priest and a rabbi were sharing a compartment on a train. After a while, the priest put down his book and said to the rabbi, 'I know that in your religion you're not supposed to eat pork – but have you really never ever tasted it?'

The rabbi closed his newspaper and replied, 'I must tell you the truth. Yes I have, on the odd occasion.'

The rabbi then had his turn to interrogate. He asked, 'I know that in your religion you're supposed to be celibate – but - '

The priest interrupted, 'Yes, I know what you are going to ask, and yes, I have succumbed to temptation once or twice.'

The two continued with their reading and there was silence for a while. Then the rabbi peeked around his newspaper and said, 'Better than pork, isn't it?'

***

Rabbi Bloom and Father Michael are involved in a car accident and it's a bad one. Both cars are crushed but amazingly neither of the clerics is hurt. After they crawl out of their cars, Rabbi Bloom sees the priest's dog collar and says, 'Just look at our cars – there's nothing left, but we're unhurt. You're a priest and I'm a rabbi so it must be a sign from God. He must have meant that we should meet and be friends and live together in peace the rest of our days.'

Father Michael replies, 'I agree with you completely. This truly must be a sign from God.'

Rabbi Bloom then says, 'Look – here's another miracle. Although my car is wrecked, this bottle of wine didn't break. God must want us to drink this wine and celebrate our good fortune.'

He hands the bottle to the priest. Father Michael takes a few big swigs and passes the bottle back to Rabbi Bloom who puts the cork back in and hands it back to the priest. Father Michael asks, 'Aren't you having any wine?'

'No. I think I'll just wait for the police,' says Rabbi Bloom.

***

A rabbi and a priest are the lone passengers on a plane. Suddenly, the plane's engines conk out. Immediately, the priest grabs the only parachute and jumps out.

The pilot asks the rabbi, 'How will you survive?'

The rabbi answers, 'Don't worry about me, the priest took my *tallis* bag by mistake.'

***

Two five-year-olds, one Jewish, the other Catholic, are playing in a sandpit. Sean says to David, 'Our priest knows more about things than your rabbi!'

To which David replies, 'Of course he does, you tell him everything.'

***

A rabbi, a priest and a minister are discussing when life begins.

The priest says: 'In our religion, life begins at conception.'

The minister says: 'We disagree. We believe that life begins when the foetus is viable away from the mother's womb.'

The rabbi responds: 'You both are wrong. In our religion, life begins when the kids graduate college and the dog dies.'

***

A rabbi, a priest and a minister are out fishing in the middle of a lake. The priest tells his two colleagues, 'I left my fishing rod in the car; I'll be right back.' He gets out of the boat, walks across the water to the beach, goes to the car, walks back across the lake, and gets into the boat. The rabbi stares at this in amazement.

Thirty minutes later, the minister says, 'I need to go to the toilet.' He, too, gets out of the boat, walks across the water, finds the nearest men's room, walks back across the water and gets into the boat. The rabbi is absolutely dumbfounded.

The rabbi keeps thinking, 'My faith is as great as theirs.' So he speaks up and says, 'I need to get something to drink; there's a refreshment stand on the beach.'

He stands up, puts his feet on the water, and SPLASH, he goes straight down under the water. The priest and minister help him back into the boat. He is embarrassed, not to mention wet, but he knows he can do it if the other two can. So, he stands up again, steps out onto the water, and again, SPLASH. Again, he is dragged out and again he decides to try. As he is going down for the third time, the priest turns to the minister and asks, 'Do you think we should show him where the stepping-stones are?'

***

A rabbi, a priest and a minister were talking one day. The priest told of an occasion when he was caught in a snowstorm so terrible that he couldn't see a foot in front of him. He was completely confused, unsure even of which direction he needed to walk. He prayed to God, and miraculously, while the storm continued for miles in every direction, he could clearly see his home twenty feet away.

The minister told a similar story. He had been out on a small boat when a heavy storm struck. There were 20-foot high waves, and the boat was sure to capsize. He prayed to God, and, while the storm continued all around, for several feet in each direction, the sea calmed, and the minister was able to return safely to port.

The rabbi, too, had such a story. One Shabbes morning, on the way home from his *shul*, he saw a very thick wad of £20 notes in the gutter. Of course, since it was Shabbes, the rabbi wasn't able to touch the money. So he prayed to God, and everywhere, for miles in every direction, it was still Shabbes, but for ten feet around him, it was Thursday.

***

A rabbi, a priest and a minister are discussing what they do with donations to their respective religious organizations. The minister says that he draws a circle on the floor, throws the money up in the air, and whatever lands in the circle, he gives to God, and whatever lands outside the circle, he keeps.

The priest uses a similar method. He draws the circle, but whatever lands outside the circle, he gives to God, and whatever lands inside, he keeps.

The rabbi has a slightly different method of dividing the money. He throws all the money up in the air. Whatever God wants, he keeps -

***

A minister, a priest and Rabbi Samuels went for a walk in the country. It was a very hot day. They were sweating and exhausted when they came upon a small lake. Since it was fairly secluded, they took off all their clothes and jumped in the water naked. When they came out, they were feeling so refreshed that the trio decided to pick a few berries while enjoying their 'freedom'.

But as they were crossing an open area, who should come along but a group of ladies from town. Unable to get to their clothes in time, the minister and the priest covered their privates and Rabbi Samuels covered his face.

After the ladies had left and the men had got their clothes back on, the minister and the priest asked Rabbi Samuels why he covered his face rather than his privates.

Rabbi Samuels replied, 'I don't know about you, but in my congregation, it's my face they would recognise.'

* * *

A priest goes to a hairdressing salon, has a haircut, thanks the hairdresser and asks him how much he owes. The hairdresser replies, 'Father, you're a holy man, a man of the cloth, I just couldn't charge you anything, it's on the house.' The priest is most grateful and says, 'Thank you, my son,' and leaves. When the hairdresser goes to open his shop next morning, almost by magic, he finds twelve gold coins on his doorstep.

Some days later, a Buddhist monk goes to the same hairdressing salon for a shave and a wax. When he goes to pay, the hairdresser says, 'You don't have to give me any money, you're a spiritual leader, a man of the people, I just couldn't charge you anything, it's on the house.' The monk bows, shakes his hand and thanks him. When the hairdresser goes to open his shop next morning, almost by magic, he finds twelve rubies on his doorstep.

The following week a rabbi goes into the hairdressing salon to have a haircut and a beard trim. When he goes to pay, the hairdresser says, 'No, Rabbi, I couldn't ask you to pay anything, it's on the house. You are a learned and wise man, go in peace.' The rabbi blesses him and leaves. When the hairdresser goes to open his shop next morning, almost by magic, he finds twelve rabbis on his doorstep.

* * *

Rabbi Bloom and Father O'Reilly were arguing one day about religion. They went on for some time and very soon, things began to get out of hand.

Then Rabbi Bloom said, 'We must not quarrel in this way. It's not right. We are both doing God's work, you in your way and I in His.'

***

At a conference on religion a priest, a minister and a rabbi were all asked the same question, 'What would you like people to say about you after you die?'

The priest said, 'I hope that people will say that I was able to rise above the scandals that are plaguing the Catholic Church at this time. I hope that people would say that I was able to shepherd my flock through this crisis and help them to understand the absolute love that God the Father, the Son and the Holy Spirit have for all of them as Catholics.'

The minister then said, 'When I die I hope that people will say that I saved many souls by bringing them to Christ. I hope that I will be remembered as a caring, thoughtful man who always spread the Word, the love of Christ and a faith everlasting in God. I hope that my preaching and converting will be carried on in my memory and to the glory of Christ.'

Finally, the rabbi was asked, 'Rabbi, what do you hope people will say about you after you have died?'

Without pausing, the rabbi answered, 'Look. He's breathing.'

Sermons

Kol Nidre was fast approaching and the rabbi remembered his dissatisfaction with the donations given by his congregation last year. He wasn't confident that he could get more from them this year. The synagogue Treasurer suggested to him that perhaps he might be able to hypnotise the congregation into giving more.

'And just how would I go about doing that?' he asked.

'It is very simple. First you ensure all windows are shut so that the *shul* is warmer than usual. Then you give your usual sermon, but in a monotone voice. Meanwhile, you dangle a watch on a chain and swing it in a slow arc backwards and forwards and suggest to the congregation that they pledge ten times more than they did last year.'

So on Kol Nidre night, the rabbi did as suggested and, lo and behold, they pledged ten times more than normal.

Now, the rabbi did not want to take advantage of this technique each and every year, so he waited two years before trying mass hypnosis again. Just as the last of the congregation was becoming mesmerised, the chain on the watch broke and the watch hit the floor with a loud thud and springs and parts flew everywhere.

'Shit!' exclaimed the rabbi.

It took them a week to clean up the synagogue.

***

One Shabbes morning, Rabbi Landau is giving a sermon on 'the *mitzvah* of forgiving your enemies'. He talks at length on the subject for nearly fifteen minutes and then asks his congregation, 'Please raise your hand if you are willing to forgive your enemies.'

About fifty per cent raise their hand. This upsets Rabbi Landau so he decides to lecture for another ten minutes. He then repeats his question. This time about eighty per cent raise their hand. But the rabbi is still not satisfied, lectures a bit longer and repeats his question. This time everybody raises their hand, except an old lady at the back of the *shul*.

Rabbi Landau asks, 'Mrs Levy, aren't you willing to forgive your enemies?'

'I don't have any enemies,' she replies.

'That's very unusual Mrs Levy. How old are you?'

'I'm 98, Rabbi.'

'Please, Mrs Levy, come to the front and tell us how you have lived to 98 and don't have an enemy in the world.'

Mrs Levy hobbles down the aisle, faces the congregation and says, with a smile, 'I outlived the *momzers*, that's how.'

***

Rabbi Josephs was cleaning up the house when he came across a box he didn't recognise. His wife told him to leave it alone as it was personal. One day, when she was out, his curiosity got the best of him. He opened the box and inside found three eggs and £2,000. When his wife came home, he admitted that he had opened the box and he asked her to explain the contents to him. She told him that every time he had a bad sermon, she would put an egg in the box ...

He interrupted, 'In twenty years, only three bad sermons, that's not bad.'

His wife continued ... and every time I got a dozen eggs, I would sell them.

***

Yankele was watching his father, a rabbi, write one of his Shabbes speeches.

'How do you know what to say, Daddy?' Yankele asked.

'Why, son, God tells me,' said the rabbi.

'Oh, then why do you keep crossing things out?'

***

Rabbi Bloom had just accepted a junior role at a north London synagogue for his first posting. The senior rabbi there, Rabbi Gold, was well loved by his congregation and considered to be very wise with a wicked sense of humour. One day, not long after he joined, Rabbi Bloom said to Rabbi Gold, 'You know I told you during my interview that I had won many prizes in the *yeshiva* for my sermons? Well, I don't think there is a subject in the world that I could not instantly find a Biblical text for and then incorporate into a sermon.'

Rabbi Gold couldn't help but decide to put him to the test.

'Rabbi Bloom,' he said, 'I want you to give my sermon next Shabbes. But there will be no need for you to prepare it in advance. Instead, when you get into the pulpit, you will find a sealed envelope and inside the envelope will be a single sheet of paper on which I will have written a one-word topic. I challenge you to find any kind of text that will fit.'

Rabbi Bloom thanked Rabbi Gold for the opportunity and said he looked forward to the challenge with relish. The day came. Rabbi Bloom walked up the stairs to the pulpit, opened the envelope, looked at the sheet of paper on which was written 'constipation', and started his sermon. 'And Moses took the two tablets and went off down the mountain - '

***

One Friday morning, a letter dropped through Rabbi Bloom's letterbox. He opened it and took out a single sheet of paper. On it was written just one word: '*SHMUCK*'.

Next day, at the end of his Shabbes sermon, Rabbi Bloom announced to his congregation, 'I have previously come across people who have written to me but have forgotten to sign the letter. This week, however, I received a letter from someone who signed it but forgot to write the letter.'

***

One Friday night I was in the synagogue and the rabbi was giving his usual sermon. At the end of his speech he told the congregation, 'Before we continue, I would like to inform you that our synagogue has decided to collect goods for the most needy people in our area. It's for a good cause and we need your help. Please bring us this Sunday anything you have lying around your house that you can spare or have no great need for. For example, I'm sure that you can all think of something that you have excess of.'

Behind me I heard the voice of an old lady saying to her neighbour seated next to her, 'Yes, worries.'

***

Rabbi Bloom was getting quite a reputation for his sermons. His synagogue was always packed because his congregation didn't want to miss a single one of his words. One Sabbath, one member had to go to another synagogue to attend a nephew's Bar Mitzvah. Because he didn't want to miss the sermon, he asked one of his non-Jewish friends to go in his place and tape the rabbi's sermon. In that way, he could listen to it when he got back. When other members of the congregation saw what was going on, they too decided to ask their non-Jewish friends to go in their places to record the sermon. They could then do other things, such as play golf or go to football. Within a short time, there were one hundred Gentiles sitting in the synagogue recording the rabbi's sermon.

The rabbi got wise to this. So the following Sabbath, he, too, asked a non-Jewish friend to attend on his behalf. His friend brought a tape recorder and played the rabbi's pre-recorded sermon to the hundred non-Jews in the congregation who then recorded the sermon on their own machines.

This was believed to be the first incidence in history of 'artificial insermonation'.

***

One Shabbes, Rabbi Bloom told his congregation, 'Next week, my sermon will be all about the sin of lying and to help you understand it better I would like you all to read Leviticus Chapter 28 before next week.'

The following Shabbes, at the start of his sermon, Rabbi Bloom asked his congregation, 'How many of you have read Leviticus 28?'

Every hand went up. Rabbi Bloom smiled and said, 'Leviticus has only 27 chapters. I will now proceed with my sermon on the sin of lying.'

***

A rabbi dies and is waiting in line to enter heaven. In front of him is a man dressed in a loud shirt, leather jacket, jeans and sunglasses. Gabriel addresses this man, 'I need to know who you are so that I can determine whether or not to admit you to the Kingdom of Heaven?'

The man replies, 'I'm Moshe Levy, taxi driver, of London.'

Gabriel consults his list, smiles and says to the taxi driver, 'OK. Take this silken robe and golden staff and enter the Kingdom of Heaven.'

Now it's the rabbi's turn. He stands upright and says, 'I am Benjamin Himmelfarb and I had been rabbi of Neasden for forty years.'

Gabriel looks at his list and says to the rabbi, 'OK. Take this cotton robe and wooden staff and enter the Kingdom of Heaven.'

'Hold on a minute,' says Rabbi Himmelfarb, 'that man before me was a taxi driver – why did he get a silken robe and golden staff?'

'Up here, we only work by results,' says Gabriel. 'While you preached, people slept – but while he drove, people prayed.'

***

The new rabbi was in the middle of a sermon when he suddenly beckoned to the *shammes* to come over. The rabbi said to him, 'That man in the third row is asleep. Wake him up.'

The *shammes* replied, 'You put him to sleep. You wake him up.'

***

A reform rabbi was having an argument with an orthodox rabbi. He asked him, 'Why don't you let the men and women of your congregation sit together as they do in my congregation?'

The orthodox rabbi (who had a mischievous sense of humour) replied, 'If you want to know the truth, I don't really mind them sitting together at all. The trouble is, however, that I give sermons and I can't have them sleeping together.'

Shabbes

George W Bush was very curious about how the Jewish people knew everything before he did. So he called the FBI and asked them to figure it out. One week later, they came back and said, 'Mr President, the Jews have something called Shabbes. They meet each other at the synagogue and use a code. They sit, they pray, and there is a word that is the key to this secret. This word is "*nu*". When one says to another, "*Nu?*" the other tells him everything, every bit of news.'

Bush wanted to see this for himself. So the FBI dressed him like a Chassid and taught him to read from the right to the left of the Siddur. Bush arrived at a synagogue on Shabbes and sat beside Issy. He waited for a moment, and said, '*Nu?*'

Issy answered, 'Shh, don't talk now, Bush is coming.'

***

Morris and Lenny are strolling home from *shul* one Saturday morning. Suddenly, a taxi speeds past, and their friend, Irving, is running frantically behind it, flailing his arms wildly.

'Well,' said Lenny, 'I never imagined our good friend Irving was a Sabbath violator! Look at him running for that taxi.'

'Wait a minute,' Morris replied. 'Didn't you read that book I lent you, *The Other Side of the Story*, about the command to judge other people favourably? I'll bet we can think of hundreds of excuses for Irving's behaviour.'

'Yeah, like what?'

'Maybe he's sick and needs to go to the hospital.'

'Come on! He was running sixty miles an hour after that cab – he's healthier than Arnold Schwarzenegger.'

'Well, maybe his wife's having a baby.'

'She had one last week.'

'Well, maybe he needs to visit her in the hospital.'

'She's home.'

'Well, maybe he's running to the hospital to get a doctor.'

'He is a doctor.'

'Well, maybe he need supplies from the hospital.'

'The hospital is a three-minute walk in the opposite direction.'

'Well, maybe he forgot that it's Shabbes!'

'Of course he knows it's Shabbes. Didn't you see his tie? It was his paisley beige 100 per cent silk Gucci tie from Italy. He never wears it during the week.'

'Wow, you're really observant! I didn't even notice he was wearing a tie.'

'How could you not notice? Didn't you see how it was caught on the rear bumper of the taxi?'

***

We Jews are not only not allowed to conduct business on Shabbes, we are not even supposed to talk about it –

Yosef and Gidon meet in the synagogue one Shabbes morning.

Yosef says, 'Not to talk about it on Shabbes, but I'm selling my car.'

Gidon replies, 'Not to talk about it on Shabbes, but how much are you asking for it?'

'Not to talk about it on Shabbes, but £13,000.'

'Not to talk about it on Shabbes, but I'll give you £12,000 for it.'

'Not to talk about it on Shabbes, but let me think about it.'

They meet again in the synagogue Shabbes afternoon.

'Not to talk about it on Shabbes, but did you think about my offer?'

'Not to talk about it on Shabbes, but I already sold it.'

***

Issy and Hetty, a young orthodox married couple, were expecting their first baby. Unfortunately, Hetty's water broke on Shabbes and they had no choice but to call for a taxi to take them to the hospital's maternity ward. Because Issy wanted to try and minimise the Shabbes violation, he told the controller that he must send them only a non-Jewish driver. The taxi quickly arrived, but when Issy and Hetty were getting in, they overheard the controller on the two-way radio ask the driver, 'Have you picked up the anti-Semites yet?'

***

Moshe spent the week looking unsuccessfully around north London for a place to live. Now it was the eve of Shabbes and he was alone in a strange town. He found the local *shul* and after services explained his predicament to the *shammes*. Within minutes, Jacob had come over and invited him to be his Shabbes guest.

At Jacob's house, Moshe was given towels and aromatic soap and then shown to the bathroom. After a soothing hot bath, he dried himself on the soft fluffy towel, got dressed and joined Jacob and his wife for a delicious meal. He was then shown to his bedroom where he immediately fell asleep.

The same kindness was shown to Moshe the next day. On Sunday it was time to leave and Moshe told Jacob, 'This was a lovely Shabbes. How can I ever repay you?'

'By paying me,' replied Jacob and gave Moshe an invoice for:

1 hot bath,
1 bar of aromatic soap,
2 clean towels,
1 full Shabbes dinner,
3 glasses Shabbes wine,
2 nights lodging (bed & breakfast),
fresh sheets,
1 Shabbes lunch, and
1 afternoon tea.
\- - - - - - - - - - - - - - - -
Total £75.00

'You're charging me?' asked Moshe.

'I certainly am.'

'I didn't ask you to take me in – you invited me. It's outrageous!'

'Even so, please pay the bill.'

'But this is wrong!'

'OK,' sighed Jacob, 'Let's not argue. We'll go to my rabbi and let him decide.'

'That's OK with me,' said Moshe.

As the rabbi listened to their arguments, he stroked his beard and said, 'Based on numerous Talmudic precedents and on my opinion of the situation, it's my decision that Moshe should pay the bill.'

Moshe couldn't believe his ears. It made no sense at all. But a decision had been made and so, as soon as they left the rabbi, Moshe handed Jacob the money he owed.

'What's this for?' asked Jacob.

'It's what I owe you.'

'Don't be silly. Keep it. It was a pleasure to have you with us. Please come again.'

Moshe was confused. 'But you gave me your invoice, we argued, we went to the rabbi, he made a decision!'

'My dear Moshe,' said Jacob smiling, 'I was pulling your leg. I just wanted you to see what kind of *shmuck* we have for a rabbi.'

* * *

Rabbi Bloom and Rabbi Levy always greeted each other at *shul* by saying 'Good Shabbes' to each other. One Shabbes, Rabbi Bloom, the younger of the two, asked Rabbi Levy, 'What by you is a good Shabbes?'

Rabbi Levy replied, 'By me, a good Shabbes is when I wake up, have a good breakfast, go to *shul*, the Bar Mitzvah boy does a good job, my sermon goes down well, we have a Kiddush, I have a whisky, go home to lunch, have a little sleep, a little studying, and then say Havdalah. That to me is a good Shabbes. And what is a good Shabbes by you?'

Rabbi Bloom replies, 'By me a good Shabbes is when I wake up, turn around and my wife and I make mad passionate love. Get up, shower, get dressed, have breakfast, snuggle a bit with my wife, walk to *shul*, do all the things you mentioned in *shul*, and come home. My wife and I make mad passionate love, have lunch, go out for a walk hand in hand, come home, go to bed and make mad passionate love once more. Then I say Havdalah. And that by me is a good Shabbes.'

'That,' says Rabbi Levy, 'is not a good Shabbes. That is a GREAT Shabbes.'

***

One sunny Sabbath afternoon in Golders Green, Shlomo and Issy, two old friends, meet for the first time in years. After exchanging the usual amenities, they sit down on a bench to talk. Shlomo says, 'Issy, people are telling me you don't go to synagogue any more. Can it be true that you no longer believe in God?'

Issy looks uncomfortable and hurriedly changes the subject. The next afternoon, they meet on the bench again. 'You must tell me, Issy,' Shlomo says, 'Don't you believe in our God anymore?'

Issy replies, 'Here is a straight answer to a straight question. No, I don't.'

Shlomo asks, 'Why didn't you tell me that yesterday?'

Issy, deeply shocked, exclaims, 'God forbid – on Shabbes?'

***

Issy and Shlomo have been running a Jewish goods shop in Kilburn, London for over forty years but the neighbourhood is not what it was and the Jewish community has moved out. One day, Shlomo says, 'Issy, our customers are moving out. Ve haff to move to where they are going – to Golders Green or Hendon, if ve vant to survive.'

'Ve can't do dis,' replies Issy, 'dis neighbourhood iz our life. Ve've been here for foity-tree years. However, instead of moving, ve should tink about sellink Katolik articles as vell as Jewish vuns.'

'Vut? Katolik tings?' says Shlomo, 'Dat's a *meshugga* idea. Ve Jews can't sell anytink Katolik.'

But in the following week they only manage to sell one *mezuzah* and a Bar Mitzvah *tallis* and by Friday Shlomo comes round to Issy's way of thinking – they will have to stock some Catholic articles. 'OK Issy,' he says, 'You vin. Call de Katolik supplier in Cricklevood right now.' So Issy rings them.

'Hello, is dis de Katolik Supply House?'

'Yes it is. How can we be of help, sir?'

'Dis is Issy of Issy's and Shlomo's in Kilburn. Ve vant 200 daily missals, 100 pictures of the Pope, all autographed please, and 200 of dem beads, vot dey called?'

'Rosaries, sir. Will there be anything else?'

'Yes, ve also vant some crosses, a gross will do for starters, and ve vant you to deliver all of dese things to us tomorrow morning.'

'OK sir,' comes the reply, 'Let me read the list back to you to check that I've got your order right. You require a delivery tomorrow morning of 200 daily missals, 100 pictures of the Pope, each one to be personally signed by His Holiness, 200 sets of rosaries and 144 crucifixes. But about dese crucifixes – do you vant dem mit or mitout Jesuses? Ve can do either. But tomorrow ve don't deliver. It's Shabbes.'

***

Moshe, Peter and Ali were discussing who was the most religious.

'I was riding my camel in the middle of the desert,' said Ali. 'Suddenly a fierce sandstorm appeared from nowhere. I truly thought my end had come as I lay next to my camel while we were being buried deeper and deeper under the sand. But I did not lose faith in the Almighty. I prayed and prayed and suddenly for 100 yards all around me the storm had stopped. Since that day, I am a devout believer in God.'

'One day while fishing,' said Peter, 'I was in my little boat in the middle of the ocean. Suddenly a fierce storm appeared from nowhere. I truly thought my end had come as my boat was tossed around by the rough waves. But I did not lose my faith in Jesus. I prayed and prayed and suddenly for 300 yards all around me the storm had stopped. Since that day I'm a devout Christian and now teach young children about Him.'

'One Saturday, I was walking down the road to my synagogue in Hendon,' explained Moshe. 'I was in my most expensive designer outfit. Suddenly I saw a leather bag drop to the ground in front of me. It appeared out of nowhere. I put my hand inside and found that it was full of money. I truly thought my end had come as we are not allowed to handle money on the Sabbath. But I did not lose my faith in my God. I prayed and prayed and suddenly for 500 yards all around me it was Sunday.'

***

A rabbi dies. After some time has passed, his congregation decide that his wife Sarah should marry again. Since it is a small village, the only available candidate is Moshe the butcher. Although very reluctant, because she was used to living with a scholar, Sarah accepts and they are soon married. On her first Friday afternoon as a new wife, just after she had taken a bath, Moshe tells Sarah, 'My mother always said that before the start of Shabbes, it is a *mitzvah* to make love before going to the synagogue.' They do it. When they come back from *shul*, Moshe tells Sarah, 'According to my father, it is a *mitzvah* to make love as soon as you come back from *shul*.'

They do it again. Later that night, when it was time to go to sleep, Moshe tells Sarah, 'My grandfather told me that one should always make love late on Shabbes night.'

So they do. Finally, they go to sleep. As soon as they awake the next morning, Moshe tells Sarah, 'My aunt says that a religious Jew always starts the Shabbes day by making love. So lets do it.'

And once again they do. Next day, Sunday, Sarah goes out to the market and meets a friend who asks her, '*Nu*, Sarah, so how is the new husband?'

'Well, an intellectual he isn't, but Moshe comes from a wonderful family!'

***

Jeremy warned his son against marrying a *shiksa*.

The son replied, 'But she's converting to Judaism.'

'It doesn't matter,' Jeremy said, 'a *shiksa* will cause problems.'

After the wedding, Jeremy called the son, who was in business with him, and asked him why he was not at work.

'It's Shabbes,' the son replied.

Jeremy was surprised and said, 'But we always work on Saturday. It's our busiest day.'

'I won't work anymore on Saturday,' the son insisted, 'because my wife wants us to go to *shul* on Shabbes.'

'See,' Jeremy said, 'I told you marrying a *shiksa* would cause problems.'

***

Moshe went to *shul* regularly but one Sabbath forgot his *tallis* and had to borrow one from the 'visitors' spares'. It was an expensive-looking *tallis* and he was certainly not embarrassed to wear it. At the end of the service, he didn't really want to hand back this excellent *tallis* and without thinking, stuffed it down his trousers. As he was walking out, the rabbi stopped him and whispered, 'Moshe, I saw you put the *shul tallis* down your trousers. I don't want to know why you did this, but may I suggest you remove it from your trousers now and give it to me?'

Moshe was so deeply embarrassed that as he was bending over trying to pull the *tallis* out of his trouser leg, where it had slipped, he accidentally loudly broke wind. The rabbi, shocked, said, 'Moshe, you took the *shofar* as well?'

Jewish holidays

A short summary of every Jewish holiday:
They tried to kill us. We won. Let's eat.

***

London doctors have published a paper that concludes that Seder participants should not eat both chopped liver and choroses, the dip made of apples, cinnamon, almonds and wine that is eaten on Passover. Their research shows that if they do, it can lead to Choroses of the Liver.

***

Maurice and Sadie invite Nigel, their Gentile neighbour for a Passover dinner. The first course is served and Sadie says to Nigel, 'This is matzo ball soup.'

When Nigel sees the two large matzo balls in the soup, he is hesitant to taste this strange looking brew. But Maurice gently persuades him to try it. 'Just have a taste. If you don't like it, you don't have to finish it, honestly.'

So Nigel has a taste. He digs his spoon in and picks up a small piece of matzo ball with some soup. He tastes it gingerly and finds he likes it very much. Quickly he finishes his plate.

'That was delicious,' says Nigel. 'Can you eat any other part of the matzo?'

***

One Yom Kippur, during a break in synagogue service, the rabbi sees a very worried looking Morry walking towards him. His face is white and his eyes are bloodshot. He stands in front of the rabbi, sweating and out of breath. 'Please, Rabbi,' he says, 'I must have a drink of water. I'm so thirsty and dry. I can't stand it any more.'

The rabbi is astonished and replies, 'Don't you realise what you are asking? Today is Yom Kippur, when we fast and beg for forgiveness and you come to me and tell me that want to drink and break your fast? Be strong and do not give in.'

Morry is in tears, 'Please, Rabbi, just a small drink. I can't take it anymore.'

But the rabbi is not an unkind man, and is touched by Morry's suffering. He thinks for a while and says, 'Alright.' He calls over the *shammes*, 'Give Morry a teaspoon of water.'

The teaspoon of water is given to Morry who is now crazy with thirst. 'Please, please, I've got to have a real drink or I'll die!' he cries.

Although he doesn't really want to do it, the rabbi instructs the *shammes* to give Morry a full glass of water. Morry drinks the water, puts down the glass, wipes his mouth with his handkerchief, looks the rabbi in the eye and says, 'Thank you, Rabbi, I'll never eat a pickled herring on Yom Kippur morning ever again.'

***

Moshe goes to see his rabbi. 'Rabbi, last week I missed saying grace after meals.'

'Why,' asked the rabbi.

'Because I forgot to wash my hands before the meal.'

'That's twice you've broken the law but you still haven't told me why.'

'The food wasn't kosher.'

'You ate non-kosher food?' asked the rabbi.

'It wasn't a Jewish restaurant.'

'That makes it even worse,' said the now angry rabbi. 'Couldn't you have eaten in a kosher one?'

'What, on Yom Kippur?'

***

At Passover, we read the story of Moses and how God brought nine plagues on Pharaoh and the Egyptians. And we read that because Pharaoh was stubborn and still wouldn't let the Jews leave Egypt, God had to unleash Plague number ten, despite his previous warning. This was the death of the first-born of every Egyptian family. Only then, after this greatest of terrors, did Pharaoh release the Jews from slavery and let them leave Egypt to journey to the Promised Land.

But in the face of such convincing evidence that something really bad would happen, why didn't Pharaoh release the Jews after the first nine plagues? It took years of research by leading Israeli scholars studying the Dead Sea Scrolls to find the answer. 'The Pharaoh was still in deNile.'

***

One Succoth, or Jewish harvest festival, as two African-Americans are standing on Brooklyn Bridge, Moshe walks past carrying a *luluv* (a palm branch and myrtle branch) and an *estrog* (a citrus fruit), to be used during the Succoth service.

'Hey man, Jew, where you goin' with that palm tree and that lemon?' they ask.

'I'm going to *shul*,' Moshe replied.

'What's "*shul*"?' they ask.

'Well, come with me and I'll show you.' Moshe said.

So one goes with Moshe to synagogue and later returns to his friend after services.

'Dem Jews is crazy,' he says. 'First dey says "oh no", den dey says "Ah don' know" and den dey says "How sh'Ah know".'

***

Holiday differences explained:

Christmas is one day. It's the same day every year, 25 December. Jews love Christmas as it's another paid day off work. We go to the cinema, eat at a Chinese restaurant and go Israeli dancing. Chanukah is eight days. It starts on the evening of 24 Kislev, whenever that falls. No one is ever sure – until that is, a Christian friend asks when Chanukah starts, forcing us to consult a calendar. We all have the same calendar, provided free with the *Jewish Chronicle* newspaper.

Christmas is a major holiday. Chanukah is a minor holiday with the same theme as most of the other Jewish holidays – 'They attempted to kill us, we survived, so let's eat already.'

There is only one way to spell Christmas. No one can decide how to spell Chanukah or Hannukah.

Christmas is a time of pressure for husbands and boyfriends because their partners expect special gifts. Jewish men are relieved of that burden because, surprisingly, no one expects a diamond ring on Chanukah.

Christians get wonderful presents such as jewellery, perfume and digital cameras. Jews get practical presents such as scarves, underwear, socks and pyjamas.

Christmas ends up in high electricity bills. But because candles are used for Chanukah, Jews are spared such high bills. We even feel good because we aren't adding to the energy crisis.

Christmas carols are beautiful ('Silent Night', 'O Come All Ye Faithful'). Chanukah songs are about clay spinning tops (*dreidels*) and similar. Nevertheless, we are proud that many carols were written and sung by Barbara Streisand and Neil Diamond.

Homes getting ready for Christmas smell great with the sweet aromas of cookies and cakes. Everyone is in a festive mood. Homes getting ready for Chanukah smell of frying oil and potatoes and onions. Everyone as usual is talking loudly and at the same time.

Women have great fun baking Christmas cookies, but Jewish women burn their eyes and cut their hands grating potatoes and onions to make *latkes* on Chanukah – a reminder of our suffering through the ages.

Many Christians believe in the virgin birth. Jews think, 'Come on Joseph, *bubbeleh*, snap out of it. Your woman is pregnant, you didn't sleep with her and now you want to blame God. Here, take the number of my psychoanalyst. He might be able to help you.'

* * *

Moshe took his Passover lunch to eat outside in the park. He sat down on a bench and began eating. A little while later a blind man came and sat down next to him. Feeling neighbourly, Moshe passed a sheet of matzo to the blind man. The blind man handled the matzo for a few minutes, looked puzzled, and finally exclaimed, 'Who wrote this shit?'

* * *

Maurice had worked most of his life helping his community and he was therefore thrilled one morning to hear that his unselfish work had been recognised by no less than the Queen. She had decided to bestow on Maurice a knighthood. But his elation soon turned to dismay when he realised that his ceremony would take place on the first night of Passover.

'What on earth should I do?' thought Maurice. 'Should I attend Seder night with my loving family or should I accept one of the highest honours in the land?'

His family soon talked him into going to the palace. 'The award is too special to turn down and you would live to regret it,' they told him.

His next worry was what to say to the Queen. He just

couldn't think of anything that would be of interest to her. He hoped that he would come up with something on the day.

The special day arrived and there was Maurice, on his knees, being knighted, with the Queen touching his shoulders with her sword and Maurice shaking with excitement.

All of a sudden, he burst out with the Passover prayer '*Ma nishtana haleila hazeh*?'

The Queen looked at Prince Philip with a surprised expression on her face and said to him, 'Why is this knight different from all other knights?'

***

Seder pick-up lines:

Let's make this night really different from all other nights!
What will you do to me for two zuzim?
What's a girl like you doing at a Seder like this?
I like my matzo thin, like my women.
Maybe when Elijah comes, we can make it a threesome.
I hear that horseradish is an aphrodisiac.
After four cups of wine, you look like Cindy Crawford.
Darling, on this night we are supposed to recline, so let's get to it.
I bet I could make you sing Dayenu.
Did that just say we were in bondage?
I could never Pass you Over.
We were strangers (with emphasis on 'were').
You're a ten in my Haggadah.
I'm going to have to search you for *chometz*.
How's about we go and re-live the 'Darkness' plague up in my room?
I'm like one of the four sons; let me show you how wicked I can be!

***

The Eight Nights Of Chanukah

On the first night of Chanukah, someone sent to me, a warm bagel topped with cream cheese.

On the second night of Chanukah, someone sent to me, two matzo balls and a warm bagel topped with cream cheese.

On the third night of Chanukah, someone sent to me, three golden *latkes*, two matzo balls and a warm bagel topped with cream cheese.

On the fourth night of Chanukah, someone sent to me, four pounds of salt beef, three golden *latkes*, two matzo balls and a warm bagel topped with cream cheese.

On the fifth night of Chanukah, someone sent to me, five pickled cucumbers, four pounds of salt beef, three golden *latkes*, two matzo balls and a warm bagel topped with cream cheese.

On the sixth night of Chanukah, someone sent to me, six *bubbehs* cooking, five pickled cucumbers, four pounds of salt beef, three golden *latkes*, two matzo balls and a warm bagel topped with cream cheese.

On the seventh night of Chanukah, someone sent to me, seven rabbis dancing, six *bubbehs* cooking, five pickled cucumbers four pounds of salt beef, three golden *latkes*, two matzo balls and a warm bagel topped with cream cheese.

On the eighth night of Chanukah, someone sent to me, eight fiddlers fiddling, seven rabbis dancing, six *bubbehs* cooking, five pickled cucumbers, four pounds of salt beef, three golden *latkes*, two matzo balls and a warm bagel topped with cream cheese.

***

There's No Seder Like Our Seder (sung to the tune of 'There's No Business Like Show Business')
There's no Seder like our Seder,
There's no Seder I know.
Everything about it is *halachic*
Nothing that the Torah won't allow.

Listen how we read the whole Haggadah
It's all in Hebrew
'Cause we know how.

There's no Seder like our Seder,
We tell a tale that is swell.
Moses took the people out into the heat
They baked the matzo
While on their feet
Now isn't that a story
That just can't be beat?
Let's go on with the show!

***

These Are a Few of Our Passover Things (sung to the tune of 'These Are a Few of My Favourite Things')

Cleaning and cooking and so many dishes
Out with the *hametz*, no pasta, no *knishes*
Fish that's gefilted, horseradish that stings
These are a few of our Passover things.

Matzo and *karpas* and chopped up *haroses*
Shankbones and Kiddush and Yiddish neuroses
Tante who *kvetches* and uncle who sings
These are a few of our Passover things.

Motzi and *maror* and trouble with Pharoahs
Famines and locusts and slaves with wheelbarrows
Matzo balls floating and eggshells that cling
These are a few of our Passover things.

When the plagues strike
When the lice bite
When we're feeling sad
We simply remember our Passover things
And then we don't feel so bad.

Synagogues

Rabbis Levy, Samuel and Kosiner were 'progressive' reform rabbis and were talking one day about the recent advances made by their synagogues. Rabbi Levy said, 'We're very modern – we allow mobile phones to be used during services – we even have re-charging points all over the synagogue.'

'Well,' said Rabbi Samuel, 'we've installed a snack bar at the back of the synagogue for those who feel hungry or thirsty during services – we serve falafel in pitta and hot salt beef with *latkes* and new green cucumbers.'

'That's nothing to what we do, my friends,' said Rabbi Kosiner. 'We close our synagogue for the Jewish holidays.'

***

Manny approaches the rabbi of his Reform Synagogue and says 'Rabbi, please make me a Cohen.'

The rabbi, taken aback, tells Manny that it is impossible. Manny offers the rabbi £10,000, but the rabbi won't budge. He offers £50,000 – then £75,000. Finally, the rabbi, reluctantly, gives in. He teaches Manny Torah. He teaches him Talmud. After six months of classes, the rabbi tells Manny, 'OK, now you can be a Cohen.'

The next Shabbes, Manny is called up for the first *aliyah* in the Torah reading. He goes up, with a big smile on his face, says the *brachot* and afterwards returns to his seat. But the rabbi is still troubled and a little curious. He approaches Manny the next day and asks him why it was so important to him to be a Cohen.

Manny answers, 'Rabbi, my father was a Cohen; my grandfather was a Cohen. I wanted to be a Cohen too!'

***

A rabbi, a cantor and a synagogue president were driving to a seminar when they were kidnapped. The hijackers asked the three of them to hand over all of their money and jewellery. When they replied that they hadn't any, the hijackers told them that immediately after their last wishes were fulfilled, they would be killed.

'My last wish,' began the rabbi, is to give a fascinating, complicated, long sermon that I have always wanted to but never been allowed to give.'

'We will grant your wish,' the hijackers replied.

'My last wish,' said the cantor, 'is to sing a beautiful, Yemenite-style song, one of my own compositions, lasting two hours. I have never been allowed to sing it.'

'We'll let you sing it,' replied the hijackers.

'What is your last wish,' the hijackers asked the *shul* president.

'Please, please shoot me now.'

***

Rabbi Landau was, as usual, standing near the synagogue exit shaking hands as his congregation left. But as Max was leaving, Rabbi Landau grabbed his hand, pulled him aside and said, 'Max, I think you need to join the Army of God!'

'But I'm already in God's Army, Rabbi,' said Max.

'So how come I don't see in *shul* except on Rosh Hashanah and Yom Kippur?' said Rabbi Landau.

Max whispered, 'I'm in the secret service.'

***

A cruise liner goes down in the Pacific and Benny is the only survivor. He manages to swim to an uninhabited island. Many years later, when a search party finally comes to rescue him, they see that he has constructed two synagogues on his tiny island.

'Why the two synagogues?' the leader asks Benny.

Benny points to the nearest one and replies, 'That's the one I go to every Saturday. The other one, I wouldn't go inside if you paid me!'

***

One Sabbath, Joseph discovers a gay *shul* in Hendon. He's very excited. It is exactly what he had been looking for. There's a gay cantor and a gay rabbi, and even the congregation is mostly gay. So with a happy heart, Joseph sits down and joins in the service. Soon, however, he just can't help noticing the handsome young man sitting next to him. Hard as he tries, he can't stop himself – Joseph puts his hand on the young man's knee. Immediately two large men rush over to Joseph, pick him up, quickly carry him out of the *shul* and forcibly throw him out into the street.

As he picks himself up, Joseph says, 'Why on earth did you have to do that? I thought this was a gay synagogue.'

'It is,' one of them replied in a deep voice. 'But nobody messes with the *rebbitsen*.'

***

You can tell the person next to you has not been to synagogue often if you hear them say:

'Hey, my book is back to front.'

'Isn't it impolite to talk when the minister is talking?'

'I get the standing and the sitting bit, but when do we kneel?'

'Does your prayer book have writing in a funny-looking alphabet, too?'

'Why do people keep coming in even after the service starts? Don't they know what time it starts?'

'Do people always get up and walk out just before the rabbi gives his sermon?'

'This food after the service is really good, but wouldn't it be better if people waited in line and then only took a little at a time?'

'Hey, I remember this part from "Fiddler on the Roof".'

'Who brings kids to a place like this?'

'You there, slow down, you're getting ahead of the soloist!'

'Why am I the only guy in the dress circle?'

'You'd think nobody has ever seen a mobile phone.'

'It's show time! They're opening the curtains.'

'Pardon me, but you have some string hanging down from your scarf.'

'The boy can't be more than twelve or thirteen – and they let him read?'

'When do they take up the collection?'

***

One Saturday morning, the rabbi noticed little David was staring up at the large plaque that hung in the foyer of the synagogue. It was covered with names and small British flags were mounted on either side of it. The seven-year-old had been staring at the plaque for some time, so the rabbi walked up, stood beside the boy, and said quietly, 'Good Shabbes, David.'

'Good Shabbes, Rabbi,' replied the young man, still focused on the plaque.

'Rabbi, what is this?' David asked.

'Well, David, it's a memorial to all the young men and women who died in the service.'

Soberly, they stood together, staring at the large plaque. Little David's voice was barely audible when he asked, 'Which one, the Friday night or the Saturday service?'

***

In his infinite wisdom, the *gabbai* gave *hagbah*, the task of lifting the Torah scroll and displaying it to the congregation, to Moshe, the puniest guy in the *shul*. With great effort, Moshe managed to complete the act but nearly faints in doing so. He then vows he will never be embarrassed like that again. He joins a local gym and commences a six-month heavy training course – push-ups, sit-ups, weight lifting, 10Ks – the whole thing.

Six months later, he's back in *shul* and the *gabbai* calls him up again. This time, Moshe immediately picks up the Torah like it were made of feathers and flips it in the air. While the Torah is spinning, Moshe does a somersault and gets on his feet just in time to catch the falling Torah. He then turns to the *gabbai* and says, 'What do you think of that, then?'

The *gabbai* replies, 'Very nice, but today I gave you shishi – the task of reading.'

***

One day, a *chazan* was bragging and boasting about the quality of his voice. He told his friend, 'Do you know that I even insured my voice for £750,000?'

His friend replied, 'So what have you done with the money?'

***

Rabbi Rabinowitz went in to beg his board of directors to buy a new synagogue chandelier. Arguing and pleading for over an hour, he eventually sat down believing he had failed.

Suddenly, the president of the board said, 'Why are we wasting time talking? First of all, a chandelier – why, we haven't got anyone who could even spell it. Second, we haven't got anyone who could even play it. And lastly, what we really need in the synagogue is more light!'

***

Synagogue Seating Request Form

Last year, many of you expressed concern over the seating arrangements in the synagogue. In order for us to place you in a seat that will best suit you, we ask you to complete the following questionnaire and return it to the synagogue secretary's office as soon as possible. Please put a tick against your choices.

1. I would prefer to sit in the:

❑Talking section ❑Non-talking section

2. If talking, which category do you prefer? (Indicate order of interest)

❑Stock market	❑Football
❑Medicine	❑Congregants' secret medical tragedies
❑Your recent holidays	
❑The *chazan*'s voice	❑The rabbi
❑What others are wearing	❑Fashion news
❑Your relatives	❑Your neighbours
❑Who's cheating on/having	❑The situation in Israel

an affair with whom ❑Jokes

❑Other:_______________________________

3. Who of the following would you like to be near for professional advice?

❑Doctor ❑Dentist
❑Psychiatrist ❑Child psychiatrist
❑Travel Agent ❑Stockbroker
❑Accountant ❑Solicitor
❑Estate agent ❑Architect
❑Plumber ❑Golf pro (tentative; we're still trying to find a Jewish one)
❑Other: _____________________________

4. I want a seat located: (Indicate order of priority)

❑On the aisle ❑Near the exit
❑Near a window ❑Near the toilets
❑Near the *bimah* [dais] ❑Near single men
❑Where no one on the *bimah* can see me talking during service ❑Where no one will notice me sleeping during service
❑Where I can sleep during the rabbi's sermon [additional charge]

5. I would like a seat where:

❑I can see my spouse ❑I cannot see my spouse
❑I can see my friend's spouse ❑My spouse cannot see me looking at my friend's spouse

6. Please do not place me anywhere near the following people. (If you require more space for your answer, you may wish to consider joining another congregation.)

____
____
____
____
____
____

7. Your name: ______________________________

8. Building fund pledge: £_____________________

***

Maurice came home from the Reform synagogue one Saturday with a black eye.

'Maurice, what ever happened?' asked his wife Beckie.

'Well,' said Maurice, 'it was like this. During the service, we had to stand several times and on one occasion I noticed that Mrs Levy, who was sitting in front of me, had her dress stuck in the crease of her *toches*, so I leaned forward and pulled it out. But Mrs Levy didn't like this at all – she turned around and hit me full in the face with her prayer book.'

The following week, Maurice came back from synagogue with the other eye blackened.

'And what happened this time, Maurice?' asked Beckie.

'Well,' says Maurice, 'it was like this. Once again Mrs Levy had her dress trapped, but this time my friend Issy saw it. He leaned over and carefully pulled out the dress. But I know that Mrs Levy doesn't like this – so I tucked it back in again!'

***

A *gabbai* approaches a guest in the synagogue and says, 'I want to give you an *aliyah*. What's your name?'

The man answers, 'Rifka *bat* Jacov.' ('Rifka, daughter of Jacob.')

The *gabbai* says, 'No, I need your name.'

The man says, 'I told you, it's Rifka *bat* Jacov.'

The *gabbai* asks, 'How can that be your name?'

The man replies, 'I've recently been in some serious financial difficulties and so everything is now in my wife's name.'

***

Bernard went to his synagogue a few hours before Yom Kippur to check that his *tallis* was all right. Whilst there, he saw the caretaker spraying the inside of the synagogue with an air freshener. As he liked the smell, Bernard asked, 'That's got a really nice smell. May I ask what it is?'

Keeping a straight face, the caretaker replied, 'Air of Yom Kippur, of course!'

***

Edgware Road synagogue wanted to help their congregation cope better with the stresses of modern life, and decided to offer a course in Time Management. Soon after the course was announced, a member telephoned the rabbi.

'What time does the course start, Rabbi?'

The rabbi replied, 'Oh – fiveish, sixish - '

HEALTH

Sight & sound

Sadie went to her doctor and confessed to an embarrassing problem. 'I fart all the time, doctor, but they're soundless and they have no odour. In fact, since I've been here, I've farted at least twenty times. What can I do?'

'Here's your prescription, Sadie. Take these pills three times a day for seven days and come back and see me in a week's time.'

The next week, an upset Sadie marched into the doctor's office. 'Doctor, I don't know what was in those pills, but the problem is worse! I'm farting just as much, and they're still soundless, but now they smell terrible! What do you have to say for yourself?'

'Calm down, Sadie,' said the doctor soothingly. 'Now that we've fixed your sinuses, we'll work on your hearing.'

***

Maurice was showing off. He said to his friend Sam, 'I bought a hearing aid yesterday. It cost me £2,000.'

Sam said, 'That's expensive, isn't it?'

Maurice replied, 'Yes, but it is state of the art.'

'What kind is it?' Sam asked.

'A quarter to twelve,' said Maurice.

***

Max was talking to Louie. 'Did you know that I'm one of eighteen children?'

Louie said, 'No, I didn't. Why do you think your parents had so many children?'

Max replies, 'The problem was that my mum was hard of hearing. When mum and dad went to bed each night, dad would ask, 'Do you want to go to sleep, or what?'

And mum would say, 'What?'

***

Sadie is in a bad way and goes to see her doctor. 'Dr Myers, what's wrong with me? Just look at the state of my face. When I woke up this morning, I glanced in the mirror and nearly fainted at what I saw. My hair has gone grey and wiry and is starting to fall out, my lovely skin has become pasty-looking and horribly wrinkled and both my eyes are bloodshot and bulging from their sockets. I look like someone who has just died. What on earth is wrong with me?'

Dr Myers gives Sadie a quick examination, looks her in the eyes and says to her, 'Well, I can say one thing I've discovered, there's nothing wrong with your eyesight!'

***

Sam was convinced that his wife Becky was getting deaf. She refused to go to an audiologist, so he asked his doctor what could be done.

'Why don't you test Becky without her knowledge. Start at the door of the room. Tell Becky something in a normal tone of voice. If she doesn't respond, keep moving nearer, still using a normal tone of voice. That should tell you just how deaf Becky is.'

'Thank you, doctor.'

Soon after, Sam saw his chance. He noticed Becky doing the dishes.

He said, 'I love you, darling.'

No response.

He moved a few steps into the room and repeated, 'I love you, darling.'

Still no response.

He moved closer, until he could almost touch her and said, 'I love you, darling.'

With this, Becky turned around and said, 'For the third time, I love you too.'

***

One day, Sadie visits a golf driving range to practise before an important game. As she is about to drive her first ball, she notices the man next to her. 'Excuse me,' she says, 'You're facing the wrong direction.'

'*Oy Vay*. Tenks for dat. Vitout you, I vouldn't have known. I'm blind, you know.'

He then turns around and starts hitting out into the range.

A few minutes later, he says to Sadie, 'How am I doing?'

'Not bad,' she replies, 'most of your shots were straight and long, but you sliced a few.'

'Tenks again,' he replies. 'Vitout you telling me, I vouldn't know dees tings.'

A few shots later, he asks, 'Do you mind I should ask a poissonal qvestion?'

'No,' Sadie replies, 'fire away.'

'I don't seem to do vell vit de ladies. Am I ugly or fett?'

'You're quite presentable,' says Sadie, smiling, 'that shouldn't be a problem.'

Smiling, he says, 'Vat a relief. I vas always afraid to ask that qvestion.'

As he was about to hit another ball, Sadie interrupts him. 'Do you mind if I give you a bit of advice?' she asks.

'Vit gladness. I vill tek all de help you hev got,' he replies.

'Lose the Jewish accent, ' Sadie says, 'you're Chinese.'

***

Benny's hearing has been getting worse of late and he finally decides to buy a hearing aid. But he doesn't want to spend too much money on it. He goes into a hearing aid shop and asks the salesgirl, 'How much do hearing aids cost?'

'That depends on the model,' she replies, 'they start from £5 and go up to £2,500.'

'So show me the £5 model, already,' says Benny.

The salesgirl puts the £5 device around Benny's neck and tells him, 'All you do is put this stud in your ear and run this length of wire down to your pocket.'

'*Nu*, so does it work?' asks Benny.

'With respect, sir, for £5, it doesn't work,' she replies, 'but when people see it on you, they'll talk louder.'

Doctors

Henry goes to the doctor's surgery to collect his wife Sarah's test results. The receptionist tells him, 'I'm sorry, but there has been a bit of a mix-up. When we sent your wife's samples to the lab, they got mixed up with samples from another Mrs Cohen and we don't know which one is your wife's. The bottom line is that the situation is either bad or terrible.'

'What do you mean?' says Henry.

'Well,' says the receptionist, 'one Mrs Cohen has tested positive for Alzheimer's disease and the other for AIDS. We can't tell which is which.'

'That's terrible,' says Henry. 'Can you do the test again?'

'Normally, yes. But your private medical insurance policy won't pay for these expensive tests more than once.'

'Well, what am I supposed to do?' says Henry.

The receptionist replies, 'The doctor recommends that you drop your wife off in the middle of Oxford Street. If she finds her way home, don't sleep with her.'

***

Shlomo goes to Dr Lewis for a check up. After extensive tests Dr Lewis tells him, 'I'm afraid I have some bad news for you. You only have six months to live.'

Shlomo is dumbstruck. After a while he replies, 'That's

terrible, doctor. But I must admit to you that I can't afford to pay your bill.'

'OK,' says Dr Lewis, 'I'll give you a year to live.'

***

Dr Jacobs finished his examination and informed Herman that he was in perfect health. 'But what about my headaches?' Herman moaned.

'I'm not at all worried about your headaches,' Dr Jacobs replied.

'If you had my headaches, doctor, I wouldn't worry about them either,' said Herman.

***

Lionel takes Freda to their doctor for a check-up. After the doctor finishes examining Freda, he takes Lionel aside and says, 'I don't like the look of your wife at all.'

'I don't either, doctor,' says Lionel, 'but she's really very good with the children and she's a great cook.'

***

At Hyman's recent medical check up, his doctor asked him a few questions. Here's how Hyman answered these questions:

Q. How do you feel?
A. How should I feel?

Q. What hurts you?
A. What doesn't hurt me?

Q. When do you feel bad?
A. When don't I feel bad?

Q. When did it start?
A. When will it end, better?

***

During the party, Beckie is introduced to Dr Selnick. 'Oh doctor,' says Beckie, sidling up to him, 'I'm so glad to meet you. You see I have this problem. Every time I raise my arm above my head, I get a pain in my right side.'

'I'm sorry,' says Dr Selnick, 'I'm afraid I can't help you. I happen to be a doctor of economics.'

'Well, in that case,' says Beckie, 'tell me, should I sell my Marks and Spencer shares now or next week?'

***

Bernard, an elderly Jew, is bumped by a car while crossing the street. He is seemingly unhurt, but Sarah, his wife, persuades him to go to the doctor, just in case.

Bernard returns home, and Sarah says, '*Nu, vos zogt der doktor?*' ['So? What did the doctor say?']

'*Der doktor zogt az ich hob a flucky.*' ['The doctor says I have a flucky.']

'*Oy Gevalt!* A flucky! Terrible. What do you do for a flucky?'

'I don't know – he didn't say and I forgot to ask.'

Well, by this time Sarah is in a state of high anxiety. She tells her neighbours, 'My Bernard was hit by a car, and now he has a flucky. I don't know what to do.'

Neighbour One says, 'In the old country, when someone had a flucky, we always applied cold. Cold is the best thing for a flucky.'

Neighbour Two says, 'What are you talking about? Cold is absolutely the worst thing you could do for a flucky. We always applied heat, that's the only thing to do for a flucky.'

Cold, heat! *Oy*! Now thoroughly agitated, Sarah decides to call the doctor herself.

'Doctor, please tell me, what's wrong with my husband?'

'I told him – nothing's wrong. He got off lucky.'

***

'You're in great shape,' says the doctor. 'You're going to live to be seventy.'

'But I am seventy,' Issy replies.

'*Nu*,' says the doctor, 'did I lie?'

* * *

Doctor to patient, 'I have good news and bad news. The good news is that you're not a hypochondriac.'

* * *

Max Levy goes to his doctor complaining of aches and pains all over his body. After a thorough examination, the doctor gives him a clean bill of health. 'Max, you're in excellent shape for an 85-year-old man. But I'm not a magician – I can't make you any younger,' says the doctor.

'Who asked you to make me younger?' says Max. ' Just make sure I get older!'

* * *

Hetty was talking to her best friend Freda. 'You know, Freda,' said Hetty, 'Being a doctor these days isn't as great as it used to be. There are now many kinds of scientist around with much more prestige than doctors. It therefore follows that in future, many Jewish boys are going to become scientists instead of doctors.'

'I can't agree with you at all on this one,' replied Freda.

'Why on earth not?' said Hetty.

'Because, my dear Hetty,' replied Freda, 'it's much more difficult to say, 'My son, the nuclear physicist.'

* * *

Moshe went to see his doctor because he was suffering from a miserable cold that wouldn't clear up. His doctor prescribed him some pills, but they didn't help. On his next visit, the doctor gave Moshe an injection, but that didn't do any good, either. On his third visit, the doctor told Moshe to go home and take a hot bath. Then, as soon as he got out the bath, he must open all the windows and stand in the draught.

'But doctor,' protested Moshe, 'I'll get pneumonia.'

'I know,' said his doctor, 'I can cure pneumonia.'

***

Yenta had to call in the doctor to check her husband Lionel. He didn't seem to be at all well. After the doctor had examined Lionel, he said to Yenta, 'Your husband is very exhausted and fatigued and needs a lot of peace and quiet. If you want to help him recover, please take one tranquilliser, four times per day.'

***

Benjy goes to see his doctor because he isn't feeling too well. After examining him, the doctor takes some samples from Benjy and asks him to come back the following week for the results.

When Benjy returns, his doctor tells him, 'I have some good news and some bad news for you, Benjy. What do you want to hear first?'

Benjy replies, 'Let me have the good news first.'

'OK,' says the doctor, 'they're going to name the disease after you.'

***

Moshe goes to see his doctor and says, 'You must help me, doctor. Sadie isn't interested in sex anymore. Do you have something I can give her?'

'I'm not really allowed to prescribe - ' the doctor starts, but is interrupted.

'Doctor, can we talk off the record please? In all the years we've known each other, have you ever seen me like this? I'm desperate. I can't concentrate, my business is failing and I'm going to pieces. I beg of you – please help me.'

The doctor takes a bottle of pills from his cabinet and says, 'I really shouldn't do this. These pills are still experimental and the results so far indicate that they're very powerful. So please don't give Sadie any more than one at a time. I suggest you put it in her coffee. Do you understand, Moshe?'

'Yes. Thanks doctor.'

Later that evening, after dinner, when Sadie goes into the kitchen to fetch the dessert, Moshe drops one pill into Sadie's coffee, hesitates, and then drops in a second pill. But Moshe couldn't forget the doctor saying they were powerful. What should he do? In a flash of inspiration, he also drops a pill into his coffee. Sadie returns with some pudding, which they both enjoy with their coffee. Five minutes after they finish, Sadie takes a deep breath, sighs and starts to shake. A strange look comes over her and in a sexy tone of voice she says, '*Oy Vay*, Moshe, do I need a man right now.'

Moshe's hands are now trembling as he replies, 'Me too.'

***

Benny is nearly eighty years old and goes to his doctor for his yearly medical checkup. His wife Beckie comes along with him. As soon as they enter the doctor's office, the doctor says to Benny, 'I need a urine sample and a stool sample.'

Benny's hearing was not as good as it used to be, so he looks at Beckie and shouts, 'What did the doctor say he wanted?'

Beckie shouts back, 'He wants your underwear.'

***

Moshe is 75 years old and goes for a medical. After the examination, his doctor says to him, 'You're in remarkable shape for a man of your age.'

'I know it,' says Moshe, 'but I've got a problem. My sex drive is too high. Have you got anything you can give me for it?'

The doctor's mouth drops open. 'Your what?' he gasped.

'My sex drive,' repeats Moshe, 'is too high and I'd like you to lower it.'

'Lower it?' exclaims the doctor, still unable to believe what his 75-year-old patient is saying. 'Just what do you consider high?'

'These days it seems like it's all in my head, doctor,' replies Moshe, 'and I'd like to have you lower it a couple of feet if you can.'

***

Sam is recovering from a recent heart attack and goes to visit Dr Myers, his cardiologist. After a full check up, Dr Myers tells Sam that he will be able to resume his sex life as soon as he can climb two flights of stairs without getting out of breath.

Sam says, 'OK, but what if I only look for women who live on the ground floor?'

***

Jacob says to his doctor, 'Doctor, my wife needs an appendix operation.'

His doctor says, 'But I took out your wife's appendix only a year ago. I've never heard of a second appendix?'

Jacob replies, 'Maybe doctor, but have you ever heard of a second wife?'

***

Hyman recently had a full medical check up. When he returned three weeks later after the exhaustive lab tests were complete, his doctor said he was doing 'fairly well' for his age. Hyman was obviously a little concerned about that comment and so asked his doctor, 'Do you think I'll live to be eighty, doctor?'

He replied, 'Well, do you smoke or drink beer?'

'Oh no,' Hyman replied, 'I've never done either.'

Then the doctor asked, 'Do you eat grilled steaks or barbecued ribs?

Hyman replied, 'No, I've heard that red meat is very unhealthy.'

'Do you spend a lot of time in the sun, like playing golf?' asked the doctor.

'No I don't,' Hyman replied.

Then the doctor asked, 'Do you gamble, drive fast cars, or mess with women?'

'No,' said Hyman, 'I've done none of those things.'

The doctor looked at Hyman and said, 'Then why do you want to live to be eighty?'

***

Rivkah wakes up one morning and utters a loud '*Oy Vay*.' She has a nagging pain in her left shoulder. She immediately books an appointment with her doctor.

After examining her, her doctor says, 'Do you own a full length mink coat?'

'Yes, doctor, mine Hymie bought me one for our silver wedding.'

'Good,' he says, 'you must wear it for three weeks, then make an appointment to see me again.'

Rivkah returns after three weeks and says, 'Well, doctor, my shoulder has cleared, but I now have a pain in my left index finger.'

After examining her, he says, 'Do you own a three- or four-carat diamond ring?'

'Yes, doctor, mine Hymie bought me a four-carat ring to celebrate the birth of Moshe, our first grandson.'

'Good,' he says, 'you must wear it for three weeks, then make an appointment to see me again.'

Rivkah returns after three weeks and says, 'Well, doctor, my finger is OK but I'm now getting terrible headaches behind my eyes.'

After examining her, he says, 'Do you own a platinum and diamond tiara?'

'Yes, doctor, mine Hymie bought me one to wear under the chuppah at our Sarah's wedding.'

'Good,' he says, 'you must wear it for three weeks, then book to see me again.'

Rivkah returns after three weeks and says, 'Well, doctor, it's a miracle. My shoulder feels great, my finger feels great and I'm not getting any further headaches. Thank you very, very much. But I have one question to ask you.'

'What is it Rivkah?' asks her doctor.

'Doctor, how do you treat your non-Jewish patients?'

***

Shlomo has been suffering from severe headaches for years with no relief. After trying all the usual cures Shlomo is referred to a headache specialist. The specialist asks Shlomo about his symptoms and he replies, 'I get these blinding headaches; kind of like a knife across my scalp and - '

He is interrupted by the specialist, 'And a heavy throbbing right behind the left ear.'

'Yes, Exactly! How did you know?'

'Well, I am the world's greatest headache specialist, you know. But I myself suffered from that same type of headache for many years. It is caused by a tension in the scalp muscles. I'm OK now. This is how I cured it. Every day I would give my wife oral sex. When she came, she would squeeze her legs together with all her strength around my head and the pressure would relieve the tension in my head. Try that every day for two weeks and come back and let me know how it goes.'

Two weeks go by and Shlomo is back.

'Well, how do you feel?' the doctor asked.

'Doc, I'm a new man! I feel great! I haven't had a headache since I started this treatment! I can't thank you enough. And, by the way you have a lovely house.'

***

Joyce was with her doctor, Sam Ginsberg. Suddenly, she asked him, 'Will you kiss me?'

'Certainly not' Sam said. 'We must preserve a distance in this sort of relationship.'

'Well,' Joyce said, 'will you hold my hand?'

'Not even that,' Sam said. 'It's important we keep this on a non-emotional basis.'

'Will you tell me that you like me a lot?'

'Try to understand,' Sam told Joyce, 'I can't kiss you, I can't hold your hand, I can't even tell you that I like you. Goodness me, we shouldn't even be in bed together!'

***

Morris, 86 years old, walked into a crowded doctor's surgery. As he approached the desk, the receptionist said, 'Yes sir, how can we help you today?'

'There's something wrong with my penis,' Morris said aloud.

The receptionist was quite shocked at his reply and said, 'You shouldn't come into a crowded surgery and talk that way.'

'Why not?' said Morris. 'You asked me what was wrong and I told you.'

The receptionist replied, 'But you've caused some embarrassment – this room is full of people. You should have said there is something wrong with your ear or something and then discussed the real problem with the doctor in private.'

So Morris walked out, waited several minutes and came in again. The receptionist smiled and said, 'Yes sir, how can we help you today?'

'There's something wrong with my ear,' Morris replied.

The receptionist nodded approvingly and smiled, knowing Morris had taken her advice. 'And what is wrong with your ear, sir?'

'I can't pee out of it,' Morris replied.

***

Sadie went to see her doctor and when he asked her about her problem, she replied that she was suffering from a discharge. The doctor said, 'OK, Undress please and go lie down on the examination table.'

She did what he asked. The doctor put on his rubber gloves and began investigating her 'private parts'.

After a couple of minutes, he asked Sadie, 'How does that feel?'

'Wonderful,' replied Sadie, 'but the discharge is from my ear.'

Hospitals

Moshe was in hospital recovering from an operation when a nun walked into his room. She said she was there to cheer up the sick. They started talking and she soon asked about his life. Moshe talks about his wife, Freda and his eleven children.

'Well, well,' the nun says, 'Eleven children, a good and proper Catholic family. I'm sure that God is very, very proud of you.'

'I'm sorry,' says Moshe, 'I'm not Catholic, I'm Jewish.'

'Jewish!' she screams, 'You're a sex maniac!'

***

Ben is in a hospital ward with two non-Jews. On his first morning, Ben puts on his *tefillin*, but the non-Jews can't figure out what he is doing. Finally, one says to the other, 'Look how smart those Jews are! He's taking his own blood pressure.'

***

A woman telephoned the Middlesex Hospital. 'Hello, I'd like to talk to someone who can give me some up-to-date information about one of your patients.'

The operator said, 'Please hold while I find someone who can help.'

Soon, an authoritative voice said, 'I'm the hospital manager. Are you the lady who is asking about one of our patients?'

'Yes,' she replied, 'I'd like to know exactly how Rifka Levy in Room 23 is doing.' He replied, 'Levy, now let me see – Lewis, Levine, Levy – yes, I have Mrs Levy's details here. It says she is doing very well. She's eaten two full meals and her doctor says if she continues improving, he is going to release her on Tuesday. Is that the information you need?'

The woman said, 'Yes, it's wonderful news that she's going home on Tuesday. I'm so happy.'

The manager then asked, 'From your excitement, you must be one of Mrs Levy's close family.'

She said, 'What close family? I am Rifka Levy. My doctor won't tell me anything.'

* * *

Howard had been a good Jew all his life. Now, ninety years old, he was very ill and in hospital. His family were with him. Then his rabbi arrived. As the rabbi walked up to the bed, Howard's condition began to deteriorate and he motioned frantically for something to write on. When the rabbi gave him a pencil and a piece of paper, Howard used his last ounce of energy to write a short note. Then he died. The rabbi placed the note in his jacket pocket and said prayers. Later, at Howard's funeral, as the rabbi was finishing the eulogy, he suddenly remembered the note.

'I've just remembered,' said the rabbi to those present, 'that Howard handed me a note just before he died. I haven't looked at it yet, but knowing Howard, I'm sure there's a word of comfort in it for all of us.'

The rabbi opened the note and read, 'Help, you're standing on my oxygen tube!'

* * *

Rabbi Levy was running behind with his daily schedule because he had attended a number of unforeseen events. His next port of call was Mrs Gold. As soon as he arrived at the nursing home, the matron said, 'Rabbi, Mrs Gold has been waiting to see you all day. She was afraid you had forgotten all about her.'

The rabbi apologised, and went straight to Mrs Gold's room. He sat down in the chair next to her bed and after he had said a few words of encouragement to her, she began to talk about her day.

Whilst he was listening, he noticed a small bowl of peanuts next to her, so he interrupted and asked her if she would mind if he took a few of the peanuts.

'No, of course not,' she replied and continued talking at length about her day.

A few minutes later, Rabbi Levy interrupted her again and

said, 'Mrs Gold, I'm sorry but I've eaten almost all of your peanuts.'

Mrs Gold smiled at him and said, 'Don't worry about it Rabbi, I can't eat peanuts – I just like to nibble the chocolate off them.'

***

Recovering from major heart surgery, Moshe awoke to find the curtains in his private ward drawn. When his surgeon arrived, he immediately saw the perplexed look on Moshe's face. So he said, 'Please don't be alarmed, Moshe. There's a large fire in the garden right outside your window and we didn't want you to wake up and think the surgery was a failure.'

***

Abe was 75 years old and had a medical problem that needed complicated surgery. Because his son Jacob was a renowned surgeon, Abe insisted that Jacob perform the operation. On the day of his operation, as he lay on the operating table waiting for the anaesthetic, Abe asked to speak to his son.

'Yes dad, what is it?'

'Don't be nervous, Jacob, do your best and just remember, if it doesn't go well, if God forbid something should happen to me, your mother is going to come and live with you and your wife.'

***

Beckie was talking to her friend Sadie. 'Just remember, Sadie to be nice to your children.'

'Why is that?' replied Sadie.

'Because,' said Beckie, 'They'll be choosing your nursing home!'

***

Hyman is lying in bed in hospital with an oxygen mask over his face. A young nurse is sponging his chest. 'Nurse,' Hyman mumbles from behind his mask, 'Are my testicles black?'

Embarrassed, the nurse replies, 'I don't know, I'm only here to sponge you.'

Hyman struggles again to ask, 'Nurse, are my testicles black?'

Again the nurse replies, 'I can't tell. I'm only here to sponge you.'

Then the matron arrives and sees how distraught Hyman is getting.

'Matron,' Hyman mumbles, 'Are my testicles black?'

Matron whips back Hyman's blankets, pulls down his pyjama trousers, moves his penis out of the way, has a good look and announces, 'There's nothing wrong with your testicles.'

Hyman pulls off his oxygen mask and asks again, 'Are my test results back?'

***

Issy has just had a minor operation at a private hospital and is having a rest when a young, attractive and smartly dressed woman knocks on his door.

The door opens a bit and a woman's voice from within says, 'Yes, vat do you vant?'

'Hello,' says the young lady, 'I have come to see how Issy's doing after his operation.'

'He's doing vell, but he's asleep,' says the voice from within. 'Who are you?'

'Oh, I'm his – sister,' replies the young lady.

'How very nice. I am pleased to meet you. So for you, I vill wake him up.'

With that, she walks over to the bed, taps Issy on the shoulder and says, 'Issy, vake up. Vake up Issy, you *shyster*. Vhy you not tell me? I am your mama! Your *shiksa* – she's so much better than your wife?'

***

Rabbi Levy had to spend time in a Catholic hospital. He became friends with the sister who was a nurse there. One day, she came into his room and noticed that the crucifix on the wall was missing.

She asked him good-naturedly, 'Rabbi, what have you done with the crucifix?'

'Oh, sister,' chuckled Rabbi Levy, 'I just figured one suffering Jew in this room was enough.'

***

Irwin was just coming out of anaesthesia after a series of tests in the hospital, and his wife, Kitty, was sitting at his bedside. His eyes fluttered open, and he murmured, 'You're beautiful.'

Flattered, Kitty continued her vigil while he drifted back to sleep.

Later he woke up and said, 'You're cute.'

'What happened to "beautiful"?' Kitty asked Irwin.

'The drugs are wearing off,' he replied.

Health

Issy is walking down the High Street with his friend, Jacob, when he suddenly says, 'Did you know, Jacob, that I'm a walking economy.'

Jacob answers, 'What do you mean by that?'

'Well it's like this Jacob,' says Issy. 'My hair line is in recession, my stomach is a victim of inflation and the combination of these factors is putting me into a deep depression.'

***

Kitty and Harry, a middle-aged couple, are watching TV one evening when an evangelist comes on and promises to heal the sick. A voice on the TV says, 'If you would like to pray with him, place your right hand in the air and place your left hand on the afflicted area.'

So Harry places his right hand in the air and his left hand on his crotch.

When she sees Harry do this, Kitty says, 'Gee, honey. He said heal the sick, not raise the dead!'

***

One day, Moshe is walking past the wooden fence at the side of the local mental care home when he hears the residents inside chanting, 'Thirteen! Thirteen! Thirteen!'

Moshe is quite a curious kind of man and wonders whether a Bar Mitzvah is taking place. So he searches for a suitable hole in the fence and then he looks in. But immediately, someone inside pokes him in the eye with their finger.

Then the chanting begins again, 'Fourteen! Fourteen! Fourteen!'

***

Issy and Rabbi Samuel were sitting next to each other on the tube train one night. Issy was returning home after another wild leaving party in the City, where he worked, and Rabbi Samuel was going to the *yeshiva* to study. They often saw each other on the tube train and not for the first time, Issy smelled of beer, his shirt was stained, and his face was covered in lipstick. Issy unfolded his *Jewish Chronicle* and began to read. After a few minutes, he turned to the rabbi and asked, 'What causes arthritis, Rabbi?'

Rabbi Samuel replied, 'It's caused by loose living, being with cheap, uninhibited women, drinking too much alcohol and showing contempt for your fellow man.'

'Really?' replied Issy, 'It says here in my paper that the well-known Rabbi Jacobs has a very bad case of arthritis.'

***

Abe came home one day and found his wife Esther in tears.

'Darling, what's the matter?'

'Oh Abe,' cried Esther, 'Dr Cohen says I have tuberculosis.'

'What! A big healthy woman like you has tuberculosis? Ridiculous,' said Abe, 'I'll call Dr Cohen and get this sorted out right now.'

So Abe called his doctor. 'Doctor, Esther said you told her she has tuberculosis.'

The doctor said something to Abe and with that, Abe began laughing.

'So what's so funny about my having such a dreadful disease?' asked Esther.

'Esther, Dr Cohen didn't say "tuberculosis", he said "too big a *toches*".'

***

Max and Leah visit a plastic surgeon. When asked what they would like done, Max replies, 'It's her *toches*, doctor; her backside is getting so large that I can no longer get my hands around it.'

'So,' says the doctor, 'you would like me to perform a *toches* reduction?'

'No, no,' replies Max, 'I need a hand enlargement.'

***

Shlomo was talking to his friend Moshe, who had just moved to a house near him in Hampstead Garden Suburb. 'Why don't you join our local synagogue, Moshe?' asked Shlomo.

'Why should I?' replied Moshe?'

'So that your children will realise they're Jewish,' said Shlomo.

'But they already realise they're Jewish,' said Moshe. 'They have heartburn.'

***

'It's been a rough day. I got up this morning, put on a shirt and a button fell off. I picked up my briefcase and the handle came off. I'm afraid to go to the bathroom.' – Rodney Dangerfield

***

Shlomo and Moshe are out hunting in the woods of New Jersey when Moshe suddenly collapses. Shlomo rushes over to him but he doesn't seem to be breathing and his eyes are all glazed. Shlomo is in a panic. He takes out his phone, calls the emergency services and shouts, 'Help, please help me. My friend Moshe is dead! What on earth should I do?'

The operator tells Shlomo, 'Sir, please calm down. I can help you. First of all, let's make sure he's really dead.'

After a short silence, the operator hears a shot. Then Shlomo gets back on the phone, 'OK, now what?'

***

Morris decides to have a facelift for his birthday. He spends £5,000 at Bushey hospital and feels really good about the result. But would others see how good he looked? So he thought he would put this to the test. On his way home, he stops off at Brent Cross shopping centre. First of all, he goes into W. H. Smith, buys a newspaper and says to the girl behind the cash desk, 'I hope you don't mind me asking, but how old do you think I am?'

'About 35,' comes the reply.

'I'm actually 47,' Morris says, feeling really happy.

Then he goes into Fenwick's for lunch and asks the waitress the same question, to which the reply is, 'Oh you look about 29.'

'I am actually 47.' This makes him feel really good.

In the car park on the way out, Morris meets two elderly ladies and asks them the same question. One of them winks to the other and replies, 'I can't really tell. I am seventy years old and my eyesight is not as good as it used to be. But when I was younger, there was a sure way of telling a man's age. If you let me put my hand down your trousers for a few minutes, I will certainly be able to tell your exact age.'

As there is no one around, Morris thinks why not and lets her slip her hand down his trousers. Five minutes later, the lady says, 'OK, it's done. I've felt your penis all over and I now know that you are 47.'

Stunned, Morris says to her, 'That was brilliant. How did you do that?'

She replies, giggling, 'We were behind you in the Fenwick's restaurant.'

***

Moshe was moderately successful in his career, but as he got older he was increasingly hampered by appalling headaches. So he sought medical help. After being referred from one specialist to another, he finally came across a doctor who solved the problem.

'The good news is I can cure your headaches. The bad news is that it will require castration. You have a very rare condition that causes your testicles to press up against the base of your spine. The pressure creates one hell of a headache. The only way to relieve the pressure is to remove the testicles.'

Moshe was shocked and depressed. He wondered if he had anything to live for. However, he couldn't concentrate long enough to answer, so he decided he had no choice but to go under the knife. When he left the hospital, Moshe's head was clear for the first time for ages. As he was walking down Golders Green High Street, he realised that he could make a new beginning and live a new life. As he walked past a clothes shop, Moshe thought, 'That's what I need – a new suit.' He entered the shop and told the salesman, 'I'd like a new suit.'

The salesman eyed him briefly and said, 'Let's see, size 44 long.'

Moshe laughed, 'That's right, how did you know?'

'It's my job.'

Moshe tried on the suit. It fitted perfectly. As Moshe admired himself in the mirror, the salesman asked, 'How about a new shirt?'

Moshe thought for a moment and then said, 'Sure.'

The salesman eyed Moshe and said, 'Let's see, 34 sleeve and 16½ neck.'

Moshe was surprised, 'That's right, how did you know?'

'It's my job.'

Moshe tried on the shirt. It fitted perfectly. As Moshe adjusted the collar in the mirror, the salesman asked, 'How about new shoes?'

Moshe was on a roll and said, 'Sure!'

The salesman eyed Moshe's feet and said, 'Let's see, 9½ E fitting.'

Moshe was astonished, 'That's right, how did you know?'

'It's my job.'

Moshe tried on the shoes and they fitted perfectly. Moshe walked comfortably around the shop and the salesman asked, 'How about a new hat?'

Without hesitating, Moshe said, 'Sure.'

The salesman eyed Moshe's head and said, 'Let's see, 7⅝.'

Moshe was incredulous, 'That's right, how did you know?'

'It's my job.'

The hat fitted perfectly. Moshe was feeling great, when the salesman asked, 'How about some new underwear?'

Moshe thought for a second and said, 'Sure.'

The salesman stepped back, eyed Moshe's waist and said, 'Let's see, size 36.'

Moshe laughed, 'No, you're wrong this time. I've worn size 34 since I was eighteen years old.'

The salesman shook his head, 'You can't wear a size 34. It would press your testicles up against the base of your spine and give you one hell of a headache.'

***

Rifka suffered from terrible headaches, so she went to a doctor in Edgware who was excellent at curing headaches. The doctor listened to her and said, 'Don't worry. Here's what you do. When you feel a headache coming on, sit down for five minutes in a private place. Take deep breaths for one minute, massage the middle of your forehead for another minute and then finish by repeatedly saying aloud for three minutes, "I haven't got a headache, I haven't got a headache, I haven't got a headache". That's all there is to it.'

Later that week, Rifka soon had to follow the doctor's advice and surprisingly, her headache went. Over the months that followed, this method always worked for her. One morning, Rifka thought, 'If the doctor was able to help me with my headaches, maybe he could also sort out my Moshe's impotence problems – he was not much good to me last night.'

She discussed her idea with Moshe and to her surprise he agreed to see the doctor that very day. That night, as they got into bed, Rifka said, 'Let's make love Moshe,' and was pleasantly surprised to hear him say, 'OK, but first I'll need five minutes alone.' Moshe then disappeared into the bathroom and five minutes later came out, got back in bed and then – Well, Rifka couldn't believe it. Moshe was making love just like he did twenty-five years ago.

The same thing happened every night and Rifka couldn't believe how good Moshe now was in bed. But she soon began to wonder what he was doing in the bathroom to overcome his problem. So one night, she told Moshe she wanted to make love. As usual, he said, 'I need my five minutes first, though.'

This time, as soon as Moshe disappeared into the bathroom, Rifka went to the door and peeked inside. There was Moshe sitting on the edge of the bath massaging his forehead and murmuring, 'It's not my wife, it's not my wife - '

Psychiatry

Shlomo goes to see his psychiatrist. 'Doctor, my wife Fay is being unfaithful to me. Every night, she goes to Palwin's Wine Bar and picks up a man. She sleeps with anybody who asks her to. I'm going crazy with worry. What on earth should I do?'

'Relax,' says the doctor, 'take a couple of deep breaths and try to calm down. Now, first of all tell me exactly where Palwin's Wine Bar is.'

***

Issy was talking to his psychiatrist, 'I grew up to have my father's looks, my father's speech patterns, my father's posture, my father's opinions and my mother's contempt for my father.'

***

Freda Cohen is having a very troublesome time with her teenage son. They are always screaming at each other and sometimes even fighting. So Freda takes him to see a psychoanalyst. After several sessions, the doctor calls Freda into his office and tells her, 'Your son has an Oedipus complex.'

'Oedipus, Shmedipus,' answers Freda, 'As long as he loves his mother.'

* * *

Yenta went to see her doctor. 'Doctor, I need your help,' she said, 'I just can't help talking to myself.'

'Do you suffer any pain?' asked her doctor.

'No.'

'In that case,' said the doctor, 'go home and don't worry. Millions of people talk to themselves – It's nothing to worry about.'

'But doctor,' cried Yenta, 'you don't know what a boring person I am!'

* * *

Moshe is having a session with his psychiatrist. Dr Cohen draws a picture of a triangle and asks Moshe what it looks like to him. Moshe shows some excitement and says, 'It looks like a man and a woman in bed.'

'Hmmm,' says Dr Cohen, stroking his beard. He then draws another picture, this time of a square, and again asks Moshe what it looks like to him. Moshe gets more excited and says again, 'It looks like a man and a woman in bed.'

Again Dr Cohen says, 'Hmmm,' strokes his beard and then draws another picture, this one a circle. He asks Moshe what this looks like to him. Moshe is agitated and replies, 'It looks like a man and a woman having intercourse.'

Dr Cohen says, 'Young man, I think you have too much sex on your mind.'

Moshe replies, 'That's unfair – it's you who's drawing the dirty pictures.'

* * *

Sidney goes to see his psychiatrist. As soon as he lies down on the couch, he says, 'I needed to have this appointment because I'm sure I'm gay.'

Dr Myers says, 'And what, please tell me, makes you think you're gay?'

'Well,' says Sidney, 'my father Hershel was gay and so was my grandfather.'

'So what?' says Dr Myers. 'That doesn't make you gay as well. No one has proven that homosexuality is hereditary.'

'Well what if I told you that my two younger brothers are also gay?' says Sidney.

'Well that would be interesting,' says Dr Myers. 'Is there anyone else in your family whom you think is gay?'

'My cousin and uncle are,' replies Sidney.

'I must admit,' says Dr Myers, 'that I've never come across this before. Is there anyone in your family who has sex with women?'

'Yes,' replied Sidney, 'my sister.'

***

Cyril was eighty years old and was visiting his psychiatrist. 'Doctor, I'm suffering from a lot of anxiety. What's going to happen to me? I'm very worried about my future.'

'Cyril,' said the doctor, 'Don't worry, I can help you. All you need do is come and see me twice a week for the next three months. My charges will be £100 a visit and you'll need to pay in advance, of course.'

'OK, doctor,' said Cyril. 'Now that your future is assured, what about mine?'

***

Hyman is 25 and leads the most over-examined life you can imagine. Each day, he spends his time thinking about those he met that day, worrying about everything said to him, wondering about every look, gesture and expression made, and hoping he came across OK. Even when he goes to bed, he has to write at least two pages in his diary about his conclusions and how he will improve his actions the following day to make people like him more.

One day, Hyman goes to Max, one of his few friends, in a very agitated state. 'What's wrong?' asks Max.

'Well,' replies Hyman, 'my father and I never had much of a relationship whilst I was growing up. He's always ignored me and he's never encouraged me to succeed. I've been trying to get him to talk to me for some time now, but without success. Then last night, out of the blue, he rings me and invites me out to dinner. I was gobsmacked. I tried to work out – why now, why dinner, why - '

'But did you go?' says Max.

'Yes, but during dinner, I said the wrong thing. It was just a slip of the tongue really and I didn't mean it the way it sounded.'

'Well, so what did you say?' asks Max.

Hyman replies, 'I meant to say, "please pass the salt", but it came out as, "you miserable old sod, you've ruined my life".'

***

One day, Benny the psychiatrist was coming home from work on the Underground when he saw an elderly gentleman talking to himself and then laughing aloud. Every so often, the man would put up his hand, stop talking then start all over again. Benny had to find out more. 'Excuse me, I hope you don't mind me asking, but is there anything I can do to help?'

'Thank you but no. To keep myself awake, I tell myself jokes when I'm travelling.'

'But why do you keep raising your hand?' asked Benny.

'Oh, that's to stop me telling myself a joke I've heard before.'

***

Q: What is the definition of a psychiatrist?

A: A Jew who wanted to be a doctor, to make his mother happy, but faints at the sight of blood.

***

Benny the psychiatrist got a postcard one morning from one of his patients. It read, 'Having a wonderful time. Wish you were here so you could tell me why.'

***

Sadie took her husband Bernie to see a psychiatrist for a checkup. After examining him, the doctor took Sadie to one side and said, 'I have some very bad news for you. There is nothing I can do to help your husband. His mind has completely gone.'

'I'm not really surprised,' Sadie replied, 'Bernie's been giving me a piece of it every day for the last fifty years.'

***

One day, Moshe the psychiatrist takes a call from a woman asking for help. She has been having hallucinations and he makes an appointment to see her. When Moshe sees her for the first time, he is so smitten by her beauty that he says to her, 'Please undress and go and lie down on my couch. I'll be with you soon.'

As soon as she does what she was told, Moshe gets onto the couch and makes love to her. As he gets off the couch, Moshe says to her, 'Well that's my problems taken care of, now let's hear yours.'

Dentists & teeth

The dentist told Melvyn that he needed a tooth removed right away. The dentist asked, 'Do you want a local anaesthetic?'

Melvyn shook his head and said, 'Let's not pinch pennies, Doctor. Get the best – use imported.'

***

Hetty and Hannah hadn't seen each other for some time when they bumped into each other in Brent Cross shopping centre. 'So

Hetty, how is your grandson, the proctologist, doing?'

'My grandson is no longer a proctologist, Hannah. He decided to become a dentist instead.'

'A dentist! Why the change in career?'

'Business is business, Hannah,' replied Hetty, 'Let's face it, everyone starts off with 32 teeth but have you ever heard of anybody who has more than one *toches*?'

* * *

Hannah goes to visit her dentist. When Moshe finishes examining her teeth, he says, 'I'm sorry to have to tell you this, but you need root canal treatment to one of your molars.'

Hannah cries, '*Oy Vay iz meer!* I'd rather have a baby!'

Moshe replies, 'Well, let me know what you decide – I'll have to adjust the chair either way.'

* * *

After being married for over sixty years, Rivkah is filing for divorce against Cyril.

At the court hearing, the judge is very surprised that this seemingly nice elderly couple are experiencing marital problems. So he turns to Rivkah and asks, 'Why do you want a divorce?'

'Vell,' replies Rivkah, 'Mine husband is now not alvays very nice to me. And lately it has become unbearable.'

'So can you give me an example please?' asks the judge.

'Yes I can,' replies Rivkah, 'Ve both vear dentures and many times in the last six months, vhen I'm asleep at night, he steals mine to eat garlic.'

* * *

Moshe was eating in Solly's restaurant one day when he saw an elderly couple on another table. They had ordered one plate of salt beef and chips, one drink and one extra glass. As he watched, the old man carefully divided the salt beef into two portions, then counted the chips and divided them equally as well. Then he poured half the drink into the extra glass and put it in front of his wife. The old man then began to eat and his wife just sat there watching, her hands folded in her lap. Moshe had to ask them whether they would accept him buying them an extra meal so that they didn't have to split theirs.

The old man said, 'Oh, no, that's very kind. We've been married fifty years now, and everything has always been and will always be shared fifty-fifty.'

Moshe then asks the old lady why she wasn't eating. She replied, 'it's his turn with the teeth.'

***

Shlomo and Rifka had now been married for fifty years and that night, after the celebrations were over, they were in bed and in a pretty romantic mood. Rifka looked at Shlomo and said, 'I remember when you used to kiss me every chance you had.'

Shlomo felt a bit obliged, so he leaned over and gave her a gentle peck on the cheek.

Then Rifka said, 'I also remember, Shlomo, when you used to hold my hand at every opportunity.'

Again feeling obliged, Shlomo gently placed his hand on hers.

Then Rifka said, 'I also remember, Shlomo, when you used to nibble on my neck and send chills up and down my spine. It was lovely.'

This time, with a blank stare on his face, Shlomo got out of the bed and as he began to walk out of the bedroom, Rifka asked him, 'Was it something I said, Shlomo, where are you going?'

Shlomo looked at Rifka and replied, 'I'm going to the bathroom to get my teeth!'

***

Arnold and Isaac were residents in a nursing home. Even though they were best of friends, they were still prone to argue with each other. One day, they were queuing up at the canteen to get their lunch. Because Arnold was taking his time, Isaac said to him, 'Hey you! Hurry up already before I punch you in the teeth.'

Arnold turns round, looks at Isaac and says, 'OK. Go ahead. Make my day! My teeth are upstairs in the glass by my bed.'

* * *

When the air raid siren went off in Tel Aviv, Hannah rushed down the stairs towards the basement of their block of flats. Isaac was much slower so she stopped and shouted back up the stairs, 'Come on, Isaac, get moving will you?'

Isaac shouted down to her, 'Wait a minute, Hannah. I'm looking for my teeth.'

'Never mind your silly teeth, Isaac,' Hannah shouted back, 'what do you think they'll drop on us – smoked salmon bagels?'

Weight loss

One of life's mysteries is when a Jewish woman hangs something in her wardrobe for a while and it shrinks two sizes. Another of life's mysteries is how a two-pound box of chocolates can make a Jewish woman gain five pounds.

* * *

Q: Why are single Jewish women skinnier than married Jewish women?
A: Single women go to the fridge, see nothing nice and then go to bed. Married women go to bed, see nothing nice and then go to the fridge.

* * *

Issy is on another of his weight reduction diets and goes to see his doctor with a *hamishe* cucumber up his nose, a bagel shoved in his right ear and a wine glass sticking out of his left ear.

Issy says, 'Doctor, I'm not feeling very well.'

The doctor replies, 'It's no wonder – you're not eating right.'

* * *

Rachel was talking to her best friend Sadie. Rachel asked, 'So, Sadie, how's your daughter the bride?'

Sadie replied, 'To tell you the truth, Rachel, not good. She's so unhappy, she's lost two stone already.'

Rachel then asked, 'So why doesn't she leave him?'

Sadie replied, 'Because she wants to lose two and a half stone!'

***

David is visiting his parents for dinner one Friday night. Whilst she is getting the table ready, his mother asks him to get the olives from the fridge. He opens the fridge to look for the olives and notices that taped to the inside of the door is a risqué photo of a lovely, slender, perfectly built, but naked young woman. David asks, 'Mum, what's the photo for?'

She replies, 'Oh, I put that there to remind me not to eat too much.'

David then asks, 'So, is it working?'

'Yes and no,' she replies. 'I've lost fifteen pounds but your father has gained twenty pounds!'

Nudity

Ruth had just stepped out of the shower when she heard her doorbell ring.

'Who is it?' she shouted downstairs.

'It's the blind man,' came the reply.

Ruth decided it didn't matter if she opened the door without any clothes on because the man was blind. In fact she thought it would be a rather daring thing to do. So she opened the door wide and he said, 'It's John Lewis Department Store, Brent Cross. Where do you want me to put these blinds?'

***

One hot summer's day in Golders Green, Jack steps out of his shower and says to his wife, Hetty, 'It's just too hot to wear any clothes today, honey. What do you think the neighbours would say if I mowed the lawn without anything on?'

Hetty replies, 'That I married you for your money.'

* * *

Moshe was an elderly man and resided in a nursing home in Hendon. One day he went into the office and informed his nurse that his penis had died. Realising that Moshe was old and forgetful, she decided to play along with him. 'It did? I'm sorry to hear that, Moshe,' she replied.

Two days later, Moshe was walking down the hall at the nursing home with his penis hanging outside his pants. His nurse saw him and said, 'Moshe, I thought you told me your penis had died.'

'It has,' Moshe replied, 'today is the viewing.'

* * *

Little nine-year-old Ira was walking home from Grodzinski's Bakery with one hand in his pocket and carrying a huge *challah* with the other hand. As he strolled up the path to his house, his mother and their local rabbi came to meet him at the door.

The rabbi said to Ira, 'Hello Ira! How are you today? What do you have there, the staff of life?'

To which Ira replied, 'Yeah, and a loaf of bread, too!'

* * *

An Israeli girl marries an Englishman and they decide to live in London. Although she cannot speak much English, she manages to communicate with her husband. However, problems always arise whenever she goes out shopping. One day, she goes to the butchers to buy some chicken legs, but she doesn't know how to ask for them. In desperation, she lifts up her skirt and shows him her thighs. The butcher gets the message and she leaves with chicken legs.

The next day she needs some chicken breasts. Again, she can't describe in words what she needs to buy, so she unbuttons her blouse and shows the butcher her breasts. Again, she gets what she wants.

On the third day she goes out to buy some sausages. She brings her husband to the butcher shop and – so what does she do?

What were you thinking? Her husband speaks English.

***

Beckie, Rifka and Estelle are passing by the half-open door to the men's changing rooms at the Mazeltov Golf Club when they can't help noticing a man with his face obscured by the towel he is using to dry his hair. However, they do get quite a good view of his nakedness from his waist down.

Later, Beckie says, 'Well, I didn't see his face, but he's certainly not my husband!'

Rifka says, 'And he isn't mine, either!'

Estelle says, 'Hell, he isn't even a member of the club!'

***

Moshe had always wanted a pair of alligator shoes but had never been able to afford them. One day he sees a pair in the Selfridges Sale priced at only £39.99. He can't believe it. They even have his size. So he buys them and proudly wears them to go home. When he gets home, he stands in front of his wife and says, 'Sadie, do you notice anything different about me?'

She looks him up and down and says, 'Moshe, you look the same to me. You're wearing the same shirt you wore yesterday and the same trousers. So you tell me, what's different?'

But Moshe won't give up easily. He goes into the bedroom, undresses and comes out completely naked, other than his new shoes. Once again he stands in front of Sadie and says, 'Sadie, now do you notice anything different about me?'

Once again she looks him up and down, then says, 'Moshe,

it looks the same to me. It's hanging down just as it was hanging down yesterday. No doubt it will be still hanging down tomorrow.'

Angrily, Moshe says, 'Do you know why it's hanging down, Sadie? It's hanging down because it's looking directly at my new shoes.'

Sadie replies, 'Moshe, I wish you had bought a new hat.'

* * *

Abe is an old Jewish guy who sells cloth. He lives next door to Smith, the biggest anti-Semite in town. One day Smith calls on Abe and says, 'Hey Jew!!! I need a piece of orange cloth. Its length must be from the tip of your nose to the tip of your penis, and I want it delivered tomorrow.'

Abe says, 'OK.'

The next morning Smith is awakened at seven a.m. by the sound of running engines. He runs outside to see a row of lorries lined up one after the other dumping loads and loads of orange cloth in his front garden. Soon his garden is five feet deep in orange cloth. Abe then presents Smith with a bill for £15,000.

Smith starts yelling and screaming at Abe. 'What is this, Jew? This is not what I asked for. I told you I needed a piece of cloth from the end of your nose to the tip of your penis. Look at this place. What do you have to say for yourself?'

With a straight face, Abe replies, 'I'm very careful when I deal with people like you. That's why I've got a few witnesses here with me. I may be off by a few miles, so I gave you a five per cent discount; but – the tip of my penis was left in Poland after my circumcision.'

* * *

Once again, Moshe and Sarah are having an argument. Moshe says to Sarah, 'I don't know why you bother to wear a bra – you've obviously got nothing to put in it.'

Sarah replies, 'So you can talk – you wear pants don't you?'

* * *

Shlomo is in his house, standing near an open window. He is obviously wearing nothing but a tie around his neck. Jacob is walking past the house, sees Shlomo and asks, 'Why are you standing there all naked?'

'Why can't I be naked?' replies Shlomo, 'this is mine house. There is no one else here.'

'But why are you wearing a tie?' asks Jacob.

'Well,' replies Shlomo, 'what if someone drops in to visit me?'

***

Sadie, an elderly Jewish lady, is leaving the Garment District to go home from work. Suddenly a man who has been walking towards her stands in front of her, blocks her path, opens up his raincoat and flashes his wares in all their sordid glory. Unruffled, Sadie takes a look and remarks, 'This you call a lining?'

***

Sarah had been married six times and divorced six times. There was something wrong with every one of her ex-husbands, so she put an advert in the *Jewish Chronicle* that said she needed a man who would not beat her, who would not run away from her and who was good in bed. Two weeks later, Sarah was quietly reading a book when she heard her doorbell ring. She opens the door and there is a guy with no arms or legs.

'Hello, how may I help you?' she said.

'Hi, I'm Bernard, and I'm here about your advert in the *JC*.'

'How do I know you meet my requirements?' Sarah said.

'Well, I can't beat you because I have no arms, and I can't run away from you because I have no legs.' he replied.

'But how do I know you're good in bed?' she asks.

Bernard replies, 'How do you think I rang the doorbell?'

***

Did you hear about the Jewish flasher who was thinking about retiring?

He decided to stick it out for one more year.

***

Moshe, tired of his wife Hetty asking him how she looks, buys her a full-length mirror. This does little to help, as now Hetty just stands in front of the mirror, looking at herself, asking him how she looks. One day, fresh out of the shower, Hetty is yet again in front of the mirror, now complaining that her breasts are too small.

Uncharacteristically, Moshe comes up with a suggestion. 'If you want your breasts to grow, then every day take a piece of toilet paper and rub it between your breasts for a few seconds.'

Willing to try anything, Hetty fetches a piece of toilet paper, and stands in front of the mirror, rubbing it between her breasts. 'How long will this take?' Hetty asks.

'They'll grow larger over a period of years,' Moshe replies.

Hetty stops. 'Why do you think rubbing a piece of toilet paper between my breasts every day will make my breasts grow over the years?' she asks.

Moshe shrugs. 'It worked for your *toches*, didn't it?'

Bodily functions

Bernie was almost ninety years old and found it difficult to keep his balance. After his latest fall, his daughter thought it was now time for her dad to have a full-time nurse looking after him. Freda duly arrived and on her first night, Bernie was, as usual, sitting on his plastic-covered couch watching TV. All of a sudden, he started to lean over to the right. Freda quickly pulled him upright. Then Bernie started slowly to lean over to the left and Freda once again rushed over and straightened him up. This rigmarole went on for some time. Later that evening, the telephone rang. Bernie picked it up.

'Hello Dad, it's me, Hetty,' said his daughter. 'Is the new

nurse doing her job properly?'

'Oh Hetty, I'm so glad you rang. You must get over here as soon as you can,' Bernie answered.

Hetty replied, 'Why, Dad, whatever's wrong?'

Bernie then whispered into the phone, 'The tyrant won't let me fart.'

***

Maurice is seventy years old and makes an appointment to see his doctor. His doctor asks him a few questions.

'Mr Levy, what about urination? Do you have any problems?'

Maurice replies, 'No, Doctor, it's very regular, every morning at precisely 7 a.m.'

'And what about your bowel movements?'

Maurice replies, 'They're fine also, Doctor, every morning at precisely 8 a.m.'

The doctor asks, 'So then why did you come to see me, Mr Levy?'

Maurice replies, '*Oy*, doctor, I don't wake up before 10 a.m.'

***

Abe, David and Bernard are not only the best of friends but also the top doctors in the neighbourhood. One day, they are out walking in Golders Green when they see this little old Jewish man walking rather strangely. He is hunched over on one side, dragging his right leg, and he has his left hand on his lower back.

Abe says, 'It's peritonitis.'

David says, 'It's an orthopaedic problem, with flat arches and a touch of chondromalacia patellae.'

Bernard says, 'It's a nerve irritation at the level of L5.'

They argue a bit and then decide to go over and ask the old man what his problem is. So they do just that.

The man replies, 'You're all wrong. I thought I was about to fart when I made in my pants instead.'

***

Esther goes to her doctor because she hasn't been 'regular' for some time. The doctor examines her, finds nothing unusual and attributes her problem to her diet. He recommends she take a laxative.

'Don't forget I keep kosher,' she says, 'whatever you prescribe must be kosher.'

'I want you to take Serutan,' says the doctor, 'and don't worry, it's kosher.'

'You're sure, Doctor?' says Esther, 'you're absolutely positive it's kosher? If it's not kosher I can't take it and I'd be very mad if I were to find out it wasn't kosher.'

'Of course it's kosher. Serutan spelled backwards is natures and what could be more kosher than nature?' replies the doctor.

Two weeks later, Esther comes storming back.

'Doctor,' she shouts, 'I'm so angry with you that I'm going to sue you.'

'What's wrong?' the doctor asks, very concerned.

'That medicine you told me to take – it's not kosher,' replies Esther.

'Of course it's kosher,' replies the doctor. 'It's called Serutan, and as I told you, serutan spelled backwards is natures.'

'Well, doctor,' Esther says, 'Serutan spelled backwards may be natures, but taking Serutan gave me such gas! And fart spelled backwards is *traf*.'

***

SEXUAL JOKES

Affairs

Sadie was in her garden hanging up her washing when Sharon, her next door neighbour, poked her head over the fence and said, 'I don't like being the one to have to tell you this Sadie, but there's a rumour going around that your husband Cyril is chasing the *shiksas*.'

'So what?' said Sadie.

'But at his age!' said Sharon, 'He's over seventy isn't he?'

'*Nu*, so he's 72, so what?' replied Sadie, 'Let him chase girls. Dogs chase cars, but when they catch one, can they drive it?'

***

Moshe tells Abe one day, 'I'm having an affair with a married woman called Freda.'

Abe replies, '*Mazeltov*. I've been in the same situation myself so I'm in a good position to give you a piece of valuable advice.'

So tell me this advice, already,' says Moshe.

'Well,' replies Abe, 'You must keep your affair a secret under pain of death. Only you, Freda and every one of her best friends must know.'

***

Abe says to Moshe, 'Another strange thing about having affairs with older women is that within minutes of you making love to them, they feel this compulsion to phone their daughter.'

***

Gary was poking through his wife Suzy's bureau one day when he came across two golf balls and £5,000 in cash. He just didn't know what to make of these, so he confronted Suzy with this evidence. 'You don't even play golf!'

'I know dear,' Suzy said, 'we've had some difficult times during our marriage and – well – there were other men. Each time I was unfaithful to you, I put a golf ball in that drawer to remind me of my error.'

'I see,' replied Gary, 'that explains the two golf balls. What about the £5,000?'

'Oh,' smiles Suzy, 'every time I collected a dozen golf balls, I sold them.'

***

Moshe and Bernie are walking down Regent's Street when Moshe suddenly says to Bernie, 'Don't look! Don't look! Here comes my wife and my mistress.'

Bernie sneaks a peak and says, 'What a coincidence, I was going to say the same thing!'

***

Morris was manager of a local estate agents. One day, he hired a new secretary. She was so good-looking and sexy that he decided he just had to try and go out with her, even though this meant he would be doing it behind his wife's back. He was very surprised how successful he was in his new 'venture'.

But within a few weeks, he was feeling very unhappy at the way she was working during the day. Her attitude was one of not caring, being rude to clients and coming in to work late. After two more weeks, Morris couldn't let her behaviour continue and he asked her to come into his office for a little chat.

'Listen, Marlene, we may have gone to bed together a few times, but who told you that you could start coming into work late and slacking off?'

Marlene replied, 'My solicitor.'

***

Sam, Abe and Moshe are waiting in line to get into Heaven. When Sam gets to the front of the queue, the Angel Gabriel says, 'Heaven is nearly full today and I can only admit those who have had horrible deaths. What's your story?'

'I suspected my wife was cheating on me,' says Sam, 'so I came home early to try to catch her red-handed. I knew something was wrong as soon as I entered my flat, but I couldn't find where the other man was hiding. However, when I went out onto my balcony, there was this man hanging onto my railings. I was furious and started kicking him but he held on so I got a hammer and battered his fingers. He couldn't take that and had to let go. He fell twenty storeys but he somehow landed in some thick bushes and only stunned himself so I ran into my kitchen, grabbed the fridge and threw it over the balcony. My aim was perfect – it landed right on top of him, killing him instantly. Unfortunately, all the raw anger got to me. I had a massive heart attack and died on my balcony.'

'That sounds quite bad to me,' says the Angel Gabriel and lets Sam in. He then explains to Abe about Heaven being full and asks for his story.

'It's been a very unusual day for me. I live on the 21st floor of a Docklands tower block and every morning I do exercises on my balcony. Unfortunately, this morning I slipped on the wet floor and fell over the edge. Luckily, I managed to grab the railing of the balcony below mine. All of a sudden, a man burst out on to the balcony and just for a moment I thought I was saved. But he was a madman and started beating me. I somehow held on but when he started hammering at my hands, I had to let go. But I got lucky and fell into the bushes below, winded but OK. But my luck ran out when a fridge fell on me. Now I'm here.'

Once again, Angel Gabriel agrees that that sounds like a pretty horrible death. Moshe comes to the front of the line and again the whole process is repeated. Angel Gabriel explains that Heaven was full and asks for his story.

'Picture this,' says Moshe, 'I'm hiding naked inside a refrigerator - '

***

Melvyn was a very likeable person and his quick wittedness had served him well in business – he was now a financial director in the City. One day his wife Rebecca was shopping close by his office and decided to pay him a surprise visit. But when she got there and opened his door, she was shocked to find him sitting at his desk with his secretary on his lap. Melvyn looked up at her and without hesitating dictated:

'And in conclusion, gentlemen, whether we have budget cuts or not, there is absolutely no way I can continue to run my office effectively with just one desk and chair.'

* * *

Benjamin returned home early from an overseas business trip and quietly let himself into his house. He crept upstairs – and found his wife in bed with a strange man. The stranger was sprawled naked on top of the sheets and was looking very pleased with himself. 'Rifka, how could you do this to me?' Benjamin shouted.

'Wait, darling,' said Rifka. 'You know that soft blue leather jacket I've been wearing recently? Well this is the kind man who gave it to me. And that pearl and diamond gold necklace you always like me wearing? Well this is the generous man who gave it to me. And do you remember when you couldn't afford to buy me my own car and I came home with an Audi? Well this is the caring man who gave it to me.'

Benjamin thought about this for a few moments, looked again at the scene before him and then said, 'For goodness' sake, Rifka, don't you know it's freezing in here. Cover him up at once. We don't want him to catch a cold.'

* * *

Maurice and his wife Sadie were asleep one night when suddenly, at 2 a.m., the phone rang. Sadie picked it up. She listened to the caller then said, 'How the hell should I know? It's 95 miles away.' She then hung up.

Maurice asked, 'Who was that?'

Sadie replied, 'Some mad woman wanting to know if the coast was clear.'

***

Two Japanese businessmen are taking their afternoon dip in the hot baths at the Geisha House. The first businessman says, 'Hiroko-san, I have some unpleasant news for you. Your wife is dishonouring you.'

Hiroko-san can't believe what he hears, and asks for more information.

'Your wife is dishonouring you and she's doing it with a foreigner of the Jewish faith.'

Shocked, Hiroko-san goes home and confronts his wife. 'I'm told that you're dishonouring me with a foreigner of the Jewish faith.'

She replied, 'That's a lie. Where did you hear such a *mishegass*?'

***

Moshe was recovering in hospital from prostate surgery. To make matters worse, his surgeon had told him that it would be six weeks before he could be sexually active again. Peter visited him to wish him well. Robert visited him to wish him a speedy recovery. His partner Abe visited his wife.

***

Three friends are at the bar talking, and after many rounds of beer, one of them suggests that everyone admit something they have never admitted to anyone.

OK,' says Peter, 'I've never told anybody I'm gay!'

John confesses, 'I'm having an affair with my boss's wife.'

Moshe, begins, 'I don't know how to tell you - '

'Don't be shy,' say Peter and John.

Well,' says Moshe, 'I can't keep secrets.'

***

Hymie enters a Catholic church and confronts the priest. 'I am 93 years old. My wife is 91. We have been happily married for 64 years. Last week I had crazy, joyous sex with a 27-year-old super-model.'

The priest is aghast. 'Why don't you go to confession, old man?'

Hymie replies, 'Why should a Jewish man such as myself go to confession?'

The priest is confused. 'If you're Jewish, why then are you telling me this story?'

Hymie replies, 'I'm telling everyone!'

* * *

Morris and Beckie are chatting one evening. Morris says, 'Beckie, it's our fiftieth wedding anniversary soon, so tell me, have you ever been unfaithful to me?'

Beckie hesitates for a moment, then says, 'Yes, darling, three times.'

'Three times? How did this happen?' Morris asks her.

'Well, Morris, You remember you lost your job a year after we got married and we had no money and we thought we might have to sell our house? Do you also remember that I went to see the bank manager to ask for an overdraft? Well, we got our overdraft and that's when it happened.'

'It's hard to accept,' Morris says, 'but as you did this for us, I can forgive you.'

Beckie continues, 'And you remember years later when you almost died from your heart problem because we couldn't afford the operation? Remember that immediately after I went to see the surgeon at his house, he did your operation for nothing? Well, that's when it happened.'

'Yes,' Morris said, 'that shocks me too, but as you did it because you loved me, I forgive you. But tell me, Beckie, what was the third time?'

Beckie responds, 'Do you remember, Morris, when you were trying to get elected as the synagogue Chairman – and you needed just twelve more votes?'

* * *

Benny comes home early from work and hears strange noises coming from his bedroom. He rushes upstairs to find his wife, Sarah, naked on the bed, sweating and panting. 'What's up?' he says. 'I'm having a heart attack,' cries Sarah.

Benny rushes downstairs to grab the phone, but just as he's dialling, his four-year-old son comes up and says, 'Daddy! Daddy! Uncle Maurice is hiding in your wardrobe and he's got no clothes on!'

Benny slams the phone down and storms upstairs into the bedroom, past his screaming wife, and rips open the wardrobe door. Sure enough, there is his brother Maurice, totally naked, cowering on the wardrobe floor. 'You bonehead!' says Benny, 'Sarah's having a heart attack and you're running around with no clothes on scaring the kids!'

Birth control

Cyril was talking to his friend Hymie. 'Do you know that women can sometimes be very silly?'

'You're telling me,' replied Hymie, 'My friend Yetta has been confusing her Valium pills with her birth control pills for years. As a result, she has had ten children but she doesn't really care.'

***

'I've had it with my wife,' said Moshe to his friend Sam. 'I'm filing for divorce.'

'Sorry to hear that Moshe,' said Sam. 'May I ask why?'

'I found her supply of birth control pills,' said Moshe.

'So what, Moshe? How can you leave her just for that? My wife also has her supply of pills.'

'It's not just that,' said Moshe. 'I had a vasectomy over five years ago.'

***

Moshe, 85 years old and recently arrived in the UK from Russia, is walking down Golders Green Road one day when he sees his cousin Max coming towards him. Max is smoking a cigarette in a cigarette-holder. As Moshe had never seen such a thing before, he asks, 'Vass iss duss, Max?'

'Dots a protector, Moshe,' replies Max. 'It protects mine clothing from di eshes and mine beard from di flame.'

Moshe says, 'I gotta hev one a dem, too. Where you geddit?'

Max replies, 'I got it from a chemist.'

So Moshe shuffles down the road till he comes to a chemist. He goes up to the assistant and says, 'So gimme a protector.'

The assistant looks at the little wizened old man and decides to have some fun with him. 'So what size do you want, mister?'

Moshe shrugs his shoulders and replies, 'Size? It should fit a Camel.'

***

Abe walks into a chemist and asks for some condoms.

'Yes sir, do you want the Catholic pack, the Protestant pack or the Jewish pack?'

Abe asks, 'What's the difference?'

The chemist replies, 'The Catholic pack has six, one for each day of the week but never on Sunday. The Protestant pack has eight, one for each day of the week and twice on Sunday. And of course the Jewish pack has twelve.'

'Why twelve?' asks Abe.

The chemist sighs and counts on his fingers, 'January, February, March - '

***

Barry telephoned his doctor and began shouting hysterically down the line. 'Help me, Doctor. What can I do? My five-year-old son David has just swallowed a condom.'

'Don't worry, I'll be right over.'

Just as the doctor was leaving the office, the phone rang. It was Barry again. He said, 'Don't worry, Doctor, I found another one.'

***

Little Yitzhak and Rivkah are only ten years old and think they are in love. So they decide to get married. Yitzhak bravely goes to Rivkah's father and says, 'Mr Levy, me and Rivkah are in love and I want to ask you for her hand in marriage.'

Keeping a serious face, Mr Levy replies, 'Well Yitzhak, you are ten, I believe. Where will you both live?'

Yitzhak replies, 'In Rivkah's room. It's bigger than mine so we can both fit nicely.'

Still trying not to smile, Mr Levy says, 'OK then, where will you get enough money to support Rivkah? You're not old enough to get a job.'

Yitzhak replies, 'Rivkah gets £8 a week pocket money and I get £7.50 a week pocket money. That's over £65 a month and that should be enough.'

Mr Levy is surprised that Yitzhak has put so much thinking into the marriage, so he tries to come up with something that Yitzhak won't be able to answer. He says, 'Well Yitzhak, it seems like you've got everything worked out. I have just one more question for you. What will you do if you should have little ones of your own?'

Yitzhak shrugs his shoulders and replies, 'Well, we've been lucky so far.'

Brothels & prostitutes

David and his friend Paul were talking. David says, 'You and I use the same call-girl and I've discovered she is charging you, an accountant, twice as much as she charges me. Aren't you angry?'

'No,' replies Paul, 'I use the double entry system.'

***

Moshe, an elderly man, goes to a brothel and tells the madam that he would like a beautiful, young lady for the night. The madam gives him a quick look-over and is rather puzzled. So she asks him, 'How old are you?'

'Why,' replies Moshe, 'I'm ninety-eight years old today.'

'Ninety-eight!' the madam exclaims. 'Don't you realise you've had it?'

'Oh,' he says, 'in that case, how much do I owe you?'

* * *

Deborah had left home to go to London to work as a secretary. Soon after, she began regularly sending money to her parents, Moshe and Sadie. Some years later, Sadie asked Deborah to come home for a visit, as her father was getting frail. Deborah said she would come to see them that weekend. You can imagine Moshe and Sadie's surprise when Deborah pulled up outside their house in a Rolls Royce and stepped out wearing fur and diamonds.

As she walked into the house, Moshe muttered aloud, 'It seems that London secretaries get well paid.'

Deborah walked over to him, took his hands and said, 'Daddy – I've been meaning to tell you something for years but I just didn't want to put it in a letter. I can't hide it from you any longer. I've become a prostitute.'

Moshe gasped, put his hand over his heart and fell to the floor. The doctor was called immediately but could not help – Moshe had clearly lost the will to live. He was put to bed and the rabbi was called. As the rabbi was comforting Sadie and Deborah, Moshe muttered weakly, 'What a way to go – murdered by my own daughter, killed by the shame of what you've become!'

'Daddy, please, please forgive me,' Deborah sobbed. 'I wanted to have nice things to wear and to have enough money to be able to send you some. The only way I could think of doing that was to become a prostitute.'

On hearing this, Moshe sat bolt upright in bed, looking already so much better. Smiling he said, 'Deborah, did you say prostitute? I thought you said "Protestant".'

* * *

Daniel and Hetty are out shopping in London when they come across a smart clothes shop. Hetty goes in. While Daniel is waiting outside, a prostitute comes up to him and says, 'Would you like to come back to my place?'

Being a bit of a joker, Daniel decides to string her along. He replies, 'How much do you charge?'

'One hundred pounds,' she says.

'I'll give you £10,' Daniel says with a wink.

She gives him the V sign and walks away.

Hetty comes out of the shop and they continue their shopping expedition. But then they pass the prostitute on the corner of the road. She takes one look at Hetty and says to Daniel, 'You see? You see what you get for £10?'

***

The madam opened the brothel door to see Hyman, an elderly man, standing there. His clothes were all dishevelled and he looked needy.

'Can I help you?' the madam asked.

'I want Natalie,' Hyman replied.

'Sir, Natalie is one of our most expensive ladies, perhaps someone else - '

'No, I must see Natalie.'

Just then Natalie appeared and announced to Hyman that she charges £1,000 per visit. Hyman never blinked and reached into his pocket and handed her ten £100 notes. The two went up to a room for an hour, whereupon Hyman calmly left. The next night he appeared again at the door of the brothel, demanding Natalie. She came down and explained to him that no one had ever come back two nights in a row and that there were no discounts – it was still £1,000. Again Hyman took out the money, the two went up to the room and he calmly left an hour later. When he showed up the third consecutive night, no one could believe it. Again he handed Natalie the money and up to the room they went.

At the end of the hour Natalie questioned the old man, 'No one has ever used my services three nights in a row – where are you from?'

Hyman replied, 'I'm from Minsk.'

'Really?' replied Natalie, 'I have a sister who lives there.'

'Yes, I know,' said Hyman. 'She gave me £3,000 to give to you.'

***

Whilst walking to the Brent Cross shopping centre, Moshe passes by an old people's home. Sitting on deckchairs outside the front door of the home are six old ladies and they are as naked as the day they were born. Moshe thinks this is a bit unusual, but continues on his way to the shops. On his return, he passes the same old people's home with the same six old ladies sitting naked on deckchairs. This time Moshe's curiosity gets the better of him and he goes inside to talk to the manager.

'Do you know there are six ladies sitting naked on deckchairs outside your front door?'

'Yes I do,' says the manager, 'they're retired prostitutes and they're having a garage sale.'

Lovemaking

One day, God and Adam were walking in the Garden of Eden. God told Adam that it was time to populate the world. 'Adam,' he said, 'you can start by kissing Eve.'

'What's a kiss?' asked Adam.

God explained and then Adam took Eve behind a bush and kissed her. Adam returned with a big smile on his face and said, 'Lord, that was great! What's next?'

'Now you must caress Eve.'

'What's caress?' asked Adam.

God explained and then Adam took Eve behind a bush and lovingly caressed her. Adam returned with a bigger smile and said, 'Lord, that was even better than a kiss! What's next?'

'Here is what gets the deed done. Now I want you to make love to Eve.'

'What is make love?' asked Adam.

God explained and then Adam took Eve behind the bush. A few seconds later, Adam returned and asked, 'Lord, what is a headache?'

***

A priest, a minister and a rabbi are talking about whether sex is work, God's work, or pleasure.

The priest says, 'It is God's work – to procreate and produce more creatures in his image.'

The minister says, 'It is a pleasure that God gave us, so that we could be fruitful and multiply.'

The rabbi says 'I'm not really sure, but I do know that if it is work my wife would hire someone to come in and do it for her.'

***

'A girl phoned me the other day and said, "Come on over, there's nobody home." I went right over – and nobody was home!'

'During sex, my girlfriend always wants to talk to me. Just the other night she called me from a hotel!'

'One day, as I came home early from work, I saw a guy jogging naked. I asked him, "Hey buddy, why are you doing that?" He said, "Because you came home early."' – Rodney Dangerfield

***

One day, whilst Hetty was out shopping in Brent Cross, she noticed an old lady sitting on a bench sobbing her eyes out. Hetty stopped and asked her what was wrong. The old lady said, 'I have a 22-year-old husband at home. He makes love to me every morning and then gets up and makes me pancakes, sausage, fresh fruit and freshly ground coffee.'

Hetty said, 'Well, then why are you crying?'

The old lady continued, 'He makes me homemade soup for

lunch and my favourite cake and then makes love to me for half the afternoon.'

Hetty asked again, 'Well, why are you crying?'

The old lady continued, 'For dinner he makes me a gourmet meal with wine and my favourite dessert and then makes love to me until two o'clock in the morning.

Hetty asked yet again, 'Well, why in the world would you be crying?'

The old lady replied, 'I can't remember where I live!'

* * *

Moshe had been married four times. He was now approaching eighty years old and went to see his doctor. When he was shown in to see the doctor, he said, 'Doctor, I have to let you know that I am soon to get married for a fifth time – to an eighteen-year-old girl.'

His doctor replied, 'This could be fatal, you know.'

Moshe replied, 'Well, if she dies, then she dies.'

* * *

Moshe again visits his doctor. 'Doctor, I think I'm going impotent.'

His doctor says, 'Oh, and when did you first notice this?'

Moshe replies, 'Last night and again this morning.'

* * *

Benny was in conversation with his friend Victor. 'So Victor, how's your sex life?'

'Oh, nothing special,' replied Victor, 'I'm having Social Security Sex.'

'Social Security Sex?' said Benny, 'What's that?'

'You know, Benny, you get a little each month, but not enough to live on.'

* * *

Moshe was eighty years old and his family decided he needed a full medical check-up. The doctor listened to his heart and then said, 'Uh uh!'

Moshe did not like what he had heard and asked the doctor what the problem was.

'Well,' said the doctor, 'I can quite clearly hear a serious heart murmur. Do you drink?'

'No,' replied Moshe.

'Do you smoke?'

'No.' replied Moshe.

'Well then, do you have a sex life?'

'Well, now that you ask me, yes.' said Moshe.

'Well then, Moshe, that's the problem,' said the doctor, 'I'm afraid you'll have to give up half your sex life if you want your heart to last.'

Moshe asked, 'Which half should I give up, the looking or the thinking?'

***

Moshe and Sadie were touring the Middle East. As part of the day's itinerary, they took a trip to the local bazaar. The couple visited many of the shops there and spoke to numerous vendors who were dotted around the square. One of the stalls was selling sandals. But not any old sandals, said the owner. 'My sandals will increase the lovemaking ability of whoever wears them. I guarantee this.'

Moshe told the owner that he wasn't interested, but Sadie looked at Moshe and insisted that he buy a pair. She said it might help him. Seeing that look in her eyes, he decided it was futile to argue.

Before paying for them, Moshe wanted to make sure that they fitted him, so he tried them on. Immediately, Moshe grabbed hold of the owner, threw him on the table, and started to rip his clothes off.

'Stop, stop,' yelled the owner. 'You've put them on the wrong feet!'

***

Rifka says to her friend Hetty, 'My Moshe is useless.'

'Why do you say that?' says Hetty.

'Because the way he goes about foreplay is a total waste of time. All he manages to do is make me feel like a light switch someone's trying to find in the dark.'

***

Moshe Cohen was 82 years old and had made an appointment with Dr Michaels who was very well known for his work in curing impotence. Dr Michaels examined Moshe carefully and then said to him, 'Mr Cohen, I've examined every part of you and I can honestly say that you're in excellent condition for a man of your age. So tell me, why are you really here?'

Moshe replied, 'My friend Bernie has told me he makes love to his wife five times a week, and I can't do that, Doctor.'

Dr Michaels smiled and said, 'Yes you can. You can also say you make love as many times a week as you like.'

***

Moshe and Freda are sitting together one evening watching a DVD movie, as they do every night. But on this occasion, Moshe suddenly says, 'So, darling, whatever happened to our sexual relations?'

Freda doesn't answer straight away, but when she does, she replies, 'You know, I don't even think we got a New Year card from them this year.'

***

Maurice and Hetty are approaching their golden wedding anniversary. One summer evening, as they are taking a slow walk in their local park, Hetty suddenly takes her walking stick and hits Maurice hard across his back with it.

'What on earth did you do that for? It really hurts,' he shouts at her.

Hetty replies, 'That's for fifty years of poor sex.'

Maurice thinks for a while and then takes his walking stick and hits Hetty hard across her *toches* with it.

'Ouch,' she screams. 'What was that for?'

Maurice looks at her and replies, 'That's for knowing the difference.'

***

Sadie, an elderly lady, is sitting at home one day when her phone rings. She picks it up and says, 'Hello.'

A male voice says, 'Hello. I can tell from your voice that you would love me to come round to your house, take off your blouse, bra and panties, throw you on to your bed and make mad passionate love to you.'

Sadie replies, 'From one "hello" you can tell all this?'

***

Rifka goes to her son's house and rings the doorbell. When the maid lets her in, she is surprised to find her daughter-in-law Sarah lying on the couch, totally naked. Soft music is playing and the aroma of expensive perfume fills the air. 'Sarah, what are you doing?' Rifka asks.

'I'm waiting for David to come home from work,' replies Sarah.

'But you're naked!' says Rifka.

'I know,' says Sarah, 'this is my love-dress. David loves me to wear this dress. It excites him no end. Every time he sees me in this dress, he instantly becomes virile and makes love to me for hours on end. Why don't you try it with Benjy?'

Rifka goes home, undresses, has a bath and puts on her best perfume. Then, still naked, she dims the lights, puts on a romantic CD and lies on the settee waiting for Benjy to arrive. Benjy comes home and sees Rifka laying there, ever so provocatively.

'What on earth are you doing, Rifka?' he asks.

'This is my love-dress,' she whispers, sensually.

'It needs ironing,' he says.

***

Myron, in his mid-fifties, had a relatively minor heart attack, and while he was in hospital, he complained to his cardiologist that he thought that his sex life was now once and for all over and done with. The cardiologist said, 'Not true, Myron. Sex is a wonderful exercise for your heart. After you get home, you should have sex three or four times a week. It'll be the best thing you can do for your recovery.'

So after his discharge, Myron tells his wife what the doctor had said. His wife looked at him and said, 'That's wonderful, Myron! Sign me up for twice.'

***

Issy was making love to his wife when suddenly, to his intense surprise, Sadie wiggled and let out a short cry of delight.

'My God, honey!' he exclaimed. 'What happened?'

'It's wonderful,' Sadie said. 'I finally decided that those curtains would look much better in peach.'

***

Freda walks into a wine bar and asks the barman to give her a double entendre. So he gives her one.

***

Moshe moves into an old age home but he is just as randy as ever. As he looks over the list of the other people living in the home, he realises that there are three times as many women as men. What luck! Moshe decides this is a good time to make some money, so he posts a sign on his door: 'SEX FOR SALE.'

On the very first night, someone knocks on his door. It is Sadie. She says to Moshe, 'What does your sign mean?'

'I am selling sex,' he replies.

'Well,' says Sadie, 'how much do you charge?'

Moshe replies, 'I haven't thought much about prices, but I suppose it will be £5 on the floor, £10 on the chair and £20 on the bed.'

Sadie reaches into her purse and pulls out a £20 note.

'Oh, you want it on the bed?'

'No,' says Sadie, 'Four on the floor please!'

***

Reluctantly, the Segal family had to put their grandfather in a nursing home. As all the Jewish homes were full, they had to put him in a Catholic home. After a few weeks in the home, they came to visit him. 'How do you like it here, *Zaydeh*?' asked the grandson.

'It's wonderful. Everyone here is so courteous and respectful,' said his *zaydeh*.

'We're so happy for you,' said one of the children on hearing this. 'We were worried that this was the wrong place for you.'

'Let me tell you about how wonderfully they treat the residents here,' his *zaydeh* said with a big smile. 'There's a musician here – he's 85 years old. Although he hasn't played the violin in twenty years, everyone still calls him "Maestro". And there's a physician here – ninety years old. Although he hasn't been practising medicine for 25 years, everyone still calls him "Doctor". And me, although I haven't had sex for twenty years, they still call me the "F**king Jew".'

***

Three couples, one elderly, one middle-aged and one newly-wed, all wanted to join a synagogue in Hendon. The rabbi said to them, 'We have special requirements for new members. To be accepted, you must abstain from having sex for two weeks.'

The couples all agreed to the terms and came back at the end of the two weeks. The rabbi turned to the elderly couple and asked, 'Were you able to abstain from sex for two weeks?'

The old man replied, 'No problem at all, Rabbi.'

'Congratulations! Welcome to the synagogue!' said the rabbi.

The rabbi then asked the middle-aged couple, 'Were you able to abstain from sex for two weeks?'

The man replied, 'Well, the first week wasn't too bad. The

second week I had to sleep on the couch for a couple of nights; but yes, we made it.'

'Congratulations! Welcome to the synagogue!' said the rabbi.

The rabbi then turned to the newly-wed couple and asked, 'Were you able to abstain from sex for two weeks?'

'No Rabbi, we weren't able to go without sex for the entire two weeks,' the young man replied sadly.

'What happened?' inquired the rabbi.

'Well, six days into the two weeks, my wife was reaching for a book from the top shelf and she dropped it. When she bent over to pick it up, I was suddenly overcome with lust and I took advantage of her right there and then.'

'You do understand, of course, that this means you will not be welcome in our synagogue,' stated the rabbi.

'We know that, Rabbi,' said the young man, grimly. 'We're no longer welcome at the Hendon library either.'

***

An elderly Italian-Jewish man wanted to unburden his guilty conscience by talking to his rabbi. 'Rabbi, during World War II, when the Germans entered Italy, I pretended to be a *goy* and changed my name from Levi to Spamoni and I am alive today because of it.'

'Self-preservation is important and the fact that you never forgot that you were a Jew is admirable,' said the rabbi.

'Rabbi, a beautiful Jewish woman knocked on my door and asked me to hide her from the Germans. I hid her in my attic and they never found her.'

'That was a wonderful thing you did and you have no need to feel guilty.'

'It's worse, Rabbi. I was weak and allowed her to repay me for my efforts with her sexual favours.'

'You were both in great danger and would have suffered terribly if the Germans had found her. There is a favourable balance between good and evil and you will be judged kindly. Give up your feelings of guilt.'

'Thank you, Rabbi. That's a great load off my mind. But I have one more question.'

'And what is that?'
'Should I tell her the war is over?'

***

Q: What do you call a Jewish waterbed?

A: The Dead Sea.

Q: How can you tell that Maurice is losing interest in his wife Hetty?

A: Because Maurice's favourite sexual position is next door.

Q: What's the difference between a Catholic wife and a Jewish wife?

A: The Catholic wife has real orgasms and fake jewellery.

***

Rivkah meets her friend Leah in Brent Cross shopping centre. 'Leah, you're looking so radiant. How come?'

Leah replies, 'You won't believe me but on Tuesday, a handsome young man rings my doorbell and asks whether my husband Cyril is home. I say no and he immediately schleps me upstairs and makes love to me for one hour. On Wednesday, he again rings my doorbell and asks whether my husband is home. I say no and once again he schleps me upstairs and makes love to me, this time for two hours. Yesterday, he rings my doorbell and again asks whether my husband is home. I say no and yet again he schleps me upstairs and makes love to me, this time for three hours.'

'*Oy Vay*,' says Rivkah, 'That's amazing.'

'Yes, it was very satisfying,' replies Leah, 'But there's just one thing that's puzzling me. What does this man want with mine Cyril?'

***

Leah meets Cyril at a dance. They have a great time and end up leaving together. When they get back to his place, Cyril shows Leah around his house. Leah notices that Cyril's bedroom is full of teddy bears – hundreds of them. There are cute small ones on a shelf all the way along the floor, cuddly medium-sized ones on the next shelf up and huge bears on the top shelf. Leah is surprised that such a handsome and virile looking man should have such an extensive collection of teddy bears. Nevertheless, she decides not to mention it to him. As times goes by, his sensitive side turns her on. Soon they kiss and then they make love.

Later, as Leah is lying there in the afterglow of some intense lovemaking, she says to him, smiling, 'Well, Cyril, how was it for you?'

Cyril replies, 'Help yourself to any prize from the bottom shelf.'

Naughtier jokes

Three men are discussing their previous night's lovemaking.

Alberto the Italian says, 'My wife, I rubbed her all over with fine olive oil, then we made wonderful love. She screamed for five minutes.'

Marcel the Frenchman says, 'I smoothed sweet butter on my wife's body, then we made passionate love. She screamed for half an hour.'

Maurice Cohen says, 'I covered my wife's body with *shmaltz*. We made love and she screamed for six hours. '

The others say, 'Six hours? How did you make her scream for six hours?'

Maurice shrugs. 'I wiped my hands on the curtains.'

***

Millie accompanied her husband Maurice to the doctor's office. After he had given Maurice a full checkup, the doctor called Millie into his office, alone. He said, 'Maurice is suffering from a very severe disease, combined with horrible stress. If you don't do the following, your husband will surely die. Each morning, wake him up gently with a long and passionate kiss, then fix him a healthy breakfast. Be pleasant at all times and make sure he is always in a good mood. Cook him only his favourite meals, lunch and dinner and allow him to relax fully after each. Don't burden him with any chores and don't discuss your problems with him, it will only make his stress worse. Don't argue with him, even if he criticises you or makes fun of you. Let him be as arrogant as he wants to be. Try to relax him in the evening by wearing see-through lingerie. Give him plenty of "full relief" body massages. Encourage him to watch all the sport he can on the TV, even if it means missing your favourite programmes. And most importantly, make full and passionate love with Maurice every evening after dinner and satisfy his every whim. I suggest you also make oral love to him mid-morning and mid-afternoon. If you can do all of this, every day, for the next six months, I think Maurice will regain his health completely.'

On the way home, Maurice asks Millie: 'What did the doctor say?'

'He said you're going to die,' she replied.

***

A customs agent stopped Sam, an elderly Jewish man who had just immigrated to Israel and asked him to open his two suitcases. In the first suitcase, the agent found over £1 million in £10 notes. 'Excuse me, sir,' he asked Sam, 'where did you get all this money?'

'Vell, I'll tell you,' Sam began, 'I love Israel. For many years I travelled all around the world and stopped off at all of the public toilets in all the major cities. I vent to New York, I vent to London, I vent to Madrid, to Prague, to Paris, everywhere. As soon as I arrived, I vent into all the cubicles where the men were peeing and I say to them, 'Give me £10 for Israel or I'll cut off your testicles vit my knife.'

'That's quite a story,' the customs agent said, 'what's in the second suitcase?'

'Vell, you know,' said Sam, shaking his head, 'not everyone likes to give - '

***

The madam of a brothel answered the ring of the bell and on opening the door she found standing there an old bearded gentleman. 'May I come in?' he said in a quavering voice, 'I'm Rabbi Bloom.'

Confused, the madam said, 'But Rabbi, surely you must be in the wrong place. Here is where we - '

'I know what you do here,' interrupted Rabbi Bloom, 'you don't think I came here for chopped liver, do you? Bring on the girls.'

Understanding her professional duties, the madam lined up several of her girls. Rabbi Bloom tottered from one girl to another until he reached Rosie, a large redhead with enormous breasts. He looked at her with appreciation and pointed, 'Good! I'll take those.'

Rabbi Bloom paid out the necessary money and Rosie led him upstairs. She helped him off with his coat and hung it up carefully on the nail on the door. Then she helped him off with the rest of his clothes and got into bed. Then, to Rosie's astonishment, Rabbi Bloom performed with an adroitness and skill that was unbelievable. In fact, Rosie, a hardened professional, found herself surprised into orgasm. As they lay in bed a few minutes afterwards, relaxing, Rosie said, 'How old are you, Rabbi Bloom?'

Rabbi Bloom replied, 'God has been good to me. I am 85 years old.'

'That is certainly amazing. Listen, if you're ever in the neighbourhood again and if you should feel in the mood, please ask for me. I would be delighted to oblige you.'

Rabbi Bloom said, 'What do you mean "if" I should be in the mood again? Let me sleep for five minutes right now and I'll be in the mood again, believe me.'

'Really, Rabbi? OK, please take a nap.'

Rabbi Bloom got himself into a relaxed position, face up,

placed his arms across his chest and said, 'Wait, this is important. While I'm sleeping, scoop up my testicles with your right hand and hold them an inch above the sheet. Don't move them – keep them absolutely still.'

And Rosie did as she was told, holding Rabbi Bloom's testicles above the sheet as he slept. Then, after five minutes, he woke with a start and said, 'I'm ready.'

And so he was, for to her delight he was even better the second time around. As she lay panting, Rosie said, 'It was wonderful, Rabbi, but I don't understand why it was necessary to hold your testicles motionless above the sheet while you were sleeping?'

'Oh that,' said Rabbi Bloom, 'well, you're a nice girl and I like you a lot, but the truth is I don't know you very well, and over there, in my coat, hanging on the hook on the door, is a thousand pounds in cash.'

***

Mrs Murphy and Mrs Cohen had lived next door to one another for over forty years and over the years they had become loving friends. One day Mrs Murphy came to Mrs Cohen and said, 'These houses are becoming too much for us. Let's sell them and we can each move into a home for the aged.'

They agreed and some months later, each went into a retirement home of their respective religions. But not long after, Mrs Murphy felt very lonesome for Mrs Cohen, so she asked to be driven to the Jewish Home to visit her old friend Mrs Cohen. When she arrived, she was greeted with open arms, hugs and kisses.

Mrs Murphy asked, 'So how do you like it here?'

Mrs Cohen went on and on about the wonderful food, the wonderful facilities and the wonderful carers. She then said, 'And that's not all. You know the best thing is that I now have a boyfriend.'

Mrs Murphy said, 'That's wonderful. Tell me what you do.'

Mrs Cohen said, 'After lunch we go up to my room and sit on the edge of my bed. I let him touch me on the top and then down below and then we sing Jewish songs.'

Mrs Cohen said, 'And how is it with you, Mrs Murphy?'

Mrs Murphy said it was also nice at her new home and that she also had a boyfriend.

Mrs Cohen said, 'That's wonderful. So what do you do?'

'We also go up to my room after lunch and sit on the edge of my bed. I let him touch me on top and then let him touch me down below.'

Mrs Cohen said, 'And then what do you do?'

Mrs Murphy said, 'Since we don't know any Jewish songs, we f**k.'

* * *

Issy and Sadie are celebrating their wedding anniversary in a small country pub. Issy leans over and says, 'Do you remember, Sadie, the first time we made love together over fifty years ago? We went behind this pub where you leaned against the fence and I made love to you.'

'Oh yes,' Sadie replies, 'I remember it very well.'

'So how about you and I taking a stroll round the back and doing it again for old times' sake?' says Issy.

'Oooooooh Issy, that sounds like a good idea,' she answers and off they go.

On the next table, Sam has heard this and says to himself, 'I've got to see this – two elderly people making love against a fence.' So he follows them. Issy and Sadie walk along together, leaning on each other for support, aided by walking sticks. When they get to the fence, Sadie turns around and as she hangs onto the fence, Issy moves in. Suddenly they erupt into action. They are *shtupping* like eighteen-year-olds. This goes on for ages with Sadie yelling 'Ohhhh God', and Issy hanging on to her for dear life. Finally, they both collapse onto the ground. When they recover, Issy and Sadie struggle to their feet. Sam, still watching, thinks, 'That was truly amazing, I must ask them what their secret is.'

As Issy and Sadie make their way back past him, Sam says, 'That was something else, you must have been making love for about forty minutes. How do you manage it? You must have had a fantastic life together. Is there some sort of secret?'

'No, there's no secret,' Issy replies. 'Fifty years ago that fence wasn't electrified.'

***

Rachel and Sam, on their honeymoon in Bournemouth, go to a bar one night and ask the bartender if there is any entertainment. He replies, 'Do we have entertainment? Of course we do, in fact The Amazing Benny is performing this very night!'

With that, the lights lower and a seventy-year-old man hobbles on stage dragging a card table. He proceeds to set up the table and places three walnuts on it. He then takes out his penis and WHACK, WHACK, WHACK, breaks all three walnuts. The crowd cheer, the lights come on and the old man hobbles off stage, dragging his card table.

On their twentieth anniversary, Rachel and Sam go back to Bournemouth and to the same bar for a drink. The bartender is the same guy from twenty years before. They begin chatting about how twenty years ago they saw this unbelievable act in this bar. The bartender says, 'Yes, The Amazing Benny! He is performing here tonight!'

With that, the lights lower and a ninety-year-old man hobbles on stage, slowly dragging a card table. He proceeds to set up the table and places three coconuts on it. He takes out his penis and WHACK, WHACK, WHACK, breaks all three coconuts. The crowd cheer, the lights come on and the old man hobbles off stage, slowly dragging his card table.

Rachel and Sam are amazed. Sam says to the bartender, 'He did that act twenty years ago when we were here, but then he did it with walnuts. *Nu?* So now he does this with coconuts?'

The bartender apologetically replies, 'Well yes, twenty years ago he did use walnuts, but of course, twenty years is twenty years and The Amazing Benny is not what he used to be – his eyes aren't so good now!'

***

A *mohel* had been busy all his life collecting all the little snippets he cut off at each *bris*. By the time he retired, he had a huge plastic bag full of these cut-offs. What to do with them? Someone referred him to a tradesman down the street and he took his huge bag there, asking if this could be turned into something.

'Sure,' said the tradesman, 'just leave it here and come back in four weeks' time.'

When the *mohel* came back, the tradesman presented him with a tiny little wallet. The *mohel* could hardly hide his disappointment and said, 'I brought you such an enormous bag full of snippets, and you make but the tiniest of wallets out of it?'

Replied the tradesman: 'Just wait till you stroke it a bit, and it turns into a huge suitcase!'

***

Maurice was very distraught at the fact that he had not had a date or any sex in quite some time. He was afraid he might have something wrong with him, so he decided to seek the medical expertise of a sex therapist. Maurice's doctor recommended that he see a well-known Chinese sex therapist, so Maurice went to see him.

Upon entering the examination room, Dr Chang said, 'OK, take off all you crose.' Maurice did as he was told.

'Now, get down and craw reery, reery fass to odder side of room.'

Again, Maurice did as he was instructed.

Dr Chang then said, 'OK, now craw reery, reery fass back to me.'

So Maurice did.

Dr Chang shook his head slowly and said, 'Your probrem vewy bad. You haf Ed Zachary Disease. Worse case I ever see. Dat why you no haf sex or dates.'

Worried, Maurice asked anxiously, 'Oh my God, Dr Chang, what is Ed Zachary Disease?'

Dr Chang looked Maurice in the eye and replied, 'Ed Zachary Disease is when your face rook Ed Zachary rike your arse.'

***

This useful tool is found in most married Jewish households. It is commonly found in the range of six to eight inches long. Its functioning is enjoyed by members of both sexes. It is usually found hung, dangling loosely, ready for instant action. It boasts of a clump of little hairy things at one end and a small hole at the other. In use, it is inserted, almost always willingly, sometimes slowly, sometimes quickly, into a warm, fleshy, moist opening where it is thrust in and drawn out again and again many times in succession, often quickly and accompanied by squirming bodily movements. Anyone found listening in will most surely recognise the rhythmic, pulsing sound, resulting from the well lubricated movements. When finally withdrawn, it leaves behind a juicy, frothy, sticky white substance, some of which will need cleaning from the outer surfaces of the opening and some from its long glistening shaft. After everything has ceased emanating, it is returned to its freely hanging state of rest, ready for yet another bit of action, hopefully reaching its bristling climax two or three times a day, but often much less.

WHAT IS IT? A toothbrush. (What were you thinking?)

***

Sonia enrolled in nursing school and was attending an anatomy class. The subject of the day was 'involuntary muscles'. The instructor, hoping to perk up the students a bit, asks Sonia if she knows what her arsehole does when she has an orgasm.

'Sure!' Sonia says, 'He's at home taking care of the kids - '

***

Moshe was getting really quite old and one of his problems was that he hadn't had any sex for a long time. So one day, he decided to go to an old-timer's dance. He'd been dancing with all the grandmas all night, but still hadn't scored. Frustrated, he approached Hetty, another grandma, and told her, straight out, 'I'm having no luck finding someone I can sleep with. How about coming back to my place, I'll give you £100.'

Hetty surprised him, saying, 'I'm willing, Moshe, let's go.'

They got back to his place and after a bit of foreplay, they headed for the bedroom. Moshe loved the sex and couldn't get over how tight she was for such an old woman. He thought that she had got to be a virgin. After the wonderful performance, Moshe rolls off of her and says, 'Wow!!! Hetty, if I had known you were a virgin, I would have given you £200.'

Surprised, Hetty replies, 'If I had known you were actually going to get an erection, I would have taken my pantyhose off!'

***

Goldie was sitting on a beach in Florida, attempting to strike up a conversation with the attractive gentleman reading on the blanket beside hers. 'Hello,' she said, 'Do you like movies?'

'Yes, I do,' he responded, then returned to his book.

Goldie persisted. 'Do you like gardening?'

The man again looked up from his book. 'Yes, I do,' he said politely, before returning to his reading.

Undaunted, Goldie asked. 'Do you like pussycats?'

With that, the man dropped his book and pounced on Goldie, ravaging her as she'd never been ravaged before. As the cloud of sand began to settle, Goldie dragged herself to a sitting position and panted, 'How did you know that was what I wanted?'

The man thought for a moment and replied, 'How did you know my name was Katz?'

***

One morning, while she was making their breakfast, Harold walked up to his wife, Hetty, pinched her on the *toches* and said, 'You know, if you firmed this up, we could get rid of your girdle.'

Although she thought this was a terrible thing to say, she refrained from responding.

Next morning, Harold woke Hetty by squeezing her breast. He said, 'You know, if you firmed these up, we could get rid of your bra.'

Hetty thought this was unacceptable and had to respond this time. So she rolled over and grabbed him by his penis. With a strong grip, she said, 'You know, if you firmed this up, we could get rid of the postman, the gardener and your brother.'

***

Three fourth-form schoolboys – Paolo, an Italian, Andreas, a Greek, and Moshe – are in the playground when Paolo suggests that they play a new game. 'Lets see who has the largest penis,' he says.

Paolo pulls down his zip and takes it out.

'That's nothing,' says Andreas and takes his out. His is a couple of inches longer.

Not to be outdone, Moshe whips his out. It is by far the biggest, dwarfing the other two in both length and girth. Paolo and Andreas are stunned.

'Wow that thing is huge!' they exclaim.

That night, during dinner, Moshe's mother asks him what he did at school that day. 'Oh, we worked on a science project, had a maths test and read out loud from a new book – and during our lunch hour, my friends and I played "Let's see who has the largest penis".'

'What kind of game is that, darling?' says the mother.

'Well, me, Paolo and Andreas each pulled out our penises and I had the biggest. They said it must be that big because I'm Jewish. Is that true, Mum?'

The mother replies: 'No, *bubbeleh*. It's because you're 23 years old.'

***

After nearly forty years of marriage, Rebecca loses her husband, Bernie. She soon becomes very depressed and is hardly ever seen outside her house. A whole year passes. One day she is out doing her weekly shopping in Hendon when she meets Moshe in her local delicatessen. Moshe, she knows, is a recent widower. They get talking and agree to go out for a meal. Over the weeks that follow, they get on so well with each other that Moshe suggests a weekend in a five-star Brighton hotel.

On their first night in the hotel, Moshe is lying naked in bed and Rebecca emerges from the bathroom naked except for a pair of black panties.

'What is this?' asks Moshe. 'What's with the underwear?'

Rebecca replies, 'You can have mine lips, mine breasts and mine tummy. But down there, well, I'm still mourning.'

The next night the same thing happens.

On the third night, Rebecca comes out of the bathroom again wearing only the pair of black panties. She looks at Moshe on the bed, sees his erection and black condom and says, 'Moshe, I told you yesterday that down there I'm still in mourning.'

'I know,' replies Moshe. 'I'm planning to make a *shivah* call.'

***

Issy goes to his doctor to arrange a sperm count. The doctor gives Issy a small plastic tub and says, 'Use this and bring me a sample tomorrow.'

Next day, Issy goes back and gives the doctor an empty, pristine clean tub. The doctor asks, 'So? Why is it empty?'

Issy explains: 'Well, Doctor, first I tried it with my right hand, but nothing. Then I tried it with my left hand, but still nothing. Then I asked my wife Rifka for help. She tried it with her right hand, then with her left, but nothing. Rifka even tried with her mouth – with her teeth in, then with her teeth out, but still no luck. We then called in our next-door neighbour and she tried it with both hands, and with her mouth too, but with no results, I'm sad to say.'

The doctor is shocked. 'You mean you asked your neighbour to try?'

Issy replies, 'Yes, Doctor, but no matter what we tried, we just couldn't open the tub.'

***

There is a raffle at the local Jewish Community Centre and prizes are being drawn.

'Fourth prize, which goes to Hymie Himmelfarb, is a Rolls Royce.' Huge applause. Hymie goes up to collect his keys and shake hands.

'Third prize, which goes to Frank Myers, is a Rolls Royce

and a cheque for £10,000.' Huge applause. Frank goes up to collect his keys and cheque and shake hands.

'Second prize, which goes to Abe Epstein, is a piece of fruit cake!' Ghastly silence. Abe goes up to the stage to the presenter.

'What do you mean, a piece of fruit cake? Fourth prize was a Rolls Royce, third prize was a Rolls Royce plus a cheque for £10,000, so what the hell do you mean a piece of fruit cake for the second prize?'

'Ah,' says the presenter, 'This is special fruit cake. It's made by the rabbi's wife.'

'F**k the rabbi's wife!' says Abe, hysterically.

'What? You want the first prize as well?' came the reply.

***

Nathan is 75 years old and has just married Rose, a 35-year-old. They are very much in love, but no matter what Nathan does sexually, Rose can't achieve an orgasm. Since a Jewish wife is entitled to sexual pleasure, they decide to ask their rabbi for some advice. When Rabbi Bloom hears their story, he says, 'Here's what you can do. Hire a handsome young man and during your lovemaking, get him to wave a white towel over you both. That will help Rose let her imagination run wild and should bring on an orgasm.'

Nathan and Rose follow Rabbi Bloom's suggestion. They hire a handsome young man and next time they are making love, he waves a white towel over them as instructed. But it doesn't help Rose – she is still left unsatisfied. So back to Rabbi Bloom they go.

Rabbi Bloom looks at Nathan and says, 'OK. Let's try it another way round. Get your young man to make love to Rose and you wave the white towel over them.'

Once again, Nathan and Rose follow Rabbi Bloom's advice. That night, as soon as the young man gets into bed with Rose, Nathan starts waving the white towel. The young man 'works' with great enthusiasm and soon Rose has an enormous orgasm. Nathan smiles, looks at the young man and says to him smugly, 'See – that's how to wave a towel.'

***

Sadie was participating in a family survey. The interviewer asked her, 'How do you feel about condoms?'

Sadie replied, 'Depends on what's in it for me.'

* * *

Hetty is having afternoon tea in a Hendon café. On an adjacent table, Mary is also having tea. Mary leans over towards Hetty and says, 'Excuse me asking, but are you Jewish?'

'Why yes I am,' replies Hetty.

'I thought so,' says Mary, 'you have a Jewish holiday this week, don't you?'

'Yes we do, it's called Rosh Hashanah.'

'Is that when you light a different coloured candle every night?' asks Mary.

'Oh no,' says Hetty, 'that's Chanukah.'

'Then is it the one when you're not allowed to eat any bread?' asks Mary.

'No, that's Passover,' says Hetty, 'Rosh Hashanah is when we blow the *shofar*.'

'That's really nice,' says Mary, 'that's what I admire about you Jewish people – you're so good to the staff.'

* * *

Hyman decides to take his secretary Sharon to dinner one night, so he rings his wife Beckie and tells her he is going to an important business dinner. After a good meal, Hyman drives Sharon back to her flat and she, in turn, offers him some coffee. Soon, one thing leads to another and they find themselves in bed. But no matter how hard he tries, poor Hyman can't get an erection. So shamefaced, he apologises to Sharon and goes home.

As he quietly gets into bed next to his snoring Beckie, Hyman's thigh touches hers and he instantly gets an erection. He gets back out of bed, goes into the bathroom, looks at his penis and says, 'Now I know why they call you a *shmuck*.'

* * *

Chaim and Moshe come from a small Jewish village in eastern Europe and both go to America. Although they travel to different cities, they decide to meet up in New York after a year. They meet at the agreed date. Moshe comes in rags but Chaim arrives driving a large Lexus. Moshe tells Chaim how he spent his year. 'It was terrible. I couldn't find any work and I'm still starving. But I see you've done really well, Chaim. Good for you.'

Chaim replies, 'You're right. I invented a cream, but as it's patented, my invention can't help you. The cream smells like banana and is spread over a penis.'

When they depart, they decide to meet again in the same place one year later. When they meet again, Chaim comes in his Lexus but this time Moshe arrives in a chauffeured Rolls Royce with three servants who come in a separate Rolls Royce.

'I see you've made a fortune. Good for you, Moshe,' says Chaim.

Moshe replies, 'You're right. I invented a cream, but as it's patented, my invention can't help you. The cream smells like penis and is spread over a banana.'

***

Avrahom and David were such innocent young men that on their eighteenth birthdays, they decide to celebrate by getting their first 'piece of *toches*'. They make arrangements with Beckie, the neighbourhood floozy, for the following Sunday. Over the following days, the forthcoming event begins to weigh heavily on Avrahom's mind so he decides to confide in his father to find out everything he should know. His father asks him, 'Do you have condoms, Avrahom?'

Avrahom replies, 'What's a condom, dad?'

His father goes to his bedside table and takes out a pack of three. 'Here. You take one of these and unroll it over your *putz* before you put it in. Even if you don't like wearing it, don't take it off. It not only helps prevent children, but also, most important of all, it prevents you from getting all those bad venereal diseases you've heard about.'

So on Sunday morning, Avrahom meets David, gives him a condom and explains word for word everything his father had told him. Then they go to Beckie for their first indoctrination into the joys of life. A week later Avrahom asks David if he feels like he's caught a disease.

David replies, 'No.'

Avrahom says, 'Neither do I. Let's take the damn condom off, I have to *pish*.'

Viagra

Did you hear about the Israeli doctor who has invented a pill that is a combination of a tranquilliser and Viagra? Soon after you take it, you get an urge to make love to a woman – but if you can't find one, you just don't care.

***

Grandpa David and Grandma Andrea were staying overnight at their grandson Paul's house when Grandpa David saw a bottle of Viagra pills in the bathroom cabinet. He asked Paul whether he could use one of the pills.

Paul said, 'I don't think you should take one, *Zaydeh*, they're potent and expensive.'

'How much?' asked Grandpa David.

'Ten pounds for each pill,' Paul replied.

'I don't care,' said Grandpa David, 'I'd like to try Viagra at least once before I die. But don't worry, if I do take one, I'll pay you for it.'

The next morning Paul found a cheque for £110 on the kitchen table. He said to Grandpa David, '*Zaydeh*, I told you each pill was £10, not £110.'

'I know,' said Grandpa David, 'The extra hundred is from your *bubbeh*.'

***

It's breakfast time. Sadie asks her husband Moshe, 'Would you like some scrambled eggs, perhaps a piece of toast and grapefruit and coffee to follow?'

Moshe replies, 'No thanks, it's this Viagra, it's really taken the edge off my appetite.'

At lunchtime, Sadie asks Moshe if he would like something to eat. 'How about a bowl of your favourite home-made chicken soup, followed by a smoked salmon sandwich on rye?' she inquires.

Moshe again declines. 'It's this Viagra, it's really taken the edge off my appetite.'

Come dinnertime, Sadie asks Moshe if he wants anything to eat. She'll go to the delicatessen and buy him some food. Would he like a nice juicy lamb chop with potato *latkes* followed by strawberry *blintzes*?

Again, Moshe says, 'No thanks, it's this Viagra, it's really taken the edge off my appetite.'

'Well,' Sadie says, 'Would you mind getting off me and letting me up? I'm starving.'

***

One day, the elderly Moshe decided to go to his local chemist and ask the pharmacist for some Viagra. The pharmacist said, 'Certainly sir, how many pills do you want?'

Moshe answered, 'I don't want many, maybe half a dozen at most. But please, can you cut each one into four pieces?'

The pharmacist said, 'One quarter of a pill won't do you any good, sir.'

Moshe replied, 'That's OK. I don't need the pills for sex. I am 75 years old. I just want them to help me to stop *pishing* on my shoes.'

***

Morris goes into his local chemist and asks the assistant behind the counter, 'What's this Viagra like, then?'

'It's very good sir,' says the assistant, 'I use it myself.'

'Good,' says Morris. 'Can you get it over the counter?'

To which the assistant answers, 'Only if I take six, sir.'

***

Moshe goes to visit his 85-year-old grandpa in hospital. 'How are you, *Zaydeh*?' he asks.

'Feeling fine,' says the old man.

'What's the food like?'

'Terrific, wonderful menus.'

'And the nursing?'

'Just couldn't be better, Moshe. These young nurses really take care of you.'

'What about sleeping? Do you sleep OK, *Zaydeh*?'

'No problem at all, nine hours solid every night. At ten o'clock they bring me a cup of hot chocolate and a Viagra tablet – and that's it. I go out like a light.'

Moshe is alarmed at this and rushes off to question the nurse in charge. 'What on earth are you doing?' he says. 'I'm told you're giving an 85-year-old man Viagra on a daily basis. Surely that can't be correct?'

'Oh yes,' replies the Sister. 'Every night at ten o'clock we give him a cup of chocolate and a Viagra tablet. It works wonderfully well. The chocolate makes him sleep and the Viagra stops him from rolling out of bed.'

***

In pharmacology, all drugs tend to have a generic name. For example, Tylenol is called *acetamophen*, Aleve is *naproxen*, Amoxil is *amoxicillin* and Advil is called *ibuprofen*.

The Israeli drug agency had been looking for some time for a generic name for Viagra and after many months, they settled on the generic name *mycoxafloppin*. They had also given thought to these other generic names: *mycoxafailin*, *mydixadrupin*, *mydixarizin*, *mydixadud*, *dixafix* and *ibepokin*.

SPORTS & RECREATION

Sports

The police are called to Avrahom's house in Hampstead Garden Suburb – the neighbours have heard some screaming. When the police arrive, they find Avrahom's wife Sadie standing over Avrahom's lifeless body holding a 6-iron in her hand. The club is still dripping blood.

A police constable asks Sadie, 'Is that your husband, madam?'

'Yes it is,' replies Sadie.

'And did you hit him with that golf club you're holding, madam?'

'Certainly,' replies Sadie. She then drops the golf club, puts her hands over her face and begins to cry. 'We only just got back from playing at a golf tournament,' she sobs.

'How many times did you hit your husband, madam?' asks the constable.

'I don't know,' replies Sadie. 'Six, seven, maybe even eight times – but just put me down for a six.'

***

O'Brien kept nudging Cohen to let him play at his Jewish Country Club. Cohen told him that only Jews could play golf there. O'Brien drove him crazy for months and Cohen finally gave in but warned him that if anyone asked, his name was Goldberg. If asked what his occupation was, he was a manufacturer. O'Brien asked what kind of a manufacturer he should be and Cohen told him to say that he made *tallis*.

Sure enough, after playing eighteen holes, he is approached by one of the members, who says that he hadn't seen him before and asked his name.

He replies, 'My name is Goldberg.'

'What do you do for a living, Mr Goldberg?'

O'Brien replies, 'I'm a manufacturer.'

'What do you manufacture?'

'I make *tallis*.'

'You know, I always wanted to know what the Hebrew letters on the neck of the *tallis* meant. Can you tell me?'

O'Brien said, 'To tell the truth, I only make the sleeves.'

***

Gary stood over his tee shot for what seemed like an eternity. He looked up, looked down, measured the distance, figured the wind direction and speed. Then he started over again. All this was driving his partner Benny nuts. Finally Benny said, '*Oy Vay!* What's taking you so long? Hit the blasted ball will you already!'

Gary replied, 'But Benny, my wife Suzie is up there watching me from the clubhouse. I want to make this a perfect shot.'

'Forget it, Gary, you'll never hit her from here!'

***

A priest, a minister, and a rabbi are playing a round of golf but are having to play very slowly because there is a foursome ahead of them. At long last they complete their round and each of them tramps back to the clubhouse to complain to the golf pro. The pro tells the priest, 'They're blind – that's why they were slow.'

The priest replies, 'That's very inspiring. I'm so impressed that I'm going to collect some money for them by organizing a blind golfers' tournament.'

The pro then tells the minister, 'They're blind – that's why they were slow.'

The minister replies, 'That's so uplifting that I'm going to use them as my theme for next Sunday's sermon.'

The pro then tells the rabbi, 'They're blind – that's why they were slow.'

The rabbi replies, 'If that's so, then why can't they play in the dark?'

***

Avrahom has done very well in business and is now very rich. One day, to show off his new Bentley Continental car, he tells his driver to take him to the exclusive Neasden Golf Club. But when they get there, a sign over the door clearly states that Jews are not permitted access.

Undeterred, Avrahom says to his driver, 'Wait here for me.'

His driver replies, 'But sir, the sign – they'll kick you out immediately.'

'But I don't have to tell them I'm Jewish,' says Avrahom, as he walks to the gate.

So his driver waits. One hour goes by, then two and soon three. Then, after three and a half hours, Avrahom is thrown out by two tough looking security guards. His driver asks, 'So what happened, sir?'

'Everything was OK until we got to the eighth hole,' replies Avrahom. 'I sliced my drive and the ball dropped into the lake. I shouted out, "Oh, my God, what shall I do now?" and then the waters separated – and everybody knew.'

***

The night before their wedding, Alf and Bette were sharing confidences. Alf said, 'You must know something before we get married. I am a fanatic golfer. I eat, sleep and drink golf. Golf is my whole life. After we are married, I'll try for some balance but I doubt whether I'll succeed. Just understand – you're marrying a golf addict.'

'I can live with that,' said Bette, 'now I'll tell you my secret – I'm a hooker.'

'A hooker?' Alf repeated. 'I can live with that. Next time, keep your head down and your left arm straight, then swing through the ball ...'

***

As you may know, in a slalom race the skier must pass through about twenty gates as quickly as possible. Surprisingly, one year Israel had Avrahom, the fastest slalom-skier in the world, and had great expectations for a Winter Olympics gold medal. The day of the final came, and the crowd waited in anticipation. The French champion sped down the course in 58 seconds. The Swiss was clocked at 58.7 seconds, the German at 61.8 seconds, and the Italian at 61.1 seconds. Then came the turn of Avrahom. The crowd waited, and waited – and then Avrahom crossed the line – in three minutes!

'What happened to you?' asked the team coach when Avrahom finally got back.

Avrahom replied, 'Which one of those bastards fixed a *mezuzah* to each gate?'

***

The Jewish Olympics

Oyga vault (with sound):

Vaulters must clear the bar then yell '*Oy*' upon hitting the foam cushion below. Any heights cleared without an '*Oy*' will be disallowed. Points will be added for more enthusiastic exclamations of '*Oy*', such as '*Oy Vay iz mir!*' and '*Oy*, I've just landed on my *toches*.'

Synchronised Swimming (ladies only):

Takes place in an Olympic-size *mikvah* (an indoor pool used for Jewish women's ritual purification). This event is sure to make a splash.

Synchronised Tanning:

Follows immediately after Synchronised Swimming. Swimmers are given ten minutes to sunbathe. Their routine must include at least two rollovers as well as the application of sunscreen to the ears and nose. An SPF of fifteen is the required minimum, but the judges will award additional points to those who can get a tan with a higher SPF number. Points will be deducted for burns or blotches.

Team Handball:

The aim is to create the perfect matzo ball. Each team will prepare a large bowl of matzo ball soup. The three winning

batches will be fed to the athletes recovering in the first aid tent. The hardest matzo balls will be used in the shot put.
Bagel Toss:
The winner is the one who first lands a bagel on each of the seven branches of the Chanukah candlestick.
Balance Beam:
The winner will be the accountant who can balance the president's wife's bank account quickest.
Mohel Marathon:
Each *mohel* must run a marathon and perform a *bris* at each mile mark. This is the only event that allows alcohol – for the babies of course.
Rings (newlywed brides only):
This event caters for those who wish to show off their diamond rings. Diamonds will be judged on the three C's: colour, clarity and cut. Contestants will also be judged on the three S's: smile, sophistication and *simchas*.

***

The Yeshiva University in Golders Green decided to put together a rowing team. Unfortunately, they lost race after race. They practised for hours every day, but never managed to come in any better than dead last. The head of the *yeshiva* finally decided he couldn't stand any more embarrassment so he sent Yankel to spy on the Oxford University team.

So Yankel schlepped off to Oxford and hid in the bullrushes off the river from where he carefully watched the Oxford team as they practised.

Yankel finally returned to the *yeshiva*. 'I have figured out their secret,' he announced. 'They have eight guys rowing and only one guy shouting.'

***

One summer, Abe Cohen went swimming in the sea at Margate and almost drowned.

Luckily, when he cried out for help, some swimmers came to his aid. As he was helped out of the water, he took a solemn oath:

'I swear I shall never to go into the water again until I learn how to swim!'

***

A Sunday League Jewish football team is desperate for players. So desperate, in fact, that one Sunday they are forced to play a kosher chicken in their team. Rather surprisingly, the chicken has a brilliant first half. One minute it's clearing off its own line, the next it's threading the perfect through ball, the next it's putting in a perfect cross.

At half time, all its team-mates are very pleased and everyone runs back onto the pitch for the second half. On the way back, the referee starts chatting to the chicken.

'Great first half mate, you must be really fit.'

'Thanks,' said the chicken, 'I try to keep myself fit but its difficult finding the time so I try to do an hour in the gym each morning before work.'

'What do you do then?' asked the referee.

'I'm a chartered accountant,' replies the chicken. At which point the referee immediately brandishes the red card and sends the chicken off.

The concerned team-mates gather round the ref and start complaining.

'Sorry lads,' says the ref, 'I had no choice – Professional fowl.'

Fitness

Freda from London was visiting some friends in Florida when she saw a little old man rocking merrily away on his front porch. He had a lovely smile on his face. She just had to go over to him. 'I couldn't help noticing how happy you look. I would love to know your secret for a long and happy life.'

'I smoke four packets of cigarettes a day, drink five bottles of scotch whisky a week, eat lots and lots of fatty food and I never, I mean never, exercise.'

'Why, that's absolutely amazing. I've never heard anything like this before. How old are you?'

'I'm 26,' he replied.

***

This letter of complaint was received by the creators of a bodybuilding course.

Dear Sir,

Since taking your bodybuilding course, I now have a 44-inch chest, a 32-inch waist, 17-inch biceps and an 18-inch neck. I feel absolutely marvellous but at the same time, I do feel that my chances of marriage are spoiled.

Yours faithfully
Mary Goldberg

***

Maurice, 53 years old, thought he was quite fit so he decided to join David's Place, the up-market London health club. It seemed all the Jews in North London went there. On his first day, Maurice went to Room 50, the exercise room for over-fifties, and tried out their stair-step machine. He told the instructor what he wanted to do and the instructor asked, 'Shall I set it for five, ten or twenty minutes?'

'Make it ten,' Maurice replied conservatively.

But after only a few minutes on the machine, his legs felt like lead and he could hardly breathe. So he got off the machine. As he limped past some of the other men in Room 50 who were resting from their workouts, Maurice said to them, 'I could only take three minutes on that thing.'

'OK, OK,' replied one of them, 'You don't have to brag about it.'

***

Morris had reached sixty, so he went to see his doctor for a full medical check-up. When he had finished, the doctor said, 'Relax, Morris, you're in very good shape. I can't find anything wrong with you. You'll probably live till you're a hundred. So how old was your father when he died?'

Morris replied, 'Did I say he was dead?'

The doctor then asked, 'How old is your father, is he still active?'

'He's 83 and goes jogging and Israeli dancing every week,' Morris replied.

The doctor was very surprised. 'How old was your grand father when he died?'

Morris again answered, 'Did I say he was dead, Doctor?'

The doctor was astonished. 'You mean to tell me that you are sixty years old and both your father and grandfather are alive? Is your grandfather active?'

Morris replied, 'He goes swimming twice a week, and plays a full round of golf every Sunday, weather permitting. Not only that, he is 107 years old and next month he is getting married again.'

The doctor said, 'If he's 107 years old, why on earth would your grandfather want to get married?'

Morris looked him in the eye and said, 'Did I say he wanted to?'

***

The *Jewish Chronicle* had heard that Benjy was coming up to his 108th birthday so they sent one of their reporters to interview him. 'How do you account for your longevity?' asked the reporter.

'You could say that I am a health nut,' Benjy answered. 'I have never smoked or drunk alcohol, I am always in bed by ten o'clock, I've been going to Israeli dance classes since I was a teenager and I've always walked three miles a day, even in rain or snow.'

'But,' said the reporter, 'my uncle Shlomo followed exactly the same routine and he died when he was seventy. So how come it didn't work for him?'

'All I can say,' replied Benjy, 'is that he didn't keep it up long enough.'

***

Morris was out jogging one Sunday afternoon when he saw a new-looking tennis ball in the road. He stopped to pick it up and as he had no pockets, he put it down the front of his running shorts. He then continued with his run. He soon came up to Sadie, who was also out jogging.

Sadie looked at him and pointed to the bulge in his shorts. 'What's that?' Sadie asked, smiling.

'Tennis ball,' replied Morris.

'I know how you must feel,' Sadie said, 'I had tennis elbow once and that was bloody painful.'

Games

Grandma Andrea was babysitting and was playing junior scrabble with Emma. Emma had just drawn her second letter 'O' and was trying to make a word with her other letters. Suddenly with a shout, Emma said, 'Look grandma, I've made a word.'

Grandma Andrea looked at Emma's tiles and saw they had been lined up to spell KOOB. So she asked, 'What kind of word is KOOB, Emma?'

'No grandma,' said Emma, 'you're not saying it right. It says BOOK.'

Grandma Andrea had a sinking feeling. Did Emma have dyslexia, she wondered? So she said, gently, 'But, darling, you've spelled it backwards.'

With a sigh reserved only for dumb adults, Emma explained, 'Of course I have, grandma, I'm Jewish!'

***

Four Jewish ladies are playing bridge in a house in Hendon.

Bette sighs and says, '*Oy* ...'

Freda nods, sighs, and says, '*Oy Vay!*'

Kitty says, '*Oy Vay iz meer!*'

Charlotte chimes in: 'Enough talk about the children already. Let's get back to the game.'

***

Issy has read that fishing was a therapeutic pastime. So he buys the necessary equipment and goes to his local lake. But as it's his first time, he has no idea what bait to use. He looks around and sees three men casting their lines. Almost immediately, they begin to catch an awful lot of fish. So Issy goes up to them. 'Excuse me,' he asks the first man, 'What bait are you using?'

'Well, I'm a doctor and I use tonsils,' he replies. 'You really can't beat them – the fish here love tonsils.'

Well Issy hasn't brought any tonsils with him, so he goes to the second fisherman. 'Excuse me,' he asks, 'What bait are you using?'

'I'm also a doctor and I have a great deal of success using bits of appendix.'

Issy then turns to the third fisherman and can't help but notice that he too is very successful at catching fish. 'Let me guess,' Issy says to him. 'You're also a doctor.'

'Actually I'm not,' came the reply. 'I'm a *mohel*.'

***

Harry and Alf are bragging about their recent fishing expeditions.

'Harry says, 'I caught a fish so huge, it must have weighed fifty pounds!'

'That's nothing,' scoffs Alf, 'I caught an antique lamp. It had a date of 1837 engraved on it: the date when Queen Victoria came to the throne. And you know what? The lamp was still lit!'

Harry stares at his friend incredulously and then replies, slowly, 'Listen Alf, I'll tell you what, we must stop this boasting – so how's this for a compromise? I will say my fish weighed only five pounds and you – well, you put your light out!'

Entertainment

Jewish film titles:
Oy of the Beholder – Singles *kvetch* about their awful partners.
Girls Interrupted – Women's section of *shul* are told to be quiet during *davening*.
Seder House Rules – *Zaydeh* explains the law on Passover.
Angela's Kashas – Woman tells all her secret recipes.
Supernova – Rocket scientists discover powerful strain of *lox*.
Dreidel Will Rock – Toy comes alive during the festival of Purim.
Sleepy Halah – It's Friday and dad fills up on bread then dozes off.
Goys Don't Cry – Rabbi explains why only Jews celebrate Tisha B'av.
Goy Story 2 – Issy divorces *shiksa*, then marries another.
Mun on the Moon – Astronauts find the poppyseed filling of *hamentashen* (a sweet cake) on the moon.
Stuart Ladle – Mouse makes chicken soup for Shabbes.
The End of the Affair – The Sheva Brochos (wedding blessings) finish at 3 a.m.

***

From the masters
'I once wanted to become an atheist, but I gave up – they have no holidays.' – Henny Youngman

'I told my psychiatrist that everyone hates me – he said I was being ridiculous, everyone hasn't met me yet.' – Rodney Dangerfield

'Marriage is a wonderful institution – but who wants to live in an institution?' – Groucho Marx

'This is the sixth book I've written – not bad for a guy who's read only two.' – George Burns

'Tragedy is when I cut my finger – comedy is if you fall into an sewer and die.' – Mel Brooks

'It's not that I'm afraid to die – I just don't want to be there when it happens.' – Woody Allen

'The pen is mightier than the sword – and considerably easier to write with.' – Marty Feldman

* * *

Yitzhak and Freda go out to see *The Producers* on stage. This is the most sold-out show of the year. Somehow, they've been lucky and manage to get best seats in the front row. But they notice that there's an empty seat in the row behind them. When intermission comes and no one has sat in that seat, Freda turns to the woman sitting next to the empty seat and asks, 'Pardon me, but as this is such a sold-out show and in such demand, we were wondering why that seat is empty.'

The woman says, 'That's my late husband's seat.'

Freda is horrified and apologises for being so insensitive. But a few minutes later, she turns around again. 'Without meaning to be rude or anything, this is an incredibly hard show to get into. Surely you must have a friend or a relative who would have wanted to come and see the show?'

The woman nods, but explains, 'They're all at the *shivah*.'

* * *

Jewish *Big Brother*:

On a new TV show, sixteen Jews are put in a two-bedroom flat near Brent Cross in London. Each week they vote out one member until there is a final survivor who gets £1 million (but placed into a trust that does not mature until they are aged 59).

The rules are:

No maid service, no au-pairs.

No use of ATMs or credit cards.

No food to be bought in or be delivered, including Chinese food.

All purchases to be retail.
Outside trips to be by foot, bus or underground. No cars or taxis allowed.
All workouts/exercise to be done in regular sweatshirts – no designer labels.
There will only be one phone for all sixteen and no call to last more than three minutes.
No mobile phones allowed.
No telephone calls to mother (for women), or the office (for men).
Maintenance problems to be resolved without help from any gentile.
No consulting with lawyers.
There is only one problem: we hear there have been no applicants as yet.

***

Sharon had lived a good life, having been married four times. Now she stood before the Pearly Gates. The angel at the gates said to her, 'I see that you first of all married a banker, then an actor, next a rabbi and lastly an undertaker. Why? This does not seem appropriate for a Jewish woman.'

'Oh yes it is,' Sharon replied. 'It's one for the money, two for the show, three to make ready and four to go.'

***

Once upon a time, a young Jewish composer was trying desperately to write a hit song. He had been at it for an entire day, without food or water, but the inspiration was taking a long time coming. Then his mother came into his room and said, 'You must eat something. I'll make you a smoked salmon sandwich.'

But he pushed her out of the room, shouting, 'Go away.'

Within fifteen minutes, she was back. 'Please, you must eat some food or you'll be ill,' she cried.

Again he shoved her out of the room, this time shouting, 'Will you please leave me alone, you silly moo. Stop bothering me, will you?'

But she took no notice. Ten minutes later, she came into the room carrying a tray full of food and drink. All his favourites were there. But it had no effect on him. She was still holding the tray of food when he angrily threw her out of the room and locked the door. He heard the crash of the tray hitting the wall and the sound of breaking chinaware. Then he heard his mother crying.

Suddenly, he shouted, 'I've got it, I know what to write.'

With that he went to his piano and composed 'My Yiddishe Mama'.

***

Moshe Magic (a Jewish magician, would you believe?) was playing to a packed London variety theatre. When he came to the point in his act where he needed someone to help him, he called up the biggest, strongest-looking man he could find in the audience. When the helper came up on stage, Moshe Magic handed him a rubber mallet and said, 'When I put my head on this wooden block, hit me as hard as you can. And don't worry about hurting me – it won't affect me at all. It's my act.'

The man said, 'OK, if you say so.'

So Moshe Magic put his head on the block and said, 'OK, you can hit me now.'

Ten years later, Moshe Magic woke up in a hospital bed from a coma and yelled, 'Ta-Da!'

***

Lionel was a ventriloquist, and not a good one at that. In fact business was so bad that he was trying his luck as a medium. One day, a widow came into his office and said that she wanted to contact her dear departed husband and asked Lionel what he charged.

'If you only want to hear him speak,' said Lionel, 'I charge £30. If you want to have a conversation with him, I charge £50. But I charge £70 if you want a conversation with him while I'm drinking a glass of water.'

Jewish culture

The 23rd Psalm for Jewish princesses

The Lord is my shepherd, I shall not want
He leadeth me to Brent Cross
He giveth me energy for shopping
He restoreth my credit card
He teacheth me to make restaurant reservations
He leadeth me past Woolworths for mine own sake
Yea, though I walk by Next, I shall not go in, for thou art with me
Thy fashionable clothes they comfort me
Thou preparest diamond jewellery for me in the presence of mine enemies
Thou anointest my face with Chanel cosmetics
My cup overflows
Surely designer clothes shall follow me to the end of my days
And I will walk along Golders Green Road forever.

***

Rifka was the original 'Jewish princess'. One day, she drives her pink Renault Clio to a garage and asks one of the mechanics, 'Do you charge batteries?'

He replies, 'Of course we do, darling.'

'Great,' says Rifka. 'Could you change my battery please and charge it to my daddy.'

***

Q: What's a Jewish princess's favourite position?
A: Inside Brent Cross shopping centre.

Q: What is a Jewish princess's idea of a dream home?
A: One that's 6,000 square feet, with no kitchen and no bedrooms.

***

Emma is nearly ten years old. One day, she comes home from school and says to her father, 'Daddy, I need a national costume. My teacher told all of the class to come to school next Monday wearing our national costumes.'

'*Oy Vay!*' he cries. 'She's not even ten, already, and she wants a mink coat.'

***

Abe is sitting on a bench in Green Park reading an anti-Semitic newsheet. Solomon, his best friend walks by, sees the paper, and stops – in shock.

'What are you doing reading that paper?' he says. 'You should be reading the *Jewish Chronicle*!'

Abe replies, 'The *Jewish Chronicle* has stories about intermarriage, anti-Semitism, problems in Israel- – all kinds troubles of the Jewish people. I like to read about good news. This paper says the Jews have all the money – the Jews control the banks – the Jews control the press – the Jews control Hollywood. Better to read nothing but good news!'

***

A Jewish quiz

If you are Jewish, or an aspiring Jew, or married into a Jewish family, or work with Jews, or dating someone Jewish, there are certain things you must know in order to survive! Take this quiz to see if you've learned enough to function as a Jew:

There are no Jews living in:
a) sin;
b) Cornwall;
c) caravan parks.

In a Jewish household, the cleaning lady is expected to:
a) do the windows;
b) make *latkes*;
c) attend all Bar Mitzvahs and weddings.

To make a good pet for a Jewish child, an animal must be:
a) gentle;
b) housebroken;
c) stuffed.

Jews spend their holidays:
a) sightseeing;
b) sunbathing;
c) discussing where they spent their last holiday and where they'll go next.

If there's a hairdresser in your immediate family, you are:
a) up on the latest style;
b) entitled to free haircuts;
c) not Jewish.

Wilderness means:
a) no running water;
b) no electricity;
c) no hot-and-sour soup.

The most popular outdoor sport among Jews is:
a) jogging;
b) tennis;
c) gasping over the neighbours' swimming pool.

Jews never drive:
a) unsafely;
b) on Saturdays;
c) eighteen-wheel lorries.

A Jewish skydiver is:
a) careful;
b) insured;
c) an apparition.

No Jewish person in history has ever been known to:
a) become a prostitute;
b) deface a synagogue;
c) remove the back of a TV set.

Jews never sing:
a) off-key;
b) 'Nel Blù di Pinto di Blù';
c) around a piano bar.

Scoring: One point for each 'a)' answer, two for each 'b)' and three for each 'c)'.
30-33 points: *Mazeltov!* You know a lot about Jews. Either you've studied your loved one's family carefully out of desire for true closeness plus your respect for their traditions, or else you're from Golders Green or Edgware.

***

Young Morris asked his father, 'Dad, was Adam Jewish?'

His father put down his newspaper and thought for a moment. He was an expert at Talmudic reasoning and in the art of making a point by an unanswerable question. He replied, 'If we can determine that Eve was Jewish, my son, we would at once see that Adam was Jewish, for who but a Jew could bring himself to marry a Jewish girl?' (Here he nervously turned his head a bit to make sure his wife wasn't listening.) 'Therefore, we can drop the Adam problem and instead ask ourselves, "Was Eve Jewish?" To answer that, we have only to ask the question, "Would anyone but a Jewish girl say, *Here, have a piece of fruit*"?'

***

Issy and his wife were taking a car trip when Issy noticed that he was getting low on petrol. Up ahead was a combination fast food outlet and petrol station. So he pulled in. As he was thirsty, Issy walked up to the juice bar.

The young kid who was wiping down the counter looked up and said, 'Juice?'

Issy replied, 'So what if we are, don't we get no petrol?'

***

Peter and Patrick are visiting Stamford Hill for the first time when they come across two Jewish men wearing long black coats, wide-brimmed hats, and who have long beards and sidelocks. Patrick turns to Peter, who is an educated gentleman, and says, 'What are they?'

Peter replies, 'Chassidim.'

Patrick responds, 'I see them, too, but what are dey?'

***

You know you grew up Jewish when:

You spent your entire childhood thinking that everyone calls roast beef brisket.

Your family dog responds to complaints uttered in Yiddish.

Every Sunday afternoon of your childhood was spent visiting your grandparents.

You were as tall as your grandmother by the age of seven.

You never knew anyone whose last name didn't end in one of five standard suffixes.

You can look at gefilte fish and not turn green.

Your mother smacked you really hard and continues to make you feel bad for hurting her hand.

You know how to pronounce numerous Yiddish words and use them correctly in context, yet you don't exactly know what they mean. *Kin-a-hora.*

You have at least one ancestor who is related to your spouse's ancestor.

You grew up thinking it's normal for someone to shout, 'Are you OK? Are you OK?' through the bathroom door if you're in there for longer than three minutes.

You have at least six male relatives named David.

You feel a sense of pride after seeing a Stephen Spielberg movie.

You think that speaking loudly is normal.

***

Some forms of Judaism:

Cardiac Judaism: 'In my heart I am a Jew.'

Gastronomic Judaism: 'I eat Jewish foods.'
Chequebook Judaism: 'I give to Jewish causes.'
Drop-off Judaism: 'I drop the kids off at Sunday Hebrew classes.'
Twice-a-year Judaism: 'I attend services on Rosh Hashanah and Yom Kippur.'

***

May you be granted every wish; and always have gefilte fish.
May you stay safe from winds and hails; and always shop at Bloomingdales.
May you always understand every detail; and never have to pay retail.
May you regard every man as your brother; and always remember to call your mother.

***

Two Jewish princesses were having lunch. Suzy complained that every time she and her husband Gary had sex, he hollered and yelled when he climaxed.

Miriam said, 'So what's wrong with that?'

Suzy answered, 'He wakes me up!'

***

All we ever hear are Jewish jokes, so here are some Gentile ones:

A Gentile goes into a men's clothes shop and says, 'This is a very fine jacket. How much is it?' The salesman says, 'It's £900.' The Gentile says, 'OK, I'll take it.'

Two Gentiles meet on the street. The first one says, 'You own your own business, don't you? How's it going?' The other Gentile says, 'Just great! Thanks for asking!'

Two Gentile mothers meet on the street and start talking about children. Gentile mother one says with pride, 'My son is a builder!' Gentile mother two says with more pride, 'My son is a truck driver!'

A Gentile calls his mother and says, 'Mum, I know you're

expecting me for dinner tonight, but something important has come up and I can't make it.' His mother says, 'OK.'

A Gentile couple goes to a nice restaurant. The man says, 'I'll have the steak and a baked potato and my wife will have the Julienne salad with house dressing. And we'll both have coffee.' The waiter says, 'How would you like your steak and salad prepared?' The man says, 'I'd like the steak medium. The salad is fine as is.' The waiter says, 'Thank you.'

A Gentile calls his elderly mother and asks, ' Mum, how are you feeling? Do you need anything?' She says, 'I feel fine, and I don't need anything. Thanks for calling.'

A Gentile woman meets an old Gentile friend. The friend asks, 'How is your son getting along?' The Gentile woman says, 'He's just fine. He just turned 35.' 'And where does he live?' asks the friend. 'He lives at home with me. I don't think he'll ever get married.' The friend says, 'How nice.'

***

Jewish dictionary extracts

Bagela. A gay Jewish baker.

Bialyache. Result of lunch at mother's and dinner at your mother-in-law's.

Blintzkrieg. A late-night assault on the refrigerator in search of leftovers.

Bubbehgum. Sweets that a grandma gives to her grandchildren.

Chutzpapa. A father who wakes his wife at 4 am so she can change the baby's nappy.

Deja nu. Having the feeling you've seen the same exasperated look on your mother's face but not knowing exactly when.

Diskvellified. To drop out of law school, medical school, or business school, as seen through the eyes of parents and grandparents.

Disoriyenta. When Aunt Sadie gets lost in Harrods and strikes up a conversation with everyone she passes.

Hebort. To forget all the Hebrew you ever learned immediately after your Bar Mitzvah.

Hebrute. Israeli aftershave.

Impasta. Someone who eats leavened foods during Passover

while maintaining he/she is observant.
Jewbilation. Pride in finding out that your favourite celebrity is Jewish.
Jewdo. Traditional form of self-defence based on talking way out of a tight spot.
Mamatzoh balls. Matzo balls that are as good as mother used to make.
Matzilation. Smashing a piece of matzo to bits while trying to butter it.
Meinstein. 'My son, the genius.'
Minyastics. Going to incredible lengths to find a tenth person for a *minyan*.
Mishpochehmarks. The assorted lipstick and makeup stains found on your face and collar after kissing all your aunts and cousins at a reception.
Re-shtetlement. Moving from Ilford to Edgware and finding all your old neighbours live in the same road as you.
Santashmanta. The explanation Jewish children get for why they celebrate Chanukah while the rest of humanity celebrates Christmas.
Shmuckluck. Finding out your wife is pregnant after you've had a vasectomy.
Shofarsogut. The relief you feel when after many attempts, the *shofar* is finally blown at the end of Yom Kippur.
Torahfied. Inability to remember your lines when called to read from the Torah at your Bar Mitzvah.
Trayffic accident. An appetiser that you find out contains prawn after you have eaten it.

***

I give you the answer, you give me the question:
A: Midrash.
Q: What is a Middle East skin disease?

A: The Gaza Strip.
Q: What is an Egyptian belly dance?

A: A classroom, a Passover ceremony, and a *latke*.
Q: What is a cheder, a seder, and a tater?

A: Sofer.
Q: On what do Jews recline on Passover?

A: Babylon.
Q: What does the rabbi do during some sermons?

A: *Kishka, succah* and *bris*.
Q: What are a gut, a hut, and a cut?

***

Abe Goldberg ran a thriving business and was very wealthy. Many of his customers were gentiles and he was therefore proud of his success. But he was worried about his teenage son, Issy, the heir to his business. Issy often used Yiddish words and phrases, some of them vulgar, in front of customers and greatly upset them. For weeks, Abe struggled with his problem. He was a widower and knew of no classy woman he felt could help. At last, the answer came to him. It was the perfect solution.

Abe went to see Father Brown, the local Catholic priest and a highly educated cleric whose command of English was flawless. As the church was having financial problems, Abe offered Father Brown £25,000 if the priest would agree to take Issy under his wing for a week and teach the boy to speak English the way he did. So, protesting loudly every step of the way, Issy went to board with the eloquent priest.

A day passed, then two, but Abe heard nothing. Finally, on the third day, he couldn't stand the suspense and he called the church. Father Brown answered the phone himself. Hoping for a miracle, but far from convinced, Abe asked how Issy was getting on.

'*Oy*,' replied the priest, 'let me tell you, the first few days with Issy were hell. He called me "*meshugga*", he said my cassock was an ugly *shmatta*, and he never stopped complaining about my *kvetching*.'

Father Brown sighed audibly. 'But don't despair, Mr

Goldberg. I haven't given up. And after all, won't any improvement be better than *bupkes*?'

***

Sadie, an elderly lady, goes up to a man at a bus stop in Golders Green, tugs on the sleeve of his coat and asks, '*Farshtayn* Yiddish?' ('Do you understand Yiddish?')

The man answers, '*Yaw, ich farshtay.*'

Sadie then says, 'Vot time is it?'

***

Benjamin and Morris are sitting in a wonderful kosher restaurant in Hendon. They are talking among themselves in Yiddish. A Chinese waiter comes up and in fluent and impeccable Yiddish asks them if everything is OK, can he get them anything, and so forth. Benjamin and Morris are dumbfounded.

'My God, where did he learn such perfect Yiddish?' they both think. After they pay the bill they ask the manager, an old friend of theirs, also fluent in Yiddish, 'Where did your waiter learn such fabulous Yiddish?'

The owner looks around and leans over to them so no one will hear and says, 'Shhhh. He thinks we're teaching him English.'

Cowboys & Indians

In the days of the Old West, Moshe had to go to Omaha on business. He went to the stagecoach office and asked, 'How much ah teeket to Omaha?' The clerk told him $5.

'Too much,' he complained. 'Anyvay, I ain't got $5, I only got $2 – Liss'n, I got ta get ta Omaha. I got very imput'n business dere. Pliess. Maybe you could do sumtink for me?'

'I'll tell you what I can do,' said the clerk. 'We need somebody to ride shotgun. Gimme the $2 and you can ride shotgun. You ride up on the top with the driver, you hold this rifle and if you see any Indians, you shoot 'em.'

'Vut you talkin' shoot Indians? I ain't never shot no Indians,' replied Moshe.

'It's easy. You see an Indian, you point the gun at him and pull this trigger. Just give me the $2 and get up there with the driver,' demanded the clerk.

So Moshe climbed up with the driver and off they rode into the prairie. About three hours into the trip, the driver asked, 'Ya see any Injuns?'

'Yep, I see vone,' said Moshe.

'How far away is he?' asked the driver.

'How could I know dis?' asked Moshe, who then held his thumb and forefinger about half an inch apart and said, 'He looks dis big – should I shoot 'im?'

'Not yet,' said the driver, 'you'll never hit him, he's too far away. Wait till he gets closer.'

Another couple of hours passed and the driver asked, 'Do ya still see the Injun?'

'Yep, I still see 'im.' Again Moshe held up his hand, this time with his thumb and forefinger about an inch apart, and said, 'He looks dis big – should I shoot 'im yet?'

'Not yet,' said the driver. 'He's still too far away. Wait till he gets closer. I'll tell you when to shoot 'im.'

Well, this continued every few hours for several days. On the third day of their journey when asked if he still saw the Indian, Moshe demonstrated the size of the Indian by spreading his arms as far as he could from top to bottom, indicating that the Indian now looked very big. The driver said, 'OK, now he's close enough. Now you can shoot 'im!'

Moshe hesitated and then said, 'Nah, I coulden shoot 'im.'

'Whaddya mean you can't shoot 'im? Why not?' demanded the driver angrily.

Moshe held his thumb and forefinger about half an inch apart, and said, 'How could I shoot 'im? I've known 'im since 'e was dis big.'

***

Back in the cowboy days, the westbound wagon train was lost and low on food. No other humans had been seen for days. And then they saw an old Jew sitting beneath a tree. The leader rushed up to him and said, 'We're lost and running out of food. Is there someplace ahead where we can get food?'

'Vell,' the old Jew said, 'I vouldn't go up dat hill und down de other side. Somevun told me you'll run into a big bacon tree.'

'A bacon tree?' asked the wagon train leader.

'Yah, ah bacon tree. Trust me. For nuttin vud I lie.'

The leader goes back and tells his people that if nothing else, they might be able to find food on the other side of the next ridge.

'So why did he say not to go there?' some pioneers asked.

'Oh, you know those Jews – they don't eat bacon.'

So the wagon train goes up the hill and down the other side. Suddenly, Indians attack and massacre everyone except the leader, who manages to escape back to the old Jew, who's enjoying a 'glassel tea'.

The near-dead man starts shouting. 'You old fool! You sent us to our deaths! We followed your instructions, but there was no bacon tree. Just hundreds of Indians who killed everyone.'

The old Jew holds up his hand and says, '*Oy*, vait a minute.'

He then gets out an English-Yiddish dictionary, and begins thumbing through it.

'Gevalt, I made myself ah big mistake. It vuz not a bacon tree. It vuz a ham bush.'

* * *

A family of Schmohawk Indians are sitting around the fire one night. There is papa Geronowitz, mama Pocayenta and the beautiful daughter, Minihorowitz.

'So, *nu*,' says Minihorowitz, 'You'll never believe.'

'What?' says Pocayenta.

'Today, at high noon, someone proposed to me.'

'So what did you say?' says Pocayenta.

'I said yes.'

'That's wonderful,' says Pocayenta. 'She said yes! Did you hear that Geronowitz? Our little Minihorowitz is getting married.'

'I heard,' says Geronowitz, 'I'm *kvelling*. So who's the lucky boy?'

'Sittin' Bialy.'

'Sittin' Bialy?' says Pocayenta, 'of the SoSiouxMe tribe?'

'That's the one,' says Minihorowitz.

'*Oy*, Geronowitz! The SoSiouxMes! There are so many of them. How can we feed them? How can we get them all in our teepee for the wedding?'

'We'll think of something,' says Geronowitz.

'Geronowitz, get me a buffalo for the wedding. I can make buffalo casserole from the meat and we can make an extra teepee from the hide. Get me a buffalo.'

So Geronowitz goes out to hunt a buffalo. A day and night goes by and Geronowitz has not come back. Another day and half the night and Geronowitz comes home exhausted, staggering and empty-handed.

'Geronowitz, I've been worried sick. Where have you been? Where's my buffalo?'

'It's like this,' he says. 'On my first day out, I hunted high and I hunted low and I finally found a buffalo. But this buffalo was scrawny with no meat on his bones for buffalo casserole and barely enough hide for a rain hat. So I settled in for the night to try again the next day. The second day, I looked high and I looked low, from this way and that way and I finally found a buffalo. He was big with lots of meat and lots of hide, but I tell you, Pocayenta, this was the ugliest buffalo I ever saw in my life. This, I thought to myself, is not the buffalo for my daughter's wedding. So I carried on looking. I went up hills and I went down hills and I found a big buffalo. It was, as buffaloes go, a beautiful buffalo. If I say so myself, it was the perfect buffalo. This, I said to myself, is the buffalo Pocayenta wants for Minihorowitz's wedding. So I reach into my backpack quietly for my tomahawk as I tip-toe over to the buffalo. I raise my tomahawk slowly over the buffalo's neck when suddenly, like a bolt of lightning from the sky, I see it.'

'See what?' says Pocayenta.

'I'd brought the dairy tomahawk by mistake!'

***

Natalie had three very active sons and they were quite a handful. One summer evening she was playing cowboys and Indians with them in her front garden when one of the boys 'shot' her and shouted, 'Bang! You're dead, mum.' So Natalie fell down.

Her next-door neighbour had been watching all this and when Natalie didn't get up straight away, he ran over to see if she had been hurt in the fall. When the neighbour bent over her, Natalie opened one eye and said to him, 'Shhh. Please don't give me away. It's the only chance I've had to have a rest all day.'

* * *

Sam calls his grandma from New Mexico. She says, 'It's so nice to hear your voice, my Sammeleh. Tell me, what's new?'

'I'm getting married, grandma.'

'My Sammeleh is getting married, how wonderful. Tell me all about her, tell me about her family.'

'Well, they're not like our people, grandma, they're native Americans.'

'So, they're first generation?'

'No, grandma, you don't understand. They live on a reservation.'

'Sammeleh, so what. Your own mother couldn't cook at all until I taught her, and she was always making reservations.'

'No, grandma, you don't understand. We are getting married in a teepee.'

'Oh, that's nice. *Nu*, so when is the wedding?'

'But grandma, I have to tell you that you won't be able to come to the wedding.'

'But why Sammeleh, your grandma has to be at your wedding?'

'I'm sorry, but only native Americans and persons with Indian names can attend.'

'Well, then, I will be there.'

'How grandma, you don't have an Indian name.'

'Yes Sammeleh, I do.'

'What, grandma, what's your Indian name?'

'Sitting Shivah.'

Philosophy

A group of elderly Jewish men meet every Wednesday in Brent Cross for a coffee and a chat. They drink their coffee and then sit for hours discussing the world situation. Usually, their discussion is very negative.

One day, Moshe surprises his friends by announcing, loud and clear, 'You know what? I've now become an optimist.'

Everyone is totally shocked and all conversation dries up.

But then Sam notices something isn't quite right and he says to Moshe, 'Hold on a minute, if you're an optimist, why are you looking so worried?'

Moshe replies, 'Do you think it's easy being an optimist?'

***

Maurice, Sam and Benny always met once a week in Edgware to discuss the world's situation. On one occasion, they tried to solve the problem of life.

'What is the problem of life?' asked Benny.

The more they talked about it, the more they thought they knew the answer. The problem of life is that everyone has worries. 'If people didn't have any worries,' said Sam, 'then life would be easy.'

But now that they knew, another question remained: how could the three of them end their worries?

They thought for a while and then Maurice said, 'Why don't we hire somebody to do all the worrying for us so that we can then have it easy?'

Sam said, 'Great idea. It wouldn't be easy, I know, but between us, we could pay him well to make up for the difficulty of the role.'

So they all agreed to chip in to pay someone £600 a month to do all their worrying for them. They were very happy with this decision until Sam pointed out the flaw.

'Tell me,' he said, 'If the man is making £600 each month, what has he got to worry about?'

***

Two *shlemiels* are *kvetching* about life. One of them sighs and says to the other, 'Considering how hard life is, death isn't such a bad thing. In fact, I think sometimes it's better not to have been born at all.'

'True,' says his friend. 'But how many men are that lucky? Maybe one in ten thousand!'

***

If a married Jewish man is walking alone in a park, and expresses an opinion, without anybody around to hear him, is he still wrong?

***

Abe went to see his rabbi. 'Rabbi,' he said, 'I would be grateful if you could explain the Talmud to me.'

'Very well, Abe,' said the rabbi, 'First, I need to ask you a simple question. If two men climb inside a chimney and one comes out dirty and the other comes out clean, which one washes himself?'

'The dirty one,' replied Abe.

'No, Abe. They look at each other. The dirty man thinks he is clean but the clean man thinks he is dirty and washes.'

'Now another question,' said the rabbi. 'If two men climb inside a chimney and one comes out dirty and the other comes out clean, which one washes himself?'

Abe smiled, 'You just told me that one, Rabbi. The clean man, because he thinks he is dirty.'

'No, Abe,' said the rabbi. 'They each look at themselves. The clean man knows he doesn't have to wash and the dirty man washes himself.'

'Now one final question,' said the rabbi. 'If two men climb inside a chimney and one comes out dirty and the other one comes out clean, which one washes himself?'

This time Abe frowned, 'I don't know, Rabbi. It could be either one, depending on your point of view.'

'No Abe,' said the rabbi. 'If two men climb inside a chimney, how could either of them come out clean? They are obviously both dirty and so they both wash.'

Abe was now thoroughly confused, 'Rabbi, you asked me exactly the same question three times, yet you gave me three different answers. Are you playing games with me?'

'No, Abe, I would never joke with you. This is Talmud.'

***

Moshe was talking to his friend Issy. 'Issy, I'm nearly forty years old. Do you think I should marry?'

'By all means get married,' replied Issy. 'If you get a good a wife, you'll be happy. If you don't, you'll become a philosopher – and that's a good thing for any man.'

***

Mogadishu Yogi is visiting north London. During one of his walks, in full costume and beard, he passes a small snack bar called Benjy's Hot Dogs and as he wants to try everything, he goes into the shop and says, 'Make me a hot dog with everything.'

Benjy goes to work and soon puts together a loaded hot dog. He hands it to the spiritual master who pays him with a £10 note, which Benjy quickly puts into his pocket.

'So,' asks Mogadishu Yogi, 'where's my change?'

Benjy replies, 'Change must come from within.'

***

Issy and Jacob are walking down Golders Green High Street when it starts to rain, and in no time at all, it's raining quite hard. Luckily, Issy is carrying an umbrella.

'*Nu*,' says Jacob. 'So when are you going to open the umbrella?'

'It won't do us any good,' says Issy. 'It's full of holes.'

'So why then did you bring it?' replies Jacob.

'Because,' Issy says with shrug, 'I didn't think it would rain.'

***

Moshe and his friends had been arguing for some days and eventually, in desperation, they all agreed that he should go to the rabbi and get his verdict on the question that had them all baffled. 'Which is more important, the sun or the moon?' Moshe asked the rabbi.

'Why the moon, of course,' replied the rabbi after some pondering. 'It shines at night, when it is needed. The sun, however, shines only during the day, when there is no need of it at all.'

Drinking

Maurice and Isaac find themselves sitting next to each other in a New York bar. After a while, Maurice looks at Isaac and says, 'I can't help but think, from listening to you, that you're from Israel.'

Isaac responds proudly, 'I am!'

Maurice says, 'So am I! And where might you be from?'

Isaac answers, 'I'm from Jerusalem.'

Maurice responds, 'So am I! And where did you live?'

Isaac says, 'A lovely little area two miles east of King David's Hotel. Not too far from the Old City.'

Maurice says, 'Unbelievable! What school did you attend?'

Isaac answers, 'Well, I attended Yeshiva University.'

Maurice gets really excited, and says, 'And so did I. Tell me, what year did you graduate?'

Isaac answers, 'I graduated in 1984.'

Maurice exclaims, 'Amazing! This was destined by fate. God wanted us to meet! I can hardly believe our good luck at winding up in the same bar tonight. Can you believe it, I graduated from Yeshiva University in 1984 also.'

About this time, Moshe enters the bar, sits down, and orders a beer. The bartender walks over to him shaking his head and mutters, 'It's going to be a long night tonight, the Goldberg twins are drunk again.'

***

Ben had been drinking in a pub all night. The bartender finally said that the bar was closing. So Ben stood up to leave and fell flat on his face. He tried to stand one more time; same result. Ben figured he'd crawl outside and get some fresh air and maybe that would sober him up.

Once outside, Ben stood up but fell flat on his face again. So he decided to crawl the four blocks to his home. When he arrived at the door, Ben stood up and again fell flat on his face. He crawled through the door and into his bedroom. When he reached his bed, Ben tried one more time to stand up. This time he managed to pull himself upright, but he quickly fell right into bed and fell sound asleep as soon as his head hit the pillow.

He was awakened the next morning to his wife, Yente, standing over him, shouting, 'So, you've been out drinking again!'

'What makes you say that?' Ben asked, putting on an innocent look.

Yente replied 'The pub called – you left your wheelchair there again.'

***

I found twelve bottles of old Passover wine but I wasn't sure they could still be drunk. I then got into an argument with my wife and lost. She instructed me to empty each and every bottle down the drain, so I proceeded with the task. I opened the first bottle and poured the contents down the sink, with the exception of one glass, which I drank. I opened the second and third bottles and did likewise, with the exception of one glass from each, which I drank. I then opened the fourth sink, poured the bottles down the glass, which I drank. I pulled the bottle from the next and drank one sink out of it and threw the rest down the glass. I pulled the sink out of the glass and poured the cork from the bottle. Then I corked the sink with the glass, bottled the drink and drank the pour.

When I had everything emptied, I steadied the house with one hand, counted the bottles, corks, glasses and sinks with the other, which were 29 and put the house in the bottle, which I drank. I'm Jewish I am so I'm not under the affluence of incahol, but thinkle peep I am. I'm not half as thunk as you might drink. I fool so feelish I don't know who is me, and the drunker I stand here the longer I get.

***

Q: Why don't Jews drink?

A: It interferes with their suffering.

***

It is Saturday night and Sean is in an Irish pub in Cricklewood. He soon strikes up a conversation with the fellow next to him at the bar. Sean says, 'I must stop drinking all this Irish whiskey.'

'Why do you want to do that?' asks his companion.

'Because every Saturday night I go out and drink a half a bottle of the stuff, come home drunk, make mad passionate love to my wife, wake up Sunday morning, and go to church.'

'What's wrong with that?' the friend asks. 'A lot of good Irishmen go out on Saturday night, drink a half bottle of good Irish whiskey, come home drunk, make love to the wife, and go to mass on Sunday.'

'I know,' says Sean, 'but I'm Jewish.'

***

Alf arrives home from work and as soon as he sets foot in the house, Sadie is on to him, telling him that their friend Michael Bloom has finally quit smoking. 'Imagine that, Alf,' she says, 'someone who smoked three packs a day for twenty years has stopped smoking all of a sudden. Now that's what I call willpower – something that you definitely don't have.'

But Sadie hadn't finished. 'And that's not all. I hear that Bernard, that drunken friend of yours, is finally giving up drinking – another example of the kind of willpower that you don't have.'

'OK, Sadie,' said Alf, 'you want to see willpower, do you? Well here's willpower. I am going to sleep in the spare room from now on. I am going to prove to you that I won't be affected at all by not sleeping with a woman.'

Alf keeps to his word. One night, when he had been sleeping alone for a week, there was a knock on his bedroom door. Alf shouted out, 'What do you want?'

Sadie replied, 'Bloom has started smoking again.'

***

Shlomo was walking down Hendon High Street one day when a filthy-looking, smelly tramp came up to him and asked, 'Could you spare one pound, please mister?'

Shlomo replied, 'Will you buy alcohol with it?'

The tramp answered, 'No, certainly not. I don't drink.'

Shlomo then asked, 'Will you gamble it away?'

The tramp again replied, 'No, I don't gamble.'

So Shlomo said to the tramp, 'OK, I'll give you your pound, but first of all you have to come home with me so my wife Beckie can see what happens to a man who doesn't drink or gamble!'

***

Rabbi Bloom caught two of his rabbinical students gambling and drinking on Sabbath. Next day, Rabbi Bloom called them into his office and asked them what was going on. They immediately confessed to having given in to weakness and agreed that they deserved some form of punishment for their sin. Rabbi Bloom thought a lot about this and then came up with the answer. He bought two bags of dried peas from the delicatessen and told them, 'Put these in your shoes and walk on them for a week to remind yourselves how hard life can be when you turn away from God.'

A few days later, the two students met each other in the

street. One had a pronounced limp and had dark circles under his eyes. He looked very tired and weary. On the other hand, the other was the same as he had been before. 'Hey,' said the first. 'How is it that you are walking so easily? Why didn't you do as the rabbi asked and put the peas in your shoes?'

'I did,' said the other. 'But I boiled them first.'

***

Bernie and Abe are having a drink together in a City wine bar to celebrate Abe's recent promotion. They have been drinking for some time when Bernie begins to insult Abe. He shouts, 'I slept with your mother, Abe.'

There is a hush as everyone listens.

Bernie again shouts at Abe, 'I slept with your mother, Abe.'

Abe replies, 'I know. Why don't you go home now, Dad, you're drunk.'

***

Arnold and Estelle have been engaged for over fifteen years. She won't marry him while he is drunk and he won't marry her while he is sober.

Gambling

Rabbi Levine is walking slowly out of a *shul* in Golders Green when a gust of wind blows his hat down the street. He's an old man and can't walk fast enough to catch his hat. Across the street, Bernie sees what's happening, rushes over, grabs the hat and returns it to Rabbi Levine.

'I don't think I would have been able to catch my hat,' Rabbi Levine says. He places his hand on Bernie's shoulder and says, 'May God bless you.'

Bernie thinks, 'I've just been blessed by the rabbi, this must be my lucky day.' So he goes into a betting shop and sees in the first race a horse named Top Hat at 20 to 1.

He bets £50 and the horse comes in first. In the second race, Bernie sees a horse named Fedora at 30 to 1 so he bets it all and this horse comes in first also. When Bernie finally returns home to his wife, she asks him where he's been. He explains how he caught the rabbi's hat and was blessed by him and then went to a betting office and started winning on horses that had a hat in their names.

'So where's the money?' she asks.

'I lost it all in the ninth race. I bet on a horse named Chateau and it lost.'

'You fool, chateau is a house, chapeau is a hat.'

'It doesn't matter,' Bernie said. 'The winner was some Japanese horse named Yarmulka.'

***

The local pub was so sure that its barman was the strongest man around that they offered a standing £1,000 bet. The barman would squeeze a lemon until all the juice ran into a glass and then hand the lemon to a customer. Anyone who could squeeze one more drop of juice out would win the money. Many people had tried over time (weight-lifters, rowers, wrestlers, etc.), but nobody could do it.

One day Hyman, a scrawny little man, came into the bar wearing thick glasses and a cheap jacket. Hyman went up to the barman and said in a squeaky voice, 'I'd like to try the bet.'

After the laughter had died down, the barman said, 'OK,' grabbed a lemon and squeezed away. Then he handed the wrinkled remains of the rind to Hyman. But the laughter turned to silence as Hyman clenched his fist around the lemon and four more drops fell into the glass.

As the crowd cheered, the barman paid the £1,000 and asked, 'What do you do for a living? Are you a professional strong man, or what?'

Hyman replied, 'No. I'm not, I work for the Jewish National Fund.'

***

An archaeologist was digging in the Negev Desert in Israel and came upon a casket containing a mummy, a rather rare occurrence in Israel, to say the least. After examining it, he called Abe, the curator of the Israel Museum in Jerusalem.

'I've just discovered a 3,000-year-old mummy of a man who died of heart failure,' the excited scientist exclaimed.

Abe replied, 'Bring him in. We'll check it out.'

A week later, the amazed Abe called the archaeologist. 'You were right about both the mummy's age and cause of death. How in the world did you know?'

'Easy. There was a piece of paper in his hand that said, "10,000 Shekels on Goliath."'

* * *

Sidney, a Jewish scientist, wanted to know where the sun went after it set. He went around asking the other scientists, but they didn't know either. Pretty soon he had the whole of his science department trying to figure it out. They puzzled over it for a long time but they couldn't come up with an answer. In fact they sat up all night thinking about it until finally it dawned on them.

* * *

Abe ran into Moshe one afternoon. 'Moshe, *nu*? What's new?'

'Abe, I'm into racehorses at the moment. I have a couple of real winners and have won a lot of money already.'

'How can I get into it, Moshe?'

'Well, I have a horse I'm looking to sell. It has had 24 starts and won nine of them. I'll let you have it for £120,000.'

Abe agreed and gave Moshe a cheque for £120,000.

Three days later, Abe was excitedly waiting at the front gate for his horse to arrive. The horse van pulled up and inside was a dead racehorse.

A month later, Abe runs into Moshe, who has been avoiding him the last few weeks.

'Moshe, *nu*? What's new?'

'Umm, things are well. And with you?'

'Things are great!'

'Abe, you're not upset I sold you a dead racehorse?'

'Not at all Moshe. In fact, it made me a lot of money.'

'How is that? It was dead!'

'Well, I had a raffle. I sold 100,000 tickets at £5 a ticket with the horse as the prize.'

'Wasn't the winner upset he won a dead racehorse?'

Abe shrugs, 'So, I gave him back his £5!'

***

Naomi, being still unmarried, was bored one evening. So she decided to go to a London casino for the first time ever and was persuaded to play roulette. She asked someone at the table the best way to pick a number. He suggested putting her money on her age. So, she put ten chips on the number 28. When the number 34 came up, she fainted.

***

Six retired Edgware men are playing poker one evening in Abe's house when Shlomo loses £650 on one big hand, clutches his chest and drops dead at the table. The other five continue playing but this time standing up to show respect for their departed friend.

Later, Abe asks, 'Who's going to tell his wife, Hetty?'

They cut cards and Moshe loses. Before he leaves, he is advised to be discreet and kind and to try hard not to make a terrible situation any worse. 'Discreet?' says Moshe, 'I'm the most discreet man there is. Discretion is my middle name. Just leave it to me and don't worry about a thing.'

So Moshe goes over to Shlomo's house and rings the doorbell. Hetty opens the door and asks, '*Nu*, so what do you want?'

Moshe replies, 'Your husband just lost £650 and is afraid to come home.'

On hearing this, Hetty yells, 'SO TELL HIM HE SHOULD DROP DEAD.'

'OK I'll go and tell him,' says Moshe.

***

Moshe just couldn't believe it – he had won a top prize in the National Lottery. He just had to tell his best friend. Maurice congratulated Moshe and asked how he had picked his six numbers.

'I chose my age and the ages of my wife and three children,' replied Moshe.

'But that's only five numbers,' said Maurice. 'What about the sixth number?'

'Well, it was a miracle,' replied Moshe. 'Six sevens appeared to me in a dream and danced before my very eyes. Six times seven is 49 and so I chose 49.'

'Hey, wait a minute,' said Maurice, 'six times seven is 42 not 49.'

'Huh? ... All right, so you be the mathematical genius.'

***

Beckie walks into Coutts Bank in the Strand and opens an account with £500,000 in cash. Because of the amount of money, the deputy manager goes over to her, gives her his card and says, 'If there's any service you need in future, please call me directly.'

A few days later, Beckie returns and deposits a further £800,000. This time, the manager goes over to her, gives her his card and says, 'If there's any service you need in future, please call me directly on my private line.'

A week later, Beckie returns and sees the manager. 'You told me that I should just ask if I wanted anything. Well. I want to meet Lord Coutts in person.'

The manager makes a phone call and then escorts Beckie to Lord Coutts' office. She is welcomed in. 'What do you do for a living?' Lord Coutts asks Beckie.

'I gamble, your lordship. I bet on almost everything and with almost anyone.'

'Well,' he says, 'would you like to make a bet with me and if so, about what?'

Beckie replies, 'OK. I bet your lordship £100,000 that two weeks from today, your testicles will become cube-shaped.'

Lord Coutts is embarrassed, but figures she's an important client and in any case, he can't lose. So he accepts the bet. Two weeks later Beckie returns accompanied by her associate carrying a large bag. She says that they have come to collect her bet.

Lord Coutts laughs. 'But you've lost. My testicles are still perfectly round.'

'Your lordship,' says Beckie, 'because of the size of our bet, I have a right to personally check.'

Reluctantly, Lord Coutts opens his trousers and pulls down his pants. Beckie grasps his testicles, at which point her associate says, 'Damn, Beckie, you've won yet again.'

'Won?' says Lord Coutts, 'but she hasn't won.'

'Oh yes she has,' says the associate. 'She bet me £500,000 that by this afternoon, she'd be holding Lord Coutts by the balls.'

***

A rabbi, a minister and a priest, played cards every Wednesday for small stakes, but their problem was that they lived in a 'no gambling allowed' town. One day, the sheriff raided their game and took them before the judge. After hearing the sheriff's story, the judge asked the priest, 'Were you gambling, Father?'

The priest looked toward heaven, whispered, 'Oh, Lord, forgive me,' and then replied aloud, 'No, your honour, I was not gambling.'

'Were you gambling, Reverend?' the judge then asked the minister.

The minister replied, 'No, your honour, I was not.'

Turning to the third clergyman, the judge asked, 'Were you gambling, Rabbi?'

The rabbi eyed him coolly and replied, 'With whom?'

Magic & mystery

For months, Leah had been nagging her husband to go with her to the séance parlour of Madame Sadie. 'Cyril, Madame Sadie is a Jewish gypsy and she brings the voices of the dead from the other world. We all talk to them. Last week, I talked with my mother, may she rest in peace. Cyril, for only £30 you can talk to your *zaydeh* whom you miss so much.'

Cyril could not resist and at the next séance, there was Cyril sitting under the coloured light at the green table, holding hands with the person on each side of him. All were humming. Madame Sadie, her eyes lost in trance, was making passes over a crystal ball. 'My medium Vashtri, who is that with you? Mr Himmelfarb? Cyril's *zaydeh*?'

Cyril swallowed the lump in his throat and called, 'Grandpa? *Zaydeh?*'

'Ah, Cyril?' a thin voice quavered.

'Yes, yes,' cried Cyril, 'This is your Cyril, *Zaydeh*, are you happy in the other world?'

'Cyril, I am in bliss. I'm with your *bubbeh*. We laugh, we sing, we gaze upon the shining face of the Lord.'

Cyril asks his *zaydeh* many questions and his *zaydeh* answers each, until – 'So now, Cyril, I have to go. The angels are calling. Just one more question I can answer. Ask. Ask.'

'*Zaydeh*,' sighed Cyril, 'when did you learn to speak English?'

***

Abe lives in Tel Aviv. One day, he takes the day off work and decides to go out golfing. He is on the second hole when he notices a frog sitting next to the green.

Abe thinks nothing of it and is about to shoot when he hears, 'Ribbit, 9 Iron.'

Abe looks around and doesn't see anyone.

'Ribbit, 9 Iron.'

And then Abe realises that the frog is doing the talking. He looks at the frog and decides to prove the frog wrong, puts his other club away and grabs a 9 iron. Boom! He hits it ten inches from the hole. He is shocked. He says to the frog, 'Wow, that's amazing. You must be a lucky frog, eh?'

The frog replies, 'Ribbit. Lucky frog.'

Abe decides to take the frog with him to the next hole. 'What do you think, frog?' 'Ribbit, 3 wood.' Abe takes out a 3 wood and Boom! Hole in one. Abe is befuddled and doesn't know what to say. By the end of the day, Abe has played the best game of golf in his life and asks the frog, 'OK where to next?'

'Ribbit. Las Vegas.'

They go to Las Vegas and Abe says, 'OK frog, now what?'

'Ribbit. Roulette.'

Upon approaching the roulette table, Abe asks,' What do you think I should bet?'

'Ribbit, $3,000, black 6.'

Now, this is a million-to-one shot to win, but after the golf game, Abe figures what the heck. Boom! Tons of cash comes sliding back across the table. Abe takes his winnings and buys the best room in the hotel. He sits the frog down and says, 'Frog, I don't know how to repay you. You've won me all this money and I am forever grateful.'

The frog replies, 'Ribbit, kiss me.'

Abe figures why not, since after all the frog did for him he deserves it. With a kiss, the frog turns into a gorgeous fifteen-year-old girl.

'And that, your honour, is how the girl ended up in my room.'

***

Mrs Goldstein was out golfing one day when she hit her ball into the woods. She went into the woods to look for it and found a frog in a trap. The frog looked up at her and said, 'If you release me from this trap, I will grant you three wishes.'

Not a person to miss a trick, Mrs Goldstein immediately freed the frog.

The frog thanked her and said, 'I'm sorry but I failed to mention that there is a condition to your wishes – that whatever you wish for yourself, Mr Goldstein will get ten times more or better!'

Mrs Goldstein replied, 'That's OK – I'm happy to accept your condition. For my first wish, I want to be the most beautiful woman in the world.' The frog warned her, 'You do realise that this wish will also make Mr Goldstein the most handsome man in the world, women will flock to him like bees to honey.'

Mrs Goldstein replied, 'It's not a problem, because I will be the most beautiful woman and he will only have eyes for me.'

So, KAZAM – Mrs Goldstein is the most beautiful woman in the world!

For her second wish, Mrs Goldstein asked to be the richest woman in the world. The frog said, 'That will make Mr Goldstein the richest man in the world and he will be ten times richer than you.'

Mrs Goldstein said, 'It's not a problem, because what's mine is his and what's his is mine.'

So, KAZAM – Mrs Goldstein is the richest woman in the world!

The frog then inquired about her third wish to which Mrs Goldstein answered, 'I'd like a mild heart attack.'

***

One Shabbes morning, during prayers, there was a loud BOOM and a sudden flash of smoke appeared in the front of the synagogue. When the smoke cleared, the astonished congregation saw this frightening figure in red, complete with horns, pitchfork and tail and a Jewish *yarmulka*. Immediately, the congregation panicked. People rushed to the back of the synagogue trying to get away. The devil watched the retreat with great glee, but his mood was disturbed by the sight of one man still relaxing comfortably in the third row right side in his pew.

Angrily the devil thundered, 'Do you not know who I am?'

Morris replied in a nonchalant way, 'Sure I do.'

The devil was extremely puzzled. 'Do you not fear me?'

'No. Not at all!' came the reply.

'Why not?'

Morris snorted, 'What for? I've been married to your sister for 35 years!'

***

Rifka goes to see a famous wizard and asks, 'Is it possible to remove a curse I've been living with for the last 35 years?'

The wizard replies, 'It's possible, but you must tell me the exact words that were used to put the curse on you in the first place.'

Rifka says, 'I now pronounce you man and wife.'

***

Two Jewish curses:

May you sell candles for a living and then may the sun never set.
May you be like a chandelier, hang by day and burn by night.

***

Shlomo, 75 years old, was taking a walk when he saw a frog in the gutter. He was shocked when the frog began to speak to him. The frog said, 'Old man, if you kiss me, I'll turn into a beautiful princess, I'll be yours forever and we can make mad passionate love every night.'

Shlomo bent down and put the frog into his pocket and continued walking.

The frog said, 'Hey, I don't think you heard me. I said if you kiss me, I'll turn into a beautiful princess and we can make passionate love every night.'

Shlomo took the frog out of his pocket and said, 'I heard you, but at my age I'd rather have a talking frog.'

***

Nicholas and Abe found themselves delivered together to Hell. A little confused at their present situation, they were startled to see a door in the wall open, and behind the door was perhaps the ugliest woman they had ever seen. She was 3ft 4in, dirty and covered in thick black hair. Flies circled her and you could smell her even over the brimstone.

The voice of the Devil was heard, 'Nicholas, you have sinned! You are condemned to spend the rest of eternity in bed with this woman!'

Nicholas groaned as he was whisked through the door by a group of lesser demons to his torment. This understandably shook up Abe and so he jumped when a second door opened. And as the door inched open, he strained to see the figure of – Cindy Crawford. Delighted, Abe jumped up, taking in the sight of this beautiful woman, barely dressed in a skimpy bikini.

Then he heard the voice of the Devil saying, 'Cindy, you have sinned - '

***

Sadie and Benny were both 65 years old and were celebrating their fortieth wedding anniversary. When all the family and guests had left their house, a fairy appeared from nowhere and said to them, 'Congratulations, you two. I'm here to grant you both one wish each.'

Sadie said, 'I want to travel around the world.'

The fairy waved her magic wand and POW – Sadie had tickets in her hand for a round-the-world cruise on a Cunard liner.

Then the fairy asked Benny what he wanted.

Benny replied. 'I wish I had a wife thirty years younger than me.'

So the fairy picked up her wand and POW – Benny was 95 years old.

***

Freda is walking down Hendon Road one morning when she hears a voice shout in her ear, 'Stop at once. Don't take another step.'

She stops at once and a brick smashes into the pavement just in front of her. She has had a narrow escape. A few minutes later, Freda is at a pedestrian crossing and just as she's about to step across the road, the same voice shouts in her ear, 'Stay where you are. Don't cross the road.'

She stays where she is and a bus goes across the red light at speed, just where she would have been had she crossed. Freda is shaking at her second narrow escape and says aloud, 'Who are you? Why are you helping me?'

'I'm your guardian angel,' came the reply, 'and I'm just doing my job looking after you. Is there any other question you would like to ask me?'

'Yes,' replied Freda, 'Where were you on my wedding day?'

***

Harry walks into a pub carrying a small box. He puts the box down on the bar, opens the lid and music wafts out into the room. The man sitting next to Harry looks into the box and is amazed to find that the music is coming from a tiny man playing a tiny grand piano inside the box. So he asks Harry about it. Harry says, 'I found a magic lamp, read the inscription and rubbed it. I've got the lamp right here.'

Harry takes the lamp out of his pocket and reads the inscription aloud, 'Rub this lamp and it will grant you one wish.'

The other guy asks, 'Can I rub the lamp too?'

Harry shrugs and says, 'I must point out that it doesn't work as well as it should.'

'Never mind.' says the other guy, so Harry hands him the lamp.

After rubbing it for a moment, the bar starts to fill up with hound dogs. Literally thousands upon thousands of hound dogs. The guy looks totally stunned and says to Harry, 'I didn't wish for hounds. I wished for a million pounds.'

Harry looks at him and says, 'I told you it didn't always work. Do you think I wished for a ten-inch pianist?'

TRAVEL & TECHNOLOGY

Holidays

Isaac and Hetty were planning a holiday. As usual, they ended up arguing. 'It's "Hawaii" I'm telling you.' Hetty said.

'*Oy Vay*, I never knew anyone so stubborn. "Havaii" is how it's pronounced,' Isaac says. And so it went on all the way until they got there. As soon as they got off the plane, they asked a porter, 'Now that we're on the island, you can settle an argument between my wife and I. Is this "Hawaii" or "Havaii"?'

'This is Havaii,' replied the porter.

'Ha!' Isaac said, turning to Hetty, 'See, didn't I tell you never to argue with me? I'm always right.'

Just before they began to walk away, Isaac gave the porter a hearty 'Thank you.'

'You're velcome!'

***

Manny was out with his best friends, Joe and Bette, one evening when he suddenly collapsed and died. His friends were naturally totally shocked. Joe pointed to Manny and said to Bette, 'How good he looks, how relaxed, how tanned, how healthy!'

'And why not?' replied Bette, 'He just spent three weeks in Eilat.'

***

One day, Freda said to her husband Tony, 'If we were rich, we'd spend six months a year in Florida, six months a year in Eilat, and six months a year in Spain.'

'But dear, I make that eighteen months in a year on holiday!' said Tony.

'Absolutely, darling. Isn't is wonderful what one can do with money these days?'

***

From Israel comes the story of a guide who was showing some visitors around a small local museum. 'That fossil in the glass case over there is two million and nine years old,' he told them.

'How can you date it so precisely?' someone asked admiringly.

'That's easy,' said the guide. 'I've been working here nine years and it was two million years old when I came.'

***

Mrs Stein, a rich tourist, goes to Paris to visit the art galleries. She decides to hire the services of a guide to show her around the Louvre.

'Oh!' said Mrs Stein looking at a painting, 'That's a Monet isn't it?'

'No, Madame, almost, it's a Manet,' replied the guide.

'And that one, it's a Pissaro?'

'Er – no, I'm sorry Madame, that's a Monet.'

'Oh, I see. Now that one I'm sure of – that's a Picasso isn't it?'

'No, Madame, that's a mirror.'

***

Beckie, an elderly Jewish lady from London, goes to her travel agent and says, 'I want to go to India.'

'Why India? It's filthy, very hot and it's filled to the brim with Indians. It's a long journey, and those trains, how will you manage? What will you eat? The food is too hot and spicy for you. You can't drink the water. You must not eat fresh fruit and vegetables. You'll get sick – hepatitis, cholera, typhoid, malaria, God only knows. What will you do? Can you imagine the hospital, no Jewish doctors? Why torture yourself?'

'I want to go to India.'

The necessary arrangements are made and off she goes. Beckie arrives in India and undeterred by the noise, smell and crowds, makes her way to an ashram. There she joins the seemingly never-ending queue of people waiting for an audience with the guru. An aide tells her that it will take at least three days of queueing to see the guru.

'That's OK, I'll wait.'

Eventually Beckie reaches the hallowed portals. There she is told firmly that she can only say three words. She is ushered into the inner sanctum where the wise guru is seated, ready to bestow spiritual blessings upon eager initiates. Just before she reaches the holy of holies, Beckie is once again reminded, 'Remember, just three words.'

Unlike the other devotees, she does not prostrate herself at his feet. She stands directly in front of him, crosses her arms over her chest, fixes her gaze on his and says, 'Sidney, come home.'

***

Hetty was on her first visit to Israel and was on a special day tour to Jerusalem. First stop was a big beautiful *shul* and she said to her guide, 'That's really special. How long did it take to build?'

The guide replied, 'About five years, madam.'

Hetty replied, 'In my country it would only have taken six months.'

They carried on with the tour and arrived at a small settlement. Hetty said to the guide, 'This is really lovely. How long did they take to build it?'

'About eight years, madam,' he replied.

Hetty said (snootily), 'Huh, in my country it would have taken less than a year.'

Then they arrived at the Wailing Wall. Hetty gasped at its size and said to the guide, 'Just look at that structure!'

The guide didn't wait for her next comment. He immediately said, 'My goodness! I just can't believe it – it wasn't here this morning!'

***

A Swiss tourist in Tel Aviv is looking for directions and pulls up at a bus stop where two Israelis are waiting.

'*Entschuldigung Sie bitte, koennen Sie Deutsch sprechen?*' he asks. The two Israelis just stare at him.

'*Excusez-moi, parlez-vous français?*' The two continue to stare.

'*Parla italiano?*' No response.

'*Habla español?*' Still nothing.

The Swiss tourist drives off, extremely disgusted and frustrated. The first Israeli turns to his friend and says, 'You know, maybe we should learn a foreign language - '

'Why?' says his friend, 'That bloke knew four languages and that didn't do him any good.'

***

Rebecca and Hyman are silently rocking on their rocking chairs in front of the fire when Hyman suddenly says, 'Rebecca, we've been married now for over fifty years and it's good that the children are all grown up, living on their own and don't disturb us much.'

They continue to rock silently for a few more minutes, then Hyman says, 'You know Rebecca, we certainly aren't getting any younger.'

They maintain their silent rocking for some more minutes, then Hyman continues, 'You know Rebecca, I've been thinking. One of these days, one of us is surely going to die.'

They maintain their silent rocking a bit longer, then Hyman says, 'You know Rebecca, if one of us does die, I'm going to take that trip to Israel we promised ourselves.'

***

Moshe left the cold climate of Edgware and went on holiday to Florida. His wife Beckie, who was in a bridge competition, was planning to join him in Florida the next day. When Moshe reached his hotel, he decided to send Beckie a quick e-mail to say he'd arrived and all was well. Unable to find the scrap of paper on which he had written the e-mail address she had given him, he did his best to type it in from memory. Unfortunately, he missed one letter and his e-mail was directed instead to an elderly woman whose husband had passed away only the day before. When the grieving woman checked her e-mail, she took one look at the screen, let out a piercing scream, fainted and fell to the floor with a thud. At the sound, her family rushed into the room and saw this email on the screen:

> Dearest Beckie, just checked in.
> Everything prepared for your arrival tomorrow.
> Your Loving Husband Moshe
> PS Sure is hot down here.

* * *

Sadie, an elderly lady, is sitting in a restaurant in Brent Cross shopping centre sipping her tea. Next to her, three nuns are discussing where to go on holiday.

The second nun says to Mother Superior, 'Let's go to Jerusalem.'

'No,' says Mother Superior, 'there are too many Jews there.'

The third nun says to Mother Superior 'Let's go to Philadelphia.'

'No,' says Mother Superior again, 'also too many Jews there.'

The second nun again speaks and says, 'Let's go to Paris.'

Yet again Mother Superior replies, 'No, too many Jews there too.'

Sadie has heard enough.

She leans over and says to them, in a thick, loud Yiddish accent, 'Vell, vhy don't you go to Hell, dere are no Jews dere!'

* * *

A north London congregation decides to honour their rabbi for his 25 years of dedicated service by giving him tickets and money for a week-long, all-expenses paid holiday to New York. When Rabbi Bloom arrives and checks into his hotel room, he is surprised to find a naked girl lying face down on his bed. Without saying a word, Rabbi Bloom picks up the phone, calls his synagogue long distance and says, 'Where is your respect? As your rabbi, I am very, very angry with you.'

On hearing this, the girl gets up and starts to get dressed.

Rabbi Bloom turns to her and says, 'Where are you going? I'm not angry with you.'

***

Jacob had just returned to Kiev after visiting London. As soon as he got home, he wrote the following letter to a friend he had met in London just before he left:

> It was so nice to meet you. If you are ever in Kiev, please come and visit me, I would be glad to see you again. It's easy to find me. Go to the main street in Kiev and start walking straight from its beginning at the station. Take the third turning on the right and continue down this road until you come to the Kiev Flats. Go through the archway and you'll find yourself in a big courtyard surrounded by apartment buildings. Then shout out as loud as you can, 'Rabbinowitz'. You'll immediately see faces looking at you from all the apartment windows in the courtyard except one! This is my window, because my name is Rosen.

***

As soon as Issy got home from work one evening, his wife Beckie came up to him and said, 'Issy, our au pair has stolen two of our towels.'

'Oh, really,' said Issy, not looking very interested, 'that wasn't a nice thing to do.'

'You're damn right it wasn't,' said Beckie, 'they were the best towels we had, the two we got from the Hilton Eilat while we were on holiday last Passover.'

***

Shlomo and Moshe are talking one day about holidays. Shlomo says, 'I think I am just about ready to book my winter holidays again, but I'm going to do it differently this time. In the past, I have always taken your advice about where to go. Three years ago you said to go to Eilat. I went to Eilat and my wife Ruth got pregnant. Then two years ago, you told me to go to Bermuda and Ruth got pregnant again. Last year you suggested the Canary Isles and as you know, Ruth got pregnant yet again.'

Moshe asks, 'So what are you going to do different this year, Shlomo?'

'This year,' replies Shlomo, 'I'm taking Ruth with me.'

***

Benjy had done very well in business. He was a multi-millionaire and had been knighted by the Queen for his endeavours. One day, after completing yet another very successful business deal, he decided on the spur of the moment to take his wife Sadie to Israel. He asked his secretary Carol to make the arrangements.

Carol rang the Tel Aviv Dan hotel and asked to speak to the manager. 'I am happy to inform you that Sir Benjy and his wife have chosen to stay at the Dan next week. But as they are very wealthy and require total privacy, they would need to book the entire hotel for their stay. Money is not a problem. Can you set this up?'

The manager didn't hesitate. 'Yes, I can move all guests to a sister hotel.'

Carol then asked, 'Is there a private beach?'

'Yes.'

'What colour is the sand?' asked Carol.

'Silver,' came the reply.

'Well that will be a problem as Sir Benjy always insists on golden sand.'

'OK. I can get round it,' said the manager. 'There's a quarry nearby and I will arrange for golden sand to be laid on the beach.'

'And finally,' said Carol, 'Sir Benjy prefers a blue sky without a cloud in it. Is the weather going to be perfect next week?'

'No problem,' said the manager, 'I will get the Israeli Air Force to seed the clouds and so disperse them.'

The following week, there were Benjy and Sadie sunbathing on the wide expanse of the private beach of the Dan hotel. Benjy looked all around him and said, 'Sadie, just look how beautiful everything is. We have privacy, there is not a sound coming from the hotel, the sand is beautifully clean and golden and the sky is so blue without a cloud in sight. Sadie, with all of this, who needs money?'

Travel

Moshe goes to Heathrow Airport to fly to New York. While he is waiting for his flight, he notices a lady sitting nearby crying. So he goes over and asks her if anything was wrong.

She says, 'My son John moved to New York some months ago and I haven't heard from him since. He's never called or written to me. So I come here from time to time because he left from this airport and I feel closer to him here than anywhere else.'

As they talk, the lady asks, 'Would you by any chance be going to New York?'

Moshe replies, 'Well, as a matter of fact I am.'

She says, 'Oh would you please find my son and ask him to call me? His name is John Dun.'

Moshe replies, 'I don't thinks it's possible to find one man in New York.'

She says, 'Oh, please try. It would mean so much to me. I miss him so very much.'

After pleading with him, he finally agreed to do his best. All the way to New York, Moshe wonders, 'How can I ever find her son?'

When the plane lands, he takes a cab to his hotel. As the cab nears his hotel, Moshe sees on the side of one of the skyscrapers the words 'DUN AND BRADSTREET' so he says to himself, 'This might be easier than I thought.'

Later that day, after unpacking, he goes to the D&B building. He goes up to reception and asks the lady there, 'Do you have a John here?'

She replies, 'Yes. Go down this hall to the right and it is the third door on the left.'

He thanks her and goes looking for the door she pointed out. He finds it and goes in. Just as he walks into the room, there is a man there, drying his hands. Moshe says to him, 'Are you Dun?'

The man replied, 'Yes.'

Moshe says, 'Call your mother.'

* * *

At the start of his flight to Tel Aviv, Abe heard the following announcement 'We are now going to show you a safety video. There may well be fifty ways to leave your lover, but there are only five ways to leave your aircraft. So please pay attention.'

* * *

It was mealtime during a flight on El Al.

'Would you like dinner?' the flight attendant asked Moshe, seated in front.

'What are my choices?' Moshe asked.

'Yes or no,' she replied.

* * *

Moshe is on a flight from New York to Los Angeles. He notices the most beautiful woman he has ever seen boarding the plane, and to his delight, she takes the seat right next to him. He is soon anxious to begin a conversation.

Moshe asks her, 'Where are you from?'

She replies, 'I'm from Miami.'

'What are you doing in New York?'

'I'm finishing my Ph.D.'

'What's it about?'

'It's a study of some of the popular myths about sexuality.'

'And what myths are those?' Moshe continues desperately.

She explains, 'Well, one popular myth is that African men are the best endowed, when in fact, the Native American man is. Also, it is widely believed that the Frenchman is the best lover, but actually men of Jewish descent make the best lovers.'

'Very interesting,' Moshe responds.

Suddenly, the woman becomes very embarrassed and blushes. 'I'm sorry,' she says. 'I feel so awkward discussing this with you when I don't even know you! What is your name?'

Moshe extends his hand and replies, 'Tonto Tonto Goldstein.'

***

Maurice had just picked up his first passenger of the evening. After about five minutes of driving, the passenger suddenly tapped Maurice on his shoulder to ask him a question. Maurice screamed, lost control of his taxi, nearly hit a bus, went up onto the pavement and stopped only inches from a shop window. For a second, everything went very quiet in the taxi, then Maurice said, 'Look mate, don't ever do that again. You scared the living daylights out of me.'

His passenger apologised and said, 'I didn't realise that a little tap could scare you so much.'

Maurice replied, 'Sorry, it's not really your fault. Today is only my second day as a taxi driver – I've been driving hearses for the past 25 years.'

***

Abe was visiting Israel for the first time. As soon as his plane landed, he got a taxi to take him to his hotel. The taxi driver was very friendly and gave Abe all kinds of useful information. Then Abe asked the driver, 'Say, is Israel a healthy place?'

'Oh, yes, it really is,' the driver answered, 'When I first came here, I couldn't say even one simple word, I had hardly any hair on my head, I didn't have the energy to walk across a small room and I even had to be helped out of bed every day.'

'That's a remarkable story, truly amazing,' Abe said, 'so how long have you been here in Israel?'

'I was born here,' said the driver, smiling

***

Issy and Daniel, the well-known anthropologists, are having a discussion. 'Daniel, do you think there are any Jewish Eskimos about?'

'I don't know,' replies Daniel, 'but why don't we go and see for ourselves?'

Two weeks later they're in Alaska. As they ask around, they are consistently directed to one particular, very ornate igloo. When they go inside, they find a family of four Eskimos sitting around an ice table munching candles – and they weren't ordinary candles. From the cardboard boxes on the table, Issy and Daniel could clearly see that they were *Yahrzeit* candles.

Surprised by this revelation, Issy turns to the Eskimo father and says, 'We've noticed the candles – are you Jewish by any chance?'

'No,' came the reply, 'we just like Jewish food.'

***

It is not generally known that a few years ago the Jewish community in Madrid discovered at the last moment that they had no horseradish for making *chrain* – horseradish and beetroot pickle – for Passover. All the countries they asked replied in the same way, 'Sorry, we have none left to send you.'

So, in desperation, the Spanish Chief Rabbi called his friend in Israel and begged him to send him immediately some horseradish by air freight. He agreed and three days before Passover, a crate of the best grade of tear-jerking Israeli horseradish was loaded onto an El Al Flight to Madrid. All seemed to be going OK, but when the Chief Rabbi went to the airport to pick up his desperately needed horseradish, he was shocked to learn that there was a strike and that no crates of any kind would be unloaded at the airport for at least four days.

So, as it is said, 'The *chrain* in Spain stayed mainly on the plane.'

***

Thirteen rabbis were on their way to Jerusalem when their flight ran into a big thunderstorm. One of the rabbis immediately called over a stewardess. Wanting to calm her nerves, he said, 'Could you please tell the pilot that everything will be all right because there are thirteen very religious men aboard this plane.'

A few minutes later, the stewardess returned from the cockpit. She told the rabbi, 'Our pilot said that although he was pleased to learn that we have thirteen holy men aboard this flight, he would still rather have just one good engine.'

***

Lionel is flying back to London. He boards his plane and sits next to the window. A few minutes later, a heavy, mean-looking giant of a man sits next to him and promptly falls asleep. During the flight, Lionel begins to feel quite sick and wants to go to the toilet, but he's afraid to wake the giant and it would be impossible to climb over him. So Lionel has to sit there trying to decide the best course of action. Suddenly, the plane hits some air turbulence and lurches around for a few seconds. A wave of nausea overcomes Lionel and he is sick all over the giant.

Some time later, the giant awakes and sees the vomit over him.

'So,' says Lionel, 'are you feeling better now?'

***

Nicola was a depressed young woman. She was so desperate that one day, she decided to end her life by throwing herself into the River Thames. When Nicola arrived at the docks, a handsome young sailor noticed her tears and took pity on her. When he found out she was Jewish, he said to her, 'Look, I'm Jewish too. You've got a lot to live for. I'm off to Europe in the morning, and if you like, I can stow you away on my ship. I'll take good care of you and bring you food every day.' Moving closer, he slipped his arm around her shoulder and added, 'I'll keep you happy, and you'll keep me happy.'

Nicola nodded 'yes'. After all, what did she have to lose?

That night, the sailor brought Nicola aboard and hid her in a lifeboat. From then on, every night he brought her three sandwiches and a piece of fruit, and they made passionate love until dawn. Three weeks later, during a routine ship-wide search, Nicola was discovered and taken to the Captain.

'What are you doing here?' the Captain asked her.

'I have an arrangement with one of the sailors,' Nicola explained. 'He's taking me to Europe, and in return, I'm making love to him.'

'Lady,' said the Captain, 'You've made a big mistake – this ship never leaves the Thames, this is the Woolwich Ferry!'

***

Bernie decided he wanted to be an aeronautical engineer and build airplanes. He studied hard, went to the best schools, and finally got his degree. It didn't take long before he gained a reputation as the finest aeronautical engineer in all the land, so he decided to start his own company to build jets.

His company was such a hit that the President of Israel called Bernie into his office. 'I want to commission your company to build an advanced Israeli jet fighter.

Needless to say, Bernie was tremendously excited at this prospect. The entire resources of his company went into building the most advanced jet fighter in history. Everything looked terrific on paper, but when they held the first test flight of the new jet, disaster struck. The wings couldn't take the strain – they broke clean off of the fuselage! (The test pilot parachuted to safety, thank God.)

Bernie was devastated; his company redesigned the jet fighter, but the same thing happened at the next test flight – the wings broke off.

Very worried, Bernie went to his *shul* to pray, to ask God where he had gone wrong. The rabbi saw Bernie's sadness, and asked him what was wrong. Bernie decided to pour his heart out to the rabbi. After hearing the problem, the rabbi put his hand on Bernie's shoulder and told him, 'Listen, I know how to solve your problem. All you have to do is drill a row of holes directly above and below where the wing meets the fuselage. If you do this, I absolutely guarantee the wings won't fall off.'

Bernie smiled and thanked the rabbi for his advice – but the more he thought about it, the more he realised he had nothing to lose. So Bernie did exactly what the rabbi told him to do. On the next design of the jet fighter, they drilled a row of holes directly above and below where the wings met the fuselage. And it worked! The next test flight went perfectly!

Brimming with joy, Bernie went to tell the rabbi that his advice had worked. 'Naturally,' said the rabbi, 'I never doubted it would.'

'But rabbi, how did you know that drilling the holes would prevent the wings from falling off?'

'Bernie,' the rabbi intoned, 'I'm an old man. I've lived for many, many years and I've celebrated Passover many, many times. And in all those years, not once – not once – has the matzo broken on the perforation!'

***

A small boat was sailing in Israeli water when Moshe's smart boat pulled alongside.

A man on the deck of the sailboat yelled, 'Ahoy.'

To which Moshe shouted back, 'Ahoy, yoi, yoi!'

***

Shlomo and Issy were queuing to buy train tickets to London. Behind them were Mick and Pete. You can imagine Mick and Pete's surprise when not only did Shlomo and Issy buy just one ticket, but also that both of them got on the train.

The train was fifteen minutes into its journey when a ticket inspector came into their carriage. Mick and Pete waited for

Shlomo and Issy to get caught, but before the inspector saw them, Shlomo and Issy ran into one of the toilets. When the inspector came to the occupied toilet and knocked on the door shouting, 'ticket please', a ticket immediately appeared under the door. The inspector clipped it and passed it back.

Mick and Pete were astounded by the trick – and mad because they had bought two tickets. They vowed to do likewise next time.

A few days later, Shlomo and Issy were in the queue to buy their ticket back home. But when they saw Mick and Pete buy just one ticket, they immediately left the queue without buying any ticket. Fifteen minutes into the train journey, when the ticket inspector entered their carriage, Mick and Pete ran into one of the toilets. Shlomo and Issy followed them and knocked on the toilet door. As soon as the ticket was passed underneath the door, Shlomo and Issy grabbed it and dashed into another toilet.

You can guess what then happened.

***

Issy had never been on a train in his life. One lovely sunny day, he decided he would try a train ride. Off he went with his *yarmulka* on his head, a piece of salami under one arm and a blackbread and some herrings in a jar in the other. He sat down in a plush compartment and got settled down to eat. Suddenly a porter popped his head in and said, 'Sir, you will have to leave this compartment. It's reserved for the Archbishop of Canterbury.'

Issy replied, 'Vell, how do you know I'm not de Archbishop of Canterbury?'

***

Daniel and Naomi, who have never met before, are travelling on the same overnight sleeper train from London to Edinburgh. The train is packed and they end up in the same sleeping carriage. Daniel has the top bunk and Naomi has the bottom bunk. After some initial embarrassment, they both get to sleep.

At 1 am in the morning, Daniel leans over and says to

Naomi, 'I'm sorry to disturb you, but I'm really very cold. Could you please pass me another blanket?'

Naomi looks up at him and says, sexily, 'I've got a much better idea – why don't we pretend we're married.'

'Why not?' says Daniel, 'that's a marvellous idea.'

'Good,' Naomi replies. 'Go and get your own blanket, then.'

***

Shlomo is travelling on the London Underground and is sitting opposite a middle-aged Jew wearing a skullcap. Shlomo says, 'Shalom. Do you have the time?'

The man ignores him.

'Excuse me,' Shlomo asks again, 'what time is it please?'

The man still doesn't answer him.

'Sir, forgive me for interrupting you again, but I need to know the time. Why won't you answer me?'

At last the man speaks. 'Son, the next stop is Edgware, the last station on this line. I haven't seen you before so you must be a stranger. If I answer you now, it's Jewish tradition that I must invite you to my home. As you're young and good looking and I have a beautiful daughter named Suzy, you will fall in love with her and will want to get married. So tell me, why on earth would I want a son-in-law who can't even afford his own watch?'

***

After months of negotiation, Avraham, a Jewish scholar from Odessa, was granted permission to visit Moscow. He boarded the train and sat down. At the next stop a young man got on and sat next to him. Avraham looked at the young man and thought:

> This fellow doesn't look like a peasant, and if he isn't a peasant he probably comes from this area. If he comes from this area, he must be Jewish because this is, after all, a Jewish area. On the other hand, if he is a Jew, where could he be going?
>
> I'm the only one from our area to be allowed to travel to Moscow. Wait – just outside Moscow there is a little village

called Samvet, and you don't need special permission to go there. But why would he be going to Samvet? He's probably going to visit one of the Jewish families there, but how many Jewish families are there in Samvet? Only two – the Bernsteins and the Steinbergs. The Bernsteins are a terrible family, so he must be visiting the Steinbergs.

But why is he going? The Steinbergs have only girls, so maybe he's their son-in-law. But if he is, then which daughter did he marry? Sarah married that nice lawyer from Budapest and Esther married a businessman from Zhadomir, so it must be Sarah's husband. Which means that his name is Alexander Cohen, if I'm not mistaken. But if he comes from Budapest, with all the anti-Semitism they have there, he must have changed his name. What's the Hungarian equivalent of Cohen? Kovacs. But if he changed his name he must have some special status. What could it be? A doctorate from the University.

At this point Avraham turned to the young man and said, 'How do you do, Dr Kovacs?'

'Very well, thank you, sir,' answered the startled passenger. 'But how is it that you know my name?'

'Oh,' replied Avraham, 'it was obvious.'

***

Hannah is taking her young daughter Judith shopping. While Hannah is getting them a taxi, Judith notices a group of scantily dressed, overly made-up women on the street corner. As they get in the taxi, Judith asks, 'Mummy, what are all those women doing over there?'

Hannah replies, 'They're waiting for their husbands to return from work, darling.'

When the taxi driver hears this, he turns to Hannah and says, 'Now come on, lady, don't lie to your daughter, why don't you tell her the truth? Educate her, for God's sake.'

Without asking permission, he then turns to Judith and says, 'They're hookers, that's who they are.'

Judith then says, 'Mummy, do these ladies have any children?'

Hannah replies, 'Of course they do, darling, where do you think taxi drivers come from?'

***

To avoid a catastrophe during a raging storm, the captain of the *Kosher Yenta*, the largest and most expensive cruise ship ever launched, decided to dock at a small port on a Caribbean island. But it was too far down to the dock below for the ship's standard gangplank to reach, so passengers who wanted to leave the ship were asked to use a makeshift narrow piece of wood as a passageway down to the dock.

All of a sudden Sadie, aged seventy, appeared at the top of the plank. The captain just stood there motionless, wondering whether she would make it down safely as there was no room for anyone to assist her. But to his great relief, Sadie edged along very slowly and eventually made it down to the dock. However, as soon as she got down, Sadie looked back up to the top of the plank and shouted, 'It's OK mummy, you can come down now.'

***

As the plane settled down at Ben Gurion airport, the voice of the Captain came over the tannoy: 'Please remain seated with your seatbelt fastened until this plane is at a complete standstill and the seat belt signs have been turned off. To those of you standing in the aisles, we wish you a Happy Chanukah. To those who have remained in their seats, we wish you a Merry Christmas.'

Immigration

Walking through London's Chinatown, Abe is fascinated with all the Chinese restaurants, shops, signs and banners. He turns a corner and sees a building with the sign: Moshe Cohen's Chinese Laundry.

'Moshe Cohen?' he muses, 'how the heck does that fit in here?' So he walks into the shop and sees an old Chinese gentleman behind the counter. Abe asks, 'How did this place get a name like Moshe Cohen's Chinese Laundry?'

The old man answers, 'Is name of owner.'

Abe asks, 'Well, who and where is the owner?'

'Me, is right here,' replies the old man.

'You? How did you ever get a name like Moshe Cohen?'

'Is simple,' says the old man. 'Many, many year ago when come to this country, was standing in line at Documentation Centre. Man in front is Jewish gentleman from Poland.

'Lady look at him and go, "What your name?" He say, "Moshe Cohen." Then she look at me and go, "What your name?" I say, "Sem Ting."'

***

When Jacob was finally given an exit visa by the Russians and allowed to immigrate to Israel, he was told he could only take what he could put into one suitcase. At Moscow airport, he was stopped by customs and an official shouted, 'Open your case at once.'

Jacob did what he was told. The official searched through his case and pulled out something wrapped in newspaper. He unwrapped it and saw it was a bust of Stalin.

'What is that?' he shouted at Jacob.

Jacob replied, 'You shouldn't ask, "What is that?" You should ask, "Who is that?" That is our glorious leader Stalin. I'm taking it to remind me of the wonderful things he did for me and the marvellous life that I am leaving behind.'

The official sneered. 'I always knew you Jews were mad. Go, and take the bust with you.'

When Jacob arrived at Ben Gurion airport, a customs officer said, 'Shalom, welcome to Israel, open your case, please!'

Jacob's case was once again searched and not surprisingly the bust was found.

'What is that?' asked the officer.

Jacob replied, 'You shouldn't ask, "What is that?" You should ask, "Who is that?" That is Stalin the bastard. I want to spit on it every day to remind me of all the suffering and misery he caused me.'

The official laughed, 'I always knew you Russians were mad. Go, and take the bust with you.'

When Jacob arrived at his new home, his young nephew watched him as he unpacked. Jacob carefully unwrapped the bust of Stalin and put it on the table. 'Who is that?' asked his nephew.

Jacob replied, 'You shouldn't ask, "Who is that?" You should ask, "What is that?" That is five kilos of gold.'

***

It might not be known by many outside Israel but new immigrants can bring in normal household items duty free, but anything that looks like it could be resold in Israel is supposed to be subject to Israeli import duty.

Moshe Cohen, a new immigrant, arrived at the Port of Haifa to claim his household goods, which had just been landed by ship. However, when he turned up, he was immediately called into the Port offices because the excise officer had noticed on the manifest that Moshe had brought in seven refrigerators.

'Mr Cohen,' said the officer, 'One refrigerator is allowed duty free, but certainly not seven of them.'

Moshe replied, 'But I'm very religiously strict. I need one refrigerator just for meat, one just for dairy, and one just for *pareveh* – foods that contain neither animal nor dairy products.'

'OK,' said the officer, 'that makes three, but what about the other four?'

'It's obvious,' replied Moshe, 'I need three for most of the year and another three, for meat, dairy and parveh, for Passover.'

'That only makes six,' replied the officer,' What's the seventh one for?'

'So, *nu*,' replied Moshe, 'What if I want to eat *trayf* once in a while?'

***

In Golders Green there is a six-star hotel called the Oy Vay Towers. It offers massage, mud baths, 24-hours-a-day kosher eating, wonderful almond Danish and best of all, gossip. The hotel pages its guests via high quality, clear sounding speakers sited all around the hotel. Listening to messages such as 'Telephone call for Moshe Cohen from his lawyer', or 'Could Sadie Levy ring her counsellor', or even 'Benny Chesnick – could you please call your parole officer', is a gossiper's dream.

One day, everyone was surprised to hear over the speakers, 'Telephone call for Shane Ferguson, telephone call for Shane Ferguson.' At once, several people went to reception to get a look at who this Gentile staying at their hotel could be. They were therefore surprised and very curious when an old man, obviously Jewish, came up to the desk. Later, one of the guests asked the old man how he came to be named Shane Ferguson when he was so obviously Jewish. This is what he told them.

'When I left my home town to come to London, my name was Samuel Mincoffski. But my uncle thought it might be best if I told immigration that my name was Sam Lyons. I practised saying my new name over and over for the entire boat trip. I asked the sailors to say it for me and I learned how to pronounce it. Time passed very quickly and soon I was standing in line at the immigration office. But while waiting, I began to worry about everything. Would I say my name properly? What if they wouldn't believe me? Would I be able to spell it? Would they arrest me and send me back? My mind started to spin and I got so confused that when I reached the front of the queue and the officer asked me my name, I panicked and said, "Schane fergessen" – I forgot already. So that's what the immigration man wrote down.'

Cars

Moshe was at his golf club and went into the clubhouse to see whether anyone could offer him a lift to Hendon. His own car was off the road being serviced.

'Sure,' said Morry, 'I'll give you a lift. My Rolls Royce is just outside.'

As they're driving along, Moshe said, 'Morry, what's that thing on the dashboard ticking all the time?'

'That's my digital clock.'

A few minutes later, Moshe asked, 'And what's that thing on the dashboard moving up and down?'

'That's my tachometer,' said Morry.

Then a few minutes after that, Moshe started to ask, 'But what's that - '

'Hold on a minute, Moshe,' said Morry, 'I can see you've never been in a Rolls Royce before.'

'Never in the front seat,' said Moshe.

***

Joseph had just passed his driving test, so he asked his father, who was a rabbi, if they could discuss the use of the car. His father took him to his study and said to him, 'Joseph, I'll make a deal with you. You bring your school grades up, study your Bible a little, get your hair cut and we'll talk about it.'

After about a month Joseph came back and again asked his father if they could discuss use of the car. They again went to the father's study where his father said, 'Joseph, I've been real proud of you. You have raised your school grades, you've studied your Bible diligently, but you didn't get your hair cut!' Joseph waited a moment and replied, 'You know Dad, I've been thinking about that. You know, Samson had long hair, Abraham had long hair, Noah had long hair, and even Moses had long hair - '

To which the rabbi replied, 'Yes, and they walked every where they went!'

***

Q: What do you call a Torah with a seat belt?

A: A Safer Torah!

***

Shlomo is driving a Yugo in Tel Aviv and pulls up at traffic lights next to a Rolls Royce. Shlomo winds down his window and smiles at the driver of the Rolls.

'Hey, buddy, that's a nice car. Have you got a phone in it? I've got one in my Yugo!'

David, the driver of the Rolls looks over and says simply, 'Yes, I have a phone.'

'OK,' says Shlomo, 'but have you also got a fridge in there? I have.'

David, looking annoyed, says, 'Yes, I have a refrigerator.'

Shlomo goes on, 'OK, but listen, have you also got a TV in there like I have?'

David, looking more annoyed, says, 'Of course I have a television. A Rolls Royce is the finest luxury car in the world.'

'OK,' says Shlomo, 'have you a bed in your car? I've one in the back of my Yugo.'

Upset that he hadn't, David immediately drove off straight to his dealer and demanded that a bed be installed in the back of his car. The next morning, David picked up his car, now with a superb bed in it and immediately went searching for the Yugo. Late in the afternoon he found it parked, with all its windows fogged up from the inside. He knocked on the Yugo and Shlomo stuck his head out, soaking wet.

'I now have a bed in the back of my Rolls Royce,' David stated arrogantly.

'Do you mean,' complained Shlomo, 'that you got me out of the shower just to tell me that?'

* * *

Hetty arrives home quite late one night and says to her worried Moshe, 'Sorry I'm late. I had to come home by train, as I couldn't get my car to start. But I'm sure I know why.'

'So what's the problem then, my mechanical engineer of a wife?' asks Moshe.

'I think there's water in the carburettor,' replies Hetty.

'How on earth can you know that?' says Moshe. 'You don't even know how to open the bonnet or to change the time on the car's clock yet alone know where the carburettor is.'

'Maybe so,' says Hetty, 'but I still think there's water in it.'

Moshe then says, 'OK, I'll go along with you. Let's check it out right now. Where did you leave the car?'

Hetty replies, 'In the lake.'

***

Bud, from Texas, is on holiday in Israel and meets farmer Shlomo there. Bud asks Shlomo what he does.

'I raise a few chickens,' says Shlomo. 'I'm also a farmer.'

'So am I. How much land do you have?' asks Bud.

'Fifty metres in front, and almost a hundred at the back.'

Now it was the turn of Shlomo to ask a question.

'You're from Texas, so what about your farm?' asks Shlomo.

Bud tells him, 'On my farm, I can drive from morning until sundown and not reach the end of my property.'

'That's too bad,' says Shlomo. 'I once had a car like that.'

***

Rifka and Abe had just left Highgate and Rifka was driving them home in their old Ford Cortina. They had just turned into Winnington Avenue, Hampstead Garden Suburb and were moving down hill when their brakes failed.

Rifka was pressing the brake pedal as hard as she can and she also tried to tear the hand brake out by the roots, but to no avail. The car continued to gather speed.

'*Oy Vay*,' she wailed, 'Abe, what should I do, what should I do?'

'For God's sake,' Abe screamed. 'Hit something cheap!'

***

One day, Bernie was trying to pull out of a parking place but to his horror, he hit the bumper of the car parked in front of him. To make matters worse, the incident was witnessed by a handful of people waiting for a bus. So Bernie got out of his car, inspected the damage carefully, took out a pen and a piece of paper and wrote a note, which he then left under the wiper blade of the other car. This is what the note said.:

Hello, I have just hit your car and there are some people here watching me. They think I am writing this note to leave you my name, phone number and car registration number, but in fact I am not. Have a good day.

***

Hetty was the local gossip and self-appointed guardian of the town's morals. One day, she accused Moshe in front of a number of people of being an alcoholic, because she saw his car parked in front of the local wine merchant.

Moshe was a wise man. He just stared at her for a moment, said nothing and walked away. Later that night, Moshe parked his car in front of Hetty's house and left it there until morning.

***

Sarah was a very successful businesswoman. Last year was such a good year that she bought herself a Rolls Royce. But a couple of weeks later, she took it back to the dealer and complained that there were odd, wheezing noises coming from the front end of the car. The dealer had the car checked and telephoned Sarah. 'We can't find anything wrong with the car, as we expected. There's only one possible explanation,' he said. 'Your chauffeur must have asthma.'

***

When Albert Einstein was young, he was regularly invited to speak at various conferences. But he nearly always found himself wishing that he was back in his laboratory carrying out further pioneering work. One day, Einstein said to his chauffeur, 'Issy, I am getting so very tired of making these speeches, but what on earth can I do?'

Issy replied, 'I have an idea, sir. I've heard you give your presentation many times before and I'll bet I could quite easily give your talk for you. Why, I even look and speak like you.'

Einstein thought for a while, then laughed and replied, 'What a good idea, why not?'

So for the next conference, they exchanged clothes. Einstein put on Issy's uniform and peaked cap and then got behind the wheel of the car. When they arrived at the conference centre, Einstein went and sat at the back of the theatre and wondered how Issy would cope. He needn't have worried. Issy gave an excellent speech and even answered the first few of the questions that followed.

But then one of the other professors asked Issy an extremely awkward question about the speed of light in relation to the formation of anti-matter. Quick as a flash, Issy replied, 'The answer to your question is easy. In fact it is so basic that I will ask my chauffeur, who is sitting at the back of the hall, to answer it for me.'

***

Rabbi Levy handed in his notice, left his synagogue and opened up a Jewish bookshop. He worked very hard for several years and then decided to buy a new car. He put on a dark suit and white shirt, which looked impressive with his long beard, and went to see John, the local car dealer.

As soon as John saw him, he said, 'Have I got a car for you, Rabbi!'

Levy looked at John and said, 'What do you mean?'

'I mean a Rolls Aviv,' said John, 'a British-built car with Israeli-designed computerised digital commands for the religious driver. Come over here and let me show you. You won't believe your eyes. It's unique.'

John opened the door of the Rolls Aviv and Levy got in.

'Notice that it has no accelerator or brake pedal,' said John.

'So how do you stop and start it?' said Levy.

'Ah, that's the wonder of the Israeli computerised technology. It has a digital VMA-box that converts words into instructions the car understands. All you have to do is to speak the right words and the car will know what to do.'

'I don't believe it,' said Levy.

'It's true. To begin driving the car, just say "*Baruch HaShem*".'

And as John spoke those words, the car began to move.

Levy was frightened. 'How do you stop it?'

'That's easy. Just say "*Shema Yisrael*", and the car will stop,' said John and as he spoke these words, the car braked to a halt.

'So there it is. Say "*Baruch HaShem*" to start and "*Shema Yisrael*" to stop.'

Levy was so impressed, he bought the car right away. He got in, said the words '*Baruch HaShem*' and soon the Rolls Aviv was heading out towards the M1 motorway. Unfortunately, Levy failed to see a sign that said, 'Warning – unfinished bridge ahead. Take next turning left,' so the car continued to move at speed towards the bridge. '*Oy Vay!* I'm going to crash. How do I stop it?'

Panicking, he couldn't remember what John told him. His mind was a blank and the car was quickly approaching the end of the unfinished bridge. 'This is the end of me,' Levy thought and preparing for death, he started reciting the Shema Yisrael. Suddenly the Rolls Aviv screeched to a halt with half of the car tilting over the bridge. Levy removed his trembling hand from his forehead, saw how close he had come to disaster and exclaimed with conviction, '*Baruch HaShem.*'

* * *

As we have all done at some time, Moshe locks himself out of his car on a hot summer day. But he manages to find a wire coat hanger in a nearby dustbin and goes back to his car to try to open the lock. As soon as he shoves the wire through the slightly open window, his wife Sadie starts telling him what to do.

'Moshe, move it more to the right – now more to the left – Higher! Lower!'

Finally, Sadie says, 'What's taking you so long, Moshe?'

Moshe replies, 'Sadie, it's easy for you to say, sitting inside an air conditioned car!'

* * *

Moshe was in a terrible car accident, which mangled his 'manhood' and tore it from his body. His doctor assured him that modern medicine could give him back his manhood, but that he would have to go privately to have this done – such an operation was not available under the National Health. Although Moshe did not have any private medical cover, he told the doctor that it was not going to be a problem – it was so important, he would pay for it out of his savings.

'So how much will it cost?' asked Moshe.

'£4,500 for a small one, £7,500 for medium and £12,000 for large.'

Moshe said, 'Then I'll have the large one, please.'

But the doctor urged him to talk it over with his wife before making such an important decision and left the room to allow Moshe to call his wife on his mobile. Moshe spent ten minutes discussing his options with Sadie and when the doctor came back into the room, he found Moshe looking utterly dejected.

'Well, what have the two of you decided?' asked the doctor.

Moshe answered, 'Sadie said she'd rather have a new kitchen.'

***

When Moshe and Sadie arrived at their local dealer to pick up their new car, they were told that there would be a delay as the keys had been accidentally locked in the car. They went to the service department and found a mechanic working feverishly to unlock the door on the driver's side.

Sadie went round to the passenger's side and as any Jewish woman would do, she instinctively tried the door handle. To her surprise, the door opened.

'Hey,' she shouted to the mechanic, 'this door's open!'

'I know,' he answered, 'I've already opened the door on that side.'

***

Issy drives his friend Hyman to the shops in Golders Green. As they get out of the car, Issy locks the doors in such a hurry that he forgets to remove the ignition key first. '*Oy Vay*,' says Issy.

'Why don't we get a coat hanger to open the door,' says Hyman.

'No, I don't think that'll work,' replies Issy, 'because passers-by will think we're breaking into the car.'

'OK,' suggests Hyman. We can use a penknife to cut the rubber seal around the driver's door, then I can stick in a finger and pull out the key.'

'No, absolutely not.' replies Issy. 'Passers-by will think we're stupid for not using a coat hanger.'

'OK,' says Hyman, 'you'd better think of something else and quick. It's starting to rain and your sun roof's still open.'

* * *

The story is told that Lord Rothschild and Sir Isaac Wolfson met one day in the City. During a pleasant conversation, they decided to treat themselves each to a new Rolls Royce and so they took a taxi to the nearest showroom. When they got there, they both fell in love with the same pale blue Rolls Royce Ecstasy on display. But there was only one of these cars in the showroom.

The sales manager heard what was going on and said to the two famous millionaires, 'It's not a problem, gentlemen. If you both want one, I can get another pale blue Ecstasy from our other branch here within 45 minutes.'

'OK,' said Lord Rothschild, 'get it. In the meantime, we're going for a coffee.'

When they returned to the showroom, there stood two beautiful, gleaming, pale blue Rolls Royce Ecstasy saloons. Sir Isaac took out his chequebook but before he could open it, Lord Rothschild waved it away and said, 'I wouldn't hear of it, my dear fellow. These are on me – you paid for the coffees.'

* * *

Q: Who, in history, had the very first motorcycle?

A: Moses – the roar of his Triumph could be heard all over Israel.

Outer space

NASA had sent many shuttles to orbit the earth and attempted to include passengers of all races, colour and creed. One day, they realised they hadn't invited anyone from the clergy so they invited a priest and a rabbi to orbit the earth. Upon their return, they were asked to go straight to the Media room to give the world their impressions of the experience.

The priest came into the room with a smile on his face. His statement was full of joy.

He said, 'It was totally amazing. I saw the sun rise and set. I saw the beautiful oceans. I'm truly in awe.'

But the rabbi came into the room completely dishevelled. His beard was tangled, his skullcap was askew and his prayer shawl was creased. The reporters asked him whether he enjoyed the experience.

He threw his hands in the air and said, 'Enjoy? *Oy Vay*, you must be joking. How could I find time to enjoy? Every few minutes the sun was rising and setting! So it was on with the *tefillin*, off with the *tefillin*, *mincha*, *maariv*, *mincha*, *maariv* – *Oy Gevalt*, service after service!'

***

Morris, the Jewish astronaut, was asked why he was packing a tie with his spacesuit.

He replied, 'My mother said that when I do a space walk I should look nice.'

Later on, during the flight, Morris became frantic and radioed mission control. 'I must make an emergency landing!'

'Why?'

'My wife called and she wants to be picked up from the hairdresser.'

***

Two astronauts, Moshe and Abe, make the first manned flight to Mars. Upon landing, they find themselves face to face with a couple of green Martians.

'How do we make contact?' asks Moshe.

'They look pretty primitive. Let's impress them with some of our technology,' says Abe.

'OK.' says Moshe. He reaches into the pocket of his spacesuit and pulls out a shiny cigarette lighter. The Martians look interested.

'I think it's working – light it!' says Abe.

Moshe turns the wheel and a flame shoots out. Immediately the faces of the Martians turn from green to red. 'Wow!' he says, 'they must really be impressed.'

Then one of the Martians reaches out his little green hand, points a finger at Moshe and Abe, frowns, and says very sternly, 'Shabbes!'

***

Freda went down for breakfast in her Miami Beach hotel. She noticed another lady and went to speak to her. 'Hello, my dear, you're not from around here, are you?'

'No,' replied the second, 'I'm from Mars.'

Freda said, 'Really, do all Martian women have blue skin like yours?'

'Yes.'

'And do all Martian women have eight fingers on each hand as you have?'

'Yes.'

'And do all Martian women have an eye on their nose as you have?'

'Yes.'

'And do all Martian women have so many diamonds?'

'No – not the *goyim*.'

***

A Martian runs into some turbulence over Earth and makes a rough landing in Golders Green. After he pulls himself out of his space ship and dusts himself off, he sees that one of his wheels is broken. Not far away are some shops, so he starts to walk towards them to see if he can find a replacement. By good luck, he comes across a store with a sign showing a wheel, and a bunch of wheels in the window. He enters the store, gets the attention of Moshe behind the counter, and says, 'Excuse me, I'd like to buy a wheel.'

'Wheel?' says Moshe. 'We don't have wheels here.'

'Then what are those things in the window?'

'Oh, those aren't wheels. They're bagels.'

'Gee, they look just like wheels. What do you use them for?'

'We eat them,' says Moshe and he hands a bagel to the Martian.

The Martian takes a taste, chews thoughtfully, and lights up. 'Hey,' he says, 'I bet these would go great with cream cheese and *lox*!'

***

One afternoon, Maurice was walking in Golders Green Park when to his utter amazement a small space ship landed in front of him. As he stared at it, a beautiful, shapely female came out and walked towards him. He couldn't believe it – she was quite like any Earth girl. She told him, in perfect English, that she was an ambassador from Venus and that she had come specifically to learn more about Earth and its customs. Being single, Maurice offered at once to escort her around London and asked her if they had nightclubs on Venus. She replied, 'What are night-clubs?'

So Maurice took her to the Café De Paris where they had an excellent meal. Then the music started. She was a quick learner and soon was dancing just like the other women there. They spent the rest of the evening dancing together and talking about the differences between Earth and Venus. At midnight, Maurice took her back to his flat for a nightcap.

As they were drinking coffee, Maurice asked her whether Venusians liked to make love. 'Of course we do,' she replied with a cheeky smile. So the two of them went into his bedroom and began to undress. Maurice soon noticed that she had emeralds for nipples, a huge blue diamond instead of a navel and hundreds of small rubies instead of pubic hair.

'Do all Venusians have jewels on their bodies?' he asked.
'No, not the Gentiles,' she replied.

Computers & mobile phones

If computer makers were Jewish:
Your PC would shut down automatically on Friday evenings.
Your 'Start' button would be replaced with a 'Let's go. I'm not getting any younger' button.
'Retry' would be replaced with 'You want I should try again?'
When disconnecting external devices from your PC, instructions would say, 'Remove from your PC's *toches* the cable.'
Your CD player would be labelled, '*Nu*, so play my music already.'
You would hear 'Hava Nagila', a well-known Israeli song, during start-up.
ScanDisk prompts you with, 'You want I should fix?' message.
When your PC is multi-tasking, you would occasionally hear an '*Oy Gevalt*.'
Manischewitz would advertise that its 'monitor cleaning solution' gets rid of the *shmaltz* on your screen.
After twenty minutes in an idle state, your PC would go '*shluffen*' (to sleep).
All computer viruses would be cured with chicken soup.
After your computer dies, you would have to dispose of it within 24 hours.
Your Web browser would have a spinning 'Star of David' in the upper right corner.
A screen saver for Chanukah would be 'Flying Dreidels'.
High capacity DVBs (digital video bagels) would supersede CD-ROMs.

***

One day God was looking down at Earth and saw all of the evil that was going on. He decided to send an angel down to Earth to check it out. When the angel returned, he told God that it was indeed bad on Earth. He reported that 95 per cent was bad and five per cent was good.

God thought a moment and decided He had better send down a female angel to get both points of view. When the female angel returned she confirmed that Earth was in decline, 95 per cent was bad and five per cent was good.

God thought about what He could do about the situation and decided to e-mail the five per cent that were good with a little pep-talk, some praise, something to encourage them, something to help keep them going.

Do you know what the e-mail said?

No?

So, you didn't get one either.

***

Sam was talking to Avrahom: 'The Internet is moving on so fast, Avrahom, you can now do more and more on it.'

'So what can you do on it?' asks Avrahom.

'Well,' replies Sam, 'for example, our rabbi is so enterprising that he's offering circumcision via the Internet. He's calling it *E-Moil*.'

***

Bernie was talking to his friend Jack about his rebellious son Yossi. 'When I was a youngster and did something wrong, my parents punished me by sending me to my bedroom without supper. I hated it. But our Yossi has his own colour TV, phone, computer and DVD player in his bedroom so we can't do that – it wouldn't be much of a punishment.'

'So what do you do, then?' asked Jack.

'We send him up to *our* bedroom without supper!'

***

Last year, as some German scientists were digging 150 feet under the ground, they were surprised to discover small pieces of copper. They studied the copper pieces very carefully and came to the conclusion that 25,000 years ago, there was a nationwide telephone network in ancient Germany. They reported this in scientific journals, worldwide.

When British scientists heard the German announcement, they were just not impressed. They immediately embarked on a project to dig even deeper. When they had dug down to 300 feet, they found small pieces of glass. They studied the glass pieces very carefully and came to the conclusion that 35,000 years ago, there was a nationwide fibre-optic network in use by the ancient Brits.

Israeli scientists were enraged when they learned of the German and British claims. They decided to dig 150 feet, 300 feet and 600 feet under the ground in Jerusalem. But unfortunately, they found nothing whatsoever. Nevertheless, they came to the conclusion that 55,000 years ago, the ancient Israelites had cell phones.

***

Moshe went to Edgware cemetery to visit his friend Daniel's grave. When he got there, he was shocked to see that Daniel's new headstone was leaning forward by some 45 degrees and could topple over. So Moshe took some wire from his car, tied one end around the headstone and fastened the other end onto a nearby telephone pole. Then he left.

Some days later, two more of Daniel's friends, Abe and Issy came to visit him. Abe took one look at the grave and said to Issy, 'That's just like Daniel. He's only been here a short while and already he's got his own phone.'

***

Issy and Sam, both elderly gentlemen, were deep in conversation. Sam said, 'So, Issy, you're the clever one, how do those so called mobile phones work?'

Issy replied, 'Well, in the left hand you take the phone, and with the right hand you push the buttons. See. Nothing magic about it is there?'

But Sam was not satisfied with this answer.

'*Nu?*' he said, 'and how can one talk with the hands so busy?'

***

Rifka, a young mother, was teaching her six-year-old daughter Ruth how to unbuckle her seat belt. Ruth asked, 'Do I click the red square, mummy?'

Rifka said, 'Yes, darling.'

Ruth then asked, 'Single click or double click?'

***

Several men are in the locker room of a golf club when a mobile phone on a bench starts to ring. Sidney picks it up, engages the hands-free speaker-function and begins to talk.

'Hello,' says Sidney.

'Honey, it's me,' says a woman, 'are you at the club?'

'Yes,' replies Sidney.

'Well I'm at the shopping centre,' she says, 'and I've found a beautiful leather coat. It's £450. Can I buy it?'

'OK,' says Sidney, 'go ahead and buy it if you like it that much.'

'Thanks,' she replies. 'I also stopped by the Mercedes dealership and had a close look at the 2005 models. I saw one that I really liked.'

'How much was it?' asks Sidney.

'£37,000,' she replies.

'For that price,' says Sidney, 'I want it with all the options.'

'Great,' she says. 'Just one more thing. That house we wanted last year is back on the market. They're only asking £750,000 for it now.'

Sidney says, 'Well then, go ahead and buy it, but don't offer more than £720,000.'

'OK,' she says, 'I'll see you later. I love you.'

'Bye, I love you too.' says Sidney and then hangs up.

The other men in the locker room who heard all of this conversation are looking at Sidney in astonishment. Then Sidney shouts out aloud, 'Does anyone know who this mobile phone belongs to?'

* * *

Yitzhak had just moved into a new flat in Hendon and was out celebrating with his friend Benny. At 2 a.m., he invited Benny back to his flat where they continued to celebrate. Then Benny said, 'Before I go, why not show me around?'

So Yitzhak proudly showed Benny his flat and all the high tech it contained. Then he took Benny into his bedroom where his friend couldn't help but notice a very large brass gong and hammer on the chest of drawers.

'Is that a dinner gong?' asked Benny.

'It's not really a gong, Benny, it's more like a talking clock,' Yitzhak replied.

'A talking clock? Are you serious?' said Benny.

'Of course,' replied Yitzhak.

'So how does it work?' said Benny.

'Watch this,' replied Yitzhak, as he picked up the hammer and gave the gong an ear shattering pounding. They stood looking at each other for a moment when suddenly, someone in the flat next door screamed, 'Stop that, you inconsiderate oaf. It's quarter to three in the morning.'

* * *

Freda, a female computer consultant, was helping a smug male set up his computer and she asked him what word he would like to use as a password for log-in.

Wanting to embarrass her, he told her to enter 'penis'.

Without blinking an eye or saying a word, Freda entered the password as he had requested. But then, Freda nearly exploded from refrained laughter as the computer displayed the message in response: 'Password rejected. Not long enough.'

FINAL YEARS

Old age

Arnold had reached the age of 105 and suddenly stopped going to synagogue. Worried by Arnold's absence after so many years of faithful attendance, his rabbi went to see him. He found him in excellent health, so the rabbi asked, 'How come after all these years we don't see you at services anymore?'

Arnold looked around and lowered his voice. 'I'll tell you, Rabbi,' he whispered. 'When I got to be ninety, I expected God to take me any day. But then I got to be 95, then 100, then 105. So I figured that God is very busy and must have forgotten about me and I don't want to remind him.'

***

David, a senior citizen, was driving along the M25 towards Edgware, when his mobile phone rang. Answering, he heard his wife's voice urgently warning him, 'David, I just heard on the news that there's a car going the wrong way down the M25. So please be careful.'

'Hell,' said David, 'It's not just one – there are dozens of them!'

***

It was coming up to Morris's eightieth birthday and his family didn't know what to buy him – he was a man who really had everything. After much discussion, they decided to hire a strip-o-gram. He had a good sense of humour and they thought he would enjoy the joke.

On the morning of his birthday, the doorbell rang. Morris opened the door and there stood a beautiful redhead wearing only black gloves and thigh-length boots. 'Happy Birthday Morris,' she said. 'Do you know why I'm here?'

'No,' said Morris.

'Well, I've come here to give you "super sex",' she said provocatively.

Just for a brief moment, Morris looked a bit confused, but then said, 'You've given me a difficult decision to make – what kind of soup is it?'

* * *

Sadie and Bernie were well into their eighties and were still able to look after themselves. Until, that is, the day a police car pulled up outside their house and out stepped Bernie. The policeman who escorted Bernie to the door was kind and understanding. He explained to Sadie that Bernie told him he was lost in the park and couldn't find his way home.

'Oh Bernie,' said Sadie, 'How on earth could you get yourself lost? You've been going to that park for over 25 years.'

Bernie went up to Sadie and whispered softly in her ear, 'Please don't tell him but I wasn't lost, I was just too tired to walk home.'

* * *

Cyril had just retired and was having a discussion with his wife Ethel on what the future might hold for them. 'What will you do if I die before you?' Cyril asks.

After some thought, Ethel replies, 'Oh, I'll probably look to share a house with three other single or widowed women. As I'm still quite active, the other three could be a little younger than me.'

Then Ethel asks Cyril, 'What will you do if I die first?'

Cyril replies, 'Probably the same thing.'

* * *

Benjamin rushes to his doctor. 'Doctor, you've got to give me something to make me young again. I've got a date with this beautiful young girl tonight.'

His doctor says, 'Hold on a second, you're seventy years old, there's really not a lot I can do for you.'

Benjamin replies, 'But, Doctor, my friend Tony is much older than I am and he says he makes love three times a week.'

'OK,' says the doctor, 'so you say it too!'

***

Sadie's thirteen discoveries of old age:

I started out with nothing and I still have most of it.

My wild oats have turned into prunes and bran flakes.

I finally got my head together. Unfortunately, now my body is falling apart.

Funny, I don't remember being absent-minded.

Funny, I don't remember being absent-minded.

If all is not lost, where is it?

It's easier to get older than to get wiser.

It's hard to make a comeback when you haven't been anywhere.

If God wanted me to touch my toes, he would have put them on my knees.

It's not hard to meet expenses – they're everywhere.

The only difference between a rut and a grave is the depth.

These days, I spend a lot of time thinking about the hereafter. I go somewhere to get something and then wonder what I'm here after.

***

When we are young, it's our parents who run our lives, but then, when we get old, it's our children who run our lives.

***

Abe and Freda had been married for fifty years. They were having breakfast one morning when Abe said to Freda, 'Just think, darling, we've now been married for fifty years.'

'Yes,' she replied. 'Just think, fifty years ago we were sitting here together at this very breakfast table.'

'I know,' said Abe, 'and we were probably sitting here naked, fifty years ago.'

Freda giggled. 'So what do you think? Should we get naked again to see how we feel now?'

So Abe and Freda got up, stripped naked and then sat down at the table again. 'You know, darling,' Freda said breathlessly, 'I think my nipples are as hot for you today as they were fifty years ago.'

'I'm not at all surprised,' replied Abe, 'one is in your tea and the other is in your porridge.'

Memory loss

Moshe, 79, was talking to Yankel, 83, who had just dropped in for a chat and a moan.

'Moshe, I'm not the same any more. I can't remember so many things!'

'It vas the same thing mit myselve! But I took a memory course.'

'Vos? Does this help?'

'Sure it does.'

'So Moshe, tell me how this vorks.'

'This is called mnemonics. You take something that reminds you of other things and so it goes.'

'I vant to take this course! Vat is it called?'

'It is called – hum – the name – *Oy Vay* – Vait! Vat do you call that flower which people in love give to their girlfriends?'

'A rose, right?'

Moshe immediately shouted upstairs, 'Rose, Rose my darling, what is the name of that memory course we took?'

***

Rabbi Herzl was visiting Mrs Gold, an elderly member of his congregation. Rabbi Herzl said, 'You know, my dear Mrs Gold, that you are getting on in years and although I pray to the Almighty that he will grant you many more years in good health, you really should now be thinking more of the hereafter.'

Mrs Gold replied, 'Thank you, Rabbi, but I am always thinking about the hereafter.'

Rabbi Herzl was rather surprised with this response.

'Really?' he said.

'Oh yes, Rabbi, every time I go upstairs, I say to myself, "What am I here after?" and every time I go into my kitchen, I say to myself, "What am I here after?" I do it all the time now.'

***

Q: What is Jewish Alzheimer's Disease?

A: It's when you forget everything but the guilt.

***

Freda and Mona, two elderly ladies, were on a park bench in Edgware enjoying the sunshine. They had been meeting in that park every sunny day for over twelve years – chatting and enjoying each other's friendship. On this day, Freda turns to Mona and says, 'Please don't be angry with me dear, but I am embarrassed, after all these years. . . What is your name? I am trying to remember, but I just can't.'

Mona stares at Freda, looking very distressed, and says nothing for two full minutes. Finally with tearful eyes, she says, 'How soon do you have to know?'

***

Shlomo, eighty, married Beckie, a lovely 25-year-old. Because of the great difference in their ages, Beckie thought it sensible to book separate hotel rooms on their honeymoon – she was worried that he might overexert himself. On the first night, Beckie was preparing herself for bed when there was a knock on her door. When she opened it, there was Shlomo ready for action. They united in conjugal union and it was good. Shlomo said goodnight and left.

Beckie once again prepared to go to bed. But five minutes later, there was a knock on her door. It was Shlomo again, once more ready for action. Pleasantly surprised, Beckie again invited him into her bed and again they made passionate love. Shlomo kissed her goodnight and left.

Beckie was now quite tired but as soon as she put her head on the pillow, there was a knock at the door and there, yet again, was Shlomo, looking very sprightly and once more ready for l-o-v-e. Again they made it. This time, before Shlomo left, Beckie said, 'I am really very impressed with you, Shlomo. I thought you were past making love, but you've proved me wrong. I've made a good choice in you – you're a special lover. Most of my other lovers could only manage it once, yet you were able to do it three times.'

On hearing this, Shlomo was very confused. He then looked her in the eyes and asked, 'Do you mean I've been here already?'

***

Sidney and Abe, both in their seventies, met in Edgware High Street one Sunday morning. Straight away, they started their gossiping and story telling.

'So, Abe, what's new?' Sidney asked.

Abe, looking very worried, replied, 'I'm sorry to have to say that only this morning I had a great story to tell you, but I've forgotten it already.'

Sidney replied, 'Well, if it's about "forgotten stories" I have a better one to tell you than that – if only I could remember it!'

***

Maurice and Rifka are a lovely elderly couple, both in their eighties. One day, Rifka says to Maurice, 'Do you know what I'd like right now – an ice cream.'

'Then I'll go and get you one,' says Maurice.

'That's sweet of you, dear,' says Rifka. 'Go and get a piece of paper so you can write down what I want. You know how bad your memory is these days.'

'Don't you worry,' says Maurice, 'I won't forget – just tell me what you want.'

'I'd rather you wrote it down,' says Rifka.

'Please don't argue,' says Maurice, 'what do you want?'

'I want a cornet with one scoop of raspberry ice cream. Please write it down.'

'I don't need to. Do you want anything else?' says Maurice.

'Yes, I'll also have a scoop of chocolate ice cream,' replies Rifka.

'Anything else?' says Maurice.

'Yes, I'll have some butterscotch sauce on top of the ice cream. But are you sure you won't write it down?' says Rifka.

'I don't need to, honest. Now do you want anything else?' says Maurice.

'Well now you ask,' says Rifka, 'I'd like a sprinkling of nuts over the sauce and to finish it off, a glace cherry on top. But will you remember all of that?'

'Yes, dear, stop nagging,' says Maurice and leaves to get the order.

Fifty minutes later, Maurice comes back with a parcel. He goes straight to Rifka and proudly announces, 'Darling, here's the fried fish you asked for!'

Rifka looks in the parcel, then at him and says, 'I knew you would forget something. So where are the chips?'

***

Benjamin and Sarah, who were both in their eighties, invited their grandson Morris to dinner one evening. Morris was impressed by the way Benjamin preceded every request to Sarah with endearing terms – Honey, My Love, Darling, Sweetheart, Sugar Plum, etc. The couple had been married over fifty years and clearly they were still very much in love. While Sarah was in the kitchen, Morris said to Benjamin, 'Grandpa. I think it's wonderful that after all these years you still call grandma those loving pet names.'

Benjamin hung his head. 'I have to tell you the truth, Benjy,' he said, 'I forgot her name about ten years ago.'

Dying

Moshe had just had a medical check-up. 'I hate to be the one to break it to you,' said the doctor, 'But you've only got about six months to live.'

'Oh my God' gasped Moshe, turning white.

A few minutes later, after the news had sunk in, Moshe said, 'Doctor, you've known me a long time. Do you have any suggestions as to how I could make the most of my remaining months?'

'Have you ever married?' asked the doctor.

Moshe replied that he had been a bachelor his whole life.

'You might think about taking a wife,' said the doctor, 'after all, you'll need someone to look after you during the final illness.'

'That's a good point,' said Moshe, 'and with only six months to live I better make the most of my remaining time.'

'May I make one more suggestion?' asked the doctor, 'marry a Jewish girl.'

'A Jewish girl? Why?' asked Moshe.

'It'll seem longer.'

***

Issy was a rich man who was near to death. He was very grieved because he had worked very hard for his money and wanted to be able to take it with him to heaven. So Issy began to pray.

An angel heard his plea and said to him, 'I'm sorry, but you can't take your wealth with you.'

Issy implored the angel to speak to God to see if he might bend the rules. He said he would try. In the meantime, Issy continued to pray.

When the angel reappeared, he informed Issy that God had decided to allow him to take one suitcase with him. Overjoyed, Issy gathered his largest suitcase and filled it with pure gold bars and placed it beside his bed. Soon afterwards he died and showed up at the Gates of Heaven.

The angel Gabriel, seeing the suitcase, said, 'Hold on, you

can't bring that in here.'

Issy explained that he had permission and suggested he verify his story with God.

Gabriel checked and said, 'You're right. You're allowed one carry-on bag, but I'm supposed to check its contents before letting it through.'

So Gabriel opened the suitcase to inspect the worldly goods that Issy found too precious to leave behind and exclaimed, 'You brought pavement?'

***

Moshe, a medieval Jewish astrologer, prophesied that the king's favourite mistress would soon die. Sure enough, the woman died a short time later. The king was outraged at the astrologer, certain that his prophecy had brought about the woman's death. He summoned Moshe and commanded him, 'Prophesy, tell me when you will die!'

Moshe realised that the king was planning to kill him immediately, no matter what answer he gave. 'I do not know when I will die,' he answered finally. 'I only know that whenever I die, the king will die three days later.'

***

Issy was dying. His wife was with him, standing next to his bed. As he was drawing his last few breaths, he gasped, 'Sadie, I have one last request.'

'Of course, Issy, what is it?' Sadie asked softly.

'Six months after I die,' he said, 'I want you to marry Louis.'

'But I thought you hated Louis,' Sadie said.

With his final breath, Issy said, 'I do.'

***

Q: Why do Jewish men die before their wives?

A: They want to.

***

The dutiful Jewish son is sitting at his father's bedside. His father is near death.
Father: 'Son.'
Son: 'Yes Dad.'
Father: (weakly) 'Son. That smell. Is your mother making my favourite cheese cake?'
Son: 'Yes Dad.'
Father: (even weaker) 'Ah, if I could just have one more piece of your mum's cheese cake. Would you get me a piece?'
Son: 'OK, Dad.'
(Son leaves and walks toward kitchen. After a while the son returns and sits down next to his father again.)
Father: 'Is that you son?'
Son: 'Yes Dad.'
Father: 'Did you bring the cheese cake?'
Son: 'No Dad.'
Father: 'Why? It's my dying wish!'
Son: 'Well Dad. Mum says the cake is for after the funeral.'

***

Beckie was dying and on her deathbed, she gave final instructions to her husband Tony. 'Tony, you've been so good to me all these years. I know you never even thought about another woman. But now that I'm going, I want you to marry again as soon as is possible and I want you to give your new wife all my expensive clothes,'

'I can't do that, darling,' Tony said. 'You're a size sixteen and she's only a ten.'

***

Benny had worked long and hard all his life and now his end was near. His family had all gathered around his hospital bed. Through half-closed and watery eyes and with a very croaky voice, Benny said, 'Sadie darling, are you here?'

'Yes, dear, I'm here.'

'Sam, are you here?'

'Yes, dad, I'm here.'

'Hannah, are you here?'

'Yes, daddy.'

'Rifka, are you here?'

'Yes, dad.'

'Harry, are you here?'

'Yes, grandpa.'

Then, struggling to sit up and using his last ounce of strength, Benny shouted, 'If you're all here, who on earth is looking after the shop?'

* * *

Rivkah is on her deathbed and the rabbi is there with her.

'Rivkah,' says the rabbi, 'do you have any last wishes?'

'Yes,' replies Rivkah, 'I want to be cremated.'

'What!' says the rabbi, 'you know that is forbidden. But, I suppose - '

'Next,' says Rivkah, 'I want my ashes spread out on the roof of Brent Cross shopping centre.'

'Rivkah,' says the rabbi, 'I must protest – why would you want to do that?'

'Well,' says Rivkah, 'that way my daughters would come and visit me once a week.'

* * *

Old Chaim is dying. His entire *mishpocheh* is sitting around his bed, subdued and not knowing what else they can do. They ask him, 'Chaim, maybe we can fulfil your last wish?'

'Yes – I'd like – a cup of tea – with two teaspoons – of sugar.'

'Why?' they ask him.

'I've had a long life – and all of that time – when I drank tea in my own house – I used one spoon of sugar – When I had tea – in someone else's house – I put three spoons of sugar in my cup – But really – really – all my life – I loved tea – with two spoonfuls of sugar.'

* * *

Sadie is dying. As she lies in her bed, she says, 'Shlomo, are you here?'

'Sadie, can't you see I'm standing right next to you?' replies Shlomo.

'Well that's a change,' says Sadie, 'I'm not used to having you at home.'

'Oh now come on darling,' says Shlomo, 'you didn't really expect me to be out of the house when you're dying?'

'Well it wouldn't have surprised me,' says Sadie.

'Please let's not argue,' says Shlomo.

'OK,' says Sadie, 'but I want you to promise me something. How many cars have you ordered to go to the cemetery?'

'Four,' replies Shlomo.

'Does that include the hearse?' asks Sadie.

'Yes,' replies Shlomo, 'but this is not the time to talk about it.'

'Shlomo, it's my funeral, remember,' says Sadie. 'Four cars are too many. If people want to come, let them find their own way there. Cancel one of the cars.'

'OK,' says Shlomo.

'And I want you to promise me something else,' says Sadie.

'Anything, darling,' says Shlomo.

'I want you and my mother to travel together in the same car,' says Sadie.

'But darling,' says Shlomo, 'you know we've not spoken to one another for at least ten years.'

'I know,' says Sadie, 'but I don't care. It's what I want. Promise me you'll do it.'

'Well, OK,' replies Shlomo, 'I'll do it, but let me tell you now, it will ruin the day for me.'

Funerals

Issy has just passed away and his wife Rifka goes to the mortuary. As soon as she sees him she starts crying. An attendant tries to comfort her. Through her tears Rifka explains that Issy is wearing a black suit and he always wanted to be buried in a blue suit. The attendant explains that they always put the bodies in a black suit as standard procedure, but he'd see what he could do. The next day, when Rifka returns to the mortuary to have one last moment with Issy, she smiles through her tears – Issy is now wearing a blue suit.

She asks the attendant, 'How did you manage to get hold of that nice blue suit?'

'Well, yesterday, after you left, a man about your husband's size was brought in and he was wearing a blue suit. His wife was very upset as he had always wanted to be buried in a black suit,' the attendant replied. 'After that, it was simply a matter of swapping the heads around.'

***

Moshe heard the loud crying of a woman and went to investigate. A woman was at a grave and was weeping 'Oh, Joseph, it's been four years since you left me but I still miss you so much.'

Moshe asked her, 'Who are you mourning?'

'My husband,' she replied, 'I miss him dearly.'

But Moshe noticed something strange, and said to her 'Your husband? But it says on the headstone IN MEMORY OF FREDA GOLDBERG'

'Oh yes,' she replied, 'he put everything in my name.'

***

Moshe has died. His solicitor is standing before the family and reads out Moshe's last Will and testament: 'To my dear wife Sadie, I leave the house, fifty acres of land, and £1 million. To my son Barry, I leave my Big Lexus and the Jaguar. To my daughter Suzy, I leave my yacht and £250,000. And to my brother-in-law Jeff, who always insisted that health is better than wealth, I leave my sun lamp.'

***

Rabbi Cohen was saying his goodbyes to his congregation after his Sabbath service, as he always did, when Esther came up to him in tears. 'What's bothering you so, dear?' inquired Rabbi Cohen.

'Oh, Rabbi, I've got terrible news,' replied Esther.

'Well what is it, Esther?'

'Well, my husband, passed away last night, Rabbi.'

'Oh, Esther,' said the rabbi, 'That's terrible. Tell me Esther, did he have any last requests?'

'Well, yes he did, Rabbi,' replied Esther.

'What did he ask, Esther?'

Esther replied, 'He said, 'Please, please Esther, put down the gun - '

* * *

Issy and Howard were brothers who had lived and worked in Golders Green all their lives. Unfortunately, nothing good could be said about them – they ran a crooked business, they womanised, they lied and they cheated the poor. But they were also very, very wealthy. When Issy died, Howard went to Rabbi Bloom and said, 'I will donate to the synagogue £100,000 if you will say at the funeral that my brother Issy was a *mensh*.'

The rabbi thought long and hard but eventually agreed.

At the funeral, the rabbi told everyone present of Issy's wrong doings. He then closed with the sentence 'But, compared to his brother, he was a *mensh*!'

* * *

Sadie is a beautiful girl. She could have been an actress but instead she decides to get married young and raise a large family. In no time at all she has ten children. Then suddenly her husband passes away – and Sadie is still only 42. But it doesn't take our Sadie long to find a new husband. She quickly remarries and finds happiness once more. She could have decided that ten children was enough, but instead has eight more by her new husband. He dies when Sadie is still only 64 years old. Maybe having so many children took it out on Sadie's poor body because only a few months later, Sadie herself passes away.

At her funeral, the rabbi looks skyward and says, 'At last they're finally together.'

Sadie's eldest son says, 'Rabbi, do you mean mum and my father, or mum and my stepfather?'

The rabbi replies, 'Neither. I mean her legs.'

***

Isaac was a very successful marketing director. Sadly, his wife Rifka died. At the cemetery, Isaac's friends and family were appalled to see that the headstone reads:

'Here lies Rifka, wife of Isaac Levy, MCIM, Post Graduate Diploma in Marketing and Marketing Director of Quality Marketing Services Ltd.'

Isaac was standing in front of Rifka's grave reading the headstone when he suddenly burst into tears. His brother said to him, 'I'm not at all surprised that you find this distasteful. It's right that you should cry, pulling a cheap stunt like this on our Rifka's headstone.'

Through his tears, Isaac sobbed, 'You don't understand. They left out the phone number.'

***

Moshe meets Arnold at their social club and asks how Abe's funeral went the other day.

'It went OK, Moshe,' replies Arnold, 'but at the end of the rabbi's eulogy, I had to try and stop myself from laughing aloud.'

'Why was that?' asks Moshe.

'Well,' says Arnold, 'throughout his marriage to Miriam, she was always telling me what a mean man he was. He never had a steady job and the money he brought home to her wasn't enough for food and clothing, let alone holidays. Yet he drank heavily and often stayed out all night gambling. Altogether, a good husband he was not. But at the funeral, the rabbi spoke of how wonderful the deceased was – so considerate, so beloved, so thoughtful to others. Then, when the rabbi had finished, I heard

Miriam say to one of her children, 'Do me a favour, David, go and see whether it's your father in the coffin.'

* * *

Rabbi Goldberg stood before the Recording Angel, who was scrutinising his page in the Golden Book.

'Fantastic!' exclaimed the Angel. 'Rabbi Goldberg, can it be? Your record shows nothing but *mitzvahs*! Tell me, in your whole life, didn't you commit one sin?'

'Mr Angel,' replied the rabbi, 'I tried to live like a God-fearing Jew.'

'But in a whole lifetime, not one single sin?'

'No, I'm s-sorry.'

'Well, I can't let you into heaven, Rabbi Goldberg! You already are an angel. I am going to have to send you back to earth for 24 hours and if you want to get into heaven, you'll appear back here with at least one sin on your record. Goodbye.'

Poor Rabbi Goldberg was scooped back to earth. He wandered about, desolate, seeking to stray from virtue, not knowing how. The hours passed and the rabbi grew uneasy. Only twelve hours now remained.

'Oh, God, blessed be your name, help me. Help me to sin. Just once!'

And then a woman signalled to him from a doorway. His prayers had been answered. How swiftly Rabbi Goldberg responded. The voluptuous woman led him to her room – and to her bed.

Hours later, the rabbi awoke. 'What time is it?'

'Half past six.'

The rabbi smiled. 'At seven o'clock, someone is picking me up.'

He started to dress, chuckling. But the chuckles froze when, from her bed, he heard the woman sigh, 'I'm over forty years old and I was a virgin. Oh, mister, what a *mitzvah* you performed last night!'

* * *

As soon as Ruth hears that her 99-year-old grandfather has died, she goes to see her 95-year-old grandmother to comfort her. 'Oh, *Bubbeh*, I'm so sorry. How did *Zaydeh* die?'

'He had a heart attack on Sunday morning while we were making love.'

'But, *Bubbeh*,' says Ruth, 'You were both nearly 100 years old. Didn't you realise that having sex would be asking for trouble?'

'Many years ago,' replies her grandma, 'realising our advanced age, we thought the best time to make love was when the church bells were ringing. It was just the right rhythm for us, nice and slow and even. Nothing too strenuous, simply down on the Ding and up on the Dong. And if that ice cream van hadn't come along, your *zaydeh* would still be alive today.'

***

The end of the world has finally come. God looks over the many billions of people and says to them, 'Welcome to Heaven. I want the women to go with St. Peter. Go now and follow him. And you men, I want you to form two lines. The line to my left is for men who dominated their women on earth. The line to my right is for men who were dominated by their women. OK, now line up all of you.'

There is then a lot of movement for some time, but eventually the women are gone and there are two lines of men. The line of men that were dominated by their women is 150 miles long. The line of men that dominated their women has only one man in it, Moshe.

God is angry with the men and says, 'You men should be ashamed of yourselves. I created you in my image and yet you were all dominated by your partners. Look at the only one of you that stood up and made me proud. Learn from him.'

He turns to Moshe and says, 'Tell them, my son. How did you manage to be the only one on that line?'

Moshe says, 'I don't know, my wife told me to stand here.'

Jewish Jokes to Tell Children

Whether you're a father, mother, grandfather, grandmother, relative or friend, telling jokes to young children can be very rewarding. To see a child smile or hear a child laugh is wonderful. So, if you have young children to visit or entertain, here are some clean, hopefully easy-to-understand jokes you can tell them – some say a child can start to understand a joke from the age of seven upwards. Note – the first joke below is the earliest joke I can remember, and it was told to me by my dear father Harry.

Mr and Mrs Levy had two sons. They were brothers, of course. One brother was called MIND YOUR OWN BUSINESS and the other brother was called TROUBLE. One day, the two brothers were playing hide and seek in the street and it was TROUBLE's turn to hide. While MIND YOUR OWN BUSINESS was counting to a hundred, TROUBLE ran down the street and hid inside a thick hedge. Then MIND YOUR OWN BUSINESS started looking for his brother. He looked behind some trees, he looked inside some cars parked in the street and he even looked under the cars, but he couldn't find his brother. But when MIND YOUR OWN BUSINESS started to look inside dustbins, a policeman saw him doing this and came over to have a word with him.

The policeman said, 'And what, may I ask, are you doing little boy?'

And the boy replied, 'Playing a game.'

The policeman then asked, 'What's your name?'

And the boy replied, 'MIND YOUR OWN BUSINESS.'

The Policeman got angry and said loudly, 'Are you looking for trouble?'

And the boy replied, 'Yes.'

* * *

'Mummy,' says little Issy, 'Why do bees have sticky hair?'

'Because they use honeycombs.'

* * *

One day, Hannah the teacher is reading out loud to her class the story of Chicken Little. Hannah soon reads out the bit where Chicken Little tries to warn the farmer. 'So Chicken Little went over to the farmer and said, "The sky is falling, the sky is falling."'

Hannah then asks her class, 'What do you think the farmer then said?'

Little Moshe raises his hand. 'I think he said, "Goodness, a talking chicken."'

* * *

Little Abe is talking to his older brother Isaac. 'Isaac,' asks Abe, 'why do bears have fur coats?'

Isaac replies, 'That's easy. It's because they'd look silly in anoraks.'

* * *

'Daddy,' says Sarah, 'Can you buy me a budgie?'

'Not now, darling,' he replies, 'now is not the right time.'

'So when is the right time to buy a budgie, Daddy?' Sarah asks.

'When they're going cheap,' replies Daddy.

* * *

Mummy and Daddy have taken little Issy to London Zoo. They are watching the lions. 'Mummy,' says Issy, 'what's a lion's favourite food?'

'Why, baked beings of course,' she replies.

***

Yitzhak is talking to his friend Harry. 'Harry,' he says, 'I was surrounded by lions in the park this afternoon.'

'What,' says Harry, 'lions in the park?'

'Yes,' replies Yitzhak, 'they were dandelions.'

***

It was Friday night and little Sam was having his Shabbes meal with his parents. They were, as usual, going to eat roast chicken. When it arrived, Sam's daddy smiled and said, 'Sam, do you know why this roast chicken is like an armchair?'

'No Daddy.'

'Because they're both full of stuffing, that's why,' said his daddy.

***

'Knock Knock.'

'Who's there?'

'Abe.'

'Abe who?'

'Abe C D E F G H - '

***

Mummy was telling little Sadie a story about a witch who arrived at a hotel without her broom because the broom was late. 'Why was the broom late, mummy?' asked Sadie.

'Because it over-swept, darling.'

'And do you know what the witch asked for when she went to reception?'

'What, Mummy?'

'Broom service.'

***

Mummy and Daddy had taken little Benjy to Blooms kosher restaurant. During their first course, Benjy says, 'This soup tastes funny, Daddy.'

His daddy replies, 'So why aren't you laughing?'

***

Morris was telling his friend Cyril all about his Chanukah presents. 'My daddy bought me a mouth organ. It's the best present I've ever had.'

'Why?'

'Because my mummy gives me extra money every week if I don't play it.'

***

Max was telling his friend Howard a riddle. 'What has a bottom at the top?'

Howard said, 'I don't know, Max. What does have a bottom at the top?'

'Why it's your legs, of course.'

***

Little Sidney is watching his mummy prepare the fish for dinner. She asks him, 'Do you know what part of a fish weighs the most, darling?'

'No,' he replies.

'It's the scales.'

***

Becky is telling her best friend Ruth all about school. Becky says, 'My teacher shouted at me today for something I didn't do.'

So what was that?' asks Ruth.

'My homework.'

***

Little Naomi goes to her kosher butchers and asks, 'Mummy wants to know how much is the duck?'

The butcher replies, 'It's £12.'

'OK,' says Naomi, 'Could you please send us the bill.'

'I'm sorry,' says the butcher, 'but you'll have to take the whole bird.'

***

Little David is staring at the clock on the mantelpiece. Then he says, 'Daddy, what do people do in clock factories?'

His daddy replies, 'They make faces all day.'

***

Benjamin was enjoying his trip to the Dead Sea.

During dinner, Benjamin says, 'Daddy, if you drop a white hat into the Dead Sea, what does it become?'

His daddy replies, 'Wet, of course.'

***

During his Hebrew lesson, little Alan asks his teacher, 'Where was King Solomon's temple, teacher?'

'On his forehead.'

***

Sarah was telling her best friend Naomi that her teacher's eyes are always crossed. 'Why is that?' asked Naomi.

'Because she can't control her pupils.'

***

Little Moshe's dad asks him one day, 'Do you know what the hat said to the scarf?'

'No, Daddy, I don't,' replies Moshe.

'You hang around while I go on ahead,' says his dad.

***

The teacher said to her class, 'Does anyone know what is white when it's dirty and black when it's clean?'

Little Sarah put up her hand and said, 'It's a blackboard, miss.'

***

One Sunday, little Benny's grandpa asks him a question, 'Do you know what one eye said to the other eye?'

'No, *Zaydeh*.'

'It said, 'Between you and me, something smells."

***

One day at school, Max was talking to his best friend David. 'David, have you heard the joke about the dustbin lorry?'

'No I haven't,' replied David.

'Don't worry,' said Max, 'it's only a load of rubbish.'

***

Little Naomi said to her mum, 'Mum, what's got four legs and one foot?'

'I don't know,' said her mum.

'A bed.'

***

One day, Rifka went up to her dad and said, 'Dad, I want to play our piano but I can't open the lid.'

'Of course you can't,' said her dad, 'the keys are inside.'

***

The teacher asks her class, 'Does anybody know what starts with T, ends with T and is full of T?'

Little Benjy puts up his hand and says, 'A teapot, miss.'

***

It was August and little Hannah was on holiday with her parents. One day, her dad says to her, 'Did you know that they don't allow elephants on this beach?'

'Why, Dad?'

'Because they can't keep their trunks up.'

***

One day at school, Morris and Henry had a race and Henry won. Morris then said to Henry, 'You won, but I know what you lost.'

'What did I lose, then?'

'Your breath.'

***

Little Leah asks her dad, 'Do you know what happened when the lion ate the comedian?'

'No, I don't, darling.'

'He felt funny.'

***

One day, Sam is out walking with his dad. Sam says, 'Do you know what runs but never walks, Dad?'

'I don't know, Sam.'

'Water.'

***

Just before she went to bed, little Ruth's mum asks her a question, 'Do you know how to make milk shake, darling?'

'No I don't, Mum.'
'You give it a good fright.'

* * *

One morning, Avrahom is eating his cheese and tomato sandwich when his mother says to him, 'Do you know what cheese is made backwards?'

'No, mum.'

'Edam.'

* * *

One day, Isaac says to his dad, 'Did you hear about the stupid fool who keeps going around saying "no"?'

'No.'

'Oh, so it's you.'

* * *

One breakfast time, Rivkah's mum asks her, 'What do cats eat for breakfast, darling?'

'I don't know, Mum.'

'Mice Crispies.'

* * *

One Sunday, little David is with his parents on a boat on the river Thames. His dad asks him, 'What do you think sea monsters eat, David?'

'I don't know, Dad.'

'Fish and ships.'

* * *

While she is eating her *lochshen* pudding, little Judith's mum says to her, 'Do you know what cries and wobbles, darling?'

'No, mum.'
'A jelly baby.'

***

Why did Arnold wear a belt on his teeth?
Because he couldn't find his braces.

***

Freda is at the Zoo with her dad when he asks her, 'What do you call a deer with no eyes, darling?'
'What, Dad?'
'No idea.'

***

One breakfast time, little Rebecca says to her mum, 'What two things can't you have for breakfast, mum?'
'I don't know?'
'Lunch and dinner, of course.'

A Kosher-Humour Test For Dating Couples

How often do you hear or read of someone saying, 'I'm looking for a partner with a gsoh (good sense of humour)'? Quite often, I suspect. So humour must be an important human characteristic and I can think of an example as to why this should be. What if a couple is watching a show, or a film, or a comedian, or see some slapstick, or are listening to someone telling a joke? What if one is laughing out loud whilst the other just has a bemused expression on their face? You've probably seen this happen. So how compatible can they be? Well, why not take this test to see how compatible you are in 'kosher humour'? You can come to your own conclusion on compatibility when you see the results.

Here follow fifteen numbered jokes. Each of you should read the fifteen jokes separately and then decide and jot down the numbers of the five that you liked the best, or laughed at loudest, or smiled at widest, or which most tickled your fancy. When both of you have done this, you can compare your selections: five jokes the same – wow! You have great kosher-humour compatibility (or you're cheats). Four jokes the same – you have very good kosher-humour compatibility; three the same – good compatibility; two jokes the same – some kosher-humour compatibility; one joke the same – there is still some hope for you both. But no jokes the same – oh dear!

WARNING: This is intended for single couples only. Married couples take this test at their peril!

1 The dream

Moshe was talking to his psychiatrist. 'I had a weird dream recently,' he says. 'I saw my mother but then I noticed she had your face. I found this so worrying that I immediately woke up and couldn't get back to sleep. I just stayed in bed thinking about my dream until 7 a.m. I got up, made myself a slice of toast and some coffee and came straight here. Can you please help me explain the meaning of my dream?'

The psychiatrist kept silent for some time, then said, 'One slice of toast and some coffee? Do you call that a breakfast?'

***

2 Kol Nidre night

Sidney telephones Rabbi Levy. He says, 'Rabbi, I know tonight is Kol Nidre night, but tonight Spurs are in the European Cup quarter finals. Rabbi, I'm a lifelong Spurs fan. I've got to watch the Spurs game on TV.'

Rabbi Levy replies, 'Sidney, that's what video recorders are for.'

Sidney is surprised. 'You mean I can tape Kol Nidre?'

***

3 Come and get me

Isaac and Sarah got married and left on their honeymoon. When they got back, Sarah immediately telephoned her mother Leah.

'Well,' said Leah, 'how was the honeymoon, darling?'

'Oh Mum,' Sarah replied, 'the honeymoon was fantastic. It was so romantic, and – and – ' then Sarah started to cry.

'Oh Mum, as soon as we got back, Isaac started using terrible language. He said things I'd never hoped to hear, all those four-letter words. Please Mum, get into your car now and come and take me home.'

'Calm down, darling,' said Leah, 'tell your mother what could be that awful. Don't be shy, tell me what four-letter words Isaac used.'

'Please Mum, I'm too embarrassed to tell you, they're terrible words. Just come and take me away,' said Sarah.

'But, *bubbeleh*, you must tell me, you must tell me what the four-letter words were.'

Still crying, Sarah replied, 'Oh mum, he used words like wash, cook, iron, dust - '

***

4 The convert

Martin Lewis converts and becomes a priest. He gives his first Mass in front of a number of high ranking priests who have come for the occasion. At the end of the new priest's sermon, a cardinal goes up to congratulate him. 'Pastor Lewis,' he said, 'That was very well done, you were just perfect. But next time, please don't start your sermon with, 'Fellow *goyim* - '

***

5 The engagement

Ruth and Golda were walking along Hendon High Street. Ruth says, 'My son Irving is getting married. He tells me he is engaged to a wonderful girl, but – he thinks she may have a disease called herpes.'

Golda says, 'Do you have any idea what this herpes is, and can he catch it?'

Ruth replies, 'No, but I am just so thrilled to hear about Irving's engagement – it's time he settled down. As far as the herpes goes – who knows?'

'Well,' says Golda, 'I have a very good medical dictionary at home. I'll look it up and call you.'

So Golda goes home, looks it up, and calls Ruth. 'Ruth, I found it. Not to worry. It says herpes is a disease of the Gentiles.'

***

6 Three Jewish Mothers

Three Jewish mothers are sitting on a bench in Brent Cross shopping centre talking about (what else?) how much their sons love them. Sadie says, 'You know the Chagall painting hanging in my living room? My son, Arnold, bought that for me for my 75th birthday. What a good boy he is and how much he loves his mother.'

Minnie says, 'You call that love? You know the Mercedes I just got for Mother's Day? That's from my son Bernie. What a doll.'

Shirley says, 'That's nothing. You know my son Stanley? He's in analysis with a psychoanalyst in Harley Street. Five sessions a week. And what does he talk about? Me.'

* * *

7 The last meal

Fabrizi, Jacques, and Abe are about to be executed and they are asked what they wish to have for their last meal. Fabrizi asks for a pepperoni pizza, which he is served. He is then executed. Jacques asks for a filet mignon, which he is served. He too is then promptly executed. Abe requests a plate of strawberries.

'Strawberries?'

'Yes,' replies Abe, 'strawberries.'

'But they are out of season.'

'So, *nu*, I'll wait.'

* * *

8 The car driver

Cyril is driving down Hendon Road when he gets pulled over by a policeman. Walking up to Cyril's car, the policeman says, 'I've come to tell you that your wife fell out of your car some two miles back.'

Cyril replies, 'Thank goodness, I thought I'd gone deaf.'

* * *

9 Are there Jews in China?

Yitzhak and Moshe were eating in a Chinese restaurant in London. 'Yitzhak,' asked Moshe, 'Are there any Jews in China?'

'I don't know,' Yitzhak replied. 'Why don't you ask the waiter? I'd be surprised if there were no Jews in China. Our people are scattered everywhere.'

When the waiter came by, Moshe asked, 'Are there any Chinese Jews?'

'I don't know sir, let me ask,' the waiter replied, and went back to the kitchen.

The waiter returned a few minutes later and said, 'No, sir. No Chinese Jews.'

'Are you sure?' Moshe asked.

'I ask everyone,' the waiter replied. 'We have orange Jews, prune Jews, tomato Jews and grape Jews, but no one ever hear of Chinese Jews!'

***

10 Meeting with the synagogue secretary

Sadly, slowly, Michael Cohen entered the synagogue. He trudged into the secretary's office and sighed, 'Shmulik, I'm here.'

He sat down. 'I have to make arrangements for my wife's burial.'

'Cohen!' exclaimed Shmulik. 'Don't you remember?' We buried your darling wife two years ago.'

Michael nodded. 'I remember, I remember. That was my first wife. I'm here about my second.'

'Second wife? *Mazeltov!* I didn't know you remarried.'

***

11 Rabbi's advice

Moshe goes to see his rabbi and says, 'I need your advice. My wife just gave birth to a girl.'

'*Mazeltov.*'

'Thank you. Can we name the baby after a relative?'

'According to Jewish custom, you can name a baby after a departed father, mother, brother - '

'But they are all still alive,' says Moshe.

'Oh, I'm terribly sorry to hear that,' says the rabbi.

***

12 The widow

Becky's husband dies. It was not until sometime after that Becky was finally able to speak about what a thoughtful and wonderful man her late husband had been.

'Sidney thought of everything,' she told some friends. 'Just before he died, Sidney called me to his bedside and handed me three envelopes. 'Becky,' he said, 'I have put all my last wishes in these three envelopes. After I am gone, open them in sequence and do exactly as I have written. Only then can I rest in peace."

'What was in the first envelope?' her friends asked.

'It contained £5,000 with a note, "Please use this money to buy me a nice coffin". So I bought a beautiful mahogany coffin for him.

'The second envelope contained £10,000 with a note, "Please use this for a nice funeral". I gave Sidney a very dignified funeral and bought all his favourite foods for the *shivah*, including some fine malt whisky.'

'And the third envelope?' asked her friends.

'The third envelope contained £25,000 with a note, "Please use this to buy a nice stone". So I did.'

Becky then held up her hand and pointed to her 5 carat diamond ring.

'So,' said Becky, 'You like my stone?'

***

13 Near to death

Leah had been slipping in and out of a coma for several months. Yet Tony, her husband, had stayed by her bedside every single day. One day, when Leah came to, she motioned for Tony to come nearer. As he sat by her, she whispered, eyes full of tears, 'You know what? You have been with me all through the bad times:

'When I got fired from my secretary's job, you were there to support me.

'When my first hairdressing business failed, you were there.

'When I got knocked down by a car, you were by my side.

'When we lost our dear Jonathan, you stayed right here.

'When my health started failing, you were still by my side -

'You know what?'

'What dear?' Tony gently asked, smiling as his heart began to fill with warmth.

'I think you bring me bad luck.'

***

14 The Garden of Eden

One day in the Garden of Eden, Eve calls out to God.

'Lord, I have a problem!'

'What's the problem, Eve?'

'Lord, I know you created me and provided this beautiful garden and all of these wonderful animals, but I'm just not happy.'

'Why is that, Eve?' comes the reply from above.

'Lord, I am lonely and I'm sick to death of apples.'

'Well Eve, in that case, I have a solution. I shall create a Man for you.'

'What's a Man, Lord?'

'This man will be a flawed creature, with many bad traits. He'll lie, cheat and be very competitive. All in all, he'll give you a hard time, but, he'll be bigger, faster and will like to hunt and kill things. He will look silly when he's aroused, but since you've been complaining, I'll create him in such a way that he will satisfy your physical needs. He will be witless and will revel in childish things like fighting and kicking a ball about. He won't be too smart, so he'll also need your advice to think properly.'

'Sounds great,' says Eve, with an ironically raised eyebrow, 'but what's the catch, Lord?'

'Well – you can have him on one condition.'

'What's that, Lord?'

'As I said, he'll be proud, arrogant, and self-admiring – so you'll have to let him believe that I made him first. Just remember, it's our little secret – you know, Woman to Woman.'

***

15 The visit to the dentist

One day, Becky goes to her dentist and asks him how much it will cost to extract a wisdom tooth.

'Eighty pounds,' the dentist says.

'That's a ridiculous amount,' Becky says. 'Isn't there a cheaper way?'

'Well,' the dentist says, 'if I don't use an anaesthetic, I can knock it down to £60.'

'That's still too expensive,' Becky says.

'OK,' says the dentist. 'If I save on anaesthesia and simply rip the tooth out with a pair of pliers, I could get away with charging you only £20.'

'No,' moans Becky, 'it's still too much.'

'Hmm,' says the dentist, scratching his head. 'If I let one of my students do it without anaesthetic and use a pair of old pliers – just for the experience, you understand, I suppose I could charge you just £10.'

'Marvellous,' says Becky, 'book my husband Moshe for next Tuesday!'

Speeches For Special Occasions

Humour can be a vital component of any speech given at a formal occasion. If you are booked to speak at events such as as a wedding, Bar Mitzvah, or an engagement or birthday party, then in the selection below you will find quips, barbs and short jokes that, if you're brave enough, you could sprinkle into your speech. Think about the person you're going to be talking about – perhaps he or she is a sports fanatic, or a bridge player, a businessperson, an intellectual, single, just married or Bar Mitzvah'ed, or a sixty-year-old birthday girl? Then choose some lines to use – if you think them funny, then you should be able to put them across confidently. I've split the material into three themes: for a sixtieth (or similar) birthday speech, and for the best man's and the bride's father's wedding speeches – but you can use them for any speech you like and modify them to suit the person or occasion. Just make sure anything you choose won't offend anyone present, for instance due to physical appearance, religion or disability.

For a sixtieth (or similar) birthday speech

For this fictitious speech, Harry is giving the speech, David is the birthday boy and Becky is his wife.

When we were planning for tonight's celebration, we went down into our local wine merchant's cellar and found something tucked away in the corner, sixty years old and covered in dust. It was David!

***

In his youth, David loved wine, women and song. He can still sing.

***

David is a man who combines the wisdom of youth with the energy of old age.

***

David likes being sixty. A young woman recently referred to him as a sexagenarian, and he figures at this stage of his life, that's the closest he'll get to flattery.

***

David didn't quite make it as a financial director. He used to look at a balance sheet and if the total assets and total liabilities were exactly the same, he would figure everything must be OK.

***

His boss once said to him, 'Be objective.' And he replied, 'I'm too knowledgeable to be objective.'

***

When David was once in Hong Kong, he bought a suit and inside the pocket he found a note written on the inspector's tag. The note began, 'Dear most honoured customer – ' and asked him to send a photo of himself to a certain address. David thought that was nice, so he did it. A month later, he got a letter from a Hong Kong tailor that read like this, 'Thank you for your photo. I have been making these cheap looking suits for many years now and I always wondered what kind of slob would wear one.'

***

At his last company medical, David's doctor said to him, 'This is a personal question, David, but at your time of life it's important to know. Do you and Becky have any trouble with mutual satisfaction?' David replied, 'No sale, Doctor, we're staying with the Prudential.'

***

David's a profound thinker. He wonders about things like, 'Is Darwin's birthday a religious holiday for apes?'

***

There are three ways to handle David. Unfortunately, none of us know what they are.

***

I don't care what David says about his conquests. On his wedding night he was a virgin. I understand that when Becky touched him, he turned his head and coughed.

***

His boss recently asked David what he had done with all the money he had earned. David replied, 'I spent quite a bit on women, drink and gambling, and the rest I spent foolishly.'

***

David is a hard boss. He recently introduced a flexible hours programme for his staff. They can come in any time they want before 7 a.m. and leave whenever they please after 6 pm.

***

David once went to language school. This is the bill he received from Berlitz: £300 for French, £250 for German, £900 for Scotch.

***

Not many of you know that David's written his memoirs. They were purchased by Waddingtons and will be released soon as a game.

***

Here's another secret David didn't want me to tell you. He is to have an entry in *Who's Through 2006*.

***

TOAST: I wish you good health, long life, continued prosperity and eventually, a measure of respectability.

***

For a best man's speech

For this fictitious speech, Vicky and Gary are the bride and groom, Paul is the best man, Harry and Helen are Gary's parents.

I suppose you are all wondering why I called you all here tonight.

***

Gary advised me to get up here, throw my script away and just ad lib. He said he likes 'textual deviates'.

***

Harry told me not to talk about football, or in-jokes, or sex. He said, 'Just talk about what a fantastic guy Gary is.'So, in conclusion -

***

I'm not here to make a fool of Gary. He'll do that himself, a little later on.

***

Perhaps only a few times in each of our lifetimes do we get a chance to say some nice things to a man of intelligence, wit and wisdom. Unfortunately, tonight is not one of those times.

***

I have spoken about many men and women in my time and tonight I will speak about Gary. In economics that's known as 'the law of diminishing returns'.

***

What can you say about a man who came from humble beginnings and is now quickly rising to the very top of his profession based solely on intelligence, grit and the willpower to push on where others might fail? A man who is beginning to distinguish himself amongst his peers and where none can say a bad word against him? Well, that's enough about me. I'm here to talk about Gary.

***

Gary, a legend in his own mind. He claims to be a self-made man. I think it's damn nice of him to take the blame.

***

As you know, Gary, I and some others play five-a-side football. Our group likes to think of ourselves as a championship football side. Robert is the full back. I'm the half back. Gary's the drawback.

***

Gary's such a football fan that when he wants a match to last for ever, he thinks of sex.

***

Gary went to see an evening football match and during the first half, the floodlights failed. Over the tannoy came a request for someone to help. So Gary went up to the offices and suggested all the spectators put their hands in the air because he knew that 'many hands make light work'.

***

I can honestly say that in all the years I've known him, no one has ever questioned Gary's intelligence. In fact, I've never heard anyone even mention it.

***

When Gary left school, he took an aptitude test. Afterwards, the examiner told him, 'You will have a splendid future working for any company where a close relative or friend holds a senior management position.

***

Gary's very classy. When we had an evening of music and drink in his house recently, I asked whether he had any Rachmaninoff. Gary replied he didn't have any vodka, only beer.

***

Gary says, 'Don't call me uncultured. I go to operas, concerts, ballet – all that crap.'

***

Gary's a big spender. He took me out for tea once. It was alright – but I hadn't planned to donate blood that day.

***

Gary's in the *Guinness Book of Records* under 'lowest recorded tippers'.

***

When he left school, Gary wanted to be a stockbroker. Gary's definition of a stockbroker is someone who invests your money and keeps on investing your money until there's nothing left to invest.

***

Gary works in customer services. One day, he had to take an internal call from someone requesting his help. Gary said he was too busy dealing with real customers. The caller angrily asked Gary if he knew who he was talking to. When Gary said no, the caller said he was the company's MD. Quick as a flash, Gary asked the MD whether he knew who he was talking to. When the MD said he didn't, Gary put the phone down.

***

Gary told me he recently attended a big overseas sales conference and gave a presentation. At the end he got a standing ovation. As he left the hall, everyone called him by his name: 'Well done, Gary,' 'Nice job, Gary.' It didn't even stop when he got into the taxi. Even the driver seemed to know him: 'Where to, Gary?' At the airport, the porter took his bags and said, 'What flight, Gary?' Strangers passed him by and said, 'Good evening, Gary.' Then when he boarded the plane, he hung up his jacket and there was this huge badge he was still wearing. It said, 'Hi, my name is Gary.'

***

Gary's currently learning Japanese using a tape machine playing under his pillow every night. He can now speak Japanese quite well, but only when he's sleeping.

***

Watching Gary at work is sort of like the piano player in a brothel. He's near the action but he doesn't get totally involved.

***

I went out to dinner with Gary once and he ordered our meals in French. I was most impressed. But you should have seen the look on the Chinese waiter's face!

* * *

Gary won't drink coffee in the morning. He says it keeps him awake all day.

* * *

Gary is so naïve that he thinks Masters & Johnson is a golf tournament.

* * *

Gary's dad said to him recently, 'Now that you're getting married, I must say you don't quite seem your usual self and it's really quite an improvement.'

* * *

If tonight you haven't yet heard a good word about Gary, it's only because we haven't let him speak yet.

* * *

Occasionally, though, Gary's had a few absolutely brilliant flashes of total silence.

* * *

Just wait until Gary gets up here. He'll have you open mouthed with his stories. You won't be able to stop yawning.

* * *

Gary, when all is said and done, you've said a whole lot more than you've done.

* * *

Gary always remembers the advice his grandfather gave him. 'Before you fall in love with a pair of bright eyes, make sure it isn't just the sun shining through the back of her head.'

***

Gary first met Vicky in 1987. That was her room number.

***

Gary, when Vicky says her food could melt in your mouth, she means that you have to defrost it.

***

When Vicky and Gary decided it was time to get married, Vicky said to Gary, 'You know, a lot of men are going to be miserable when I get married.' Gary said, 'Really, how many are you going to marry?'

***

Gary's always said that he'd never marry until he found a girl who likes what he likes. Himself! And now he's found her.

***

For a bride's father's speech

Note: In this fictitious speech, Sarah is the father's wife.

Before I begin, I want you all to know that Sarah has instructed me not to be witty, not to be humorous, and not to be intellectual. In fact she said, 'Just be yourself.'

***

Sarah has also asked me to check that my instructions on how to get here were accurate and that everyone has managed to find their way here tonight – so if I could just check by asking, 'All those not yet here, please raise a hand.' Thank you.

***

I can't tell you how good it feels to be standing here now on this special occasion. I'm so glad I cancelled that dental appointment to be here.

***

In terms of long marriages, you both have some good role models here today. Just try to avoid what happened to one married couple we know. They told us that the first part of their marriage was very happy. But then, on the way back from the wedding canopy -

***

That's all folks. My speech is over other than to give you this definition of marriage: 'Marriage is when a woman asks a man to remove his pyjamas because she wants to put them in the washing machine.'

The Best Punchlines

You've probably heard the story of the group of jokers who only tell each other the joke 'numbers' and one day one of them gets no laughs when he says 'number eight,' because he told it wrong. Well, here is the Jewish version. Why not just tell the punchlines of the jokes? All of the following can be found in this book, though they are listed here in random order.

Do you call that a breakfast?

We don't schlep on Shabbes.

It was obvious.

And what does he talk about? Me.

So, *nu*, I'll wait.

Thank goodness, I thought I'd gone deaf.

So, you like my stone?

I think you bring me bad luck.

Some of my best friends are genitals.

If she finds her way home, don't sleep with her.

He thought I said '*kvetch*'.

Does that mean you're not coming?

You're coming empty-handed?

He thinks we're teaching him English.

I said Sem Ting.

Very nice, but I gave you shishi.

Because I forgot where I put it.

Is that all you people think of?

You got me out of the shower to tell me that?

Why is this knight different from all other knights?

My mother would send me out on a night like this?

You're a sex maniac!

Can you eat any other part of the matzo?

Do you think it's easy being an optimist?

You put him to sleep. You wake him up.

So she could love you, my son.

What were the grown-ups doing all this time?

You order an apple in this restaurant and look how they serve it.

It's OK, he's single.

I can't remember where I live.

Aha, now you're talking.

Vell, I make a living.

Please put down that gun.

It's his turn with the teeth.

I don't know, my wife told me to stand here.

Señor, the bull does not always loose.

You must get such *naches* from him.

Ok, we'll take ten.

Today is the viewing.

I like ours a lot better.

Like I'm talking to a wall.

She said she'd rather have a new kitchen.

What's a headache?

We wanted to wait until all of the children were dead.

Do you mean I've been here already?

He always put everything in my name.

But nobody messes with the *rebbitsen*.

Who on earth is looking after the shop?

Did I say he wanted to?

This one is different. It's eating my popcorn.

Tell me, are you still circumcised?

It needs ironing.

Neither, I mean her legs.

He only works in egg and onion.

I wish you had bought a new hat.

This, my darling, is foranoccasion.

That's good, children, don't fight.

So I tucked it back in again.

That way my daughters would come and visit me once a week.

Look, he's breathing!

Go and get your own blanket, then.

So why didn't it say anything?

Am I my brother's *kippa*?

Then why do you want to live to be eighty?

I'll hold your monkey for you.

Look at that *shmuck* on the camel.

I think you should take the poison.

You speak to him. He wants to be a doctor.

There's nothing wrong with your eyesight.

With all this, who needs money?

Where did you hear such *mishegass*?

There are another two Bar Mitzvah safaris ahead of us.

He said you're going to die.

Not everyone likes to give.

You call this a lining?

How do you think I rang the doorbell?

Oh what a *mitzvah* you performed last night!

Certainly not! That could lead to dancing.

Tell me – what would you put in your window?

His eyes aren't so good now.

Should I tell her the war is over?

How did you know my name was Katz?

I'm planning to make a *shivah* call.

See – that's how to wave a towel.

Why, don't you have a vase?

What does this man want with my Cyril?

Glossary of Yiddish and Hebrew terms

Alav hasholom: May he or she rest in peace.
Aliyah: To be called up to read a portion of Torah scroll in synagogue; the immigration of Jews to Israel.
Bar Mitzvah: Religious ceremony marking the coming of age of a thirteen-year-old Jewish boy.
Baruch HaShem: Blessed be the name of the Lord – used like 'God willing'.
Blintzes: Pancake, usually spread with cream cheese or, jam or strawberries rolled within a thin dough pancake.
Bris; brisses (pl): Circumcision ceremony, performed on a boy on the eighth day after birth.
Bubbeh: Grandma.
Bubbeleh: Term of endearment (like dear, pet or honey).
Bupkes: Nothing; something trivial, worthless.
Challah: Braided white bread made with egg, eaten on the Sabbath.
Chanukah: The Festival of Lights, a Jewish festival that falls in December.
Chassid; Chassidic: Member of an orthodox religious sect.
Chazan: Cantor, the singer who leads synagogue services.
Chometz: Leavened food, forbidden during Passover.
Chuppah: A wedding canopy.
Chutzpah: Insolence, impudence, unmitigated cheek, effrontery.
Daven: To pray, or lead prayers, often with strong swaying from the hips.
Flayshig: Meats, poultry or foods prepared with animal fats.
Frum: Religious.
Gabbai: Synagogue warden.
Gefilte fish: Fish, ground, seasoned with spices and made into balls or patties, then shaped into fishcakes and boiled or fried. Often made from carp.
Gefilter: Play on words – *gefilte*, filled, stuffed.
Get: A Jewish religious divorce.

Goy; goyim (pl): Non-Jew.
Hanukah: see Chanukah.
HaShem: God; literally 'The Name'. Jews consider that saying the name of God is blasphemy.
Hassid: see Chassid.
Havdalah: Ceremony marking the end of the Sabbath.
Kiddush: A special blessing said before a meal on the Sabbath and festivals, and after the Sabbath synagogue service, usually including the blessing over the wine or and bread.
Kippa: Skullcap; see also *yarmulka*.
Kol Nidre: Prayer said just before sunset on eve of Yom Kippur. The name is that of the first two words of the prayer beginning 'All our vows ... '.
Kol Nidre Appeal: An appeal for charity that is made on Kol Nidre evening in the synagogue.
Kosher: Food that complies with the Jewish dietary religious laws. By extension, anything that is pure, good, whole; legitimate; genuine.
Kvell: To gush with pride.
Kvetch: To complain.
Latke: Potato pancake, a sort of hash brown made from raw, grated potatoes.
Lox: Smoked salmon.
Maariv: Daily evening religious service.
Matzo: Unleavened bread eaten during week of Passover; matzo ball is a dumpling made from ground matzos.
Mazeltov: Congratulations; good luck.
Mensh: Man of fine qualities, a real man.
Meshugga: Crazy, mad.
Mezuzah: A passage from the Torah written on a small piece of parchment and placed inside a wooden or metal case that is attached to the doorpost of a Jewish home. It is customary for an Orthodox Jew to touch his fingers to his lips, then to the mezuzah, each time he or she passes the doorpost.
Milchig: Dairy foods.
Mincha: Daily afternoon religious service.
Minyan: The quorum of ten men required for holding public prayers.
Mishegass: Madness, absurdity.
Mishpocheh: The entire family network of relatives by blood or marriage.
Mitzvah: Good deed.
Mohel; moil: The religious man who performs ritual circumcisions according to rabbinic regulations and customs.
Momzer: A bastard.
Naches: Pride, pleasure, good fortune.

Nu: Well, so.
Oy: Exclamation to denote pain, rapture, awe, astonishment, surprise, delight.
Oy Gevalt: Exclamation to denote fear, terror, astonishment.
Oy Vay [iz meer]: Oh, woe is me!
Passover: Jewish festival commemorating liberation of Jews from their bondage in Egypt.
Pish: To urinate.
Rebbitsin: Rabbi's wife.
Rosh Hashana: The Jewish New Year.
Schlep: To drag, carry; a long journey.
Schmooze: To gossip, chat up.
Seder: The traditional evening home service and meal during Passover.
Shabbes: The Sabbath, which lasts from sunset on Friday to sunset on Saturday.
Shadchen: A professional marriage broker.
Shammes: Synagogue sexton or caretaker.
Shema Yisrael: A Hebrew prayer recited three or four times daily by Orthodox Jews, and the last prayer he utters on his deathbed.
Shiksa: A non-Jewish woman.
Shivah: The seven-day period of mourning after a person's death.
Shmaltz: Cooking fat; excessive sentimentality; luxury, good luck.
Shmatta: A rag; old clothes.
Shmuck: A stupid person; a penis.
Shofar: A ram's horn blown in a synagogue during services for Rosh Hashanah and Yom Kippur.
Sholom aleichem: Hebrew for 'peace be unto you'. Used as a greeting like 'hello' or 'goodbye'.
Shtup; shtupping: Vulgar Yiddish term for having sex.
Shul: Synagogue.
Siddur: The daily and Sabbath prayer book.
Simcha: A joyous celebration.
Succah: A temporary outdoors booth in which to eat meals during the Festival of Succoth.
Tallis: A prayer shawl, usually in white silk with fringes, and worn over clothes.
Talmud: A massive compilation of writing that forms the basic body of Jewish laws and traditions.
Tefillin: Two small, black leather boxes with straps attached, that contain passages of Hebrew script. The boxes are strapped on (one on the head and one on the arm) by Orthodox Jewish men each weekday morning.
Tisha B'av: A Jewish day of fasting and mourning.
Toches: The rear end, bottom, buttocks.

Torah: The Five Books of Moses, or the scroll containing them and read in the synagogue; it can also imply all sacred Jewish literature.
Trayf; traf: Non-kosher foods.
Tsouris: Troubles, worries, suffering.
Tzitzit: The fringes at the corners of a prayer shawl, or *tallis*.
Yahrzeit: The anniversary of someone's death.
Yarmulka: Skullcap; see also *kippa*.
Yenta: A gossipy woman.
Yeshiva: A Jewish school; theological college.
Yeshiva bucher: A *yeshiva* student; a gullible or inexperienced person.
Yom Kippur: Jewish festival – the Day of Atonement.
Zaydeh: Grandpa.

Other great titles available from Robson Books

The Alan Coren Omnibus **ISBN1 86105 739 3**	**Alan Coren**
Jackie, Oy! **ISBN 1 86105 539 0**	**Jackie Mason**
The Ultimate Book of Rude and Politically Incorrect Jokes **ISBN1 86105 449 1**	**Allan Pease**
Lip Reading **ISBN1 86105 359 2**	**Maureen Lipman**

THE ALAN COREN OMNIBUS

'The funniest writer in Britain today.'
SUNDAY TIMES

The Alan Coren Omnibus
by Alan Coren

Here, quite simply, is the best of the best: a personal selection by Britain's master humorist of eighty-six dazzling pieces from the hilarious thousands with which he has delighted readers for the past forty years. It is, in every sense, essential Coren.

Alan Coren is renowned for his brilliantly funny writing. Educated at Oxford, Yale and Berkeley universities, he is a former editor of *Punch* magazine and has been a columnist for the *Daily Mail*. Previous collections of his witty writing have all been best-sellers. These include *Waiting for Jeffrey* (1861056966) and *The Cricklewood Tapestry* (1861053746), both published by Robson Books.

ISBN 1 86105 739 3

Jackie, Oy!
The Frank, Outrageously Funny Autobiography of
Jackie Mason
Jackie Mason
With Ken Gross

Jackie, Oy!
by Jackie Mason

Jackie, Oy! is Jackie Mason's extraordinary story – of overnight stardom, of his subsequent fall and of his recent spectacular rise to the top. As he contemplates this new-found success, he marvels ironically, 'The Jews said I was too Jewish. The Gentiles said I wasn't Jewish enough. Now I'm a sensation telling the same jokes that made me a failure for twenty-five years'.

Filled with irreverent commentary on his life and times, this compelling autobiography is also the ultimate immigrant's story. Jackie Mason talks openly and hilariously, with all the superb wit that has made him a cult figure.

ISBN 1 86105 539 0

THE ULTIMATE BOOK OF

RUDE AND POLITICALLY INCORRECT JOKES

ALLAN PEASE

The Ultimate Book of Rude and Politically Incorrect Jokes
by Allan Pease

Had enough of being told you're not politically correct? Fed up with others telling you what to say or how to think?

This book will give you freedom from the chains of mental and verbal bondage. And it contains every joke guaranteed to annoy the P.C. brigade – it will certainly offend prudes and those who take life too seriously.

The jokes in this book are politically incorrect, rude or both – but they're all very funny and never obscene (obscene being anything that arouses a judge).

ISBN 1 86105 449 1

MAUREEN LIPMAN

Lip Reading

Lip Reading
by Maureen Lipman

Between starring in West End and television shows, making public appearances and writing her column, quite how Maureen Lipman manages to fit anything else into her life is a mystery. But she does. Here she finds herself trussed up back-stage in Birmingham, ponders the more peculiar aspects of cricket terminology and explores the miracle of plastic table-cloths. Along the way, she stops off in southern Ireland to rest and recuperate, makes friends with a dolphin in Barbados, gets healthy in Thailand and gets stressed on the way to a health farm. The popular actress, raconteur and bestselling author returns with another slice of life as only she lives (and tells) it.

ISBN 1 86105 359 2